THE LEGACY OF MESOPOTAMIA

by
Stephanie Dalley, A. T. Reyes, David Pingree,
Alison Salvesen, and Henrietta McCall

with drawings by
Stephanie Dalley and Marion Cox

edited by
Stephanie Dalley

OXFORD UNIVERSITY PRESS

1998

Oxford University Press, Great Clarendon Street, Oxford OX2 6DP

Oxford New York

Athens Auckland Bangkok Bogota Bombay
Buenos Aires Calcutta Cape Town Dar es Salaam
Delhi Florence Hong Kong Istanbul Karachi
Kuala Lumpur Madras Madrid Melbourne
Mexico City Nairobi Paris Singapore
Taipei Tokyo Toronto Warsaw

and associated companies in
Berlin Ibadan

Oxford is a trade mark of Oxford University Press

Published in the United States
by Oxford University Press Inc., New York

© Oxford University Press 1998

British Library Cataloguing in Publication Data
Data available

Library of Congress Cataloging in Publication Data
The legacy of Mesopotamia / by Stephanie Dalley with Andres Reyes
. . . [et al.] ; with drawings by Stephanie Dalley and Marion Cox ;
edited by Stephanie Dalley.
Includes bibliographical references and index.
1. Middle East—Civilization. 2. Iraq—Civilization. 3. Greece—
Civilization—Middle Eastern influences. I. Dalley, Stephanie.
II. Title.
DS56.D33 1997 935—dc21 97–12948
ISBN 0–19–814946–8

1 3 5 7 9 10 8 6 4 2

Typeset by Graphicraft Typesetters Limited, Hong Kong
Printed in Great Britain
on acid-free paper by
St. Edmundsbury Press, Bury St. Edmunds

Preface

An unusual degree of patient co-operation between the contributors has allowed this book to reach its present form. The editor's aim has been to produce a book which can be read from beginning to end as a coherent composition; to achieve this the contributors have been exceptionally tolerant of editorial interference in harmonizing, eliminating overlaps, and incorporating suggestions, including specific material, and the editor is grateful to them.

Many people have generously contributed time, criticism, and knowledge to the final result. The authors are indebted to the following: to Dr Joan Weir and Christopher Dalley for reading numerous drafts and suggesting improvements; to Dr John Day for help with Chapter III; to Professors Sir John Boardman, Fergus Millar, Trevor Bryce, and Martin West, for Chapters IV and V; to Dr Sebastian Brock for Chapters II and VII; to Dr Helen Whitehouse and Richard Jenkyns for Chapter IX; to Dr Barry Flood, Dr Jeremy Hughes, Dr Peter Kingsley, Dr Eleanor Robson, Professor Michael Roaf, Dr St John Simpson, Dr Emilie Savage-Smith, Dr Judith Olszowy, Professor Geza Vermes, Dr Nadav Na'aman, and Professor David Hawkins for advice on specific points. We are grateful to Marion Cox for many drawings; Stephanie Dalley is responsible for others, and a few of them are joint efforts, including the maps. We are also deeply indebted to several libraries in Oxford and to their librarians for exceptional facilities and services. Chapters IV and V were first drafted by Dr Reyes who assembled the Classical and other material; Stephanie Dalley then added more Mesopotamian material and is responsible for the final draft.

Spellings of names given by Classical authors mainly conform to usage in Pauly-Wissowa's *Realencyclopädie der classischen Altertumswissenschaft* (Stuttgart, 1894–1980). Spellings of Akkadian names conform to current transliteration except when a biblical form is in common usage. In an attempt to avoid overloading the work with annotation, bibliography has been restricted and given by section within each chapter, but extensive footnotes have been allowed for Chapters IV–VI. The editor is responsible for the omissions and inconsistencies that remain.

Finally the editor would like to thank Hilary O'Shea and the Oxford University Press for suggesting the project, and for her patience in waiting for its completion.

S.D.

Oriental Institute, Oxford
April 1996

Contents

Notes on Contributors

STEPHANIE DALLEY is Shillito Fellow in Assyriology at the Oriental Institute and Senior Research Fellow at Somerville College, Oxford. She has published cuneiform archives excavated in Iraq and Syria, as well as *Mari and Karana, two Old Babylonian Cities* (1984) and *Myths from Mesopotamia* (1989).

HENRIETTA MCCALL trained as a journalist and then studied Egyptology and Akkadian at Oxford University. She has published *Mesopotamian Myths* (1990) and contributed a chapter on sphinxes to *Mythical Beasts* (1995).

DAVID PINGREE is Professor of the History of Mathematics and of Classics at Brown University, Providence, Rhode Island. He is expert in a wide range of languages and has published extensively on Greek, Islamic, pre-Islamic, and Indian subjects, including co-operative works on Mesopotamian astronomy.

A. T. REYES is a Classical scholar who has worked and travelled in countries of the Middle East. He has written *Archaic Cyprus* (1994), and teaches Latin and Greek at Groton School, Massachusetts.

ALISON SALVESEN researches in Syriac and patristic literature, and teaches in Aramaic and Syriac at the Oriental Institute, Oxford University. She has published *Symmachus in the Pentateuch* (1991).

List of Illustrations

MC denotes drawings made by Marion Cox; SMD denotes drawings made by Stephanie Dalley.

List of Maps

Abbreviations

ACT	O. Neugebauer, *Astronomical Cuneiform Texts*, 3 vols. (London, 1955)
AfO	*Archiv für Orientforschung*
AJArch.	*American Journal of Archaeology*
ANET	J. B. Pritchard, *Ancient Near Eastern Texts Relating to the Old Testament*, 3rd edn. (Princeton, 1969)
ANRW	*Aufstieg und Niedergang der römischen Welts*
BPO	E. Reiner and D. Pingree, *Babylonian Planetary Omens* i: *The Venus Tablet of Ammiṣaduqa* (Malibu, 1975); ii: *Enūma Anu Enlil Tablets 50–51* (Malibu, 1981)
CAH²	*Cambridge Ancient History*, 2nd edn. (Cambridge, 1969–)
CESS	D. Pingree, *Census of the Exact Sciences in Sanskrit*, Series A, vols. 1–5 (Philadelphia, 1970–94)
CJ	*Classical Journal*
CQ	*Classical Quarterly*
EAT	O. Neugebauer and R. A. Parker, *Egyptian Astronomical Texts*, iii (London, 1969)
FGrH	F. Jacoby (ed.), *Fragmente der griechische Historiker* (Berlin, 1923–58)
HAMA	O. Neugebauer, *History of Ancient Mathematical Astronomy* (New York, 1975)
JCS	*Journal of Cuneiform Studies*
JHS	*Journal of Hellenic Studies*
JNES	*Journal of Near Eastern Studies*
LIMC	*Lexicon Iconographicum Mythologiae Classicae* (Zurich, 1981–)
MARI	*Mari Annales de Recherches Interdisciplinaires*
MH	*Museum Helveticum*
NABU	*Notes Assyriologiques Brèves et Utilitaires*
RE	*Paulys Realencyclopädie der classischen Altertumswissenschaft* (Stuttgart and Munich, 1894–1980)
SAOC	*Studies in Ancient Oriental Civilization*
TAPA	*Transactions of the American Philosophical Association*
ZAW	*Zeitschrift für alttestamentliche Wissenschaft*
ZPE	*Zeitschrift für Papyrologie und Epigraphik*

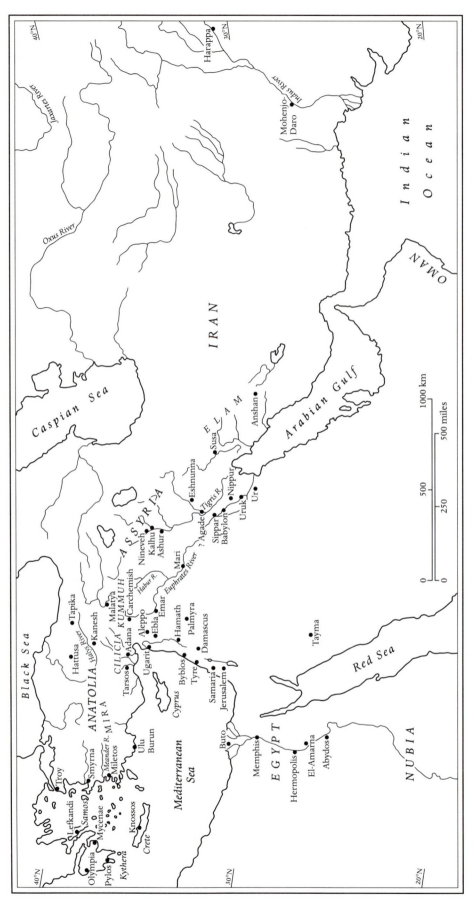

MAP 1. Sketch map of Mesopotamia and adjacent lands: the early periods

INTRODUCTION

S T E P H A N I E   D A L L E Y

Between the two rivers Tigris and Euphrates lies the alluvial land known as Mesopotamia. There one of the world's very early civilizations arose. Brick-built cities and writing are two of its distinctive hallmarks, and the ancient names of its cities still echo around the world today: Ur of the Chaldees, Babylon, and Nineveh. For the Sumerians who first lived in southern Mesopotamia, Uruk (biblical Erech) was the seat of ancient kingship and early narrative literature. For the Babylonians who superseded them, Babylon was the centre of the world. For the Assyrians, Ashur was their most ancient capital, Nineveh their most glorious royal residence, and Harran their final seat of royalty. All those people wrote upon clay using hundreds of wedge-shaped signs, first in Sumerian, later in Akkadian which is the name now given to the written language of the Babylonians and Assyrians.

What was their relationship to other early civilizations? This question has been tackled in several different ways during the last century or so, and some of the answers have contradicted others. Premature conclusions have been dismissed as better evidence has come to light; diverse religious, political, and cultural groups have argued for or against influence with equal passion.

Scholarship in ancient Near Eastern studies has made huge progress, yet the challenge still stands. This book takes up that challenge because the evidence is now more plentiful and better understood than before. The burden of proof can be tackled by combining different kinds of evidence: chronological, textual, and archaeological, from different times and places.

The ruins of Nineveh and Babylon were rediscovered by explorers from western Europe in the nineteenth century, and have been excavated in fits and starts ever since. Assyriology, which is the study of Babylonian and Assyrian culture, began with those first excavations. The pioneers who first uncovered and studied the eroded remnants of Mesopotamian civilization had a clear if general view of its influence upon the rest of the world. 'Light from the East' and 'The Cradle of Civilization' were two of the catch-phrases that excited the educated people of Europe and the USA. They perceived that so high a level of cultural attainment, so much earlier than the achievements of Classical Greece, must inevitably have been at the roots of urban, literate civilization.

Yet certain reservations remained. Egypt seemed to have blossomed into an urban, literate culture at much the same time, although without scientific dating methods it was impossible to say whether Egypt or Mesopotamia came first. India, with its Indus valley cities and its Sanskrit literature, also laid claims to priority which were hard to assess not only because the comparative dating of archaeological deposits was in its infancy, but also because the antiquity of its written traditions could only be guessed at from later survivals. Eventually it became possible to date the beginnings of culture in both India and China, where the development of cities and writing appears to be later than in the Near East.

Scholars of ancient Mesopotamian culture had the enormous advantage that its writings were impressed on clay which does not perish in the ways that most other writing materials do. On the other hand clay surfaces are easily damaged by water and knocks, and the writing system used upon them was of awful complexity. Only slowly and painfully was it possible to come to a correct understanding of important texts.

Until Assyriology presented this new challenge, the basis for our knowledge of cultural evolution had been secure since the Renaissance. People assumed that Classical Greek culture based mainly upon Athens, and the Judaeo-Christian tradition of the Bible based upon Jerusalem, comprised the two early traditions from which our own culture stemmed. The eighth century BC gave an approximate starting point to the process. Although Chaldaean wisdom supposedly featured in some of the hermetic and oracular writings of late Antiquity, most scholars agreed that they were new compositions forged during the time of the Roman empire to look as if they were much older.

True, the ancient Egyptians had written their hieroglyphic inscriptions on tombs and temples in the Nile valley at a much earlier period, and there was no denying their stupendous achievements in architecture and sculpture, still visible above ground in shining stone. The bare mounds of mud-brick rubble in Iraq could not compete with glorious granite and marble, whether in Egypt or in Greece and Ionia. But the forms of Egyptian literature, early though they were in comparison with Greek and Hebrew, seemed to have left barely a trace in Greek and Jewish culture. The worship of ibises, cats, and hippos belonged to the world of African anthropology and had no links with the Olympian gods or Israelite monotheism. It seemed that Egypt, Greece, and the Bible could keep their cultural autonomy safe after all.

The great names of kings, queens, and cities from ancient Mesopotamia were known, of course, from the pens of Greek writers and from books of the Bible. Semiramis, Sardanapalos, Ninos, and Nebuchadnezzar were legendary names. But the colours in which they were painted gave a picture of unedifying barbarity: rapacious conquerors who indulged in excesses of food, drink, and women, castrators of boys, extortionate usurers who ground the face of the oppressed into the dust, destructive empire-builders who were insensitive to adjacent cultures. Such damning hyperbole is, as we well know from modern examples, an inevitable part of the public image created against a powerful and distant alien.

During the early years of Assyriology the belief that outstanding men could change the course of history competed with a growing belief in economic forces beyond the control of individuals, and in an ethnic character that went hand in hand with language groups. According to this, exceptionally gifted men were only the tools of inexorable Fate, but some racial groups were intellectually superior to others. Archaeologists busily measured cranial capacity and proportions, applying the 'sciences' of phrenology and craniology to the skeletons of people long dead. 'The Semitic mentality' and 'the Indo-European cast of mind' were concepts applied to modern and ancient people alike, which made it rash to link achievements across ethnic boundaries. Nineveh and Memphis, Jerusalem and Athens, were sharply divided both by race and by language. In the new field of linguistics the Indo-European languages were extensively studied because their highly inflected forms were thought to be more sophisticated than the structures of other groups of language. Early translations of Mesopotamian literature were so halting and literal that they seemed to confirm that assessment, and it was easy to relegate Babylonian culture to a backwater, confined to its own small world of esoteric writing. It turns out that some of the brilliance of cuneiform texts was intimately connected to the clever manipulation of the signs, and so there were crucial features of the written literature which could not be translated into languages written in alphabetic scripts. To mock Babylonian scriptures in inadequate translation was all too simple, just as the denouncers of those early Christian heresies which had adopted pagan texts found it easy to ridicule them. Semitic languages in general were relegated to the periphery of scholarship, giving way to a core of more prestigious learning in Indo-European languages. Very few people questioned the assumption that language group and ethnic group were inextricably bonded together.

Early attempts to prove that one culture depended upon another began with that unjustified assumption: that different language groups, especially Semitic and Indo-European, stood for ethnic groups with distinct racial characteristics. Environment was thought to be a much less influential factor than language and genetic grouping, which were reckoned to be self-contained and static. One of the most outrageous applications of such assumptions was the 'pan-Babylonian' school of scholarship, led by A. Jeremias and F. Delitzsch before the First World War. They set out to show that Yahweh was originally a Babylonian god, and the Hebrew faith a mere sideline of semitic Mesopotamian paganism. Even though the attempt was soon discredited, echoes still reverberate in modern times, so that subsequent attempts to show how Mesopotamian culture influenced Israel arouse fears of a revival. To describe influence in any coherent way became for a while unacceptable because racist interpretations were suspected. It was therefore popular to maintain that analogy does not prove influence because most points of resemblance could result from independent development.

Assumptions and pressures of this kind are hard to dislodge from scholarship and from the popular mind, and sometimes they reappear in a new guise. The concept of an oriental, slave-owning society was deeply rooted and made for colourful and dramatic writing of ancient history. Marxist scholars took it up and projected it back into very early Antiquity; for example, the third dynasty of Ur (*c*.2112–2095 BC) was described by the Soviet Assyriologist Igor Dyakonov as 'one of the most repressive regimes known to man', for the evidence was sufficiently ambiguous for him to impose his interpretation upon it. On the other hand the Dane Thorkild Jacobsen envisioned early Sumerian society as a kind of golden age of primitive democracy with unrestrained and idyllic relationships between the sexes, before decadence and oppression set in. Christian traditions were unable to shake off biblical and Classical denigration, so that for instance William Blake drew Nebuchadnezzar as half man, half beast roaming the desert, insane; and Belshazzar's Feast in music and art depicted the corrupt and decadent court at Babylon getting its just deserts for sacking Jerusalem and oppressing the Hebrews.

Between the two World Wars further discoveries of archaeological evidence in the soil of the Fertile Crescent led to renewed attempts to show connections and dependence. In particular scholars tried to link the early stories in the Bible with archives excavated at Mari on the Middle Euphrates, which dated some eight centuries before the time of Solomon in the tenth century BC, and then with archives excavated at Ebla near Aleppo in Syria, which went back at least fourteen centuries before Solomon. The names of Sodom and Gomorrah, of Abraham and David, seemed at last to have come under the spotlight of contemporary record. Gradually, however, claimed connections fell away as scholars tussled with the vagaries of cuneiform readings. Hasty links with biblical characters and cities were uncoupled as time allowed more thorough research, and these retractions strengthened the case for independent

evolution. When Linear B, the writing of Bronze Age Greece, was shown in 1953 to be an early form of Greek, the decipherment meant that Greek civilization could still be viewed as an indigenous product of mainland Greece, acknowledging the introduction of the Phoenician alphabet as an isolated intrusion from the Semitic world of western Asia. In Palestine archaeologists at first enthusiastically linked material remains closely to the biblical record, but soon began to question both the links and the prejudices that had seemed to confirm them. The idea of diffusion faded once again.

Fresh evidence continues to surface from trenches in ancient mounds and from museum collections. Archaeologists, trying to fill in the gaps between early cultures, have searched further afield, finding ever more evidence of civilized settlements in early times in unexpected places: central Anatolia, Bulgaria, Oman, and Central Asia. Rescue excavations in the basins of new dams, on airport sites, or new roads have brought surprises. Intermittent political upheavals and wars have forced excavators to shift their focus to new areas. Far more numerous expeditions nowadays set out to survey and to dig, more university and museum departments, more scholars benefiting from cheap travel and electronic communication have all brought a flood of new information. Archaeology has become a respectable subject for study in its own right, separated from its traditional links with particular cultures and languages. The old picture built up by early adventurers and collectors has been revised with new kinds of scrutiny, new techniques and approaches. One particularly interesting application of the modern science of genetics has shown that genetic grouping does not necessarily give the same pattern as language grouping.

Yet there is a sense of frustration and disillusion. Masses of new data brought new problems rather than clear solutions to old ones. Cuneiformists deciphered their fragmentary sources very slowly, and produced results that seemed incomprehensible to the outsider; or they changed their interpretations and quarrelled over them. Embedded in their arcane learning, they seemed less and less to communicate clearly with non-linguists. The hope that archaeology on its own could prove the truth of holy scriptures, or give clear answers to the questions people asked of it, was often doomed to disappointment, so anthropology and pure theory were applied to archaeological study, usually without regard for real connection or factual validity. Our picture of ancient Mesopotamia in particular suffered from the uncritical use of the Ottoman court and administration as a direct model for neo-Assyrian society. Even after a century of study the accounts of Babylonian customs recorded by biblical and Greek authors had been clarified neither by excavated texts nor by other archaeological discoveries. Assyriologists still could not identify Kedor-laomer in the book of Genesis, or the sage Oannes named by Berossos, or the Assyrian goddess Mylitta named by Herodotos, or the site of the Hanging Gardens of Babylon.

The time-span involved has expanded inexorably with the researches of both excavators and epigraphists. To most people, brought up with a historical framework calculated in centuries, it is as hard to grasp the millennia of literate Antiquity as to comprehend geological time-scales or astronomical distances. This book has taken very early writing, around 3000 BC, as its starting point, yet prehistoric cultures of remarkable extent and ingenuity existed at least three thousand years earlier than that.

To assess the nature of influence and to trace the channels of diffusion from Mesopotamia to its neighbours is far from simple. The span of time is enormous, the occasions and opportunities very varied. To help eliminate accidental resemblances, one must first show how, when, and where influential contacts were made, and they are far more extensive in time and space than is often reckoned. Biblical scholars tend to focus their search for influence upon the Assyrian and Babylonian occupation of Palestine in the eighth–sixth centuries BC, and Classical scholars pick out the orientalizing period of the eighth–seventh centuries BC, but in fact the possibilities are far wider. The purpose of the first two chapters in this book is to draw attention to many of the ways and means, using both textual and archaeological sources.

By pointing to evidence for Mesopotamian influence this study inevitably tends to ignore influence that flowed in the reverse direction: into Mesopotamia from its neighbours. To do otherwise would be beyond the scope of one book. But it should be emphasized that the Mesopotamians were as receptive as adjacent cultures and they absorbed foreign ideas, foreign population groups, and foreign overlords. Even at the height of their commercial, political, and military power they combined flexibility with domination.

At various times their country was invaded or infiltrated and ruled by foreigners, from north and south, east and west.

Nor should we undervalue the creative changes that were made to Mesopotamian ideas where they were received abroad. Neighbouring cultures did not simply accept and use what came to them, but took foreign matter to heart and absorbed it into their own works so thoroughly that it was transformed. Sometimes the Mesopotamians would receive this transformed influence back again. These factors make the assessment of individual items complex at all times, and quite frequently open to question as to the direction in which influence flowed. In the following pages the aim has generally been to include only those examples which have been agreed in the past by a majority of scholars, and not to argue the case for disputed pieces of evidence. This decision has inevitably led to the omission of some enticing possibilities, but was made in the hope that most of the material presented here will prove reliable over time. However, it was not possible to use reliable studies for some areas of research that have never before been tackled. This is especially true for the period of late Antiquity and early Islam, where previously no influence was expected and so not looked for, so parts of Chapters 2, 5, and 8 make use of evidence long available to break new ground. Even when evidence and interpretation seem sure, they are subject to alteration, for new excavations and new texts are found every year in the Fertile Crescent, and any attempt to present the current state of scholarship must take its place as a mere stepping-stone across the dangerous waters that surge between the present and the very ancient past.

What was left after the death of cuneiform? Modern tradition still knows Adam and Eve, Achilles, Odysseus, and Helen of Troy. What happened to Gilgamesh and Humbaba, whose fame was broadcast throughout the very ancient world in many languages both Semitic and Indo-European? Why is every attribution to Chaldaean wisdom in texts of late Antiquity and the Middle Ages dismissed as ridiculous, evil, superstitious, or downright forgery? When did cuneiform writing end, and how could it have happened that so much learning simply vanished from the face of the earth? These questions are tackled for the first time in this book. To do so we cut across several areas of academic study that are usually kept quite separate. The answers make an extraordinary story, and one that has never been told before.

The perplexed observer might be forgiven for wondering whether very ancient material is so ambiguous that influence and connections may be found anywhere, according to the interests of the researcher; that one has only to dream up a framework and then select suitable material to fill it fairly convincingly. He can be reassured that, in the case of Mesopotamia, genuine progress has recently been made in clarifying areas of uncertainty. The enormity of the task undertaken by scholars during the past century can now be appreciated. Our difficulties in understanding and assimilating complex data had partly arisen because we underestimated the time and labour needed. Mistakes of the past may reflect the speed of discovery and the vastness of the subject rather than incompetence or wilful distortion for political or racial ends.

This introduction would not be complete without an explanation for the general reader of the methods by which scholars can use tiny pieces of evidence and begin to build up a reliable picture of contact and influence. We know from a century and a half of archaeological excavations that distinctive cultures arose early in many different parts of the Old World. They have existed for more than five thousand years. Fortunately for us their traces survive in the remains of cities where new buildings were set upon the debris of old ones in a series of levels rising higher and higher, each containing distinctive and indestructible pottery sherds. Equally luckily the earliest writing was often set upon clay 'tablets' which do not suffer the decay to which paper and parchment succumb. Gradually archaeologists have been able to build up a coherent picture from those precious remains of buildings, tombs, pottery, and writing, showing how each individual culture evolved.

This study goes further by comparing the various cultures in order to establish priority, contact, and influence. What ways can be found to trace interaction and influence among peoples and cultures so far in the past?

To establish a chronological framework is fundamental. The Mesopotamians recorded what they saw in the sky, including astronomical events for which we can calculate precise dates: these underpin the framework. The long gaps between these few dates can be filled in by the lengths of reign which are supplied by very ancient king-lists. In fixing absolute chronology in this way we can be accurate for dates going back to *c.*1000 BC. Between about 1000 and 1500 BC there is a leeway of a few years. But then, before *c.*1500 BC, there are four options for dates, each one 56 years apart. For that period Carbon 14 dating still has too large a margin of error to help. In this book the longest chronology is used, by which Hammurabi of Babylon ruled from 1848 to 1806. Cultures beyond Mesopotamia have no extant written records of this kind for such an early period, so that absolute chronology for them cannot be secured earlier than about 600 BC.

Some cultures, notably the Egyptian, Israelite, and Hittite kingdoms, have known dynastic sequences. Occasionally they can be linked to Mesopotamian chronology by a synchronism, for example when a text mentions that a certain Babylonian or Assyrian king had dealings with a certain foreign king. Synchronisms tell us that the two reigns overlapped, but not the exact point within the reign of each king.

We can gain further insight by using relative chronology, in which events happening in different countries are shown to be simultaneous or far apart in time. Relative chronology can be established in several ways. The material evidence of imports among archaeological finds is particularly useful. Archaeology is not usually precise enough to date to a particular king the context in which imports were found, but their presence proves that a level of occupation in the excavated sequence cannot be much earlier than the moment when the object was made. Especially useful are sherds of the kinds of pottery which were subject to fast-changing fashion, such as the painted wares of Minoan Crete or Attic Greece. Since they had no intrinsic value when broken, they were soon discarded. Elsewhere, however, ceramic styles stayed unchanged for many decades.

Some objects bear inscriptions of known kings —alabaster vessels and seals of officials are two examples. One might think that such items are ideal for pinpointing the influence of Mesopotamians abroad, for even without inscriptions, they were carved according to quite frequent changes in fashion out of imperishable stone. Unfortunately, however, their intrinsic value means that they were handed down the generations as heirlooms, or given away as gifts, or collected as antiques, or fell down rabbit holes— all ways in which they ended up in a time-zone quite different from the one in which they were made. So individual finds are not reliable guides to chronology, but the accumulated evidence can yield a firmer framework.

Other types of valuable object, such as statues and jewellery of particular designs and techniques, are also recognizable abroad as 'foreign'. But even when the findspot is known and clear, such as in a tomb or temple or palace (rather than dredged out of a river by chance, for instance) we cannot tell whether the treasure came directly or indirectly, as merchandise or as the dowry of a foreign princess. Again, reliable information comes only from adding together several different clues.

These are the material remains from which relative chronology is built up, gradually narrowing the margins of error as more evidence comes to light. Because these objects seldom connect with an absolute date, it is customary to express time in periods according to the leading metal technology of the time, such as 'Middle Bronze Age'. Of course the period so named for one country is only roughly equivalent to the period so named in another. But since in the Old World phases of development in metal technology are roughly parallel within each culture and are linked to recognizable imports, we can say with some confidence whether, for instance, the practice of making standard bricks or of writing in cuneiform (wedge-shaped) script spread from one place to another, rather than in the reverse direction. The quantity and quality of evidence increases for later periods, and links become much firmer from the late eighth century BC onwards.

Evidence of a quite different kind comes from languages and scripts. Some languages can be grouped by common features of structure and sound. The words that correspond to each other between languages of the same group are called cognates; within the Indo-European group *city* in English is cognate with *civitas* in Latin and *ciudad* in Spanish, but not with *polis* in Greek.

When a word from one language is borrowed by a language of another group, it is often recognizable by its shape. We can see that bungalow, jujitsu, assassin, and jamboree are foreign words in English. But we often know the language group without being able to specify exactly which language loaned the word. For instance *siglos* 'shekel' in ancient Greek is a Semitic word which may come either from Akkadian

(east Semitic) *shiqlu* or from Hebrew (west Semitic) *sheqel*. Often the borrowed word merges into the patterns of the adopting language, as the Greek *siglos* has changed the guttural sound *q*, which is foreign to it, into *g*, and has added a Greek noun ending *-os*. If several such changes take place, the loan may be hard to recognize. This is often so with names and epithets: John, Ian, Siobhan, and Johannes are all cognate. The shapes of words are sometimes distinctive: we may recognize that *fortissimo* is Italian and *Schadenfreude* German, whether or not we know the meaning. The study of comparative philology tries to work out rules for the changes that take place, for it is easy to be misled by coincidence: despite appearances, French *car* 'for' has nothing to do with English *car* 'vehicle'. Past scholarship is littered with the debris of false connections.

Personal names are especially useful for tracing contact. They all have literal meanings and were sometimes translated in Antiquity rather than being pronounced in their original language. Thus *Peter* in English is our pronunciation of Greek *Petros* 'rock', but in St John's Gospel Peter was called *Cephas*, using an Aramaic word for 'rock'. Sometimes several kinds of change work together: in Japan *Superman* has become *Ultraman* and is pronounced *Urataraman*.

Scripts are entirely distinct from language groups. The Semitic Phoenicians used an alphabet which was also used by the Indo-European Greeks, although the latter added a full system of vowels. The different alphabet used for the Semitic Arabic language was taken over and adapted for the Indo-European Persian and Altaic Turkish languages. Some languages were written from left to right, or top to bottom; other languages using the same script wrote from right to left. These are all features by which influence can be traced.

Before alphabets were developed, writing systems were more complicated. Some were mainly syllabic, so that *ab, eb, ib, ub, ba, be, bi, bu* may be 8 entirely different signs, rather than the 5 letters *b, a, e, i, u* in combination. Other scripts were mainly pictographic or ideographic in which one sign stood for a whole word or a set of ideas; English examples are % 'per cent', £ 'pound sterling' and = 'equals'. These scripts can be grouped in another way, according to the materials used for writing. Egyptian hieroglyphs and alphabetic Aramaic are generally painted with ink on to the flat surfaces of papyrus, wood, or wall-plaster, whereas the cuneiform script, used for Akkadian, Sumerian, Hittite, and several other languages from different groups, was indented with a stylus into the surface of a moist clay tablet. By taking several such characteristics into account, and checking their chronological relationship, we can confirm that the Indo-European Hittites derived their writing system from that of Semitic Akkadian, and that Herodotos was correct in saying that the Greeks acquired their alphabet from the Phoenicians.

Most complex of all is to compare different cultures for themes in literature and for religious practices. On the face of it one might suppose that certain stories or particular forms of worship are likely to have arisen by coincidence in different places at different times. Often people look at such similarities piecemeal and they ignore quite different kinds of evidence for contact and influence. We generally take for granted that literature is found in certain, easily recognized genres: poems, fables, letters, fairy-tales, and novels. In some parts of the world however, such as Australia, southern Africa, or Canada before Europeans arrived, these genres never developed. In the ancient Near East and adjacent lands the genres developed over a very long span of time, in conjunction with particular themes suitable to each genre and precise ways in which the themes are formulated. This gradual and complex development can be traced in Mesopotamia, which maintained an unbroken tradition of scholarly activity during a period of three thousand years. Its patrons came from both temples and royal courts. It is documented through hundreds of thousands of dated cuneiform writings on clay and stone. Embedded in those texts are concepts of education, law and ethics, religion, magic, and science, many of them closely associated with forms of worship and court ceremony. Natural disasters and foreign conquerors came and went, but no dark age was deep enough to break the thread of continuity. When similarities are found between adjacent cultures in respect of genre, theme, and ideas, we can often eliminate coincidence by using entirely different evidence of the kinds just described.

Ancient Mesopotamia was remarkable above all for its scholarly academic tradition, continuing into the period of the Roman empire, unbroken by political and linguistic changes. According to the evidence we have found, if one factor had to be singled out as pre-eminent in spreading influence from Mesopotamia to its neighbours, it would be that academic tradition. Scholars from Babylon and Nineveh travelled abroad and brought literary training with translation skills to foreign courts. The tradition, flexible and adaptable, began long before alphabetic scripts developed and continued long afterwards.

FURTHER READING

CAVALLI-SFORZA, L. L., MENOZZI, P., and PIAZZA, A., *The History and Geography of Human Genes* (Princeton, 1994), esp. 16–24 and 242–5.

COOPER, J. S., 'Posing the Sumerian Question: Race and Scholarship in the Early History of Assyriology', *Aula Orientalis 9*, in honour of M. Civil (1991), 47–66.

DAWKINS, R., *The Selfish Gene* (rev. edn.; Oxford, 1989), ch. 11.

GRUEN, E., 'Cultural Fictions and Cultural Identity', *TAPA* 123 (1993), 1–14.

JAUSS, H. R., *Toward an Aesthetic of Reception* (Harvester Press, 1982).

MOOREY, P. R. S., *A Century of biblical Archaeology* (Cambridge, 1991).

STOLPER, M. W., 'On Why and How', *Culture and History: The Construction of the Ancient Near East* ii (Copenhagen, 1992), 13–22.

WELLS, P. S., *Culture Contact and Culture Change: Early Iron Age Europe and the Mediterranean World* (Cambridge, 1980).

I

OCCASIONS AND OPPORTUNITIES

1. *To the Persian Conquest*

STEPHANIE DALLEY

Proto-Historic Times, *c.*3500–3000 BC

FAR BACK IN TIME WHEN THE EARLIEST FORMS of writing began, cities already sprawled along the banks of the two great rivers in lower Mesopotamia. Writing seems to have developed there out of an accounting system. Our first evidence is limited to geometric tokens of solid clay, sometimes enclosed in clay envelopes. A stone cylinder, carved with a design, was rolled over the outside surface to seal it. Sometimes the clay envelopes were also impressed with tokens of the same shape and number as those enclosed within. In this way seals and writing were inextricably linked in a union that persists to this day. Some early signs that were impressed upon clay tablets resemble the tokens. They are not specific to any one language for, like international road signs, the tokens as symbols could be understood in any language and so used abroad. Cylinder seals were a local invention which gave far better scope to artistic design than the stamp seals used in adjacent lands.

The simple signs seem to have evolved very quickly into an elaborate system using hundreds of signs, many of them not pictographic, and the development took place in the same few large cities of southern Mesopotamia where the token system of accounting had been invented. In neighbouring Iran around Susa the idea was soon taken over and adapted to local use. Records made in this way were apparently kept in huge archives and were used to keep control over the agricultural and pastoral produce that supplied big organizations. The need to invent such a system must have been overwhelming: so enormous was the extent of those very early cities—Uruk, Girsu, Kish, and Susa—that the supply and storage of foodstuffs for the teeming populace and sacrifices for their numerous deities required a rigorous system of control and an élite of administrators.

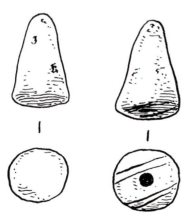

1. Clay tokens and an archaic tablet from Mesopotamia.

MAP 2. Sketch map showing major cities and regions of Mesopotamia in early Antiquity

Just as in complex modern systems, corruption, fraud, and theft were a constant temptation to insiders and outsiders, and held the potential for massive depletion. Security measures such as envelopes, duplication, and sealing evolved fast to thwart thieves. To defend against raiding, whether by hostile men or by predatory animals, defensive walls both for buildings and for cities were built. To give some idea of the size of buildings and cities at that time, one supreme example may be cited: the Early Dynastic (c.3000–2350 BC) city wall of Uruk is 9 km. long, and it contained several colossal buildings with dimensions of the order of 80 × 50 m. Such huge constructions could hardly have been created without that quintessentially Mesopotamian invention, the brick mould. This enabled the mass production of bricks in standard sizes in a land which lacked stone or good timber, but produced straw to temper the alluvial clay. The brick and early writing soon came together when inscriptions began to be stamped upon bricks to testify to their maker. Both were necessary to the development of the city, and early civic pride is clearly shown in the design of some large cylinder seals engraved with symbols that later represent the names of great cities: Larsa, Ur, Uruk, Zabala, and others. The invention of beer helped to lighten the burden of incessant labour. Sacred fermentation vats were kept in the temples of Ishtar, patron goddess of brewing. These inventions—standard bricks, beer, large cities, and administration through the written word—are still with us today.

The architecture of that very early time displays some features which are unique and easily recognized. Terracotta cones or pegs of various kinds adorned mud-brick walls, inserted into the brickwork so that their heads formed a decorative mosaic-like façade. These artefacts, together with clay sealings impressed by cylinders, are the distinctive objects which allow

2. Seal impression from Susa, *c.*3300 BC and reconstruction of the cylinder seal from which it came.

Mesopotamian contact and influence to be traced beyond the boundaries of the homeland, and they show an influence far wider than anyone suspected a few decades ago. Terracotta cones and cylinder seal impressions have now been found on numerous archaeological sites in north Syria and south-eastern Turkey, particularly in settlements along the banks of the upper Euphrates river. In Egypt too they have been found: cones at Buto in the western delta of the Nile, and cylinder-seal impressions at Abydos. For the next 3,000 years seals and sealings transported artistic motifs in miniature to far-distant regions.

We still cannot say what kind of influence from Mesopotamia affected Egypt, nor how long it persisted at this very early time. There is still no way of showing for how long an archaeological level of deposit or a building or an art style remained in use: at least a century in this case and perhaps much longer. One route by which the influence arrived was by sea from the Levant. In Egypt the traces of Mesopotamian influence are supported by close similarities in architectural forms, particularly niched façades, and in pictures carved on stone palettes used for mixing pigments. They are found in the period preced-

ing the First Dynasty, around 3500 BC, before the whole of the Nile valley in Egypt was united for the first time and when kings first appear in Egypt. The traces continue for a short time into the Egyptian Early Dynastic period (*c.*2920–2575 BC) and then vanish, but they leave behind two enduring hallmarks. First, an Egyptian hieroglyph meaning 'seal' and 'treasurer' shows a cylinder seal on a string, and it is written to convey those meanings even when the act of sealing is performed not with a cylinder but with a scarab. Second, the Egyptian system of writing has features which are identical with some in Sumerian and Akkadian cuneiform—the written languages of early Mesopotamia. It contains a mixture of logographic (one sign for a whole word) and syllabic signs. It uses determinatives, signs which are not pronounced but show the category of an adjacent sign, for example whether it stands for an object made of wood or of stone. Even the verbal system of the Egyptian language is reckoned to have had the same parent as the Semitic verbal system, having left it as an offshoot at an early age.

Because writing was only just developing out of an iconic system of tokens which did not offer a way

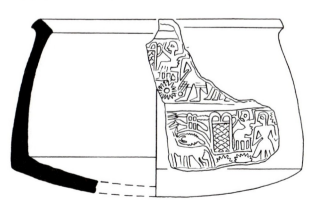

3. Cylinder seal impression on a jar.

4. Early cylinder seals in Egypt.

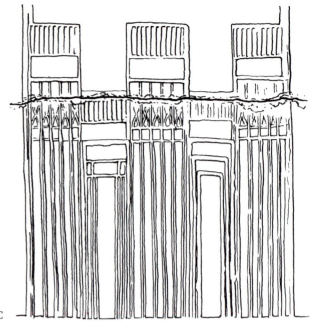

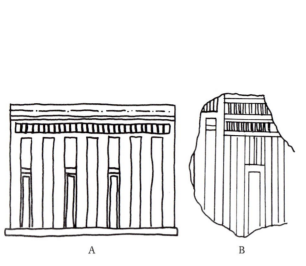

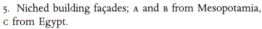

5. Niched building façades; A and B from Mesopotamia, C from Egypt.

of formulating sentences, narratives, or dialogues, different groups of peoples could apply such a writing system to their own languages. The characteristic Egyptian hieroglyphs make a sudden appearance imitating the Mesopotamian system but reflecting the language of Egypt; thus too the cuneiform script used for proto-Elamite in south-western Iran exhibits its own individuality. The stimulus was therefore a general one which inspired but did not mask indigenous culture, and would have met with a creative response only where a high level of culture already existed.

The token system and then clay tablets, engraved with pictograms which quickly developed into cuneiform signs, are attested also in eastern Iran, demonstrating that influence flowed eastwards as well as westwards. In the same way traces are coming to light of fourth-millennium settlements along the Arabian Gulf, which suggests that the much later emergence of writing and sealing in the Indus valley, coinciding with large, brick-built cities, should also be connected in some way with the culture of Mesopotamia. As elsewhere, the exact nature of the contact still eludes us.

Any guesses we may make about the nature of influence or control exerted by the inventors of writing over Syria, Anatolia, Egypt, and Iran may be supplemented by the pictures engraved on those early cylinder seals that left their clear impression upon *bullae*—the clay blobs that sealed bags of tokens, strings around the mouths of sacks and jars, leather pouches,

and door bolts. We find files of prisoners, naked and bound; rows of obedient people bringing endless produce to temples; men stripped of their clothing, receiving physical punishment: these are scenes that imply ferocious control over the local populace, and perhaps also conquest abroad by force. On seal impressions found around Susa in western Iran the sack of a fortified city is shown in a manner reminiscent of Assyrian conquests more than two thousand years later.

This period of expansion, linked to the rise of urban civilization and writing, gives rise to implications as profound as they are tantalizing. Pieces of clay in various shapes and sizes may be our only tangible evidence, but general similarities in buildings, types of literature, and some religious and royal practices between the different areas of the Near East may be explained by the early links now revealed. Each area rapidly developed its own style and made its unique contributions. To appreciate how they are related we must look at cultures elsewhere in the world and realize that not every early civilization had brick-built cities, or kings with sceptres; not every religion made representations of its gods in human form or fed them with human food and drink and chanted hymns in their praise; not every culture handed down wisdom and philosophy in the form of a dialogue between a man and his son or a master and his pupil.

But the nature of the evidence means that scholars cannot track down the way in which individuals affected society, or provide a neat chronological table showing a precise sequence of crucial events. Neither personal names, nor loan-words, nor literary echoes can be traced back to such early times. No types of written evidence are preserved without large gaps. Nevertheless, it is now beyond doubt that the late fourth millennium BC was a time when Mesopotamian influence spread far abroad and established itself at the core of urban civilization.

Merchants and Sealings in Anatolia, *c.*2300–1700 BC

Bullae as well as terracotta cone decoration are normally found associated with the first public buildings to emerge from early urban sprawl. Taking them as a guide, archaeologists have found the trail leading along the upper Euphrates through the Taurus mountains and reaching deep into Anatolia, beginning around 3500 BC and distinctly altering the nature of local settlements. Once again, there is no way to find out the nature of the contact. It can only be suggested, by working backwards from later, clearer evidence, that groups of traders set out from the big cities of southern Mesopotamia and south-western Iran to distant, foreign settlements where they lived as merchants and did business from a separate quarter of the town, calling upon their homeland for occasional military assistance as the need arose.

Evidence comes from a single Assyrian merchant colony at Kanesh near Kayseri in central Anatolia, derived from the parent city Ashur on the middle Tigris, a journey of about six weeks. It consists of business records which use a rather limited range of cuneiform signs. They date between about 2000 and 1700 BC, and were found in houses of two successive levels of occupation. These dwellings, clearly private not public, were preceded by two earlier levels built along the same lines but lacking clay tablets or sealings. The guess that they might represent an earlier settlement of Assyrian merchants has a gleam of support from fragments of extraordinary stories about two famous kings of Mesopotamia: Sargon and Naram-Sin of Agade,[1] who made legendary military forays into Anatolia around 2300 BC, in support of beleaguered merchants. These stories were found not in

Mesopotamia but at the Hittite capital city Hattusa in the heart of Anatolia. In showing that the Indo-European Hittites enjoyed them, the discovery of these tales proves that they were not merely the local, propagandist output of the heroic Semitic rulers in question.

Although the colony of Assyrian merchants at Kanesh is the only one for which we have documentary evidence, its texts refer to colonies of the same kind in other Anatolian cities, as do the fragmentary legends about the kings of Agade. Moreover, bricks stamped with an inscription of Naram-Sin have been uncovered at Tell Brak, in the plain at the foot of the Taurus mountains, providing firm material evidence along the routes from Mesopotamia into Anatolia. There is good evidence, therefore, that foreign enclaves of Mesopotamians, living abroad in order to trade, were to be found in Anatolia around 2000 BC.

In any case, when the Hittites formed their first dynasty at Hattusa around 1700 BC they did not bring a pure, Indo-European culture to a region of undeveloped barbarism. It was upon the higher culture of Mesopotamia, already 1,500 years old, that they based their model for many social and religious institutions, even if they knew about it only at second-hand from foreign traders and from sporadic encounters with soldiers from Agade until much later they conquered Syrian cities. The background of long-standing contact, whether continuous or intermittent from the late fourth millennium, explains why the Hittites adopted the cuneiform script; why Hittite myths and treaties of the mid-second millennium incorporate several major Babylonian deities in positions of high respect, as well as referring with reverence to the city of Nippur; and why their law-code texts are like those of Assyria and Babylonia both in formulation and in subject matter. Since the Hittites also had an older, hieroglyphic writing system which is more like that of Egypt, we cannot claim that Mesopotamia alone influenced their cultural development, but simply that it was a contributor; however, Egyptian gods, places, and personal names are not found in Hittite texts except in international correspondence.

The direction of influence is clear. An impression from a cylinder seal, found on an envelope of the second level at Kanesh, *c.*1700, exhibits purely Mesopotamian iconography. Hittite myths and gods

---

[1] The city Agade was located at the confluence of the Tigris and Diyala rivers.

are not found in Babylonian literature. Even when Mursili the Hittite king eventually made a lightning raid on Babylon around 1651 he left behind no marks of influence, cultural or political. Scribes at Hattusa often had Babylonian personal names, but scribes in Babylon never had Hittite names.

Mesopotamian influence in general spread mainly through trading and business activities rather than direct domination. This was helped by a major development in Mesopotamian society of that time, namely the finance of investment and insurance. The ancient Babylonians and Assyrians, inhabiting rich alluvial land with no mineral resources, used trade to build up a stock of gold, silver, copper, and lead for currency from which new enterprises could be funded. Much of the business was undertaken by private individuals who used the banking facilities of temples and palaces. Their activities were based upon ever-growing national reserves of silver; almost all transactions were notionally carried out in silver even if the metal itself did not change hands; and the word for silver came to mean 'money' in general, like the French 'argent'. Within their own society they had evolved the concept of negotiable shares or prebends, in other words individual investments for which the owner was not the one who laboured, but who took regular profit and used it to extend his business activities as an entrepreneur. Such a system was superior in scope to that of neighbouring peoples whose own concepts had barely developed beyond complex barter with the indirect exchange of goods.

Gemstones from the East and Cities of the Indus Valley

Lapis lazuli and carnelian were the most highly prized gemstones, precious luxuries used to display the wealth of the Sumerians and Babylonians of early Mesopotamia. They could be acquired only from distant lands—lapis lazuli mined in the mountains of north-east Afghanistan, and carnelian mainly extracted from the rocks of Gujarat on the Indian subcontinent. Trading ventures to procure them have left their visible results in beads and inlays among the ornaments of early graves from the late fourth millennium BC, not only in the cities of Mesopotamia and neighbouring western Iran, but also in Egypt and at urban settlements on the upper Euphrates in Syria

and Turkey. These were the means, whether by land or sea, by which Mesopotamian culture, notably the idea of writing, sealing, and monumental brick architecture, became known to the populous regions of western Pakistan, and seem to have influenced the rise of urban civilization in the Indus valley, where writing appears in archaeological remains around 2000 BC. Two of its cities, Harappa and Mohenjo-daro, built several centuries earlier using standard sizes of brick, cover more than 200 hectares each. As elsewhere, the rise of large cities was accompanied by widespread use of seals and bricks, and followed by writing. The extraction of copper from Oman, equidistant between the two Bronze Age cultures with similar needs for copper ore, also brought contact between Mesopotamia and the Indus.

Contact deduced from goods found within Mesopotamia has been traced in the form of etched carnelian beads, stamp and cylinder seals featuring elephants and characteristically Indian cattle. There are no *bullae* of clay impressed with cylinder seals from the Indus, or terracotta cone mosaics, and it appears as if the contact between the two regions was both later in time and of a kind different from that which is traceable in Egypt and along the upper Euphrates. It seems to have lasted from around 2500 BC until the Indus cities were destroyed after some 700 years of splendour, with textual evidence from the cities of lower Mesopotamia in particular revealing that textiles and foodstuffs flowed eastwards.

Just as happened earlier, some of the ideas and skills of Mesopotamian society were adopted in an area which had already become quite cultured, but the resulting development looked very different from the form it took elsewhere. Alien symbols of writing (still undeciphered) and rectangular stamp seals (not cylinders) are characteristic of Indus cities. Urban cultures in other regions such as Arabia and Central Asia, where prehistoric remains are still at a very early stage of discovery, may have contributed to the differences. After that period the links became much weaker and less direct, and the word for the Indus region, Meluhha, became an expression for a fabulous country far away. Sometimes it was applied to Ethiopia, just as to the Romans 'India' meant both the Indian subcontinent and the north-east coast of the African continent. The Indus valley abandoned both its urban tradition and literacy for the next thousand years until around the time of Alexander the Great. However, the names of gods Mitra, Indra, Varuna, and Nasatya later known in India are found in cuneiform texts of the fourteenth century BC, for they were worshipped by Mittanian (Indo-Aryan) overlords of Assyria, so the gap in evidence between the Harappan culture and the Hellenistic period is still hard to evaluate.

Implications of the Sumerian King-List

Around 2100 BC in Mesopotamia a king-list was compiled which presented the early dynasties of various cities as a simple list, as if each had succeeded another and none were contemporary. Kings before the Flood were given in the same format as kings after the Flood, except that they had stupendous numbers of years allotted to their reigns.

Although the text is written in Sumerian, it covers a much wider area than simply the cities of lower Mesopotamia; in other words, it acknowledges that early urban civilization was found outside the confines of a single ethnic or language group and beyond the alluvium of lower Mesopotamia. The five cities which precede the Flood: Eridu, Bad-tibira, Sippar, Larak, and Shuruppak, are indeed central Mesopotamian ones; but after the Flood, and after the dynasties of Kish, Uruk, and Ur, we find the distant cities of Awan, Hamazi, and Mari named.

Neither Awan nor Hamazi has been identified, but both are known to lie in Iran, and Awan is known from other texts as a traditional Elamite political centre, Elamite being neither a Semitic nor an Indo-Iranian language, and unrelated to Sumerian. Hamazi has variously been placed to the east of the Tigris, either a short or a long distance away over the Zagros mountains. The great Elamite centres of Susa and Anshan are not mentioned in the Sumerian king-list, but since a copy of the list has been unearthed at Susa, we know for certain that the king-list was part of the scribal curriculum or a library text there around 1800 BC. It was not, therefore, simply a piece of local propaganda. Anshan, which was a huge city five times larger than Susa in proto-Elamite times, is known particularly for its 'defeat' by Mesopotamian rulers of the late third millennium, and for the frequency with which it is named in messenger texts from the Third Dynasty of Ur recording

payments of silver made to envoys from abroad. The chief king of that dynasty, Shulgi, sent a daughter to marry the ruler of Marhashi, a very powerful state in central or eastern Iran. The part played by princesses who made such diplomatic marriages and their hybrid children in transmitting culture from Mesopotamia abroad is not less important for being elusive. With Anshan identified as Tell-i Malyan near Persepolis, and Marhashi even further to the east, the western regions of Iran can be seen as belonging to an area to some extent sharing its culture with Mesopotamia over more than a millennium. The kingdom of Elam, based upon Susa and Anshan, had its own language and deities, but nevertheless kept many records in Babylonian, only occasionally using the same script to write the Elamite tongue. The Babylonian hero Gilgamesh was so famous in Elam that his name was used in Elamite personal names; conversely, no recognizably Elamite or Iranian heroes are known from Mesopotamian personal names. The titles of Hittite, Elamite, and west Semitic kings are closely modelled upon the titulary of their contemporaries in the ancient cities of Babylonia, as if drawn into the area of highest prestige represented by the Sumerian king-list.

Mari on the middle Euphrates represents the westernmost city in the Sumerian king-list. It lies outside the true heartland of Sumer, and its early kings appear to have Semitic, perhaps west Semitic, names. Cuneiform texts found there have similarities with those of contemporary Ebla to the west, where early texts can now be defined as an offshoot of literary traditions centred upon Kish. They show how firmly inland Syrian cities (including Carchemish, Aleppo, and Hamath which are often named in texts from Ebla) can be placed within the orbit of Mesopotamian culture around 2300 BC. Although the coastal cities of the Levant lie outside the sphere of the Sumerian king-list, it should be noted that offerings were made in Ur to the goddess of Byblos in the late third millennium, and that a cuneiform dictionary text of the same period was found in Byblos.

To the north of Mesopotamia, in the foothills of the upper Habur river, a copy of the Sumerian king-list, dating to around the time of Hammurabi of Babylon (1848–1806), has been found at Tell Leilan. The site lies over 200 km. north of Ashur, in an area where Hurrian people predominated. Once again we see how Mesopotamia exerted a cultural supremacy through a core of cuneiform texts over an area which contained many different peoples and languages. This picture is reinforced by the use of cylinder seals by rulers in peripheral lands. For example, a ruler from Itapalhum, a city-state in the Zagros mountains, whose connections with Elam were strong, had a 3-century-old cylinder seal recut with his own name and titles in Babylonian cuneiform.

High Culture from the Sages

At the heart of Mesopotamian traditions about the origins of writing and the arts of civilized life lies the story of the Seven Sages. Briefly recounted by Berossos in the Hellenistic period for the benefit of a royal patron, confirmed by passing allusions in late cuneiform texts, the tale was fundamental to ancient belief about Babylonian origins.

The great god Ea, so the tradition runs, sent seven sages to earth, long before the Flood, in order to teach mankind all the arts and skills of civilization such as building cities, kingship, music, metallurgy, and agriculture. Each sage was associated with a different legendary king in one of the early cities such as Eridu, where kingship first arose under the patronage of Ea; Sippar, the city of Shamash the sun-god (whose early king Enmeduranki has connections with the biblical Enoch); Uruk the city of Gilgamesh; and Kish, ruled by kings with Semitic, not Sumerian, names. All these kings are listed in the Sumerian king-list.

The sages were represented as holy carp, fish who had risen up from the sweet waters of the Apsu, Ea's dwelling in the southern city of Eridu, and were banished back again after angering the gods by their bad behaviour. In addition to the original seven, there were other sages after the Flood, who were only partly divine, and were attached to the courts of historical kings, such as Asalluhi-mansum the sage of Hammurabi of Babylon.

No foreign elements can be detected in this tradition, which is closely linked, like the Sumerian king-list, to the Flood, and there is no reason to doubt that it is indigenous.

The Egyptians had sages, but they were all historical men of learning attached to the courts of known pharaohs. The earliest was Imhotep, the architect and chancellor of Djoser around 2650 BC, far later

than the pre-Flood era of Mesopotamian legend. Like those who followed him, he was of mortal birth. He was deified as a reward for his achievements, but did not arrive on earth as an immortal being sent from heaven. Therefore the Egyptian tradition does not claim either the antiquity or the divine mission that is characteristic of Mesopotamia.

Syria too had a tradition about sages. It resembles that of Mesopotamia rather than that of Egypt. Sanchuniathon, a Phoenician, is said to have written a work 'before the Trojan War' which Philo of Byblos claimed to transmit in c. AD 100; Philo's writings in turn were transmitted in extracts by Eusebios, c. AD 260–340. This tradition lists some fourteen generations of super-mortals who invented the skills needed for civilized life, particularly in its technological aspects. Until recently scholars were inclined to dismiss most of the traditions in Philo of Byblos, as well as those of Berossos. But when Canaanite myths of the Late Bronze Age were discovered at Ugarit and confirmed some of Philo's details, and when cuneiform evidence for the sages emerged from the ruins of Seleucid Uruk, Philo and Berossos were recognized as bearers of true testimony, even though the textual tradition was corrupt. The archaeological evidence for very early contact between all these areas backs up the deduction that the essential concept, civilization brought by sages, was diffused from Mesopotamia.

The School Curriculum in Cuneiform

By the late third millennium BC writing was a fairly standardized skill, taught and practised in academies of learning. By the time Shulgi ruled Ur (2150–2103 BC) a large range of signs with pictographic and syllabic values had been reduced to a more-or-less standard corpus of about 600. With them there developed a narrative capability which gradually crystallized into distinct genres used for myths, wisdom literature, chronicles of events, records of conquests, and letters both official and personal. These works of literature were still very short compositions which were occasionally collected into a group or series, just as daily records were collected into monthly and yearly records. But they did not yet have a framework as coherent collections, and the writing was

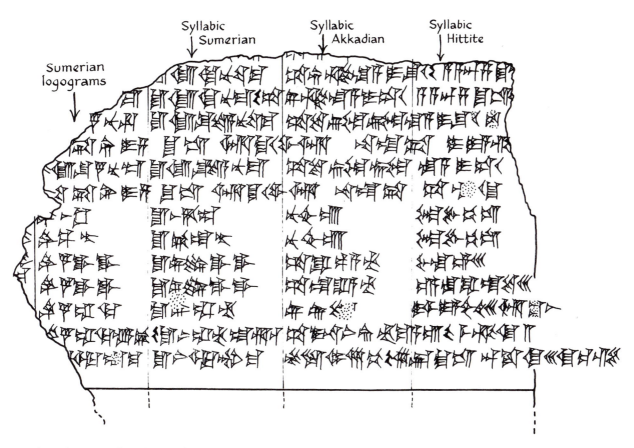

6. Trilingual version of standard professions list, from Hattusa.

still very brief and ambiguous, for it did not represent complete speech.

Shulgi was a model ruler who had received his education in a sophisticated academy of learning, and claimed a place of honour as a foremost scholar of his time. In his own translated words:

The Seven of wisdom went out (from Eridu) with me.
In the house of wisdom, the intelligence of the land,
I, Shulgi, the king of Sumer, truly profess knowledge.
My hand accurately controls the pure reed (for writing
    and measuring)
I can sing foreign songs,
I can make modulations brilliantly on the harp.
So that good people can measure fields with the lapis rod,
Heap up an abundant harvest
To satisfy appetite with best greens and grain,
I am perfect with pickaxe and brick-mould, . . . designing
    building plans, setting out foundations.
For writing cuneiform inscriptions on the pedestals of
    statues,
For elucidating the lapis tablet,
Calculating the accounts, the designs of the land,

I, the intelligent man, learned their terms in full,
I brought the gentle words of my tongue alive on the
    clay,
Large tablets [conveyed] my wishes,
By the word . . . I learned them all,
Dispensing justice with great authority.

Cuneiform was used outside Mesopotamia before 2000 BC in Syria, for instance at Ebla and at Byblos, and at Susa in Elam. Scribes there received their training along strictly Mesopotamian lines. Central to the curriculum was the study of sign manuals and lexical (dictionary) lists which grouped words by category, such as wooden objects, animals, and professions. By the late second millennium we have plenty of evidence that these lists were augmented for use in different language areas. The 'list of professions' is one of the fullest examples showing the origins and expansion of the tradition. Known first from the cities of Uruk and Shuruppak around 3200 BC, it is also found in Susa not much later. By around 1800 BC a complete text of 846 lines or entries can be

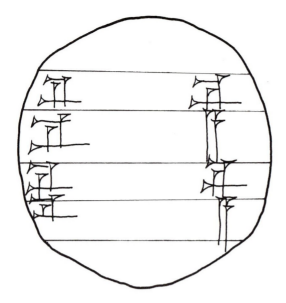

7. School exercise tablet for elementary signs.

pieced together. By 1400 BC it was being used from Ugarit on the Mediterranean to Susa in Iran and to Hattusa in the heart of Anatolia. Eight hundred years later it was still in use not only in the major Assyrian cities, but also in north Syria where scribes in the local school at Huzirina near Harran were obliged to learn and copy it. Also remarkable for its wide distribution in the Late Bronze Age was the list from which scribes learned complex logograms. Like the list of professions, it is known from El-Amarna in Egypt as well as from Ugarit and Hattusa.

The dictionary lists were based on Sumerian, to which Akkadian translations were added. Some of them became trilingual when they were used abroad. At Ugarit, Hurrian as well as alphabetic cuneiform for the Canaanite language known as Ugaritic might be added; in Anatolia Hittite was added; in Babylonia under the non-Semitic Kassite dynasty, equivalents in the Kassite language were added. One list gives common Akkadian words with rare, dialect, or foreign equivalents. This is the mechanism by which Mesopotamian literary culture travelled abroad. Since a process of translation and grammatical comparison had been essential in early lexical lists for Sumerian and Akkadian phrases written side by side, despite fundamental differences in the structure of the two languages, it was a relatively easy exercise to add another, non-Semitic language in an extra column of words or phrases. The Babylonians, through the need to translate Sumerian phrases into their own language Akkadian, had evolved the study of grammar

and syntax by the early second millennium. Evidence for this consists of specialized terms and paradigms for verbs, much of it still impossible for us to understand. The date is some 1,500 years before the lifetime of the Indian scholar Pāṇini, who was a leading figure in the study of Sanskrit grammar in India, and was once thought to be the earliest grammarian in the world.

Another element in school training was the practical mathematics needed to organize manpower and materials for digging canals, making bricks and building walls, and for sowing acres of land with barley. Methods were evolved for solving such problems and ready-reckoner tables have been found in their hundreds. Scribes were also trained to write literary letters for which epistolary models were used, recognizable from multiple copies.

In the Middle Bronze Age at Mari some records were kept in two different styles, so that duplicate texts were produced using on the one hand heavily logographic writings based on the Sumerian language, on the other a more modern, syllabic style to represent the Akkadian language. In the Late Bronze Age at Emar there were two different styles of record, each with a characteristic shape and layout, each using a slightly different syllabary. Among the Hittites, sealings with Luwian hieroglyphs were sometimes used to authorize transactions in cuneiform Hittite written on clay; the names of officials would thus be present on a single document written in two different scripts and two different languages. In other words, a bilingualism in writing was commonplace, aided by lexical lists and a rigorous scribal training, for many centuries. Scribes with Babylonian names (whether they were taken from birth or adopted for the profession) were common on all sites outside Mesopotamia where cuneiform tablets were written. They could deal professionally with a multiplicity of language and writing systems. Literature thus flowed across the borders of lands and languages, making an easy transition into new environments via the training of scribes. The Egyptians had a curriculum for scribal training which in many ways resembles that of Mesopotamia, especially in the use of lists of objects, animals, professions, etc., and in compiling texts for arithmetic and land measurement; but their texts are found from a much later date, the earliest known dating from the Middle Kingdom.

Not only were literature and scribal exercises transferred from the cities of Mesopotamia into foreign

8. Inlays of shell from Ur which imply the existence of animal fables.

countries. In the field of music, for instance, when scribes were trained in the texts which describe the tuning of the harp or lyre, they automatically learned the system later known as Pythagorean tuning. This goes back at least into the Middle Bronze Age in Babylonia, more than a thousand years before the lifetime of Pythagoras the Greek. When they learned the syllabus for quantity surveyors, and struggled through model problems of mathematical calculation, they used an approximation for *pi* and understood what was later known as Pythagoras' theorem. They used place-value notation for numbers, both decimal and sexagesimal, and they divided the circle into 360 degrees.

In the passion which the Babylonians display for collecting examples, listing, and categorizing, we can observe an extension of the recording system represented by the clay tokens, sealed envelopes, and early administrative tablets written in cuneiform script. Drawing on a tradition that went back at least to 2300 BC, the Code of Hammurabi, preserved almost intact on a stone monument, contains some 292 laws, a collection of examples from past and contemporary practice, framed with a poetic prologue and epilogue written in a high literary style. Such works as these formed the core curriculum of scribes throughout the lands where cuneiform writing was adopted. Various practices such as proving guilt or innocence by means of a river ordeal, or swearing oaths by a god while touching a sacred object, were part of the legal system to which Hammurabi's laws referred, and they were widely used beyond Mesopotamia, in Iran, Syria, and Anatolia.

Not long after Shulgi's time, in the early second millennium BC, we can discern among the infuriat-

ingly fragmentary clay tablets some longer compositions, many of them written in Akkadian. The *Epic of Gilgamesh*, incorporating some of the older Sumerian stories about the heroic king of Uruk, took the earliest form in which it qualifies as an epic. Animal fables, which are collected together with proverbs on school tablets, are found much earlier in Mesopotamia (from at least 1800 BC) than in Egypt or Iran.

Therefore not only did business, law, and administration run along lines universally recognized from the east Mediterranean to central Iran, from Anatolia to Egypt, but also a shared literature helped to override distinctions of race and language. In the mid-second millennium BC the Indo-European Hittites of central Anatolia and the Caucasian Hurrians of Armenia both possessed versions of the *Epic of Gilgamesh* translated into their own languages. They wrote in cuneiform only slightly modified to represent their tongue, using some signs purely as icons to express a concept that they would 'read' in their own language. For instance the Storm-god was known under different names and had various attributes according to his locality. A single logogram, the sign

9. Proto-Elamite seal showing animals as scribes, with tablet, styluses or sticks, cylinder seals, measuring vessels, a domed granary, and a reed hut.

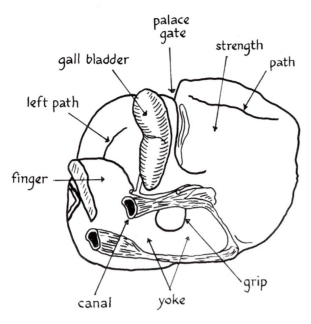

10. Sketch of a sheep's liver showing the main features as named in Akkadian.

IM, was used to write 'Storm-god' and would be read as 'Ishkur' in Sumer, 'Adad' in Assyria, 'Hadad' in Damascus, 'Tarhu' among the Hittites, and 'Teshub' among the Hurrians in the Armenian highlands. This system facilitated translation in writing, and presumably ran alongside the current of oral tradition, which cannot be traced.

The cities for which the core curriculum of cuneiform is definitely known in the mid-second millennium BC are widespread. They include El-Amarna in Egypt, Megiddo and Hazor in Palestine, Pella in Transjordan, Ugarit and Emar in Syria, Hattusa and Tapika in central Anatolia, Susa and Anshan in Iran. One might expect that scribes would have chosen to write in Egyptian or Hittite at times when each was the dominant political power in the area, but they did not do so. Sumerian and Babylonian cuneiform tradition had a cultural authority sufficient to carry it through periods of political strength and weakness alike.

Divination Priests and Doctors as Scribes

The scribes in the academies of the great cities were responsible for maintaining and updating the textbooks used in training. At some point during the late second millennium BC they modernized some of the lexical texts by adding an extra column or entry which gave the up-to-date word, as if to explain one that had fallen out of use. From at least the seventh century they also wrote commentaries on literary texts to explain archaic or erudite terms. They were also responsible for library collections, some of which were housed in temples and palaces and others in the official residence of the scribe, where they have been discovered together with records. From this evidence and from the colophons which give title-page information on literary texts, we now know that many of those scribes were also divination priests, seers who studied and elaborated the rules for discovering destiny in advance and avoiding or averting it by ritual. The divination priests were responsible for a wide variety of writings, including lexical texts, astronomical compendia, myths, epics, and medical treatises. Such men formed the backbone of the educated élite.

The gods imparted their divine decrees to mankind through omens, of which the most common kind could be elicited from the liver of a sheep, metaphorically known as 'the tablet of the gods'. The immortals took decisions in a spirit of democratic counsel and consultative legal judgement. Therefore their decrees could be changed or avoided by man's appropriate action, through rituals and incantations. It was not a question of tricking the gods, but of offering them acceptable alternatives and substitutes. A systematic set of rules for interpretation was the elaborate framework of an academic discipline which relied in part upon the application of opposites such as right–left, upper–lower, straight–curved, etc., partly on series of three such as top–middle–bottom, partly on double meanings in a word (in which the technical vocabulary for individual parts of the liver was crucial) and partly (but to a much lesser extent than used to be thought) upon the idea that a conformation registered as an omen connected with an event such as defeat will again occur when a defeat is impending. These rules were adaptable for other kinds of omens such as the flight of birds, or planetary movements.

The same system was used by the Hittites, among whom cuneiform writing was adopted. But it is also found much further afield, among Greeks and Etruscans, who used, as it were, the same terminology in translation. As we have seen, translation is

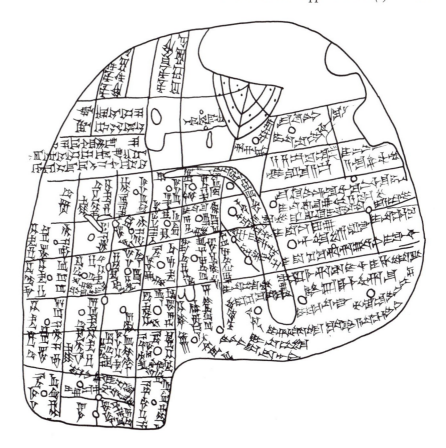

11. Clay model of a sheep's liver with omens labelled in Babylonian, max. dimension 0.145 m.

particularly easily made through a writing system that uses icons or logograms which are not specific to any one language. Omen texts are often written with a high proportion of logograms. In this way it is easy to see how, in the second millennium, the techniques and vocabulary of divination spread across the boundaries of language and geography together with cuneiform writing, under the guidance of scholarly divination priests.

Many of the scribes whose names were given as the 'authors' of famous and long-lasting works in Babylonian cuneiform were incantation priests, *mašmaššu* or lamentation priests, *kalû*. For instance, Sin-leqe-unninni, credited with authorship of the *Epic of Gilgamesh* in its standard version, was an incantation priest from whom, centuries later, other authors who were lamentation priests derived their genealogy. They sang songs designed to calm and appease angry gods, texts which often allude to myths about Ishtar and Dumuzi who periodically went down to the Underworld and died, and who seasonally revived. The chief scribe of the great Assyrian king Esarhaddon, one Adad-šum-uṣur, was also an 'exorcist', a

word which in English belies the wide range of scholarship that such a man professed.

Specialists such as these diviners, incantation priests, and lamentation singers had not only to be highly trained but were also initiated in some way before they could be entrusted with the secrets of their art, and they acknowledged themselves the servants not only of Nabu and Nisaba, traditionally god and goddess of literary skills, but also of Ereshkigal, queen of the Underworld. The clearest evidence for scribes being also diviners or incantation-priests comes from Emar, where their names are found upon dictionary texts, revealing that the educational system of cuneiform literacy was integrally linked with divination, magic, and medicine. In Hittite the logograms for divination priest and doctor are interchangeable.

The prestige of such individuals and their fame in foreign lands is well known from ancient texts. The Amarna letters show that kings of Ugarit, of the Hittites and of Cyprus all at various times summoned such men from foreign courts including Egypt and Babylon. A biblical story describes how the king of Moab sent for a seer named Balaam from Pethor,

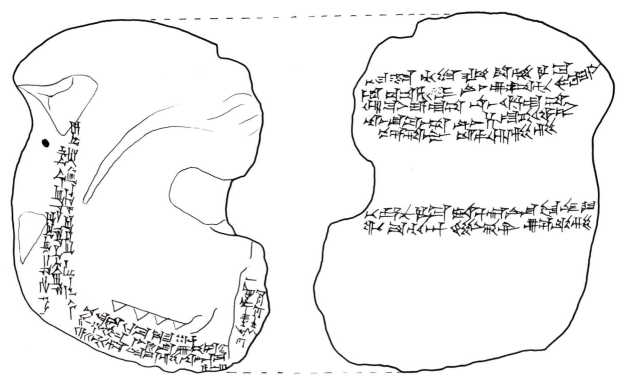

12. Clay model of a sheep's liver with omens inscribed in Akkadian and Hittite from Hattusa.

identified now as Pitru on the Euphrates to the south of Carchemish, where cuneiform Akkadian was regularly used.[2] The itinerant holy man, trained in literature, science, and religion, was an authoritative figure in the second millennium BC. Much of his prestige rested upon his mastery of the cuneiform system of writing and his initiation into the secrets of carefully guarded texts. To teach such mastery, academies of learning flourished in the cities of Mesopotamia with royal patronage, whether the kings of the moment were indigenous or foreign; the west Semitic dynasty of Hammurabi and the non-Semitic dynasty of the Kassites promoted the ancient traditions without interruption, and themselves became Babylonians by adoption.

The Late Bronze Age c.1500–1000 BC

During the Middle Bronze Age the Babylonians had used foreigners as mercenaries. They also took foreigners captive in battle and brought them back to Mesopotamia. Eventually those people might return

home, whether for retirement or because they were ransomed, taking with them reports of the marvels they had seen and learnt abroad. Some wonders were practical, such as the pilastered façades of temples, brick vaulting, and other technical skills; others were intellectual, such as the principles upon which harps were tuned, or the basis of astronomy.

According to clay tablets found in abundance at Mari from the time of Hammurabi of Babylon, various groups of semi-nomadic west Semites, known collectively as Amorites, formed the main components of the fighting force on the middle Euphrates. Babylonian records of Hammurabi's time show that both Elamites and Kassites from Iran were used as specialist units for fighting, particularly as archers and horsemen respectively. Groups of Kassites became settled in the cities of Mesopotamia as well as on the middle Euphrates, and eventually took over the kingship of Babylonia. As rulers they continued traditional practices into the Late Bronze Age.

The deportation of conquered peoples on a huge scale began at least as early as the fourteenth century BC.[3] Tukulti-Ninurta I brought 28,800 Hittites to

[2] For Balaam see Ch. VII, pp. 149–50.   [3] For a description of deportation see Ch. III, pp. 62–3.

13. Sealing of Suppiluliuma from Ugarit, inscribed in Akkadian and Luwian.

Assyria 'from beyond the Euphrates', and he settled Kassite soldiers at the northern Assyrian city of Kalhu on the Tigris, long after the fall of the Kassite dynasty in Babylon. This policy of massive deportation continued into the first millennium, and was instrumental in ensuring that a common cultural background continued through the many centuries when different alphabetic systems, each used for a different language, began to challenge the supremacy of the cuneiform script.

In Ugarit an alphabet of thirty characters written on clay in very simple cuneiform may have picked up the idea of representing letters (rather than syllables or words) from earlier, linear alphabets apparently invented in regions far to the south under Egyptian influence. The cuneiform alphabet was used alongside Akkadian cuneiform which persisted for administration and for royal correspondence. The literature diverges: Canaanite myths were written only in alphabetic cuneiform, and Babylonian compositions were written only in the traditional way. By the early Iron Age a new custom would arise which continued for many centuries: important public inscriptions would be written in two or three languages, each with a different writing system: the traditional, Babylonian cuneiform; Hittite hieroglyphs; and the new, alphabetic writing. An early example of this is inscribed upon the statue of Hadad-yish'i who flourished in the eighth century BC, using Aramaic and Babylonian cuneiform in north Syria. The ease of transfer from one language to another is demonstrated at Emar around 1200 BC where two legal records, both written in Babylonian cuneiform, provided a clear example of a personal name given in two different languages: Tattašše (Hurrian) and Ra'indu (Babylonian), both versions having the same meaning 'Beloved' in the respective tongues. In the kingdoms of upper Mesopotamia and beyond, translation or paraphrase was commonplace.

Of contact through trade, diplomatic gifts, princely exchanges, and marriages arranged for princesses at foreign courts, the Akkadian correspondence found at El-Amarna in Egypt gives many fascinating details, for it contains letters written between all the great rulers of the day: Hittite and Mittani, Babylonian and Assyrian, Cypriot and Tyrian. Just as at Ugarit, the chancellery at El-Amarna possessed its own professional translation service for royal correspondence in the various other languages. At the court of Amenophis III and IV at El-Amarna, scribes were busy learning Babylonian cuneiform through the medium of lexical lists and epics. Letters from the kings of Mittani, Indo-Aryan overlords of Hurrian-speaking people far to the north-east in Anatolia, were written in Babylonian following a preamble in the local language (Hurrian)—which was also written in cuneiform script adapted to the purpose.

Royal ideology and its icons had much in common among the major powers at that period. The symbol of the winged disk, which is the mark of a king, is also the symbol of the Sun-god. It was used by the Pharaoh, the king of Ugarit, Cypriot rulers, the Hittite king, and the Assyrian ruler.

A central belief in Mesopotamian cult practice as in Egyptian was the idea that one could make a statue of a god out of material substances and then by a magic, purifying ritual one could make the god enter the statue so that the object became divine. Two parts of this ritual were known as 'mouth washing' and 'mouth opening', for which details are given in cuneiform texts. The same ritual has been found on tablets from the Hittite capital in Anatolia, virtually translating or paraphrasing the Babylonian text.

A period of upheaval and much destruction separates the Late Bronze Age from the Iron Age. It is especially apparent in central Anatolia where cities

14. Winged disks: Hittite, neo-Assyrian, Aramaean, Urartian, and Achaemenid Persian.

were looted, burned, and abandoned. Mass migrations occasionally forced desperate people to take to the sea, from which they practised piracy and tried to seize coastal lands. Although these movements were catastrophic in some areas, they did not cause anything like a complete break in cultural traditions; indeed, one effect was to spread the knowledge of iron-working from north-eastern Anatolia into the Fertile Crescent by the forced emigration of starving blacksmiths. Although the Hittite empire broke up, Hittite kingdoms writing only Luwian hieroglyphs survived in many regions of central southern Anatolia:

from Malatya on the upper Euphrates to Karatepe in Cilicia, at Hamath on the Orontes in southern Syria and at Carchemish on the middle Euphrates. At Karatepe cuneiform lost its hold, for bilingual inscriptions there are written in Luwian hieroglyphs and the Phoenician alphabetic script. Malatya, Carchemish, and Hamath, however, continued to use cuneiform for some restricted purposes in the Iron Age. In Babylonia and Assyria there was no break whatsoever in the flow of tradition, either in architecture and settlement or in literary practice. The havoc wreaked in central Anatolia and on the coasts of the eastern Mediterranean barely affected Mesopotamia in any direct way.

The Urartian Kingdom in Armenia (*c*.1275–590 BC)

The Hurrians of eastern Anatolia had formed their own petty kingdoms and city-states up to the borders of Assyria since at least as early as 2300 BC. They were a Caucasian people who adopted cuneiform to write their own language on clay, and they worshipped principally the storm-god Teshub and his consort Hepat; also the goddess Shawushka (equivalent to Assyrian Ishtar) whose cult at Nineveh was as much Hurrian as Assyrian in very early times. In the mid-second millennium areas with Hurrian-speaking peoples had been dominated by new arrivals coming from places still unknown: the Mittani, who were Indo-Aryan and worshipped quite different gods. For a couple of centuries the Mittani had gained territory at the expense of the Assyrians, particularly east of the Tigris; but under their rule Babylonian ritual, literature, clay records, and cylinder seals continued in use as before. Eventually the tide turned and the Mittani fell victim, like the Hittite empire, to famine and destruction. We do not know what became of them, but the Hurrian population that remained in eastern Anatolia resurfaced, politically speaking, in the early Iron Age as the Urartian kingdom, once again challenging Assyria for control of the rich foothills and the ancient cities of northern Iraq and Syria.

Despite the convulsions that preceded the establishment of Urartian state power, the kingdom which emerged at the end of the second millennium is recognizably connected with what went before. The

15. Neo-Assyrian royal stamp seal, and a Urartian lion medallion.

Urartians wrote their monumental inscriptions in cuneiform in their own language, which is related to Hurrian; but in the region south-west of Lake Urmia which they controlled until the end of the eighth century they carved bilingual inscriptions so that Akkadian too could be read. Much of their design in the decorative arts is based upon Assyrian motifs, such as the human-headed winged bull. In using cylinder seals as stamps (instead of rolling them), they combined Hittite and Mesopotamian tradition, but their designs are recognizably Mesopotamian.

The earliest extant attempt to record the ancient history of Armenia is to be found in the chronicle of Moses of Khorene in late Antiquity. He has been ridiculed for relating a story about Semiramis, once dismissed as a purely legendary queen of Assyria, and for claiming that she marched to Armenia and fell in love with its ruler Ara, who was tragically slain in the war between the two nations; heartbroken, she decided to spend much of the rest of her life there, and built a fabulous city. Although the story undoubtedly contains fictional material, an Assyrian inscription has recently been found in Anatolia which proves from a contemporary record that Semiramis, historically the wife and then mother of Assyrian monarchs around 800 BC, did indeed march personally into Anatolia, so that there is a grain of truth in

the story after all (See fig. 44B). And it reinforces the observable connections between Assyrian and Urartian civilization, demonstrating that the main flow of influence ran from Mesopotamia northwards.

Urartu was later a place that harboured fugitives from Mesopotamia. When Sennacherib the king of Assyria was murdered by two of his sons in 681 BC, the criminals fled up into the Armenian highlands. When Darius I was still trying to get a firm grip on Babylon in 522 BC, two pretenders arrived from Urartu, claiming to be the sons of Nabonidus, hoping to benefit from an uprising that proved ephemeral. Thus by the time Armenia fell to the Persians around 521 BC, it was thoroughly imbued with the traditions of Babylonian and Assyrian culture, and was sometimes included under the name Assyria.

The Neo-Assyrian Empire
(*c*.1000–612 BC)

The Assyrian people of the late second and early first millennia BC absorbed many foreign influences. They owed their religious and literary eminence largely to Babylonia, filling their own great libraries with texts copied from temple libraries in Babylonian cities.

They had statues of the gods of many other lands in their temples for regular worship: Mitra and Ahura-Mazda[4] from Iran, Teshub and Hepat from Urartu, Marduk from Babylonia. Their marvellous palace sculptures were modelled upon the ones they had seen abroad in Hittite and Luwian (neo-Hittite) city-states in northern Syria and southern Anatolia, and they learned the skills of cavalry from Media to the east, of chariotry from Samaria to the west. Yet they welded these disparate contributions into a new whole that was never static, ever changing and improving. Theirs was a lively society, not embarrassed to copy, emulate, and borrow. In forming gradually a huge empire, they became the wealthiest people in the world, so that the forms of achievement which they made their own were in turn emulated by every ambitious, fashion-conscious court of lesser kings. With empire came wars, prisoners, deportees, tribute, and trade, disseminating influence which extended to the princes of Cyprus, to the Urartians in Armenia, to the Arabs at Tayma in north-west Arabia and to the horse-crazy kings of Nubia who conquered much of lower Egypt around 700 BC.

When a foreign power proved intransigent, the Assyrian monarchs deported people, whether to Mesopotamia itself or to outposts of empire: Arabs to Samaria, Israelites to the River Habur in northern Syria, people of Kummuh[5] to Babylonia. These deportees included the cream of their society: members of the royal family, priests and prophets, skilled craftsmen, and professional warriors. Not all those who came were deportees; some came of their own free will as mercenaries and served willingly the richest rulers ever known, taking a lively interest in the wonderful sights and new ideas that they encountered at Nineveh and Kalhu. Panammu, the ruler of a state in southern Anatolia, had it recorded on his memorial inscription that he had proudly served Tiglath-pileser III in battle:

This statue Bar-rakkab has set up for his father Panammu . . . He grasped the hem of his lord the great king of Assyria, and his lord the king of Assyria set him over powerful kings . . . and he ran at the wheel of his lord Tiglath-pileser in campaigns from east to west . . . over the four quarters of the earth. Then my father Panammu died while following his lord Tiglath-pileser king of Assyria on campaign . . . and the whole camp of his lord the king of Assyria wept for him, and he set up an image for him on

the road and brought my father across from Damascus to Assyria.

Others came as diplomats: wine-ration texts from Kalhu list the many different foreign envoys who drank at the courts of ninth- and eighth-century monarchs. Junior members of royal families came to Assyria as hostages: the Arab princess Tabua was raised at the court of Sennacherib and was then made queen of the Arabs by Esarhaddon; and Arukku son of Cyrus I lived for a while at the court of Ashurbanipal in Nineveh.

We are accustomed to see Assyrian conquest and rule, including deportation, through the eyes of those redactors who gave the Old Testament its final form and who have, perhaps unwittingly, given us the impression that the people of Israel were particularly targeted for harsh treatment. In fact cuneiform records, contemporary with the events that they describe, show that Israelite charioteers from Samaria worked willingly for Sargon II, and many young men in search of fame and fortune came from Nubia, Palestine, Ionia, Urartu, and Elam as specialist mercenaries and returned home having gained prestige.

The Assyrian records reveal also that by far the largest number of people uprooted from their homeland consisted of Babylonians, including citizens of Uruk, Babylon, and Ur. This great exodus and diaspora of native Babylonians from their country must have had a great effect in reinforcing the cultural contact which already existed throughout the Near East.

It has often been supposed that by the late eighth century, when the neo-Assyrian monarchs embarked upon their final and greatest era of expansion, the Aramaic language and script would have superseded cuneiform writing except in the heartland of Mesopotamia because they are simpler. In fact there are small but precious indications that this was not so.

At Huzirina, a town not far from Harran, a scribal school in which cuneiform tablets were found has been excavated, showing how pupils were still busily copying the great works of Babylonian literature even while the Assyrian empire was on the wane. Harran had been the most important centre for Assyrians in the north-west from at least the eighth century, when Sargon II granted it privileged status along with other ancient Assyrian and Babylonian cities, and it was the city to which the royal court was transferred

---

[4] If Assara-Mazaš in an Assyrian god-list is correctly identified.
[5] On the upper Euphrates in Anatolia, later known as Commagene.

when Nineveh and Kalhu were threatened by unpredictable combinations of Medes, Cimmerians, and Babylonians. Its oracle had predicted the successful invasion of Egypt under Esarhaddon, and its local version of the New Year festival was performed on behalf of the lunar deities Sin and Nikkal (Ningal) his consort.

To the south of Harran lies Neirab, near Aleppo, which was another important centre for worship of the moon-god and another key garrison city for the Assyrians in Syria. A series of legal records unearthed there dates from the reigns of the early Achaemenid kings and shows that the flow of cuneiform tradition continued after the capture of Babylon, even though public monuments there were already being inscribed in Aramaic. Fragments of cuneiform records from Tarsos date to the late Assyrian period, showing that the tradition was not restricted to the area around Harran. Hamath was a cosmopolitan centre in Syria in the early first millennium. There Yahweh was worshipped among other deities, and monumental Luwian hieroglyphic inscriptions were erected in public places. The city made an alliance with Samaria which only briefly resisted the Assyrian advance in the late eighth century. Danish excavations in the 1930s discovered cuneiform tablets which include letters as well as medical, magical, and astrological texts, marking Assyrian cultural presence. One of them is an incantation to Ea, Shamash, and Asalluhi,[6] designed to animate divine statues; duplicates of the text are known from Nineveh and Sippar. Sargon, having defeated Hamath in 720, transferred no fewer than 6,300 Assyrians as well as the Median leader Daiukku (Deioces) to Hamath. He also deported Babylonians and others to Samaria, where fragments of cuneiform texts have likewise come to light. Sargon's policy of indoctrinating foreigners with Assyrian culture is clearly and publicly stated in his cylinder inscription:

Populations of the four world quarters with strange tongues and incompatible speech, dwellers of mountain and country, . . . whom I had taken as booty at the command of Ashur my lord by the might of my sceptre, I caused to accept a single voice;[7] and I caused native Assyrians who are all expert in all kinds of knowledge to dwell among them, and I sent overseers and officers with instructions to teach them to assimilate(?) and to respect god and king.

Three generations later the policy promoted by Sargon was still being reinforced by Ashurbanipal, who in particular deported people from Babylon, Uruk and Susa to western territories. Esarhaddon had captured Memphis in 671 and took captive members of the Egyptian royal family. A major deportation of people from Qirbitu in eastern Babylonia on the border with Elam took Mesopotamians into the Nile valley in 668 BC. Mesopotamian temples at Memphis, Hermopolis, and Syene (Aswan), dedicated to Ea, Nabu, Bel, and Nergal, attested in the Achaemenid Persian period from Aramaic papyri, may go back to these manifold activities of Assyrians in Egypt. Despite vicissitudes during two decades, the Assyrians maintained their power over the lower Nile until Psammetichos I expelled them with the help of Greek and Carian mercenaries.

By late Antiquity it had become impossible to distinguish Assyrian and Chaldaean wisdom from that of Egypt. When the intermingling began may be deduced in part from evidence for cultural influence connected with the late Assyrian kings, for Esarhaddon's royal inscriptions specify the extraordinary number of top officials who lived in Egypt after the Assyrian conquest, to add to those who were already there because of the trade agreements set up by Tiglath-pileser III and Sargon II.

Over all the land of Egypt I appointed new rulers, governors, officials, market officers, temple administrators and commanders. I established forever regular offerings and sacrifices to Ashur and the great gods my lords, I levied tribute.

Stories about Assyrian kings—Esarhaddon and Ahiqar, Ashurbanipal and his rebellious brother Shamash-shum-ukin—circulated in Egypt in Aramaic as a result of this deep penetration.

We may also look to Tayma in north-west Arabia as a city where Mesopotamian influence was particularly strong, for accounts of conquest from the time of Tiglath-pileser III (744–727 BC) onwards are backed up by a fragment of stone carved in Assyrian-style relief found there. It seems to show that the Assyrians controlled and embellished the city. Two carved, monumental stelae may be a century or so later in date; inscribed with an informative text in

---

[6] Asalluhi was a god of healing and incantations from southern Mesopotamia who became equated with Marduk.

[7] The exact meaning of this phrase is uncertain; 'one command' or 'one language' have both been suggested.

16. Monumental terracotta lion which guarded a temple at Tell Harmal in Hammurabi's day.

Aramaic, they reveal that the Mesopotamian deities Ṣalmu and Sangilaya (Marduk) as well as Ashima the patron deity of Hamath were worshipped in Tayma. Recent finds have shown that caravans from Tayma and from Saba in southern Arabia were reaching the middle Euphrates during the eighth century BC.

A thousand years earlier the custom in which Assyrian merchants lived abroad in foreign cities, trading with occasional back-up from a home-based expeditionary force, had endured for several centuries. A similar practice seems to be attested from neo-Assyrian inscriptions, for Tiglath-pileser III and Sargon II both state that they opened up a market (*kārum*) on the border of Egypt. Likewise in the Levant they established trading stations (*bīt kārāni*) in Sidon, Tyre and Arvad. Assyrian public buildings or 'palaces' excavated in southern Palestine presumably supported this mercantile activity.

Around 614 BC the Assyrian king and his court abandoned Nineveh and moved westwards to Harran, which became the capital city for a few years. When Nineveh fell to the Medes and their allies in 612 BC a further scattering of the population from Assyria was inevitable. Displaced Assyrians carried abroad with them a long tradition of academic activity: teaching from a conservative syllabus, collecting literary and scientific writings into libraries, composing commentaries, and compiling catalogues. But neither Nineveh

nor Susa was destroyed as utterly as hyperbolic and legendary accounts suggest, and a late Elamite dynasty in Susa wrote letters to an administration that remained in Nineveh after 612 BC.

Architecture, Engineering, and Decorative Arts

Various hallmarks of Assyrian design spread abroad. Not all of them definitely originated in Mesopotamia, but once they had been incorporated into Mesopotamian buildings and fine arts they were identified with Assyrian culture.

Although architecture made with sun-dried bricks does not usually survive up to the level of the parapet, certain drawings and sculptures show clearly that stepped merlons or crenellations were regularly in use on palaces, temples, and city walls from the late second millennium onwards. For those defending cities against besiegers this design was never surpassed until gunpowder rendered it obsolete, and it became the norm throughout different regions of the Near East. Likewise the placing of monumental stone or metal lions, bulls, and other massive creatures at formal entrances, as if to protect them from attack, had spread probably from Assyria and Babylonia into other parts of the civilized world. There is an early version in terracotta, from Tell Harmal near Babylon which dates around the time of Hammurabi.

Several designs for arches and vaults have been found in Mesopotamia much earlier than elsewhere. Brick arches both slightly pointed and virtually flat, vaults laid both with pitched and with radial bricks, and a pitched brick vault resting on pendentives have been found on excavations from at least 2000 BC in temples and tombs. Pilastered temple façades which imitate a grove of trees also go back to the third millennium. They were made with specially moulded bricks. By about 1500 BC they were combined with the figures of deities set in between the pillar-trunks. These were common to the architecture of many major temples, in both the north and the south of the country. Similar effects are found much later in Classical and Hellenistic temples.

Sennacherib was responsible for inventing the 'Archimedean' screw for raising water, and he also built an aqueduct in well-cut stone with pointed arches. At Arbela he constructed a *qanat* to carry

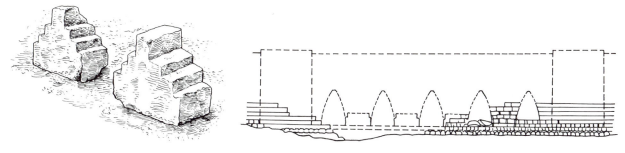

17. Stone crenellations and an aqueduct carried on stone arches, built by Sennacherib *c*.700 BC.

18. A. Goddess with radiant aura (nimbus), from a neo-Assyrian cylinder seal; B. Buddha with nimbus, from a wall painting at Bezeklik, Central Asia, found in a cave temple previously used by Manichaeans.

water underground, and recorded his achievement on an inscription there. His contemporary the Chaldaean king of Babylon Merodach-Baladan II had the first known botanical garden in which plants were grouped by type, so that for instance several types of mint were grown together.

The Assyrians used tiny glass plaques, square in outline, very thin, curved about the vertical axis, painted and decorated also with gold leaf, for purposes still unknown. They foreshadow Islamic glass vessels that are painted and gilded. Patterns and scenes made by inlaying shaped pieces of stone and mother-of-pearl into wall plaster to form a frieze, common in public buildings from the Early Dynastic period, have been found in Islamic palace rooms at Samarra, of the Abbasid period. Many fine techniques of jewellery-making were in use by the Assyrian period, and the discovery at Nineveh of a rock-crystal lens that gives good magnification shows that the finest work was not necessarily done with the naked eye.

The neo-Assyrians perfected the art of glazing bricks and tiles, and put up large panels with decorative designs, inaugurating a tradition that is still popular today in the houses and mosques of the Middle East.

Sumerian and Babylonian myths sometimes refer to the mantle of radiance worn by deities to protect them, powerful rays that emanate from their persons, and during the neo-Assyrian empire it became fashionable to draw these rays as flame-like projections encircling the upper part of a divine form. The fashion developed from one used much earlier in Syrian glyptic art around 1700 BC, when most divine statues were covered in gold leaf, and the sheen of precious metal may have stimulated the concept. As an iconographic device it proved so successful in highlighting the divine presence, especially in scenes containing a variety of human forms, that it was adopted much later in Buddhist, Christian, and Islamic art.

The Neo-Babylonian Empire
612–539 BC

When Nineveh fell in 612, the Assyrian court had already transferred to Harran. Babylon quickly seized the initiative and its Chaldaean kings, originally tribal upstarts from the South, won most of the empire formerly controlled by Assyria. The name of its great king Nebuchadnezzar came to symbolize world power and enormous wealth. That he captured Jerusalem in 587 BC and deported to Babylon the ruling family along with other important people is well known, not only from Old Testament sources but also from cuneiform administrative lists found at Babylon which name Jehoiachin as a recipient of rations. Once again we see a situation in which the exchange of information and close cultural contact could take place at the highest levels of society as a direct result of deportation. Ezekiel's famous vision of the Chariot of God which he saw while he lived in Babylonia almost certainly uses imagery from the great temples and their rituals which he witnessed in exile. His tomb in lower Mesopotamia is still a place of pilgrimage for people of different faiths.

The court of Nebuchadnezzar was famous for its cosmopolitan society. Phoenicians, Syrians, Elamites, and Egyptians rubbed shoulders with Ionians and Israelites, feasting together and conversing in Aramaic. Well-educated members of the nobility and well-travelled professional mercenaries shared experiences and ideas. Many Assyrians were drawn southwards, away from their damaged cities and abandoned courts, into the centre of world power in Babylon.

Although one might have expected political change and ethnic mixing at this time to cause the old traditions and cuneiform writing to die out, the authority of tradition was still so strong that erosion is barely perceptible. Nabonidus, the last king of the dynasty, was a dedicated antiquarian, who studied old inscriptions, followed ancient rituals, and enjoyed the museums of antiquities set up in Ur and Babylon around this time. They were filled with statues and inscriptions left by famous men of old which often came to light through building works carried out to repair and strengthen dilapidated temples. Quite apart from deliberate collections intentionally visited, old sculptures and cylinder seals were always coming to light on urban building sites, and travellers entering and leaving Mesopotamia saw numerous rock reliefs in mountain passes where earlier kings had left carvings showing themselves and a record of their deeds in cuneiform, high up on the rock face.

Not all deportees stayed at the royal court, nor even in Babylon. Many of them made a new life in the enclaves of foreigners frequently attached to other cities. As merchants and traders they could make use of links with their homeland, which became valuable contacts. When Nebuchadnezzar finally succeeded in capturing Tyre, Tyrian deportees settled in a large group on the outskirts of Nippur and made the most of new opportunities for commerce. A group of Egyptians served as oblates in the temple at Sippar. As well as feeding their own cultural traditions into an ever-receptive Mesopotamian culture, such people brought new energy and wealth to their adopted country.

An event of great importance for cultural contact was Nabonidus' residence at the Arabian oasis town of Tayma during seven or so years of his rule as the last native king of Babylon. As we have seen, the town had almost certainly housed Assyrians as well as Syrians from Hamath in the previous century, but now a section of the Babylonian court including the monarch resided there for about a decade, in a palace. There he received regular supplies and bulletins from Babylonia, as cuneiform records show. The impact that this had on local Arabian society must have been considerable. A fragment of scroll from the Dead Sea written several centuries later preserves a tradition that Nabonidus was healed of an illness there by a Jewish healer. The oasis towns that Nabonidus had to conquer in order to make a secure base at Tayma are exactly those where Jews resided a thousand years later when Muhammad began to assert the power of Islam around Medina.

Royal connections with Harran, where the court of the last Assyrian king Ashur-uballit II resided after the fall of Nineveh, continued into the neo-Babylonian period, for the mother of Nabonidus kept her position as high priestess of the Moon-god from the time of Ashurbanipal's reign in Nineveh to the reign of her own son in Babylon. Thus she stands for continuity through troubled times, and her death was marked by a memorial inscription in Babylonian cuneiform which merged the Assyrian and Chaldaean kings into a single dynastic line. This perception was to mislead later historians of Antiquity, who often failed to distinguish the Assyrian from the Babylonian empire. The oracle of the moon-god at Harran, which had successfully predicted that Esarhaddon would conquer Egypt, presumably still prophesied in Akkadian. That Harran kept up its tradition of cuneiform writing for at least another century, well into the period of Achaemenid rule, is proved by the remarkable discovery, far away in Transjordanian Moab, of one cuneiform clay tablet recording a legal agreement made in Harran under Darius. Nabonidus' formal inscriptions on stone were cherished at Harran long after Babylon passed into foreign custody: eventually they were incorporated into the mosque that the caliph Marwan II built over the site when he made his capital there.

In Anatolia too Babylonian influence must have continued where the Assyrians left off. Nabopolassar spent much time in Samsat, setting up and strengthening garrisons along the upper Euphrates, and his son Nebuchadnezzar campaigned frequently in Syria and Palestine, and attacked Egypt, although he achieved no lasting occupation.

Through trade and writing, conquest and deportation the Mesopotamians took and kept the initiative that early advantages had given them. With full storehouses, well-constructed buildings, and a specialized workforce they were able to develop systems of finance and record-keeping beyond those of their neighbours. Pride in their beautiful cities stimulated them to compete and acquire, and frequent influxes of foreigners brought in new energy.

FURTHER READING

1. Proto-Historic Times, *c.*3500–3000 BC

AURENCHE, O., *La Maison orientale: L'architecture du Proche Orient ancien des origines au milieu du quatrième millénaire* (Paris, 1981).

BIGGS, R., 'Ancient Mesopotamia and the Scholarly Traditions of the Third Millennium', *Sumer* 42 (1984), 32–3.

DREYER, G., 'Ein Siegel der frühzeitlichen Königsnekropole von Abydos', *Mitteilungen der Deutsche Archäologische Institute, Abteilung Kairo* 43 (1987), 33–43.

MOOREY, P. R. S., *From Gulf to Delta and Beyond* (Beer-Sheva, 1995).

NISSEN, H. J., *The Early History of the Ancient Near East 9000–2000 BC* (Chicago, 1988).

NISSEN, H. J., DAMEROW, P., and ENGLUND, R. K., *Archaic Bookkeeping* (Chicago, 1993).

POSTGATE, J. N., *Early Mesopotamia: Society and Economy at the Dawn of History* (London, 1992).

SCHMANDT-BESSERAT, D., *Before Writing: From Counting to Cuneiform* (Univ. Texas Press, Austin, 1992).

TEISSIER, B., 'Glyptic Evidence for a Connection between Iran, Syro-Palestine and Egypt in the Fourth and Third Millennia', *Iran* 25 (1987), 27–53.

THACKER, T. W., *The Relationship of the Semitic and Egyptian Verbal Systems* (Oxford, 1954).

2. Merchants and Sealings in Anatolia, *c.*2300–1700 BC

LARSEN, M. T., *The Old Assyrian City State and its Colonies* (Copenhagen, 1976).

VAN DE MIEROOP, M., *Economy and Social Organization in OB Ur* (Leuven, 1992).

YAKAR, J., *The Later Prehistory of Anatolia, British Archaeological Reports* (Oxford, 1985).

3. Gemstones from the East and the Cities of the Indus Valley

ALLCHIN, B. and R., *The Rise of Civilization in India and Pakistan* (Cambridge, 1982).

HERRMANN, G., 'Lapis Lazuli: The Early Phases of its Trade', *Iraq* 30 (1968), 21–57.

JARRIGE, J. F., *Les Cités oubliées de l'Indus* (Paris, 1988).

POTTS, D., *The Arabian Gulf in Antiquity*, i: *From Prehistory to the Fall of the Achaemenid empire* (Oxford, 1990).

4. Implications of the Sumerian King-List

CARTER, E., and STOLPER, M., *Elam: Surveys of Political History and Archaeology* (Chicago, 1984).

CHARPIN, D., 'Tablettes présargoniques de Mari', *MARI* 5 (1987), 65–126.

EDZARD, D.-O., 'Amarna und die Archive seiner Korrespondenten zwischen Ugarit und Gaza', in J. Amitai, (ed.) *Biblical Archaeology Today*, Proceedings of the International Congress on Biblical Archaeology, Jerusalem, April 1984, (Jerusalem, 1985), 248–59.

EIDEM, J., and MOLLER, E., 'A Royal Seal from the Ancient Zagros'. *MARI* 6 (1990), 635–9.

KUPPER, J-R., 'Mari', *RlA* vii (1987–90), 382–90.

SIGRIST, M., *Messenger Texts from the British Museum* (Potomac, 1990).

VINCENTE, C., 'Tell Leilan Recension of the Sumerian King List', *NABU* no. 11 1 (1990), 8–9.

WILCKE, C., 'Genealogical and Geographical Thought in the Sumerian King List', in *DUMU-E2-DUB-BA-A, Studies in Honor of Åke W. Sjöberg* (Philadelphia, 1989), 557–71.

5. High Culture from the Sages

ATTRIDGE, H. W., and ODEN, R. A., *The Syrian Goddess* (Scholars Press, Missoula, Mont., 1976).

BURSTEIN, S., *The Babyloniaca of Berossus*, Sources and Monographs: sources from the ancient near east 1: 5 (Malibu, 1978).

FINKEL, I., 'Adad-apla-iddina, Esagil-kin-apli and the series SA.GIG', in *A Scientific Humanist, Studies in Honor of Abraham Sachs* (Philadelphia, 1988), 143–60.

FOSTER, B. R., 'Wisdom and the Gods in Ancient Mesopotamia', *Orientalia* 43 (1974), 344–54.

VANDERKAM, J. C., *Enoch and the Growth of an Apocalyptic Tradition*, Catholic Biblical Quarterly Monograph, series 16 (Washington, DC, 1984).

6. The School Curriculum in Cuneiform

BIGGS, R. D., 'Ancient Mesopotamia and the Scholarly Tra-
    ditions of the Third Millennium', *Sumer* 42 (1984), 32–3.

BLACK, J., *Sumerian Grammar in Babylonian Theory* (Rome,
    1991).

CAVIGNEAUX, A., 'Lexikalische Listen', *RlA* vi (1980–3).

CIVIL, M., 'Bilingualism in Logographically Written Lan-
    guages, Sumerian in Ebla', in L. Cagni (ed.), *Il bilinguismo
    a Ebla* (Naples, 1984).

DURAND, J.-M., 'La Situation historique des Šakkanakku',
    MARI 4 (1985), esp. p. 162.

GURNEY, O. R., 'Babylonian Music Again', *Iraq* 56 (1994),
    101–6.

HAWKINS, J. D., 'Writing in Western Asia', in P. R. S. Moorey
    (ed.), *The Origins of Civilization* (Oxford, 1979).

KRECHER, J., 'Kommentare', *RlA* vi (1980–3), 188–91.

——— 'Schreiberschulung in Ugarit. Die Tradition von Listen
    und sumerischen Texten', *Ugarit Forschungen* 1 (1969),
    131–58.

LANDSBERGER, B., REINER, E., and CIVIL, M., *Materials for the
    Sumerian Lexicon* XII Pontifical Biblical Institute (Rome,
    1969).

SOLLBERGER, E., 'Byblos sous les rois d'Ur', *AfO* 19 (1959–
    60), 120–2.

WESTBROOK, R., *Studies in Biblical and Cuneiform Law* (Paris,
    1988).

WILLIAMS, R. J., 'Scribal Training in Ancient Egypt', *Journal
    of the American Oriental Society* 92 (1972), 214–21.

7. Divination Priests and Doctors as Scribes

ARNAUD, D., *Recherches au pays d'Ashtata*, Emar vi: 4 (Paris,
    1987), esp. no. 604.

BECKMAN, G., 'Mesopotamians and Mesopotamian Learn-
    ing at Hattusha', *JCS* 35 (1983), 97–114.

BOTTÉRO, J., *Mesopotamia: Writing, Reasoning, and the Gods*
    (Chicago, 1992).

BURKERT, W., *The Orientalizing Revolution: Near Eastern In-
    fluence on Greek Culture in the Early Archaic Age* (Harvard,
    1992), 41–87.

FLEMING, D., 'The Voice of the Ugaritic Incantation Priest',
    Ugarit Forschungen 23 (1991), 141–54.

KOROŠEC, V., 'Die hethitischen Gesetze in ihren Wechsel-
    beziehungen zu den Nachbarvölkern', in H. Nissen and
    J. Renger (eds.), *Mesopotamien und seine Nachbarn* (Berlin,
    1982), 295–310.

PARPOLA, S., *Letters from Assyrian Scholars to the Kings Esar-
    haddon and Assurbanipal*, Alte Orient und Altes Testament
    5/1, (Neukirchen-Vluyn, 1970), commentary vol. 5: 2 (1983).

8. The Late Bronze Age

ABOU ASSAF, A., BORDREUIL, P., and MILLARD, A., *La Statue
    de Tell Fekherye et son inscription bilingue assyro-araméenne*
    (Paris, 1982) with redating by H. Sader, *Les États
    araméens* (Beirut 1987) and A. Spycket, 'La Statue bilingue
    de Tell Fekheriyé', *Revue d'Assyriologie* 79 (1985), 67–8.

HARRIS, R., *Ancient Sippar* (Istanbul, 1975).

LAROCHE, E., 'Luwier, Luwisch, Lu(w)iya', *RlA* vii (1988).

MORAN, W., *The Amarna Letters* (Baltimore and London, 1992).

NAVEH, J., *The Early History of the Alphabet* (Jerusalem, 1987).

SASSON, M., *The Military Establishments at Mari* (Rome, 1969).

WEIDNER, E., 'Studien zur Zeitgeschichte Tukulti-Ninurtas
    I', *AfO* 13 (1939–41), 122.

9. The Urartian Kingdom in Armenia

BARNETT, R. D., 'Urartu', in *CAH*² iii: 1 (1982), 314–71.

DONBAZ, V., 'Two Neo-Assyrian Stelae in the Antakya and
    Kahramanmaras Museums', *Annual Review of the Royal
    Inscriptions of Mesopotamia Project* 8 (1990), 5–15.

KÖNIG, F. W., *Die chaldischen Inschriften*, AfO Beiheft (Graz,
    1955–7).

THOMSON, R. W., *Moses Khorenats'i, History of the Armenians*
    (Harvard, 1978).

WILHELM, G., *The Hurrians* (Warminster, 198).

10. The Neo-Assyrian Empire

AL-RAWI, F. N. H., and GEORGE, A. R., 'Tablets from the
    Sippar Library V', *Iraq* 57 (1995), 225.

CAVIGNEAUX, A., and ISMAIL, B. K., 'Die Stadthalter von
    Suhu und Mari', text no. 2 *Baghdader Mitteilungen* 21
    (1990).

DALLEY, S., 'Foreign Chariotry and Cavalry in the Armies
    of Tiglath-Pileser III and Sargon II', *Iraq* 47 (1985), 31–48.

ELAT, M., 'The Political Status of the Kingdom of Judah
    within the Assyrian Empire in the 7th *c.* BCE', in *Lachish*
    v (Tel Aviv, 1975), 61–70.

GIBSON, J. C. L., *Syrian Semitic Inscriptions*, ii: *Aramaic
    Inscriptions* (Oxford, 1975).

GRAYSON, A. K., *Assyrian Royal Inscriptions*, i–ii (Wiesbaden,
    1976).

LIVINGSTONE, A., 'Taimā': Recent Soundings and New In-
    scribed Material', *Atlal* 7 (1983), 108–11.

ODED, B., *Mass Deportations and Deportees in the Neo-
    Assyrian Empire* (Wiesbaden, 1979).

POTTS, D., 'Tayma and the Assyrian Empire', *Arab.arch.epig.*2
    (1991), 10–23.

RIIS, P. J., *Hama. Fouilles et recherches de la Fondation
    Carlsberg 1931–38*, ii: 2 (Copenhagen, 1990), 257.

RÖLLIG, W., 'Miṣir', *RlA* viii (1994).

11. Architecture, Engineering and Decorative Arts

DALLEY, S., 'Nineveh, Babylon and the Hanging Gardens',
    Iraq 56 (1994), 45–58 (for the Archimedes screw).

FALES, F. M., and POSTGATE, J. N., *Imperial Administrative
    Records*, Part I, 'State Archives of Assyria VII' (Helsinki,
    1992), esp. fig 20 (photograph of the rock crystal lens
    from Nineveh).

GARBINI, G., 'The Stepped Pinnacle in the Ancient Near
    East', *East and West* 9 (Rome, 1958), 85–91.

JACOBSEN, T., and LLOYD, S., *Sennacherib's Aqueduct at Jerwan*
    (Chicago, 1935).

LAESSØE, J., 'Reflexions on Modern and Ancient Oriental Water Works', *JCS* 7 (1953) 5–26.

LAMM, C. J., *Das Glas von Samarra* (Berlin, 1928), esp. pl. XI.

LAYARD, A. H., *Nineveh and Babylon* (London, 1853), 197 (for rock-crystal lens).

OATES, D., 'Innovations in Mud-Brick: Decorative and Structural Techniques in Ancient Mesopotamia', *World Archaeology* 21: 3 (1990), 388–406.

ORCHARD, J. J., 'Glass Plaques from Fort Shalmaneser, Nimrud', *Iraq* 40 (1978), 1–22.

RAWSON, J., *Chinese Ornament: The Lotus and the Dragon* (London, 1984).

READE, J., 'A Glazed Brick Panel from Nimrud', *Iraq* 25 (1963), 38–47.

SAFAR, F., and BASMACHI, A., 'Sennacherib's Qanat at Arbela', *Sumer* 3 (1947), Arabic section.

12. The Neo-Babylonian Empire

BAWDEN, G., EDENS, C., and MILLER, R., 'Preliminary Archaeological Investigations at Tayma', *Atlal* 4 (1980), 69–106.

BONGENAAR, A. C. V. M., and HARING, B. J. J., 'Egyptians in Neo-Babylonian Sippar', *JCS* 46 (1994), 59–72.

DANDAMAEV, M., 'Neo-Babylonian Society and Economy', in *CAH*[2] iii: 2, 2nd edn. (1991), 252–75.

DHORME, P., 'Les Tablettes de Neirab', *Revue d'Assyriologie* 25 (1928), with some redating by F. M. FALES, *Oriens Antiquus* 12 (1973), and I. EPHAL, *Orientalia* 47 (1978).

GADD, C. J., 'The Harran Stelae of Nabonidus', *Anatolian Studies* 8 (1958), 35–92.

KOLDEWEY, R., *Das wiedererstehende Babylon*, 4th rev. edn., ed. B. Hrouda (Munich, 1990).

TALBOT RICE, D., *Illustrated London News* (Sept. 1957), 466 ff.

II

OCCASIONS AND OPPORTUNITIES

2. Persian, Greek, and Parthian overlords

Stephanie Dalley

Achaemenid Persian Rule 538–331 BC

WHEN CYRUS II CONQUERED BABYLON IN 539 BC he brought to an end the rule of kings who took Babylonian names. However, adopting the title 'king of Babylon', he espoused local customs, celebrating the Babylonian festival of the New Year in which he 'took the hands' of Bel–Marduk, and heard the *Epic of Creation (Enūma Elish)* recited. Even before he captured Babylon, Cyrus was hailed by the Babylonians as a fine ruler chosen by Marduk. It was nothing new for Babylon to have foreign rulers. Hammurabi's Amorite dynasty had come from the west; the Kassite rulers originally came from western Iran, and the Chaldeans of more recent times were tribal people who had not long settled in southern Mesopotamia.

Cyrus belonged to an Iranian tribe which had migrated southwards during previous centuries, coming either from the Caucasus or from Central Asia. The movement was a gradual one, and many migrants had assimilated with Urartian, Hurrian, and Elamite peoples and customs on their way into north and west Iran. They had no tradition of writing their own language, but adopted writing from the people they conquered, so Cyrus, even though he was Iranian not Semitic, and was obliged as a usurper to denigrate the deposed king of Babylon in the time-honoured way, adopted Babylonian and Elamite cuneiform as well as alphabetic Aramaic.

Whether in Mesopotamia or at Persepolis where many of the top administrators were Mesopotamians or west Semites, most official inscriptions and daily records were not written in Persian. Ethnic Iranians were in the minority in posts that required literacy. Darius I invented a simplified cuneiform script for the Old Persian language, but it was not a great success, and was soon abandoned. His famous rock inscription high up in the mountain pass of Behistun was written in Babylonian and Elamite first of all; the Old Persian version was squeezed in afterwards.

The Achaemenids acknowledged Ahura-Mazda as their chief god whose prophet Zoroaster probably lived many centuries before the lifetime of Cyrus, but became a key figure in much later Persian religion. No reference to Zoroaster's life and sayings has come to us from the Achaemenid dynasty, and it is still impossible to tell whether later Iranian ideas had already been formulated. But a text dated around 700 BC seems to show that the Assyrians recognized Ahura-Mazda and allowed him a place in their temples along with other foreign gods.

The Achaemenid kings did not resist Babylonian influence. They celebrated Mesopotamian festivals according to the Babylonian system of lunar months with intercalation to calibrate them with the solar year, and they often used Babylonian and Elamite month names in their records, names which reflect indigenous festivals. They did not attempt to replace the native priests and administrators of the great temples with Iranian nationals, but allowed cult and culture to continue in Babylonia uninterrupted. Business was still carried on there without coinage, using silver and gold by weight that could be assayed as required; but when the Persian daric was minted as the coin of the dynasty, it was based upon the Babylonian system

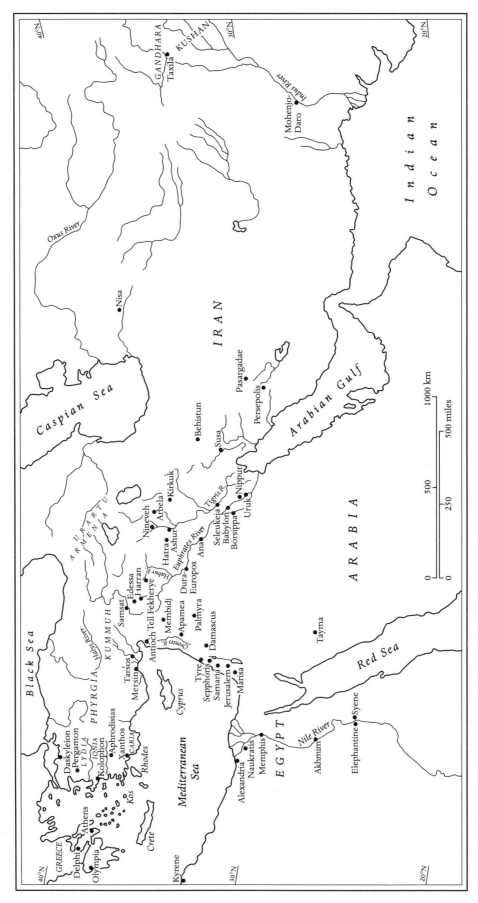

MAP 3. Sketch map of Mesopotamia and adjacent lands: the later periods

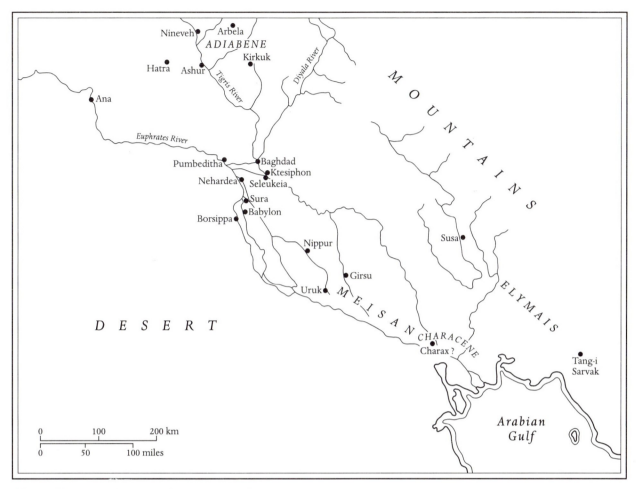

MAP 4. Sketch map showing major cities and regions of Mesopotamia in late Antiquity

of weights, corresponding to one-sixtieth of a mina. In Babylonia at least, the laws of older times continued to be in force, and the ancient Code of Hammurabi was still studied and copied. Those Persians and Medes who lived in Babylonia often gave their children Babylonian names. They used cylinder and stamp seals with traditional designs just as their Assyrian and Babylonian predecessors had done.

Achaemenid rule in Babylon lasted for more than two centuries, during which business and scholarship continued as usual in the great cities, much of it conducted in cuneiform. Until recently it was thought that shrines and cities were irrevocably damaged and neglected by Achaemenid kings and that the use of cuneiform for local records fell into disuse, or was only permitted in exceptional circumstances. This view was based largely on the gross over-interpretation of an incident which Herodotos reported: 'Xerxes, however, took it (a subsidiary gold statue of Marduk)

and killed the priest who tried to prevent the sacrilege.' But recent work has shown that the incident did not end in widespread damage or a change of attitude, and has given rise to a reassessment of how the Persians ruled Babylon, and how they allowed religious, scholarly, and commercial activities to continue and to flourish.

Neither Cyrus nor his successors changed the names of cities or built new ones in Mesopotamia. Susa was refurbished as a royal city, and Babylonian specialists were employed for the brickwork, much of it glazed as Nebuchadnezzar had had done in Babylon. The cult of the Babylonian goddess Nanay flourished there, and a library of cuneiform works was still maintained. Arbela too was important, for it was connected directly to Susa by the royal road running northwards to Armenia, and Darius chose it as one of the main cities in which the corpses of unsuccessful rebel kings were displayed. Presumably one reason for its continuing prestige was the great temple of Ishtar with its famous oracle, by then very ancient. The city became the capital of the province Adiabene in Parthian times, and later tradition claimed that the Parthian kings were buried there. The oracle probably flourished until the fourth century AD, when a priest of 'Sharbel'[1] was converted to Christianity.

Babylon and Assyria provided the model from which the Achaemenids moulded their kingship. Throne and footstool, crown and sceptre, titles and epithets, military and ritual duties all conform to the style of their predecessors within Mesopotamia, and the winged disk, as an emblem of royalty associated with the national deity, they adopted as their own. In administration too they took over from the Babylonians and Assyrians road and courier systems, and the allocation of fields as a reward for military service. Closely connected with kingship and the court rather than with religious institutions, Achaemenid art was created by collecting Babylonian, Assyrian, Ionian, and other elements and fusing them into a new but essentially eclectic form. One can seldom pick out elements that belonged to the Persians before they became a world power. When Cyrus built his new royal residence at Pasargadae, he decorated his palace with relief sculptures resembling those of Sennacherib at Nineveh, which he visited in person, despite the damage done to it in the siege of 612 BC. His successors did likewise at Persepolis. Only the design of gardens, particularly at Pasargadae, seems to be distinctively Iranian. An Achaemenid style in glyptic art emerges gradually out of previous Babylonian and Elamite styles, in which even the introduction of the fire-altar (often seen as a hallmark of purely Persian practice) seems to be a motif taken up from much earlier iconography in the Zagros area.

The Persians have managed to achieve a favourable public image by comparison with the Assyrians through the bias of Old Testament writers, but in fact their own inscriptions show that they tortured and killed rebels and deported people from conquered lands in much the same way, although they encouraged deportees from previous regimes to return: Ninevites to Nineveh, Tyrians to Tyre, and Judaeans to Jerusalem. Those who went took with them knowledge of Mesopotamian customs, ideas, and skills, but many chose to remain, having put down firm

roots during the decades of exile. Mesopotamia itself became even more cosmopolitan than before, since not only did the Persian court at times visit and contribute to local administration, but also foreign levies and mercenaries did tours of military service there. Anti-Persian feeling in conquered lands led to scurrilous rumours, such as the tale that Xerxes destroyed the statue of Marduk–Bel in Babylon. This story has proved to be a fabrication: the cult statue continued unscathed to embody the presence of the god in his undamaged temple in Babylon during subsequent centuries, and so Herodotos' description of the golden statue of Marduk–Bel in the time of Artaxerxes I (464–424 BC) need not be doubted. Continuity of cult and architecture are thoroughly attested by the written sources for this and the subsequent period.

In Egypt there was a massive influx of foreigners who came and stayed. A high official named Oudjahorresne complained that when Cambyses arrived in Egypt, 'Foreigners from every foreign land were with him. (When) he had taken possession of this entire land, they made their homes there.' At this period there is clear evidence that groups of Mesopotamians still lived permanently in Egypt and maintained their own religious and cultural traditions except that they no longer used cuneiform writing. At Memphis an international company of ship-builders, and the treasury for the whole satrapy of Egypt, brought in foreigners who wrote their records in Aramaic and supported a temple to the Babylonian god Nabu. At Elephantine and next-door Syene on the border with Nubia, existing military posts were manned by soldiers from western Asia— Hebrews, Syrians, and Babylonians—who enjoyed their literature, now in Aramaic, in works that harked back to the great days of the Assyrian kings. They read the story of Ahiqar the sage of Esarhaddon, and the tale of the two brothers Ashurbanipal and Shamash-shum-ukin who ruled Assyria and Babylonia respectively and became bitter enemies. They worshipped there in temples dedicated to Mesopotamian gods: Nabu, Bel, Shamash, and Nergal. From this period onwards Assyrians living in Egypt are mentioned in demotic papyri; for instance, fifteen of them took part in a campaign to Nubia led by the Pharaoh Amasis in 528/9 BC.

---

[1] This is a corruption of Ishtar (Assyrian Issar)–Bel.

This information is crucial for showing that Assyrian and Babylonian culture still continued to flourish in some Egyptian cities, whereas Egyptian culture is not attested in Mesopotamia, not even in Susa despite the enforced residence there of the Pharaoh-in-exile and 6,000 Egyptians after Cambyses deported them.

The Buddha, heir to a kingdom in southern Nepal, was born around the mid-fifth century, probably when Persian rule had reached the Indus. According to the later legend of Barlaam and Ioasaph (Budhasaf), which is a Christianized life of the Buddha, his father's court had 'fifty-five men schooled in the star-lore of the Chaldaeans'. The Buddha's chamberlain in the story bears the name Zardan, which is likely to be Akkadian, and his wise teacher Barlaam came from Senaar, Babylonia, according to the Greek version. This background, legendary though it is, fits with the undoubted fact that the Buddha knew in detail two Akkadian manuals of omens and celestial lore, *Šumma ālu* and *Enūma Anu Enlil*, and used material from them in a sermon of which the text survives.[2] This is the best evidence we have for Chaldaean scholars living far abroad as experts and tutors in royal courts at this time, to add to the earlier example of the seer Balaam.

Remarkably little evidence for cultural impact from Iran on Mesopotamia can be shown. An apsidal temple at Uruk which has many different building phases may perhaps be identified as a temple to Mitra, but neither the god nor the precise period are certain. One Persian-type pillared hall has been found in Babylon. The Persian kings did not attempt to turn the ancient cities of Babylonia into 'Iranian' cities like Pasargadae and Persepolis. In general it is clear that the Iranian conquerors were themselves conquered by the higher culture which they found in Mesopotamia, just as the Kassites had been a millennium earlier. As Herodotos wrote: 'No race is so ready to adopt foreign ways as the Persians.' The Babylonian word 'Chaldaeans' became virtually synonymous with the Persian word 'Magi' meaning men of wisdom and magic.

Alexander the Great and his Seleucid Successors, 330–c.128 BC

Alexander conquered Babylon in 330 BC and treated the city with great respect. He approved a programme of renovation for its shrines and took part in the New Year festival, as some at least of his Persian predecessors had done. Not long before his death, as he marched from northern Mesopotamia towards Babylon, he gave audience to embassies which came from all over the world to honour him. They included Celts, Ethiopians, and Iberians who would all have returned home having admired Mesopotamian temples and palaces, decorative motifs and fine arts, at first hand.

After Alexander died in Babylon the eastern part of his empire was inherited by the Seleucids who ruled Babylonia for almost 200 years until the Parthians captured it. Around the heroic figure of Alexander there grew up a romantic legend known as the *Alexander Romance*, to which in its Greek versions the name of Kallisthenes is spuriously attached. Although many versions in other languages depend upon the Greek version for some episodes, one Hebrew version clearly does not stem from the Greek, and in almost all versions there is a sequence derived from the *Epic of Gilgamesh*, and therefore not Greek in origin. Both the *Epic of Gilgamesh* and the *Alexander Romance* explore the nature of divinity as claimed by a mortal.[3] Alexander and his successors were sometimes portrayed on coins and statues as having horns upon their heads, which in Mesopotamia was the traditional way of showing that divine nature was claimed. An early instance of the custom comes from Naram-Sin king of Agade around 2250 BC whose monumental rock reliefs were still visible in Alexander's day, carved in prominent positions on mountain passes.

Alexander had some Babylonian works translated into Greek. A commentary on a work of Aristotle, written much later, claimed that Kallisthenes, one of his pupils, sent back home Chaldaean celestial observations which covered 1,903 years before the fall of Babylon. Even before the death of Alexander, an account of Babylonian beliefs regarding the creation of the world was written in Athens by Eudemos, a contemporary of Aristotle. Although the writing of Eudemos does not now survive, it was still available to the philosopher Damaskios about 800 years later when the latter, who served as head of the Platonic Academy at Athens, wrote a brief account of Babylonian ideas about cosmogony. This testimony has a faint echo in the Armenian account by Moses of

---

[2] See Ch. VI, p. 131.   [3] See Ch. VIII, pp. 170–1 for more detail.

Khorene[4] who wrote that Alexander had books from Nineveh translated into Greek. Eudemos' writings included a *History of Astronomy*, which would have enabled some Babylonian astronomical knowledge to bridge the gap between Mesopotamia and the Greek world. During the rule of Alexander's immediate successors, Chaldaean works were translated into Greek in Egypt under the patronage of Ptolemy II Philadelphos (285–246 BC) along with Egyptian works, according to George the Synkellos, a Byzantine chronicler of the early ninth century AD. From then onwards it was often difficult for Greeks to distinguish Egyptian and Chaldaean works, although the geographer and astronomer Ptolemy (AD *c.*100–78) made clear distinctions between their methods of astrology in his *Tetrabiblos*.

Greek though the Seleucid dynasty was in name, it did not remodel the ancient cities along Hellenic lines. A Greek theatre was built in Babylon, but essentially the city remained faithful to the plan of Nebuchadnezzar's time. In general the public buildings and streets in Mesopotamian cities do not reflect the adoption or imposition of Greek taste, nor were they refounded and renamed. This is in contrast to new cities such as Seleukeia-on-Tigris which was, of course, laid out according to Greek practice with colonnaded streets, an agora, and typically Greek public buildings. Under Seleukos II in 236 BC the Babylonian assembly of the temple of Bel in Babylon had received an official letter in cuneiform about land holdings, and a tablet dated 229 BC describes the shrine of Marduk and enjoins its readers to secrecy. These two documents imply that the main religious institution there still flourished. Babylon struck its own temple coins, the silver lion-staters, but had stopped doing so by the time Parthian rulers took control.

Some local officials, to be sure, took a Greek name in addition to their Babylonian one to signify their homage. But essentially the change from Persian to Greek rule had little effect upon the great institutions of Babylonia, and cuneiform libraries were maintained and updated. At this period it was often supposed that all the Greek philosophers before Plato had gained their learning from Orientals, and so Chaldaean learning was highly regarded. Several languages were used for official purposes, and Greek did not supplant Babylonian and Aramaic in this region. Thus Antiochos I, in writing a Babylonian inscription to commemorate the refoundation of the temple Ezida at Borsippa, modelled it upon a similar inscription written by Nebuchadnezzar. Astronomical diaries, which briefly relate contemporary events in cuneiform, have shown that in 187 BC Antiochos III, resplendent in the purple garment once worn by Nebuchadnezzar, took a full part in rituals at Babylon and Borsippa as his predecessor Seleukos I had done. 'That day he went up to Esangil and prostrated himself. That day he entered the temple of the New Year Festival. . . . Cattle and sheep [he sacrificed] to Bel, Beltiya and the great gods.' This event shows that shrines and their traditional rituals still attracted royal patronage.

The last decades of Seleucid rule were marked by instability from both inside and outside the empire, for a split in the line of succession led to a series of struggles that amounted at times to civil war. Meanwhile in parts of Anatolia, in Armenia, in Maccabean Judah, and in southern Mesopotamia, independent rulers arose and established local kingdoms. The Romans were expanding into the Levant and Asia Minor, while the Arsacid Parthians—tribal Persians from the East—had driven the Seleucids out of Iran by about 142 BC. Then began a period in which Seleucids and Parthians fought for control of Mesopotamia itself, with short-lived gains and retreats on both sides. The period between about 141 and 126 BC is agreed to have been one of constant chaos and conflict.

Despite this unrest, cuneiform writing and scholarly activity continued, the latest known Akkadian text being dated AD 75. An extraordinary group of tablets has recently been assembled from a scattering among collections in several museums. Each one has Babylonian cuneiform on one side, and a Greek alphabetic transcription, to give a phonetic approximation, on the other. Instead of turning from obverse to reverse from top to bottom, as one normally does, they turn like the pages of a book, from side to side. All the texts seem to belong to the cuneiform academic curriculum, for they consist of lexical lists, syllabaries, and literary pieces, and they do not include day-to-day records and contracts. Undated, they are thought to belong to the Seleucid or even Parthian period, and may show either that Greeks were trying to

---

[4] He is traditionally dated to the 5th cent. AD, but most scholars think he lived at least two centuries later.

19. Lion stater of Babylon.

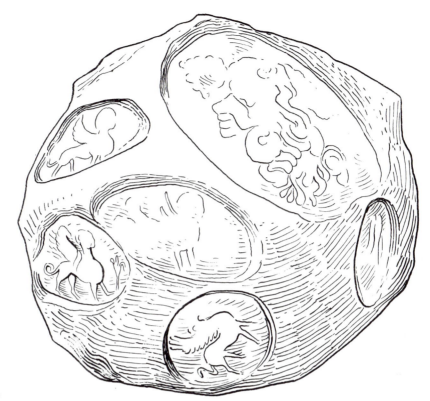

20. Clay sealing with impressions from several stamp seals, reign of Seleukos III.

learn Chaldaean texts in transcription, or that Babylonians were trying to write their own language with Greek letters.

Babylon was not the only city that continued to flourish at this time. Through Seleucid rule and into Parthian times the ancient city of Uruk maintained its religious and literary eminence. A large library was kept up to date with new copies of old literature and ongoing chronicles and astronomical observations. A huge temple complex known as the *bīt rēš* was restored and improved by several governors of the city. According to an inscription of Anu-uballit Nikarchos in 244 BC the inner sanctum was dedicated to Anu and his consort Antum, and the outer buildings had significant symbolic features: 'three gates which open outwards, and seven courts around the courtyard in which the Shrine of Destinies is.' The new work was consecrated on the eighth day of Nisan, while the New Year festival was being celebrated in Babylon. Its plan[5] seems to reflect the arrangement of the universe as it was conceived at that time, in which there were seven heavens or palace courts to be crossed before a worshipper could come face to

face with the enthroned deity who wrote the fates for each year. The governors of Uruk had both Babylonian and Greek names: Anu-uballit was also called Nikarchos by royal decree of Antiochos II (261–246 BC), and another Anu-uballit was also called Kephalon in the reign of Antiochos III (223–187). They were considered virtually independent rulers. Recent work has shown that these great men were buried with golden wreaths in huge tumuli outside Uruk; meanwhile the temple of Ishtar and Nanay was restored in the city, the cult statue of Ishtar was repaired, and a temple for the New Year festival, celebrated there in the month of Teshrit, was maintained to a high standard outside the city walls. The circumstances surrounding the decline of the city and the cessation of religious and intellectual life are not known; the latest evidence for activity by a descendant of Anu-uballit Kephalon dates to 132 BC.

Borsippa, with its shrine dedicated to Nabu, and Kutha with its shrine to Nergal, both flourished in the vicinity of Babylon. Borsippa still boasted an important school of astronomy, according to Strabo, who wrote: 'There are also several tribes of Chaldaean

---

[5] As with descriptions of Babylon, the text presents the ideal which does not correspond to the excavated building.

astronomers. For example, some are called Orcheni, others Borsippeni.'[6]

Susa also maintained a cuneiform library. The evidence for this is slight but firm: the colophon of a clay tablet found at Uruk and dated between 292 and 281 BC reveals that a scholar from Uruk went to Elam (presumably to Susa) and made a copy of a tablet that had been taken there by Nabopolassar 300 years earlier: 'According to tablets which Nabu-apal-usur the king of the Sealand looted from Uruk and now Kidinānu of Uruk saw them in Elam and wrote (copied) them in the reign of Seleukos and Antiochos and brought (the copies) into Uruk.'

Not every city flourished. Sippar seems to have been more or less abandoned, and late astronomical texts once thought to come from there have now been attributed to Babylon. Ur went into decline, perhaps as a result of a change in the coastline and the silting up of its approaches to the sea; its place was taken by the new city of Charax Spasinu, which Alexander had founded and settled with disabled Macedonian soldiers, thus introducing a nucleus of Greeks into the south of the country.

The Parthian Period, c.141 BC–AD 226

Even while the Parthians were edging out the old order, the late Seleucid king Demetrios II (145–141 and 129–125 BC) authorized a new cuneiform king list which ended with his own name, following tradition. Recent research has shown that this period, far from being one of decadence and decay, still indicates continuity in the old cities as well as innovation in new ones. Under Parthian rule all forms of religious life were allowed to flourish. The clearest evidence for this comes from the words of Rav, the great Jewish rabbi, who came from southern Mesopotamia and began to teach and write around AD 219: he named Babylon's temple of Bel and Borsippa's temple of Nabu as leading centres of idolatry with regular festivals in his time. His plain statement allows us to re-evaluate the misleading comment which Pliny made in the mid-first century AD:

'The temple of Jupiter Belus in Babylon is still standing . . . but in all other respects the place has gone back to a desert, having been drained of its population by the proximity of Seleukeia. There are in addition the following towns in Mesopotamia: Hippareni—this is also a school of Chaldaean learning like Babylon; . . . also Orcheni (Uruk). A third seat of Chaldaean learning is situated in the same neighbourhood towards the south.'[7]

The change was probably exaggerated by Pliny, since Babylon, lying beside the Euphrates, had its own economy that was scarcely altered by the foundation upon the Tigris of Seleukeia, for each river had its distinct pattern of economic life. In Babylon the Greek theatre (or an adjacent gymnasium) was still being used for athletic competitions, for an inscription, still written in Greek in 109 BC, records the prizes awarded to two classes of athletes in various competitive events which took place in that year. The building itself appears to have been rebuilt during the Roman period, and the Amran quarter of the city was quite wealthy, as archaeological remains show. Palmyrene merchants of great personal wealth were still resident in Babylon in the early years of the Christian era, and sent money for rebuilding the temple of Bel in Palmyra. The Arab kings of Hatra in the north near Ashur named their main temple Esagila after the temple of Marduk in Babylon, and called its Sun-god Shamash 'Bel'.

At Uruk the library with its learned men continued to exist: the *Epic of Gilgamesh* was copied anew and astronomical records containing chronicle entries were still regularly kept at the beginning of this period, although we do not yet know why or when these customs came to an end. There the temple of Anu and Antu as well as the temple of Ishtar were still used for regular rituals and festivals. At Nippur the temple of Inanna appears to have been rebuilt.[8] At Nineveh a part of the old palace of Sennacherib,

21. Parthian door lintel from the palace of Sennacherib at Nineveh.

---

[6] Orcheni means men of Uruk.
[7] Hippareni was originally thought to be Sippar, but has now been established as a pronunciation of Nippur.

[8] See Ch. VII, pp. 151–2 for details about Hatra and Ashur at this time.

now 700 years old, was refurbished with a new, decorated lintel.

The Parthians exercised a loose and flexible control over their huge territories. They did not make Babylon their capital, and seem not to have interfered in its way of life. Very little is known about their institutions, for almost no records of their kings survive, but they seem to have tolerated a very great degree of independence by local rulers, of whom two outstanding examples are the dynasts of Hatra and Palmyra.

Independent Kingdoms

Another such realm, which enjoyed a brief independence from AD 20 to 35 within the heartland of Mesopotamia, was the Jewish kingdom of Nehardea. Not far from ancient Sippar (which by now lay in ruins), it lay on the left bank of the Euphrates. Tradition related that Jehoiachin founded it using earth and stones brought from Jerusalem. For a long time Jews were buried on the right bank of the Euphrates in burial grounds that were considered to lie within the land of Israel, for rabbinic tradition shows that the Jews of Babylonia erroneously believed rainfall in Palestine supplied the Euphrates with its water. Though its independence was short-lived, Nehardea survived as an important centre until it was sacked in AD 259, when nearby Pumbedita took over as a centre for Jewish orthodoxy and developed as an academy of learning. Those numerous Jews who already lived in Mesopotamia were joined by a fresh influx after Trajan quelled a rebellion in Palestine in AD 117, and both Kabbalistic mysticism and rabbinic Judaism developed not only in Palestine but also in Mesopotamia, the two areas having close contact. Rabbi Judah put the finishing touches to his work on the Mishnah (the text upon which the Babylonian and Palestinian Talmuds are based) in the city of Sepphoris near Nazareth, around AD 200–17. It was a city where paganism flourished late, yet the Sanhedrin (the central council for Jewish lawgiving) had moved there from Jerusalem. Jewish sages went there from Babylonia to converse with the great Rabbi, to such an extent that there was a synagogue 'of the Babylonians' in Sepphoris.

Around the time when the Parthians first began to dominate Mesopotamia, an unorthodox Jewish community was flourishing at Qumran in Palestine. Definite Mesopotamian influence has been recognized in the version of the *Book of Enoch* which the Qumran community used. One chapter of it, known as the Book of the Watchers, contained a story about Gilgamesh and his monstrous opponent Humbaba. Although it is only known in tiny fragments, an episode about the Flood has also been recognized, and a later version of the chapter, found in Central Asia, shows that the survivor of the Flood was called not Noah but Atambish, a form of Ut-napishtim's name. Therefore a Babylonian, not a biblical version of the Flood story was adopted. Even more recently another episode has been pieced together from Qumran which relates a dream of Gilgamesh about a divine court of judgement set in a heavenly garden with trees. The interpreter of the dream is Enoch, who takes the part that Enkidu played in the Akkadian *Epic of Gilgamesh*.

The books of Enoch and Ezekiel both played an important role in the development of Jewish mysticism, especially the mysteries of the Kabbalah known as Hekhalot 'palaces' and Merkabah 'chariot'. Visions of God in human form as a huge man seated on a throne, of concentric walls with gates through which one must pass with great danger in order to gain access to God, details of materials of crystal and blue gemstone, of cherubim and seraphim, of the divine chariot in which the god was carried, all have their counterparts in Babylonian cult and myth which Ezekiel would have witnessed or heard about during his exile in Babylonia, and which would have been familiar to Babylonian Jews in later centuries. The mystical text *Shi'ur Qomah* which describes the body of God in terms of various precious materials has been compared with similar texts from the library of Ashurbanipal at Nineveh.[9]

Two kingdoms which probably owed their independence to the long period of uncertainty in the late second century BC are Characene in lower Mesopotamia and Elymais south of Susa in Iran. Both give evidence of Babylonian culture re-emerging with renewed vigour.

An unexpected and charming monument of the period is a new palace built on the mound of ancient

[9] See also Ch. III, pp. 75–6.

22. Baked brick from Tello with bilingual Aramaic–Greek inscription of Adad-nadin-ahi, *c.* first century AD.

Girsu. This city, long deserted, had been one of the most important in lower Mesopotamia in very early times, for around 2100 BC a Sumerian governor named Gudea had built a splendid new temple there and raised Sumerian to new heights as a literary language. Highly polished statues of him in black diorite can be seen in several of the world's great museums. The new palace was built by a man with a good Babylonian name: Adad-nadin-ahe, which he inscribed on his bricks in Aramaic and in Greek.

More than this, in preparing the foundations he dug out statues of Gudea, already 2,000 years old, and used them to furnish the courtyard of his palace, where French archaeologists eventually uncovered them.

Adad-nadin-ahe was probably father to the man who founded the independent dynasty of Characene centred on the city of Charax, and engaged in prosperous trade with Palmyra and with India. Its coins show that Nergal Herakles was the patron god of the state. Some of the rulers took Persian names, but others followed Babylonian custom with names such as Abi-Nerglos and Attambelos. Because none of these names is taken from a famous king of the past (not a single one calls himself Nebuchadnezzar!), we may deduce that many men of Characene still had Babylonian names as a matter of course.

In the closing years of the pre-Christian era Charax was home to an indigenous historian and geographer known as Isidore of Charax. Among the remnants of his surviving works is one known as 'Parthian Stations', written in Greek, which describes the main route from the Levant to the western borders of India. The unadorned, repetitive style of the itinerary is just like cuneiform Akkadian itineraries known from the early second millennium BC onwards.

The name Elam, by the addition of a Greek ending and a slight modification of vowels, was known as Elymais in Seleucid times. At about the same time as the local dynast in Characene formed an independent kingdom, not far away around Susa another independent dynasty arose. Its kings, like those of Characene, were conscious of their debt to an illustrious past, for in taking the royal title *kamnaskires* they were resurrecting the Elamite title *kapniškir* meaning 'treasurer', which had been used for the satrap of Susa in Achaemenid times, when Susa housed one of the largest royal treasuries in the empire. Even at this period the temples of Elymais must have guarded considerable treasures, for both Antiochos III and IV tried to raid temples of Bel and of Nanay in Elymais to replenish their coffers, and both died in the attempt. The title Bel for the chief god implies that a local version of the *Epic of Creation* was part of annual ceremonies.

A group of rock reliefs with Aramaic inscriptions shows the investiture of Orodes (III or IV) in the open-air sanctuary at Tang-i Sarvak in south-west Iran, where Bel holds out the ring of kingship to the new king according to Mesopotamian precedents 2,000 years old.

Helped by the guiding hand of Nanay, a goddess known early from an oracle which she uttered in 2000 BC in Uruk, we can trace Mesopotamian influence leading up through Characene and Elymais into distant regions. She was above all the goddess of wisdom. In Arbela she was equated with Ishtar from the late Assyrian period. On coins minted in the Kushan kingdom near Kabul and Peshawar, whose empire stretched to the Ganges in the first three centuries AD, she appears with her Babylonian name written incongruously in Greek letters, and bears a lunar crescent on her head. At the Parthian capital of Nisa she had a temple which has been excavated. In Armenia she was worshipped until her temple was

23. Investiture scene showing ring of kingship, on rock at Tang-i Sarvak, Elymais.

destroyed by St Gregory the Illuminator in the fourth century. She was invoked on an incantation bowl found at Nippur, where her name was written in Aramaic. Among early Arabs her name was sometimes used for the planet Venus, rendered in Arabic. There was a temple to Nanay in Alexandria and in the Fayum; she was worshipped in Greece according to a Greek inscription from the Piraeus, where she was equated, as at Susa, Palmyra, and Dura-Europos, with Artemis. The people of Hatra and of Samarkand revered her.

Scholarship in Seleucid and Parthian Babylonia

Greek became the main language of philosophy and literature in Babylon. It was used by Babylonian

24. Coins showing Nanay on reverse, from Kushan kingdom, second century AD.

scholars who developed and adapted their native traditions in a changing world.

Berossos was a priest of Marduk in Babylon who dedicated to Antiochos I (281–261 BC) an account in Greek of Babylonian traditions. His work, the *Babyloniaka*, is known in short and garbled extracts quoted by later authors, some of whom used an unreliable synthesis made by Alexander Polyhistor. Nevertheless the extant passages show that the Sumerian king-list, a Sumerian version of the Flood story, and royal inscriptions of Sennacherib, were at his disposal. He is said to have settled on the Aegean island of Kos in a community of philosophers, and to have had a daughter who was a sibyl. He seems to have had a colleague named Kritodemos, who apparently helped to transfer Babylonian astrological literature to the Greek world. This may imply that a programme of translation from cuneiform Babylonian to Greek continued under Antiochos I. Berossos, like Eudemos two generations earlier, used Akkadian names for the primeval deities who play a part in the *Epic of Creation*.

Chief among the famous scholars of Babylonia whose international standing ensured the transmission of culture was Diogenes the Stoic. We do not know whether he was a Greek or a Babylonian by parentage. He was born around 240 BC. Strabo says, ambiguously, that he was called the Babylonian because 'we do not call men after Seleukeia if they are from there'. If he was a native Babylonian, his

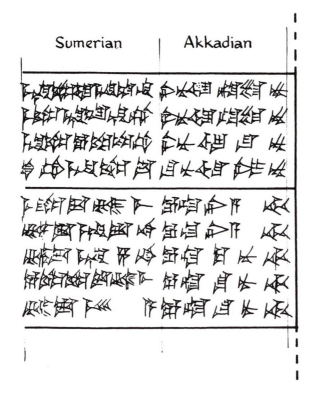

Sumerian	Akkadian

25. Two sections from a bilingual Sumerian–Akkadian grammatical paradigm for the verb, from mid-second millennium Nippur. The order 'we, you, they' is the same as used in English formal grammar.

Greek name would have been used in addition to a Babylonian name according to the practice attested for two local governors at Uruk.

Diogenes grew up in Mesopotamia perhaps two generations after Berossos. He was eventually appointed head of the flourishing school of Stoic philosophers in Athens. There he had many influential pupils including Archidemos of Tarsos who later founded a school of Stoic philosophy in Babylonia, according to Plutarch. As a venerable scholar in his mid-eighties Diogenes led a mission of Stoic scholars from Athens to Rome in 156/5 BC, together with Carneades, who was head of the Platonic Academy at Athens. There he made a great impression, so that Cicero, writing more than two centuries later, called him 'a great and important Stoic'. He was the first Stoic teacher to visit Rome, where he lectured extensively. Some of his best work was done in grammar, and many modern scholars claim that traditional grammar began within the Stoic movement, Diogenes'

treatise *Techne peri phones* being the source for later handbooks. Thus he continued the tradition known from the cuneiform study of Sumerian and Babylonian grammar, extant from around 1800 BC, and this background helps to explain why the Stoics in general were so interested in studying grammar. At about the same time the Indian grammarian Pāṇini, born in north-west India, wrote his grammar of Sanskrit. The appendices to that work listed words by classification as parts of speech, in the same way as some cuneiform lists give groups of words by parts of speech. Like the Stoic grammarians, Pāṇini's work tried to establish the proper use of language, using the analysis to determine what was correct.

The early Stoic tradition is poorly known because none of the early philosophical writings are now extant. The movement was founded in Athens by Zeno, a non-Greek from Cyprus and none of its early heads were mainland Greeks. Babylon, Seleukeia, Tarsos, and Apamea-on-Orontes where the cult and oracle of Babylonian Bel flourished in the Roman period, provided some of its most celebrated men. It is especially noteworthy that Diogenes and his follower Apollodoros 'from the Tigris' emerged from 'Babylon' or Seleukeia before any known philosophical school was founded there; it was their successor Archidemos who set up a Stoic school in Babylonia. If it is right to connect Berossos' *Babyloniaka* with the precursor of that school, we seem to have a parallel to the way in which, at Apamea-on-Orontes, the priest of Bel acted as head of Epicurean philosophers, thus ensuring that Babylonian learning penetrated the apparently Greek philosophical traditions.[10]

Educational practices in Rome and Egypt followed the models established long ago in ancient Mesopotamia. Using an alphabet instead of complex cuneiform, pupils first learned letters, practising them by writing them down vertical columns in the Babylonian way, and then they proceeded to write syllables such as *ba be bē bi bo bu bō* (in capital letters which do not require ligatures) just as was required for learning cuneiform. Thus the old *tu-ta-ti* exercises of Babylon were retained despite the alphabetic system. Two- or three-line exercises written on ruled lines by the teacher were copied on the same tablet or slate by the pupil just as had been done in Mesopotamia for over 2,000 years. Lists of words by category

---

[10] See pp. 51–2 below.

26. Part of a commentary on the Babylonian Theodicy (dividing marks showing junction of extract and comment are black on this drawing).

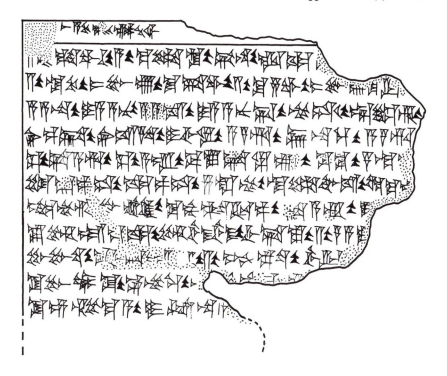

—fish, trees, birds, etc.—were learned and practised by the pupil, continuing the tradition of cuneiform lexical lists, and colophons are identical in content and format; only the language and writing system are different. An advanced stage of academic work was to write or study learned commentaries on old texts in which, for example, modern words were given to explain archaic words, or etymologies were suggested. Such commentaries had been composed and used since the neo-Assyrian period in cuneiform. It was easy for a Babylonian such as Diogenes to communicate with educated men in Athens and Rome because their educational training was so similar.

One of the Stoic techniques used to investigate connections between the gods and earthly matter, the links between macrocosm and microcosm, was based on the theory that the names of things, regardless of language, contain cryptic evidence from which the essential substance can be extracted. It uses the kind of etymological play enjoyed by modern crossword puzzlers; for example, the goddess *Athena* is equated with 'air', *aither*, because both words contain the letters ATHE. The same kind of technique is found in the Babylonian *Epic of Creation*, in which the epithets of Marduk are dissected one by one into various syllables and logographic elements, which can each be given independent meanings of their own. For instance, the name Marduk could be understood as *mar* 'son' and *duku* 'holy mountain'. Likewise Bardaisan of Edessa (AD 154–222)[11] believed that composition and formation of words was analogous to the composition of essential natures. Much later the same technique was used by Michael Scot, the remarkable scholar who served Frederick II of Sicily from AD 1224. He had studied in Toledo where he would have read, for instance, the encyclopaedic work *Etymologies* written by Isidore of Seville in the sixth century AD, and widely popular in the Middle Ages, a compilation showing the technique used in simplistic ways.

Diogenes was contemporary with another Babylonian scholar named Sudines, who was famous, according to Pliny, particularly for the study of the magical properties of stones. The attempt to link stones with aspects of divine influence is well known in cuneiform from at least late Assyrian times, and it continued into the Parthian period under Zachalias, whom Pliny also names. Various different powers were ascribed to stones, and they were used in certain combinations in order to cure illness or avert impending harm. Strings of stones in specific numbers and order acted as amulets, and the knots tied

[11] See Ch. VII, p. 154.

between each stone or bead represented a prayer or incantation, the sequence varying according to the prescription. Sudines visited the court of Attalos I (241–197 BC), the king of Pergamon who made its famous library rival that of Alexandria. The name of Sudines is known now from a fragment of Greek papyrus from Egypt which confirms his fame.

A pupil of Diogenes was Apollodoros of Seleukeia-on-Tigris, a Stoic like his master. He is known to have written treatises on ethics and physics. Around the same time lived Kritodemos, of whose work an introduction is extant in the writings of Vettius Valens. It recounts the long wanderings of the scholar, and his initiation into secret lore, in a manner reminiscent of Zosimos of Akhmim.[12]

'Seleukos the Babylonian' was a contemporary of the Greek astronomer Hipparchos and is credited by Posidonios, the Stoic philosopher from Apamea-on-Orontes, with postulating that the Sun was the centre of the universe, for which he tried to find proofs, and for demonstrating that tidal movements were connected with the movements of the Moon.

Kidenas (Babylonian Kidinnu) of Nippur was known as a famous scholar to Pliny, Strabo, and Vettius Valens, and to Hipparchos who used his work. Kidinnu is known from contemporary cuneiform astronomical tablets, and may have invented the arithmetical method which modern scholars call System B, designed to represent deviations from the mean solar, lunar, and planetary movements. Naburiannos was a Babylonian astronomer whose fame was also known to Classical authors.[13]

One might suppose that academic activity in Babylon and its vicinity would have come to an end when the Parthians took control of Babylon. But this was not the case. There is clear evidence that the region still produced world-class scholars, some with Greek and some with non-Greek names.

Teukros 'of Babylon' lived in the first century AD, and made a register of stars that rose to the north and south of each zodiacal sign. It is thought to be his work which influenced Arab and medieval European astrology. A fragment of his work, discovered early this century, equates the twelve signs of the zodiac with major countries of the world. This tradition is represented in the biblical Book of Daniel, set in Babylon, in which the major political powers

of the world in chapter 8 are described in terms of the animals in the signs of the zodiac.[14]

During the second century AD lived Herodikos 'the Babylonian' who wrote a scurrilous work mocking Plato and Sokrates, and showed a strong preference for Homer; his writing seems to be the first of a long-lived type in which the writings of Plato and Homer were compared and judged. Lucian of Samsat (a Mesopotamian by virtue of his home on the Euphrates) wrote in the same way much later. One of Herodikos' famous epigrams is extant:

Away with you from Greece, ye scholars of Aristarchos;
Take flight over the broad back of the sea,
More fearful than the brown antelope,
Ye who buzz in corners and talk of monosyllables,
Whose business is *sphin* and *sphoin* and *min* and *nin*.
Let these things be yours, ye fretful men,
But may Hellas and divine Babylon ever remain for
    Herodikos.

Herodikos also compiled a reference work listing the people named in Greek comedies—not a characteristic composition for a Greek author; perhaps one can see in this work a legacy of the list-making habits of earlier academies in Babylonia.

Around the same time Zachalias 'of Babylon' wrote works which ascribed to stones the ability to influence fate and the affairs of those who wore them. We are indebted to Pliny for this brief information and for telling us that his patron was Mithridates (IV of Pontus? AD 128–47). The scanty information is just sufficient for us to deduce that Zachalias was reworking an old, cuneiform manual on the properties and uses of stone, known as *Abnu Šikinšu*, which is attested from Assyrian libraries at Ashur and Sultantepe, and to link him with Sudines whose interests were in the same field three centuries earlier.

A Greek poem known as *Lithika*, attributed in the Middle Ages to Orpheus, concerns the magic powers of stones and contains Babylonian-style correlations between divine powers and different stones. Together with a similar work known as the *Lithika Kerygmata*, it belongs generally in the group of literature known as Hermetic, which implies restricted access and secrecy, and is a type of work often attributed to Hermes Trismegistos.[15] Several characteristics point to a core of older, Mesopotamian material within a Hellenized end-product. The Sumerian–Akkadian

---

[12] See Ch. VIII, pp. 168–70.   [13] See Ch. VI, p. 134.   [14] See also Ch. VIII, p. 169.   [15] See Ch. VIII, p. 166.

myth *Lugal-e*, still read at the late Assyrian court, recounts how the god Ninurta defeated the stones and then blessed or cursed them according to their natures, beginning with crystal in the list of blessed stones. Likewise both Greek works are set into a mythological framework, the catalogue of stones begins with crystal, and the god often addresses the stone in question as if it were a person:

The Lord turned to crystal, and addressed chalcedony, carnelian, and lapis lazuli: 'You shall be the first to come to my workshop, be prepared for anything that is required of you.' (*Lugal-e*)

This can be compared with:

I know the powers that your sovereign potions possess
    against evil,
O wonderful stone, hailed by mortals. (*Lithika*)

Crystal also begins the Babylonian series of incantations known as *Lipšur Litanies*. Both *Lugal-e* and the *Lithika Kerygmata* attribute to (a form of) crystal both male and female manifestations. The *Lithika Kerygmata* contains very little information about places of origin with the notable exception of 'za(m)pila(m)pis' from the Euphrates and 'the Babylonian stone', probably carnelian, which it says is mainly worn by palace dignitaries. The two Greek works are thought to be of the fourth century AD. They are quite unlike Theophrastos' work on stones.

Abydenos, whose name is probably Babylonian with a Greek ending, wrote a Chaldaean History that has not survived except in a few quotations and paraphrases. It was written probably during the second century AD, and seems to contain some historical information that certainly is not derived from Herodotos or Ktesias.

It may well be asked why these Babylonian scholars with their Greek names studied Greek literature and not the earlier, Mesopotamian works that we have retrieved through archaeology. A part of the answer can be given in the words of Philo of Byblos, a Phoenician who wrote during the Hellenistic period:

'The Greeks, who surpass all men in their natural cleverness, first appropriated most of these tales. They then dramatized them in various ways with additional literary ornaments, and intending to beguile with the delights of myths, they embellished them in all sorts of ways.'

From this statement emerges the understanding of educated Semites that the Greeks had adopted and developed Semitic, Near Eastern tradition. Therefore by studying Homer and Plato, Babylonian scholars considered that they were dealing with evolved, modern versions of their own writings in one of the languages that had come to replace their own.

Babylonian Gods at Palmyra and Dura-Europos

Babylonian religion and learning flourished not only in the great centres of learning within lower Mesopotamia but moved out into cities whence cuneiform writing had long vanished. Palmyra is particularly important in this respect, for it had ancient connections with Babylonia going back to a time before the camel was domesticated for transport. Its Semitic name was Tadmor, and it was a trading station for Old Assyrian merchants as early as 2000 BC. During the Parthian period one of the largest temples in the world was dedicated to Bel, built on the highest point of a citadel mound that was already very ancient.

An inscription of 44 BC mentions priests of Bel, showing that Palmyra was already established at that time as a cult centre for Bel. By AD 24 the building or rebuilding of the temple (unfortunately displacing layers of earlier occupation) was being funded at least in part by merchants of Palmyra from 'the city of Babylon'. It was decorated with a sculpture more than 5 metres long which showed Bel in his chariot drawing his bow and shooting Tiamat, 'Sea'. The scene is surrounded by Victories, who hold palm fronds. Even this detail can now be connected with the celebration described in cuneiform, for a palm frond was presented to Bel in Babylon according to a late version of the *akītu*-festival ritual which has only recently come to light:

'In the month Kislev, fourth day . . . the singer will chant the *Epic of Creation* to Bel. At (the recitation of the line:) "For Usmu who carried your present to give the news (of victory)" the priest will raise a palm-frond and place it on a silver brick opposite Bel.'

Many terracotta tesserae were found in the temple of Bel. They are thought to be tickets to the banquet held during the festival. This event was presided over by a Chief of Feasts who not only provided the wine but may also have taken charge of the divination by which the annual destinies were decreed, as they

27. Frieze from the Temple of Bel at Palmyra, showing Bel in his chariot shooting Tiamat, a scene from the Babylonian *Epic of Creation*, first or second century AD.

were in the traditional Babylonian ritual. Most of the inscriptions found there are bilingual in Palmyrene Aramaic and Greek, with fuller versions in the former. Aurelian set up a cult to Bel of Palmyra in Rome following his conquest of Queen Zenobia in AD 273. After that date the cult persisted in Palmyra, lasting until at least AD 380 when Theodosios is recorded as having put an end to pagan rites there. Although Bel was sometimes called Zeus, and Nabu Apollo, by Greeks, the Palmyrene inscriptions make it quite clear that the Semitic gods remained the focus of the cult. Phonetic writings of Bel in Greek distinguish this god from the Phoenician BaꜤal and from the local gods whose names end in Bol.

Bel was not the only Babylonian god to be worshipped publicly at Palmyra. A very large temple to Nabu has also been unearthed, together with inscriptions which name a tribe as 'sons of the priests of Nabu'. Many of the personal names used by Palmyra's citizens were formed with the names of Bel and Nabu. The Babylonian goddess Nanay and the goddess Herta (Akkadian 'bride') were also worshipped there. By contrast, two centuries of Achaemenid rule had had little observable effect upon the religious life of Palmyra.

Palmyra was a centre for learning with the patronage of Zenobia. One Longinos (probably not the man of that name who wrote about literary style in his work *On the Sublime*) was famous in the Roman world for his learning, being described as 'a living library and walking university'. A friend of the Palmyrene Longinos named Aemilius founded the great academy of philosophy and religious thought in nearby Apamea-on-Orontes, under the aegis of Zenobia.

Gods from Babylonia were also worshipped at Dura-Europos on the Euphrates. A land sale, written on a cuneiform tablet and sealed with the seal of the king of Hana in the mid-second millennium BC, was found in excavations there. It showed that a town called Damara had existed there from at least c.1500 BC with a tradition of recording in cuneiform, so the remains of the earlier town presumably lie beneath the unexcavated citadel mound. The Hellenistic city was therefore not a new foundation but a remodelling of an ancient town using the old name Damara, now pronounced Dura. Its patron deity was probably Nanay (as also at Jerash in Jordan), and her huge temple was built according to a Babylonian type of plan. Although some of the Greek inscriptions from the site refer to her as Artemis, in others she kept her name Nanay, spelt out in Greek letters. A votive terracotta chariot in the Babylonian tradition was probably dedicated to her. Among various Babylonian personal names in the inscriptions from Dura was the name of the daughter of Konon, priest of Bel; she is shown in her finery on a wallpainting from Bel's temple and conveniently labelled Bith-Nanay. Her brothers are labelled with entirely Greek names.

An Assyrian god Apladad 'Son of Adad' was worshipped at Dura in a temple built or rebuilt in AD 54, wearing the uniform of a Roman soldier on a small stone carving. He was patron god of the town 'Ana, not far downstream, and was the divine consort of the goddess Anat whose name, like Ashur and Athens, belongs both to the deity and to the town. He too was famous for oracles, and with his father played the part of the hero-god in the local *akītu*-festival, as texts of the eighth century BC, recently discovered, have shown.[16]

The Palmyrene version of Bel, together with two local Palmyrene gods Yarhibol, the god of the spring,[17] and Aglibol or Malakbel, had a temple on the edge of Dura; an inscription names Bel with Yarhibol. A fragment of wall-painting set on the wall behind the cult statues in the inner sanctum is thought to show Bel as a giant, probably with a horse and chariot, accompanied by two warriors over whom a Victory hovers with a crown. The date has been put around the late first century AD, and a scene from Bel's victory over Tiamat seems a possible subject, particularly in view of the sculpture showing another such episode from the temple of Bel in Palmyra. A separate temple was dedicated to Zeus Megistos. A wall-painting in a private house at Dura shows a hunting scene 'as if taken from late Assyrian bas-reliefs', portraying the horse in the 'flying gallop' typical of Assyrian art but not used in Classical Greek sculpture.

The Cult of Bel at Apamea-on-Orontes

The cult of Bel beyond Mesopotamia was not restricted to Palmyra and Dura, but flourished too at Apamea, a city of great Antiquity which the Seleucid kings refounded and renamed. As a centre for prophets and magicians it was notable when in *c.*140–135 BC a slave named Eunous, who was a prophet–magician from Apamea, led a revolt in Sicily. He enjoyed a brief but remarkable success, partly due to an oracle from Bel prophesying that Eunous would

become king. The oracle won international acclaim according to the Roman historian Cassius Dio:

'importance was attached to the utterance of Zeus called Belos, a god worshipped at Apamea in Syria; for this god, years before, while Severus was still a private citizen, had spoken these words to him: 'Eyes and head like those of Zeus who delights in the thunder; slender his waist like Ares, his chest like that of Poseidon.' And later, when he had become emperor, and again consulted this oracle, the god gave him this response: 'Thy house shall perish utterly in blood.'

The description suggests that Bel in this case was the storm-god Adad.[18]

Apamea was also famous for its philosophers. Long before Aemilius founded a Platonic academy there in Zenobia's time (around AD 270), the city was an international centre for Stoic thinkers, most famously Posidonios (*c.*135–50 BC), thought by many to be a key figure, although his written works have unfortunately perished. He would have worked at a time when the new Stoic school founded by Archidemos in Babylonia was persevering through times of political uncertainty, and like Babylonian scholars he took a particular interest in the study of stones. According to Seneca, Posidonios credited sages with putting primeval human society in order and making known to men certain technical skills such as metallurgy —an account which seems to reflect Mesopotamian beliefs rather than the 'Syrian' description of the origins of technology which Philo of Byblos recorded.

A new sect became popular in Apamea, together with the scripture written by its founder Elchesai. Elchesai himself is barely known; Christian writers later considered him to be a heretic. It is known that he advocated baptism for the remission of sins, and that one Alkibiades of Apamea preached to promote his teachings, taking the *Book of Elchesai* to Rome during the reign of Trajan, probably in AD 116/17.[19]

Numenios, a Neoplatonist of Apamea in the early second century AD, was the first author to refer to the 'Chaldaean Oracles', which are now known only from a few quoted extracts, but were very prestigious in late Antiquity.[20] He believed that the soul lived on in different bodies after corporeal death, following a theory first attributed to Pythagoras, although some think that the metamorphoses of Ishtar's lovers, described in the *Epic of Gilgamesh*, imply the same

---

[16] See Ch. V, p. 121.
[17] *yarhu* 'spring' or 'pool', a word long used by the Assyrians.
[18] See also Ch. V, p. 121 and fig. 60.

[19] For antecedents of baptism in Babylonia, and for the importance of Elchesai in the background to Manichaeism, see Ch. VIII, pp. 170–1.   [20] See Ch. V, pp. 119, 121.

ΕΙΘΥΝΤΗΡΙΤΥΧΗΣ
ΒΗΛΩ
ΣΕΖΖΤΟΣΘΕΤΟΒΩ
ᳵΜΟΝ
ΤΩΝΕΝΑΠΑΜΕΙΑ
ΜΝΗΣΑΜΕΝΟΣ
ΛΟΓΙΩΝ

28. Altar dedicated to Bel of Apamea, found at Vaison in France, inscribed in Greek and Latin.

belief was held in the Near East at a much earlier period. There is evidence too for an Epicurean school headed by a priest of Bel; an inscription unearthed at Apamea dating to the first half of the second century AD wrote: '. . . by the command(?) of the greatest, holy god Bel, Aurelius Belios Philippos, priest and diadochos of the Epicureans in Apamea.' This evidence directly connects the cult of Bel with philosophy, and shows one path by which Babylonian religious and wisdom traditions were able to influence the development of Hellenistic philosophy. A bilingual inscription dedicated to Bel of Apamea as 'the governor of fate' was found in southern France, which gives an indication of how widely the god's fame spread.

Iamblichos in the fourth century was based in Apamea, and he was a key figure in the Neoplatonist movement. He wrote a work called *On the Mysteries of the Egyptians, Chaldaeans and Assyrians* in which he took pains to justify divination and omens in the face of scepticism. Apamea clung to its pagan traditions late in the Christian era: Libanios of Antioch, who was born in AD 314, wrote that 'Apamea . . . is dear to Zeus and continued to reverence Zeus when punishments were reserved for reverencing the gods.' From this background of continuing rites it would be quite appropriate for a collection of oracles to be called 'Chaldaean' even if most of the collection had been written after the death of cuneiform.

The manifold traditions known as the 'Sibylline' oracles may have some connections with Seleucid Babylonia. Not only was there a tradition naming a Babylonian sibyl Sambathe (a name reminiscent of Sabitu, the wise 'ale-wife' in the *Epic of Gilgamesh*) but another tradition named as sibyl a daughter of Berossos called Sabbe—possibly a form of the same name. At Rome the Sibylline oracles were consulted from at least 218/17 BC onwards, at a time when Antiochos III was king in Babylon. These oracles are formulated in the same way as Akkadian predictions of various kinds: from the dynastic prophecies still written in cuneiform at the end of the Seleucid period, to the much older liver divination texts, bird augury, and astronomical omens: 'If a certain condition is found, a certain event will occur.' The 'science' by which the first clause was related to the second followed certain detailed rules which were already well developed in the early second millennium BC.

Just as Assyrian and later kings consulted the great astrological manual *Enūma Anu Enlil* in Nineveh and Babylon at times of uncertainty, so Roman leaders consulted the Sibylline oracles; just as Assyrian kings consulted the oracles of Ishtar of Arbela and Sin of Harran in the seventh century BC, so the Seleucid kings consulted the oracle of Apollo at Daphne near Antioch, and the Roman emperor Severus consulted Bel at Apamea. Individual oracles from Ishtar of Arbela in the seventh century BC were collected together on to large tablets, just as prophecies had been at Mari a thousand years earlier; so too, it seems, were the Sibylline and Chaldaean oracles. The 'Chaldaean' collection has sometimes been dismissed as an outright forgery dating from around the time of Julian the Apostate (AD 361–3), but it is more likely to have incorporated older material such as was still available in Apamea, Harran, and Arbela, to enhance its credibility according to precedent.

Babylonian and Assyrian culture did not die when cuneiform writing became obsolete. Scholarship persisted in central Mesopotamia, but was carried on in Greek. Babylonian cults with related literature (probably written in Aramaic) continued in Babylon, Borsippa, Uruk, Palmyra, Apamea, and were introduced into Rome; Assyrian cults persisted at Ashur, Harran, and Arbela, and were introduced into Hatra.

FURTHER READING

1. Achaemenid Persian Rule

Bechert, H. (ed.), *The Dating of the Historical Buddha* (Göttingen, 1992).

Cool Root, M., *The King and Kingship in Achaemenid Art*, Acta Iranica, 3rd. ser., Textes et mémoires 9 (Leiden, 1979).

Dalley, S., 'Nineveh after 612 BC', *Altorientalische Forschungen* 20 (1993), 134–47.

Dandamaev, M. A., and Lukonin, V. G., *The Culture and Social Institutions of Ancient Iran* (Cambridge, 1989).

Gibson, J. C. L., *Syrian Semitic Inscriptions* (Oxford, 1975), 125–43.

Giron, N. A., 'Fragments de papyrus araméens provenant de Memphis', *Journal Asiatique* 18 (1921), 56–64.

Kingsley, P., 'The Greek Origin of the Sixth-Century Dating of Zoroaster', *Bulletin of the School of Oriental and African Studies* 53 (London, 1990), 245–65.

Kuhrt, A., and Sherwin-White, S. M., ''Xerxes' Destruction of Babylonian Temples', in H. Sancisi-Weerdenburg and A. Kuhrt (eds.), *Achaemenid History, ii: The Greek Sources* (Leiden, 1987).

Pingree, D., 'Mesopotamian omens in Sanskrit', in D. Charpin and F. Joannès (eds.), *La Circulation des biens, des personnes et des idées* (Paris, 1992), 375–9.

Posener, G., *La Première domination perse en Égypte* (Cairo, 1936).

Sancisi-Weerdenburg, M., Kuhrt, A., and Cool Root, M., *Continuity and Change, Achaemenid History* viii (Leiden, 1994).

Stolper, M., 'Late Achaemenid Legal Texts from Uruk and Larsa', *Baghdader Mitteilungen* 21 (1990), 559–624.

—— 'The neo-Babylonian text from the Persepolis Fortification Tablets', *JNES* 43 (1984), 305.

Woodward, G. R., Mattingley, H., and Lang, D. M., [St John Damascene] *Barlaam and Ioasaph*, Loeb Classical Library (Harvard, 1983).

Zauzich, K. T., 'Ein Zug nach Nubien unter Amasis', in J. H. Johnson (ed.), *Life in a Multi-Cultural Society*, SAOC 51 (Chicago, 1992), 361–4.

2. Alexander the Great and his Seleucid Successors

Arrian, *Life of Alexander* 7. 15. 4.

Brinkman, J. A., 'The Akkadian words for "Ionia" and "Ionian"', in R. F. Sutton (ed.), *Daidalikon, Studies in memory of R. V. Schroder* (Illinois, 1989), 53–71.

Clay, A. T., *Miscellaneous Inscriptions in the Yale Babylonian Collection*, no. 52, Yale Oriental Series 1 (New Haven, 1915).

Doty, L. T., 'Nikarchos and Kephalon', in E. Leichty, M. de J. Ellis, and P. Gerardi (eds.), *A Scientific Humanist, Studies in Memory of A. Sachs* (Philadelphia, 1988), 95–118.

Downey, S., *Mesopotamian Religious Architecture* (Princeton, 1988).

Hopfner, T., *Orient und griechische Philosophie*, Beiheft zum alten Orient 4 (Leipzig, 1925), esp. 1–8.

Hunger, H., *Babylonische und assyrische Kolophone*, Alte Orient und Altes Testament 2 (Neukirchen-Vluyn, 1968).

Mayer, W. R., 'Seleukidische Rituale aus Warka mit Emesal-Gebeten', *Orientalia* ns 47 (1978), 431–58.

Newell, E. T., *The Coinage of the Eastern Seleucid Mints* (New York, 1938).

Pedde, F., 'Frehat en-Nufegi: Two Seleucid Tumuli near Uruk', in A. Invernizzi and J.-F. Salles (eds.), *Arabia Antiqua, Hellenistic centres around Arabia* (Rome, 1993), 205–221.

Sherwin-White, S., 'Seleucid Babylonia: A Case-Study for the Installation and Development of Greek Rule', in A. Kuhrt and S. Sherwin-White (eds.), *Hellenism in the East* (London, 1987).

—— and Kuhrt, A., *From Samarkhand to Sardis* (London, 1993).

Thureau-Dangin, F., *Rituels accadiens* (Osnabruck, 1921; repr. 1975).

Tigay, J., 'An Early Technique of Aggadic Exegesis', in H. Tadmor and M. Weinfeld (eds.), *History, Historiography and Interpretation* (Jerusalem, 1983), 169–89.

Wehrli, F., *Eudemos von Rhodos; Die Schule des Aristoteles VIII* (Basle, 1955).

3. The Parthian Period *c.* 141 BC – AD 226

Aggoula, B., *Inscriptions et graffites araméens d'Assour* (Naples, 1985).

—— *Inventaire des inscriptions hatréennes* (Paris, 1991).

Babylonian Talmud, 'Abodah Zarah 11b, ed. L. Goldschmidt, vol. vii (Haag, 1933).

Boehmer, R. M., 'Uruk 1980–1990: A Progress Report', *Antiquity* 65 (1991), 465–78.

Dalley, S., 'Nineveh after 612 BC', *Altorientalische Forschungen* 20 (1993), 134–47.

FINKBEINER, U., 'Keramik der seleukidischen und parthischen Zeit aus den Grabungen in Uruk-Warka', *Baghdader Mitteilungen* 22 (1991), 537–637.

GRAYSON, A. K., 'Königslisten und Chroniken', *RlA* vi (1980–3), 86–135.

HAUSSOULLIER, B., 'Inscriptions grecques de Babylone', *Klio* 9 (1909), 352–63.

INVERNIZZI, A., 'Hellenism in Mesopotamia: A View from Seleucia on the Tigris', *Al-Rāfidān* 15 (1994), 1–24.

LIEU, S. N. C., *Manichaeism in Mesopotamia and the Roman East* (Leiden, 1994).

MATHIESON, H. E., *Sculpture in the Parthian Empire* (Aarhus, 1992).

MEYERS, E. M., NETZER, E., and MEYERS, C. L., *Sepphoris* (Eisenbraun, 1992).

WETZEL, F., Schmidt, E., and MALLWITZ, A., *Babylon der Spätzeit* (Berlin, 1957).

4. Independent Kingdoms

AZARPAY, G., 'Nana, the Sumero-Akkadian goddess of Transoxiana', *Journal of the American Oriental Society* 96 (1976), 536–42.

BAUMGARTEN, J. M., 'The Book of Elkesai and Merkabah Mysticism', *Journal for the Study of Judaism* 17 (1986), 212–23.

BEYER, K., *Die aramäische Texte vom Toten Meer*, Ergänzungsband (Göttingen, 1994), 119–21.

CUMONT, F., *Fouilles de Dura Europos* (Paris, 1926), 195 ff.

HENNING, W., 'The Monuments and Inscriptions of Tang-i Sarvak', *Asia Major* 2 (1952), 151–78.

INGHOLT, H., *Parthian sculptures from Hatra* (New Haven, 1954).

KINGSLEY, P., 'Ezekiel by the Grand Canal between Jewish and Babylonian Tradition', *Journal of the Royal Asiatic Society* 3 (1992), 339.

LE RIDER, G., *Suse sous les Seleucides et les Parthes*, Mémoire de la Mission Archéologique en Iran 38 (Paris, 1965).

2 Maccabees 1: 13–15.

NEUSNER, J., *Judaism, Christianity and Zoroastrianism in Talmudic Babylonia* (Atlanta, 1990).

PARROT, A., *Tello. Vingt Campagnes de Fouilles (1877–1933)* (Paris, 1948).

SCHOFF, W. H., *Parthian Stations, by Isidore of Charax* (Philadelphia, 1914).

WEIDNER, E., 'Assyrische Itinerare', *AfO* 21 (1966), 42–6.

5. Scholarship in Seleucid and Parthian Babylonia

ARNIM, J. VON, *Stoicorum Veterum Fragmenta*, iii (Teubner, 1923), 210–12, 259–61.

BARB, A. A., 'The Survival of Magic Arts', in A. Momigliano (ed.), *The Conflict between Paganism and Christianity in the 4th century* (Oxford, 1963).

BIDEZ, J., 'Les Écoles chaldéennes sous Alexandre et les Seleucides', *Annuaire de l'institut de philologie et d'histoire orientales*, volume offert à Jean Capart, iii (1935), 41–89.

BONNER, S. F., *Education in Ancient Rome* (Berkeley, 1977).

BRÉHAUT, E., *An Encyclopaedist of the Dark Ages: Isidore of Seville* (New York, 1912).

CAQUOT, A., 'Sur les quatre bêtes de Daniel VII', *Semitica* 5 (1955), 5–13, with critique of J. Day, *God's Conflict with the Dragon and the Sea* (Cambridge, 1985), 154–5.

DURING, I., *Herodicus the Cratetean* (Stockholm, 1941).

FREDE, M., 'The Origins of Traditional Grammar', in *Essays in Ancient Philosophy* (Oxford, 1987).

HALLEUX, R., and SCHAMP, J., *Les Lapidaires grecs* (Paris, 1985).

HOROWITZ, W., 'Two *abnu šikinšu* Fragments and Related Matters', *Zeitschrift für Assyriologie* 82 (1992), 112–22.

KRECHER, J., 'Kommentare', *RlA* vi (1980–3), 188–91.

MAUL, S., *Zukunftsbewältigung* (Mainz, 1994), 107–10, 375–6.

OBBINK, D., and VAN DER WAERDT, P. A., 'Diogenes of Babylon', *Greek, Roman and Byzantine Studies* 32 (1991), 355–96.

OELSNER, J., *Materialen zur babylonischen Gesellschaft und Kultur in hellenistischer Zeit* (Budapest, 1986), 239–44 (on the Graeco-Babylonian tablets).

PLINY, *Natural History* 9. 115, 37. 169.

RE s.v. Zachalias and Teuker.

SANDBACH, F. H., *The Stoics*, 2nd edn. (Cambridge, 1989).

SHAFTS, B., *Grammatical method in Pānini* (New Haven, 1961).

STRABO, *Geography*.

TASSIER, E., 'Greek and Demotic school-exercises', in J. H. Johnson (ed.), *Life in a Multi-Cultural Society*, SAOC 51 (Chicago, 1992), 311–15.

WENDEL, C., *Die griechisch-römische Buchbeschreibung verglichen mit der des vorderen Orients* (Halle, 1949).

WETZEL, F., and WEISSBACH, F. H., *Das Hauptheiligtum des Marduk in Babylon, Esagila und Etemenanki*, Wissenschaftliche Veröffentlichung der Deutschen Orient-Gesellschaft 59 (Berlin, 1938), 49–56.

6. Babylonian Gods at Palmyra and Dura-Europos

BOUNNI, A., 'Nabu palmyrénien', *Orientalia* NS 45 (1976), 46–52.

CANTINEAU, J., *Inscriptions de Palmyre* ix (Beirut, 1933).

CAGIRGAN, G., and LAMBERT, W. G., 'The Late Babylonian *kislimu* Ritual for Esagila', *JCS* 43–5 (1994), 89–106.

CAVIGNEAUX, A., and ISMAIL, B. K., 'Die Staathalter von Mari und Suhu', *Baghdader Mitteilungen* 21 (1990), 343–57.

CUMONT, F., *Fouilles de Doura Europos (1922–3)* (Paris, 1926).

DALLEY, S., 'Bel at Palmyra and in the Parthian period', *ARAM* (conference 1995, forthcoming).

DU MESNIL DU BUISSON, R., 'Le Bas-Relief du combat de Bel contre Tiamat dans le temple de Bel à Palmyre', *Annales Archéologiques Arabes de la Syrie* 26 (1976), 83–100.

GAWLIKOWSKI, M., 'Les Dieux de Palmyre', *ANRW* ii/18/4 (Berlin and New York, 1990), 2605–58, esp. 2614.

HAJJAR, Y., 'Divinités oraculaires et rites divinatoires en Syrie et en Phénicie à l'époque gréco-romaine', *ANRW* ii/18/4 (1990), 2253–57.

HITTI, P., *History of Syria* (London, 1951).

ROSTOVTZEFF, M. I., *Dura Europos and its Art* (Oxford, 1938).

—— *Parthian Art and the Motive of the Flying Gallop* (Cambridge, Mass., 1937).

SEYRIG, H., 'Les Tessères palmyréniennes et le banquet rituel', *Memorial Lagrange* (Paris, 1940), 51–8.

STEPHENS, F. J., 'A Cuneiform Tablet from Dura-Europos', *Revue d'Assyriologie* 34 (1937), 183–90.

7. The Cult of Bel at Apamea-on-Orontes

BAUMGARTEN, J. M., 'The Book of Elkesai and Merkabah Mysticism', *Journal for the Study of Judaism* 17 (1986), 212–23.

DIO CASSIUS, 79. 8. 5.

DIODORUS SICULUS, 34. 2. 5–22.

GRAYSON, A. K., *Babylonian Historical-Literary Texts* (Toronto, 1975), 17–18 (for the likely Babylonian origin of Sibylline Prophecy iii. 381–7).

LIBANIUS, *Autobiography and Selected Letters* ed. A. F. Norman vol. ii, no. 104 (Harvard, 1992).

LIEBERMAN, S. J., 'A Mesopotamian Background for the So-Called Aggadic "Measures" of biblical Hermeneutics?', *Hebrew Union College Annual* 58 (1987), 157–225.

LIEU, S. N. C., *Manichaeism in the Later Roman Empire and Mediaeval China* (Tubingen 1992), 40–2.

MAJERCIK, R., *The Chaldaean Oracles* (Leiden, 1989).

REY-COQUAIS, J-P., 'Inscriptions grecques d'Apamée', *Annales Archéologiques Arabes de la Syrie* 23 (1973), 66–8.

SCHÜRER, E., *et al.*, *The History of the Jewish People in the Age of Jesus Christ*, iii: 1, rev. edn. (Edinburgh, 1986), 617–54.

SENECA, *Epistolae Morales* 90.

TAYLOR, T., *Iamblichus on the Mysteries* (London, 1895).

THOMSON, R. W., *Moses Khorenats'i, History of the Armenians* (Harvard, 1978).

WEIPPERT, M., 'Assyrische Propheteien', in F. M. Fales (ed.), *Assyrian Royal Inscriptions: New Horizons* (Rome, 1981), 71–116.

III

THE INFLUENCE OF MESOPOTAMIA UPON ISRAEL AND THE BIBLE

Stephanie Dalley

The Historical Background

Before the Hebrew tribes chose their first king at the end of the Late Bronze Age, they shared the land of Palestine with many other peoples: indigenous Canaanites and foreign Egyptians, Hittites, Hurrians, and Philistines. From their remote past the Hebrews could link their ancestry with west Semitic Amorites, of whom some groups had founded dynasties in Mesopotamia. After the monarchy was established, Judah and Israel inhabited a small country rich in sheep, olive oil, wine, certain luxury goods and specialized skills for which the great empires surrounding them had an insatiable appetite. When the Philistines came to control the southern coast of Palestine, the Phoenicians the northern coast, and Ammon, Moab, and Edom the lands east of the Jordan, Judah and Israel had restricted access to good harbours, and so they built up their wealth by land-based connections to the north and south. Hebrew tribes and kingdoms in Palestine were thus caught between several successive empires arising from Egypt, Hittite Anatolia, Assyria, Babylonia, and Iran, and were influenced by the ebb and flow of those great powers.

The theme that links early Palestine most closely to the culture of Mesopotamia is literacy. In Sumerian and Akkadian cities from around 2500 BC onwards, recording systems and literature of many different genres, written in cuneiform on clay and stone, developed in academies of learning. This type of literacy spread into Syria especially at Ebla and then into Hittite Anatolia, accompanied by cylinder seals and sealings upon which royal and religious themes were engraved.

In the nineteenth century BC Hammurabi of Babylon (c.1848–1806) conquered parts of eastern Syria, including the important city-state of Mari on the middle Euphrates. Although he was of Amorite descent, he wholly adopted Mesopotamian traditions. Mari had long used cuneiform, and almost certainly enjoyed direct relations with Hazor, later to be 'the capital of all these kingdoms' (Joshua 11: 10) and with La'ish (Tell Dan), famous for its bronze-workers.

Archaeologists have found a scatter of cuneiform texts in Palestine which are dated to the next five centuries: sheep accounts from Hebron, a fragment of the *Epic of Gilgamesh* from Megiddo, lexical, legal, and divination texts from Hazor, official letters and lists from Ta'annach, Shechem, Jericho, Pella east of Jordan, and a fragment of a clay prism with trilingual vocabulary as well as other fragments inscribed in Akkadian from Tell Aphek near Tel Aviv. Clay models of sheep's livers, some inscribed in cuneiform, were used to record omens and to instruct apprentices; examples have been found at Hazor and Megiddo. Such a wide range of Akkadian cuneiform tablets from Palestinian sites shows the penetration of Babylonian scribal habits, and implies that local scribes were trained in the practices and literary works of Mesopotamian academic tradition. This influence was apparently not linked to military or political domination.

Dates are given according to J. Hughes, *Secrets of the Times*, Journal for the Society of the Old Testament, Supplement Series 66 (1990). Biblical quotations are taken from the Jerusalem Bible.

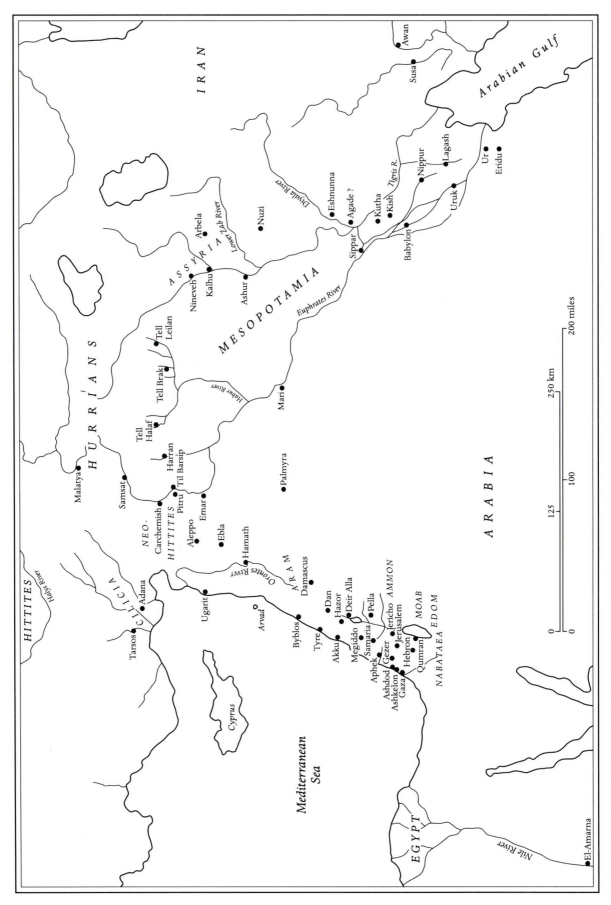

MAP 5. Sketch map showing Mesopotamia with Syro-Palestine

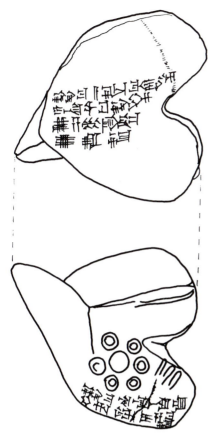

29. Clay model of a sheep's liver, inscribed with an omen in Akkadian, from Mari on the Euphrates, *c.*1800 BC.

30. Clay model of a sheep's liver, inscribed with an omen in Akkadian, from Hazor, mid-second millennium BC.

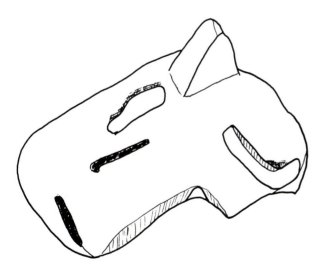

31. Uninscribed clay model of a sheep's liver, from Megiddo, Late Bronze Age.

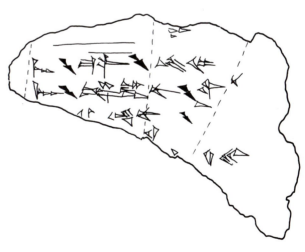

32. Fragment of trilingual vocabulary written on a clay prism, from Tell Aphek (near Tel Aviv), giving words for water and wine in Sumerian, Akkadian, and Canaanite (shown as if flattened at the dotted lines; dividing marks at junctions black on this drawing).

From the early seventeenth century onwards the Hittites expanded southwards from the centre of Anatolia into Syria, beginning with the conquests of Hattusili I, whose capture of cities there, especially Aleppo and Ebla, is now thought to have introduced the Hittites to cuneiform *belles lettres*, which they then adopted. Genesis 23 connects Abraham with Hittites; Esau married Hittite women according to Genesis 26: 34 and 36: 1–3; and these links suggest that the time of the patriarchs[1] was no earlier than the first period of Hittite expansion. At that time the Hurrians, who may be the Horites found in stories of the patriarchs, had already become an important element in the population of Syria. Rivalling the Hittites was the Hurrian kingdom of Mittani, and Hurrian cuneiform texts from Ugarit, Hattusa, and El-Amarna mark the broad extent of their influence in the west. During the second half of the millennium, therefore, Mesopotamian influence is likely to have reached Palestine indirectly, through contact with Hittites and Hurrians.

Imperial powers emerged at this time. By the fifteenth–fourteenth centuries the expanding empires of the Egyptians, Hittites, and Hurrians controlled much of Syria and Palestine. Babylon, which was not then a major imperial power, nevertheless continued to exert a powerful cultural influence because the Babylonian language and script became ever more widely used as a *lingua franca* throughout the ancient Near East. Even the Egyptians, who had their own long history of literacy, used the Babylonian language and cuneiform script to communicate both with other imperial powers and with vassal states, the latter including Jerusalem. A significant body of such correspondence, dated to the second quarter of the fourteenth century, has been found at El-Amarna. From Ugarit comes a great variety of texts. Babylonian cuneiform was used for diplomatic purposes as well as being the basis for dictionary texts (lexical lists) with which scribes were trained; wisdom literature composed in Babylon; and a fragment of the Flood story. Hurrian cuneiform was used for certain ritual texts; and Canaanite myths were written in the newly invented cuneiform alphabet. An early linear, proto-Canaanite alphabet, which had evolved in the south under Egyptian influence, seems to have been used only for names and labels. However, in time linear alphabetic writing on papyrus, parchment, and potsherds became so successful that it drove cuneiform out of local use in the Levant, but the training methods and *belles lettres* of more ancient times continued to be used.

The Hebrew language, written in a linear alphabetic script, began to evolve around 1200 BC, and soon developed its own literary tradition. Their neighbours the Aramaeans of Damascus and Moab did likewise in Aramaic and a dialect of Hebrew. The Philistines, who may have settled in Palestine around the same time as the Hebrews, included Mycenaean people who came via Cyprus. They had long abandoned their Linear B writing and eventually adopted the linear alphabetic script and west Semitic language of their new neighbours.

No direct evidence has yet come to light to help date the Exodus and the subsequent time when the tribes of Israel settled in Palestine. An uneasy consensus has settled on the thirteenth century in the reign of Rameses II (1279–1213) for the Exodus, which would allow about 200 years for the settlement to take place before the monarchy was established sometime before 1000 BC.

Although the power of the Hittites came to an abrupt end in the twelfth century, their southern kingdoms, centred upon the upper Euphrates and Cilicia, survived a Dark Age and gave rise to the neo-Hittite states of Syria without a break in dynastic tradition. However, the neo-Hittites, like the peoples of Canaan, abandoned cuneiform writing; henceforth those new kingdoms wrote both in traditional hieroglyphic Luwian, and in new alphabetic Aramaic or Phoenician. Southernmost among them was the kingdom of Hamath, which was later closely allied with Samaria until its last ruler was killed by Sargon II; Yahweh was worshipped there. So during the early first millennium neo-Hittite culture—thoroughly mixed with Canaanite, Hurrian, and Phoenician ingredients—was very close to the Hebrews. Although none of these peoples still used cuneiform writing, Akkadian with its ancient literature and academic practices persisted on the middle Euphrates. Recently discovered texts from Emar show that Mesopotamian merchants continued to pass through Palmyra dur-

---

[1] I accept that there is a historical basis behind the legendary stories of the patriarchs, although it cannot yet be separated from folkloric accretions. Many modern scholars reject all historicity for the patriarchal narratives.

ing the twelfth century as they had done in the nineteenth; the goddess of Akku (Acre) was worshipped at Emar, and Tiglath-pileser I (1115–1077) marched from Assyria through Carchemish and into Phoenicia, reaching the island of Arvad in the Mediterranean.

When the Hittite empire collapsed and Ugarit was destroyed, power in Palestine began to shift away from the older Canaanite city-states and towards tribal groups. In the eleventh century some of these tribal groups united to create a Hebrew monarchy under Saul and later (with the addition of southern tribes) under David, who flourished around 1000 BC. This tribal alliance was apparently fragile, for after the death of David's successor Solomon, divisions between the northern and southern tribes led to the creation of separate Hebrew city-states—a northern kingdom of Israel ruled from Samaria, and a southern kingdom of Judah ruled from Jerusalem by David's successors. The words used in Hebrew for 'palace' and 'throne' are loan-words from Mesopotamia, implying that the model of Israelite kingship was influenced from there.

Within Mesopotamia, Assyria emerged as the major power and began to expand westwards. Israel probably became a vassal of Shalmaneser III (859–824) and so was obliged to send envoys to Assyria and to make yearly payments of tribute. When Assyrian kings campaigned in Syria and Palestine, western vassal kings were expected to deliver their tribute in person: direct contact took place at the highest levels of society.

An Aramaic inscription from Tell Dan, written *c.*842 by king Hazael of Damascus, and the Moabite stone of *c.*830, written in a language which is closely related to biblical Hebrew, contain accounts of contemporary events. The narrative style of the latter can be compared closely with 2 Kings 3 which records the same series of events from a different point of view, and the national god Chemosh behaves just like Yahweh in forsaking his people when angry, then relenting and delivering them from their enemies. This text proves that west Semitic historical writing was already well developed, taking over forms of composition which had originated in Mesopotamia.[2]

These manifestations of cultural independence developed before the kingdoms of Damascus, Moab,

Israel, and Judah succumbed to direct Assyrian rule in the late eighth and seventh centuries. The few cuneiform tablets found in Palestine that date to the Assyrian empire belong to the administration of occupying Assyrians, and not to local, independent rulers and their scribes, in marked contrast to the preceding period.

A different kind of contact is revealed by glimpses of the Mesopotamian seer Balaam. In Numbers 22–4 he was hired from the distant town of Pethor by the king of Moab to curse Israel. In the words of Philo of Alexandria: 'There was at that time living in Mesopotamia a man famous for divination, who had been initiated into divination in all its forms.' An inscription, written in a form of Aramaic on wall plaster, was excavated at Deir 'Alla' in Transjordan and records some oracles of Balaam which are different from the biblical text. It dates perhaps to the late eighth century, several centuries after the putative lifetime of Balaam. The text gives divinely inspired answers to presumed omens in the Mesopotamian manner, and the word 'answer' is the technical term in Aramaic, equivalent to the Akkadian word used in the same technical context. Balaam's home town Pethor has been identified with Pitru, known from Assyrian texts to lie on the Euphrates. Balaam is the best known example of the wise seer trained in Babylonian methods who travelled abroad and gave his services to foreign rulers, disseminating Mesopotamian forms of ritual and literature which were thus transferred into an alphabetically written language.[3]

Cuneiform texts from the early second millennium onwards show that Mesopotamian kings, according to their public inscriptions, envisaged war as holy action. Before they began to campaign they besought their gods for divine favour; on the march and in battle their gods fought at their side; defeat meant that the gods had withdrawn their approval, and victory was attributed to their support. Likewise in Israel the concept of holy war infuses historical narratives, both before and after the monarchy was established: Yahweh is entreated, he approves the act of aggression, helps his people and delivers the victory, as a comparison between the following passages shows.

---

[2] This author does not share the opinion of some scholars, that all Old Testament text was created after the Exile.

[3] See also Ch. VII, pp. 149–50.

I, Esarhaddon, lifted my hands to the gods Ashur, Sin, Shamash, Bel, Nabu and Nergal, Ishtar of Nineveh and Ishtar of Arbela, and they heard my words. With their keen assent they sent me a repeated oracle: 'Go! Do not hold back! We will go at your side and kill the foe!' . . . The fear of the great gods my lords defeated them . . . Ishtar mistress of battle and conflict who loves my priesthood stood at my side and broke their bows and scattered their battle formation.   (Esarhaddon 680–669 BC)

David consulted Yahweh, 'Shall I attack the Philistines?' he asked. 'Will you deliver them into my power?' Yahweh answered David, 'Attack! I will most surely deliver the Philistines into your power.' Accordingly David went to Baal-perazim and there defeated them. (2 Sam. 5: 19–20)

Yahweh Sabaoth says this: 'I am going to break the bow of Elam, the source of all his might. I will bring four winds down on Elam . . . and I will scatter the Elamites to the winds.' (Jer. 49: 35–6)[4]

The names of Israelite and Judaean kings appear intermittently in Assyrian inscriptions during the ninth and eighth centuries, whenever they were induced to pay tribute to Assyria. But with the reign of Tiglath-pileser III (745–727) a closer relationship was enforced: Judah and other southern states which had previously escaped Assyrian attentions now became vassals. In 733–732 Tiglath-pileser subdued a revolt in which Pekah of Israel was involved. Pekah lost his life, and was replaced by Hoshea, the last king of Israel, who travelled in person to Babylonia to pay tribute, according to a contemporary Assyrian text. Parts of Israelite territory were annexed by Assyria. When Tiglath-pileser died in 727, Hoshea apparently took the opportunity to cease paying tribute. This led to a three-year siege of Samaria, ending in capture. At this point Israel became a province of the Assyrian empire, and ceased to exist as an independent state. A part of the population was deported to distant parts of the empire, following normal Assyrian practice, and was replaced by deportees from other captured territories; Sargon II (722–705) recorded that 27,290[5] Israelites were taken away.

Samaria became an Assyrian provincial capital, and Arabian deportees were brought in, according to Assyrian sources; 2 Kings 17 tells how 'the king of Assyria brought people from Babylon, Cuthah, Avva, Hamath, and Sepharvaim, and settled them in the towns of Samaria to replace the Israelites'. Eventu-

ally the king of Assyria allowed a priest previously deported from Samaria to return to Bethel to instruct immigrants in local forms of worship, but this led to corruption of religious practices, for 'the men of Babylon had made a Sukkoth-benoth, the men of Cuthah a Nergal, the men of Hamath an Ashima, the Avvites a Nibhaz and a Tartak, while the Sepharvites burnt their children in the fire in honour of Adrammelech and of Anammelech, gods of Sepharvaim'. Of these foreign places and their gods, Babylon and Cuthah are central Mesopotamian cities, and cuneiform texts record that more Babylonians than any other group of people were deported by the Assyrians. In later times members of the Samaritan sect were called 'Cuthim' by Josephos and in the Mishnah. Hamath and Sepharvaim are probably both cities in Syria, and Avva is Awan in western Iran, with its gods known in cuneiform as Ibnahaza and Dakdadra.[6] Shalmaneser V (726–722) is said to have deported men from Samaria to Halah (north-east of Nineveh) and to the region of the Habur River in northern Syria. Cuneiform inscriptions from ancient Guzana confirm this by supplying Israelite personal names at that time. Much later Jewish tradition used this episode: in the apocryphal book of Tobit, the *History* of Joseph ben Gorion, and in a Hebrew version of the *Alexander Romance*, attributing the deportation to Shalmaneser.

Deportation meant taking people of high rank, in particular royal and military personnel and craftsmen, keeping families and regional communities together, and sometimes giving them land and employment abroad. The royal family in exile resided at the Assyrian court, and was introduced to its life-style. Tiglath-pileser III claimed to have deported all the royal family from Samaria, and Shalmaneser V took Hoshea to Assyria before the fall of Samaria (2 Kgs. 17: 4). Although they were obliged to remain abroad, deportees were not enslaved. Top-ranking charioteers from Samaria were soon serving in a professional capacity in the exclusive Assyrian royal regiment alongside native Assyrian officers, as administrative cuneiform tablets from Kalhu show. Other deportees of various nationalities were mainly consigned to a less exclusive regiment. Sargon II's inscriptions also say that deportees who were skilled were allowed to

---

[4] Jeremiah's ministry began c.627 BC.

[5] As with most ancient records for such events, different versions of text give different numbers.

[6] Dakdadra was also known as Dirtak. They were equated by Akkadian scribes with Ea the creator god of wisdom and with Sin the Moon-god respectively.

continue doing the kinds of work in which they were expert. When the Assyrians invaded Judah in the reign of Sennacherib (705–681), the Assyrian chief cup-bearer did not threaten the people with slavery but, shouting up at the walls of Jerusalem he promised its people: 'I come to deport you to a country like your own, a land of corn and good wine, a land of bread and of vineyards, a land of oil and of honey' (2 Kgs. 18: 32).

The state of Judah continued to exist for over a century after the fall of Samaria, although both Tiglath-pileser and Sargon marched through Palestine past Judah and deported the inhabitants of Ashdod, which was an independent Philistine city-state with its own ruler. To replace the population Sargon settled there 'people from the east'. Assyrian public buildings in southern towns of Palestine may have been built for foreign administrators at that time, and Tiglath-pileser and Sargon both set up trading stations on the border with Egypt and in Phoenician cities. From the time when Hezekiah, having lost the town of Lachish to Assyrian besiegers, sent his tribute to Sennacherib, there would have been a significant presence of Assyrians within Judah as the Assyrians consolidated their gains and built up towards the invasion of Egypt.

Hezekiah's successor Manasseh (694–640) was deported to 'Babylon' (probably Nineveh is meant) in the time of Esarhaddon, but eventually he was allowed to return to his native land as king (2 Chr. 33: 11–13), probably during the reign of Ashurbanipal (669–627), having absorbed Assyrian influence at the centre of power. When Ashurbanipal put down a rebellion at the Phoenician port of Akku, he deported those men whose lives he spared to Assyria, where many of them were incorporated into the Assyrian army. When eventually the Assyrian empire began to shrink, Nineveh itself falling in 612, Josiah of Judah (639–609) reasserted Judaean independence, but died in battle while attempting to prevent Egyptian forces going to the aid of the remaining Assyrian armies.

The last years of the kingdom of Judah were dominated by the opposing empires of Babylon and Egypt. Nebuchadnezzar II (604–562) won a decisive victory over the Egyptians at Carchemish which left him in effective control of Syria and Palestine. He laid siege to Jerusalem and captured it in 598, shortly after the death of its king Jehoiakim. Jehoiakim's immediate successor Jehoiachin, who ruled for only three months, was deposed and replaced by Zedekiah, whose subsequent rebellion against Nebuchadnezzar led to the second capture of Jerusalem in 587. Judah became a province of the Babylonian empire and deportations to Babylon followed. Five years later a dated record from Babylon reveals that Jehoiachin and his five sons, together with the sons of the king of the Philistine city Ashkelon and other foreign nobles were receiving a generous ration of oil in the palace in Babylon; after 37 years of living among the Babylonians Jehoiachin was freed by Amil-Marduk, biblical Evil-Merodach. Three distinct phases of deportation are listed in Jeremiah 52: 28–30.

Unlike the Assyrians, the Babylonians apparently did not attempt to relocate large numbers of people in distant parts of their empire. The number of Judaeans who were deported was relatively small (4,600 according to Jer. 52: 30) and may have involved primarily the ruling and upper classes, including priests and scribes, for they might have provided a focus for later rebellions if they were allowed to remain. Nevertheless, it is this event of Israelite history to which 'the Exile' refers in later Judaic tradition. Among those exiled to Babylon were biblical writers such as Ezekiel. From cuneiform records it is possible to locate the 'River Chebar', where Ezekiel settled, as the Kabaru canal which linked Babylon to Nippur. Probably exiled there too were the anonymous 'Deuteronomists' who edited many of the books of the Bible including the historical books, from Deuteronomy to Kings and Jeremiah; they may also have edited the early books of the Pentateuch and other prophetic books. Many Judaeans who were exiled to Babylon retained their cultural and religious identity, and Babylonia became an important centre of Judaean culture. This continued to be the case after the Persian king Cyrus II (539–530) conquered Babylon and gave permission for Judaean exiles to return to Judah. Many did not choose to do so, or not immediately; the families that did not return there had by then lived abroad for long enough to have established businesses in a country where merchants had a high social status, and those who had been deported earlier by the Assyrians had already lived in Mesopotamia for five generations.

Under Persian rule the temple in Jerusalem was rebuilt and Judaean culture and religion in Palestine were re-established under Persian political control. During the post-exilic period, Judaean culture became

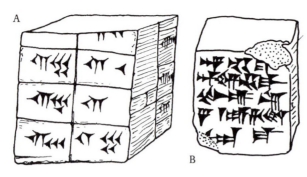

33. A. Ivory prism from Nineveh giving tables for computing the length of daylight according to seasons; B. Clay lot cast before the gods Ashur and Adad, recording the appointment of the eponym official for 833 BC.

34. Coins of Samaria, second century BC, two of which give the first syllable of the city name in cuneiform, a third imitates the Assyrian royal stamp seal.

more rather than less distinctive, perhaps because the loss of political independence increased the importance of religious tradition as a focus for ethnic identity. Nevertheless, Judah adopted the Babylonian calendar during the exile, and took over month names such as Tammuz (the name of the Sumerian god Dumuzi) and Tishri. The book of Esther, ostensibly a court narrative of the Achaemenid period,[7] may transmit a myth about Ishtar (Esther) and Marduk (Mordecai) which serves to explain the Jewish feast of Purim, which is an Akkadian word for lots drawn to allocate property and duties. As late as the fourth century BC the city of Samaria issued coins inscribed

with the city name in an abbreviation using a cuneiform sign. These are clear indications that Babylonian traditions were not entirely abhorrent to Jews, despite the Exile, and there is no evidence for religious persecution by the Babylonians, Persians, or Seleucids.

This brief sketch of the contacts between Mesopotamia and Palestine through a very long period shows how many and varied were the types of relationship that would have allowed cultural influence to enter Israelite customs and biblical literature. They may be summarized as: directly, through the education of a literate élite, through deportation and the administration of Israel and Judah by Assyrian and then Babylonian governors; by hiring diviners; indirectly through trade; through a common stock of west Semitic Amorites, and filtered through Hittite and Hurrian presence immediately to the north, people who in turn had absorbed many aspects of Mesopotamian cultural life. Against this background may be set the comparisons that follow.

Babylonian Traditions in Genesis and Exodus

Different theories compete to explain how the books of Genesis and Exodus were composed, but most scholars accept that they contain different strata, normally identified as JE (Yahwistic and Elohistic material) and P (Priestly material). In the view of most scholars J and E were written before the Exile whereas P was written during or after it, but may contain earlier material. The three sources vary in treating how the divine name was revealed—J thought it had been used from the time of Enosh (Gen. 4: 26), whereas according to E (Exod. 3: 14–15) and P (Exod. 6: 2–3) it was first revealed to Moses—and their different use of divine names corresponds to these theories: J uses the name Yahweh, while E and P mainly use the title Elohim, which is grammatically a plural and means literally 'gods'. This title is the 'plural of majesty', and its Akkadian equivalent is occasionally used in cuneiform texts to refer to the Pharaoh and to the god Nergal. Linguistic, stylistic, and theological differences also distinguish J and E from P.

[7] See Ch. VII, pp. 146–9.

The authors of Genesis described how mankind originated in the Garden of Eden, located at the source of rivers which included the Tigris and Euphrates (Gen. 2: 8–14), and how human history restarted after the Flood. There was a single language in the world after the Flood until Noah's descendants, passing through Babylon, angered Yahweh by attempting to build a tower to heaven. Yahweh then scattered the people and caused diversity of language. Abraham, the father of Israel, was believed to have emigrated from Ur to Canaan via Harran in upper Mesopotamia, and Isaac and Jacob took their wives from Harran.

In view of the important part which Mesopotamia plays in the Genesis stories, it is not surprising that there are parallels between Mesopotamian traditions and Genesis. The Babylonian Creation epic, *Enūma Eliš*, which was written during the second millennium BC, has been compared with Genesis 1 (from the P source). There are some general similarities between the two stories which include the creation of the universe by a god, and an original watery state for the universe. However, the Mesopotamian account gives Sea and the Abyss of Fresh Water as primeval parents who give birth to several pairs of deities before the creator god is born, whereas in Genesis the creator god alone exists from the very beginning. A closer comparison can be made with the *Chaldaean Cosmogony* which introduces the time before the foundation of the city of Eridu with a description of the world: 'All the lands were sea.' This cosmogony was not just local to the city Eridu, for a quarter of Babylon was called Eridu too. The Babylonian word *tiāmat* used for Sea in both accounts is cognate with the word *tehōm* 'deep' in Genesis 1: 2. In *Enūma Eliš* the god Marduk defeats Tiamat the sea-monster and fashions heaven and earth from her carcass. The sun and moon, and other heavenly bodies, are created to mark the passage of time (compare Genesis 1: 14). Following the creation of the universe, Marduk rests before the god Ea creates humans according to Marduk's 'skilful plans'; similarly in one biblical version (J, Genesis 2: 7) God created the universe and only after a rest did he create man. But the Mesopotamian story has men created to serve the gods and release them from toil, whereas in Genesis 1 men are created to rule over the earth and its denizens. So despite some similarities, there are many differences between the two stories. Genesis 1 mentions

only one God, although in verse 26 he speaks as if he were addressing a court of other heavenly beings in the same way as Marduk addresses the assembly of gods in *Enūma Eliš*: 'God said. "Let us make man in our own image, in the likeness of ourselves."' Similar allusions to the gods' assembly are found in the Psalms: 'God stands in the divine assembly, | Among the gods he dispenses justice, (Ps. 82).

Differences between *Enūma Eliš* and Genesis 1 make it hard for us to know if the biblical author was familiar with the Babylonian account, or if both stories merely draw on a common background of mythical ideas and stories. An Akkadian letter from Mari (*c.*1800 BC) refers to the defeat of the sea, Tiamat, by the Storm-god of Aleppo, and it is known that the Babylonian hero-god Marduk took over both some exploits previously attributed to Ninurta, the hero-god of Nippur in central Mesopotamia, and some of the attributes of Tishpak, patron god of Eshnunna which lies east of the Tigris. It should be noted that Genesis 1 is not the only biblical Creation story, for a second story, from the J source, occurs in Genesis 2; and there are many Sumerian and Babylonian accounts of origins which give different combinations of primeval gods and their generations.

Connections between *Enūma Eliš* and Genesis 1 are hard to evaluate, but links between the Babylonian *Epic of Atra-hasis* and early chapters of Genesis are clearer. This epic, which was composed about 1700 BC, relates the history of the world from the time when the gods were alone in the universe. Humans are created to relieve the gods of the need to work for their food, but their unchecked population increase results in such a noise that Ellil, the chief god in this story, is unable to sleep. Various control methods including plague and drought are tried without success, till the gods eventually decide to send a flood. However, Atra-hasis and his family escape by building a boat on the advice of Enki, the god of wisdom. Finally Enki suggests various measures designed to restrict mankind's population to tolerable proportions.

Similarities between the Flood story in *Atra-hasis* and the Flood story (woven from two sources: P and J) in Genesis are close, and both link creation to the Flood. Some details can be supplied from the better-preserved version of the Flood story which is told by Ut-napishtim (alias Atra-hasis) in the standard version of the *Gilgamesh* epic. In this version the gods decide to destroy humans with a flood. Their reason for

35. Assyrian sculpture, perhaps of Ashur-bel-kala (eleventh century BC), which is a visual counterpart to Gen. 9: 12–16: 'Here is the sign of the Covenant . . . I set my bow in the clouds.' Height 0.40 m.

doing so is not stated, in contrast to the *Epic of Atra-hasis* where they wish to silence noisy people, and the biblical story where God punishes mankind for being wicked or lawless. Ut-napishtim, a devotee of Ea (Enki in the *Atra-hasis* epic), is forewarned by his mentor and given detailed instructions for building a boat with which to save his life and the lives of his family and of all kinds of animals. The Flood starts after seven days, and lasts for seven days before the boat runs aground on Mount Nimush. Ut-napishtim sends out a dove which returns, followed by a swallow which also returns, and finally a raven which does not return. Having seen that the Flood has now abated, he offers a sacrifice on Mount Nimush, and the gods—who were starving because in destroying humans they had destroyed their own food supply —gather like flies around the sacrifice. Ellil is initially angry that Ut-napishtim has escaped, but he is rebuked by Ea, who complains that to destroy the innocent with the guilty is unjust (compare Abraham's intercession with Yahweh in Genesis 18), and suggests a policy of sending minor calamities instead of universal floods. Ut-napishtim and his wife are blessed and given immortality. This story and the Flood story (or stories) in Genesis are so similar that a con-

nection is certain. There are minor differences which include chronological details (the biblical Flood lasts for forty days according to J, or a year and ten days according to P), the exact measurements of the boat or ark, and the animals led into the boat, but all the main elements of the Babylonian account are present in the biblical Flood story. The word for 'pitch' *kōpher* which is used in the biblical account of the ark's construction (Genesis 6: 14) does not occur elsewhere in the Hebrew Bible, but its Akkadian cognate *kupru* is found in the Babylonian stories, and pitch occurs naturally in Mesopotamia, not in Palestine. Widespread and destructive floods were a common occurrence in the flat river plains of Mesopotamia, but not in the hills of Palestine. Following the Flood episode in the *Epic of Gilgamesh*, a snake plays a key role in depriving the hero of rejuvenation, a motif which has been compared with Genesis 3 (J source) in which a snake deprives Adam of immortality before the Flood.

The son of Cush in Genesis 10: 8–12 was

Nimrod, who was the first potentate on earth. He was a mighty hunter in the eyes of Yahweh. First to be included in his empire were Babel, Erech (Uruk), and Akkad, all of them in the land of Shinar. From this country came Ashur, the builder of Nineveh, Rehoboth-Ir, Calah and Resen . . .

Nimrod is a corruption of the Sumerian god-name Ninurta, patron of the hunt, whose exploits in the *Epic of Anzu* placed him in charge of the Tablet of Destinies—he 'won complete dominion'. His role in this respect was taken over by the Babylonian god Marduk and the Assyrian god Ashur. He was patron god of the Assyrian royal city Kalhu which is also known as Nimrud. The biblical statement about his empire may refer to the Assyrian king Tukulti-Ninurta I (1244–1208) who was the first Assyrian king to conquer Babylon, for the name may have been abbreviated. Shinar is a name for Babylonia which seems to have been used only during the Late Bronze Age. Ashur the chief god of Assyria would presumably have been the eponymous founder of Ashur city. The idea that gods originally built the great cities was common in Mesopotamia, and is applied to Kish in the *Legend of Etana*, and to Mari in an inscription of the early second millennium. Nineveh, listed first in this passage, was an Assyrian royal capital mainly from the late eighth century, and Kalhu (Calah) from the tenth century.

Names in the genealogies of Genesis 10 and 22 such as Medes and Chaldaeans (Chesed) can be linked to Iron Age history rather than to the patriarchal period. Genesis 14 presents circumstantial evidence for a genuine event with named kings from the east, 'Amraphel king of Shinar, Ariok king of Ellasar, Kedor-laomer king of Elam and Tidal king of the Goiim', who formed an alliance which fought the kings of Sodom and Gomorrah, kingdoms whose historical and geographical existence has not been substantiated from any other ancient records. Such difficulties attend its interpretation that it still eludes precise linkage. Our knowledge of political and military events of this time remains woefully deficient. However, the passage may echo events of the Late Bronze Age if the name Kedor-laomer conflates elements from the names of known Elamite rulers, if Tidal is a form of Tudhaliya (a Hittite royal name borne by at least four kings) and if Shinar is the Kassite name for Babylonia used only during that time. A group of cuneiform tablets, the so-called Kedor-laomer texts, has been linked with this episode, but they are so fragmentary that the doubtful comparisons cannot be taken further at present.[8]

An early Mesopotamian tradition seems to be related to the story of the Tower of Babel in Genesis 11. According to the Sumerian story *Enmerkar and the Lord of Aratta* all people originally worshipped Ellil with one voice until Enki (Ea), like Yahweh, introduced diversity and contention into language. According to Genesis 11, humans settled in the plain of Shinar after the Flood, and began to build a city and a tower there with its top in the heavens. The biblical writer (J) describes the strange construction of the tower, which was built from brick and bitumen rather than stone and mortar, and seems to resemble a Mesopotamian ziggurat, a temple tower. Since stone is a rare commodity on the mud plains of Babylonia, most buildings were built from brick. In J's story, Yahweh appears to regard the tower as a threat to his own security, and intervenes to confuse the languages of its builders, so that they stop building the tower and scatter over the face of the earth. The tower is subsequently known as 'Babel', which is explained by way of a pun with the Hebrew word for 'confuse', *balal*.

Other links between Mesopotamian traditions and Genesis may be found by comparing cuneiform king-lists, especially the Sumerian king-list, with the genealogies of Genesis 5 and 11 (both from P). These lists of names all ascribe super-mortal lifespans to kings or ancestors who lived before the Flood, and decreasing lifespans to postdiluvian ancestors; they centre their sequences upon the Flood, and Ziusudra (the Sumerian name for Atra-hasis) occupies a similar position to his Hebrew counterpart Noah in Genesis 5. Genesis 4 and Genesis 5 seem to contain different versions of a single list, in which Adam 'man' in Genesis 4 matches Enosh, also meaning 'man' in Genesis 5, and like the versions of the Sumerian king-list, the two biblical versions are of different lengths. Moreover, Enmeduranki king of Sippar, who is seventh in some versions of the Sumerian list, corresponds to Enoch as the seventh generation after Adam, and there is other information that seems to connect them as men who ascended to heaven and to whom divine relevations were given.

Apocalyptic works ascribed to Enoch purport to tell of visions which he received during heavenly ascents preceding his final translation. This Enoch was the son of Jared in Gen. 5: 18–24. His namesake in Genesis 4 was the son of Cain. According to Genesis 4: 17, 'Cain had intercourse with his wife, and she conceived and gave birth to Enoch. He (Cain) became builder of a town, and he gave the town the name of his son Enoch.' The statement that Cain built a city is surprising in view of the fact that a few verses earlier he was condemned to a life of wandering in punishment for his murder of Abel, and it is possible that the 'Enoch' at the end of the second sentence was added wrongly by a later scribe. Without it, we should naturally understand the subject of 'he built' to be Enoch rather than Cain, in which case the city was named after Enoch's son Irad. The oldest city according to Mesopotamian traditions (including the Sumerian king-list) was Eridu, and traditions related to Eridu seem to play a particular role in Genesis material.

Abraham's closest ancestors have names which occur in Akkadian texts as place-names in the vicinity of Harran: Serug = Sarūgi, Nahor = Nahur or Til nahīri (possibly Tell Brak), and Terah = Til turāhi. However, Abraham's father is said to have migrated with Abraham from 'Ur of the Chaldees' before settling in Harran. There is little doubt that Ur is the city in southern Mesopotamia, although it cannot have been known as 'Ur of the Chaldees' before the first millennium BC, for the Chaldaeans, a Semitic tribe like the Aramaeans, did not begin to settle in southern Mesopotamia until about the tenth century BC. Only later did they gain political power in the urban centres. Curiously, both Ur and Harran were major centres of the Mesopotamian moon-god Sin, and the names of Abraham's wife and sister-in-law (Sarah and Milkah, meaning 'princess' and 'queen' in Hebrew) are epithets of Sin's consort (šarratu 'queen') and daughter (malkatu 'princess') in Akkadian.[9] There is no way of assessing whether a historical person called Abraham migrated from Ur in southern Mesopotamia, via Harran in the north, to Canaan, or if tribes which later became known as Israelite originally came from Ur or Harran. As far as Genesis is concerned, Abraham's migration is a necessary part of the story, since it bridges the gap between primeval traditions which are centred on Mesopotamia and patriarchal traditions about events in Canaan.

Legends about Sargon of Agade, which were written in Sumerian and Akkadian cuneiform at least from the early second millennium, include themes which occur in several of the early books of the Bible. The episode of dreams which Joseph interpreted for Pharaoh in Genesis 37 bears a notable resemblance to Sargon's interpretation of the dreams of the king of Kish in the Sumerian *Legend of Sargon*; the same legend contains the motif of the messenger who carries a letter which orders his own death, comparable to the story of Uriah in 2 Sam. 11 (and of Bellerophon in *Iliad* 6). The episode in the Akkadian *Legend of Sargon's Birth*, in which Sargon as an infant was concealed and abandoned in a boat, resembles the story of the baby Moses in Exodus 2. The Sumerian story was popular in the early second millennium, and the Akkadian legend may originally have introduced it. Cuneiform scribes were trained with such works for many centuries. They enjoyed new popularity in the late eighth century when Sargon II of Assyria sought to associate himself with his famous namesake.

From the Hittites derives a practice that scholars linked at first directly to Mesopotamia. In the story of Jacob, Rachel, and Laban, the *terāphīm* 'household idols', which Rachel stole and hid, served as tokens of the right to possess family property, but the biblical account did not make it clear exactly what they were. As more texts came to light it emerged that a Hittite word *tarpi-* was the base for the Hebrew word, and that the *terāphīm* were figurines of ancestors whose links with property and inheritance were close, for the son who was dispossessed had no access to them. The figurines were also known as ghosts and as gods in Akkadian, and Old Assyrian records of merchants from the early second millennium show that they were invoked to help when a member of the family fell ill. The Babylonian king consulted the *terāphīm* for an oracle, according to Ezekiel 21: 26, and this seems to match an Assyrian text which tells that Ashurbanipal revered the ghost of his mother.

In Sumerian, Hittite, Ugaritic, and Akkadian the word *apu* (in its Akkadian form) means a hole in the ground through which one may communicate with the dead, and it plays a part in neo-Assyrian rituals, being sometimes supplied with the determinative that denotes a divinity. Hebrew *'ōb* (1 Sam. 28: 7) is cognate with *apu*, and refers to a spirit in necromancy when the woman of Endor conjures up the ghost of Samuel at Saul's request. Isaiah 29: 4 uses the word to mean a ghost, and Leviticus 20: 27 in banning magicians uses it in the sense of a necromancer. Obtaining oracles through necromancy using figurines of ancestors or numinous fissures in the ground seems therefore to have been a widespread practice from early times in the ancient Near East.

---

[9] Note the crossover in meanings.

Cuneiform Laws and Biblical Parallels

Various types of cuneiform texts in Sumerian, Akkadian, and Hittite have been compared with biblical laws for legal concepts, phrasing, and for overall literary form. Earliest are the reforms of Urukagina king of Lagash, written in Sumerian in the mid-third millennium BC. They are presented as acts authorized by the patron god of Lagash and carried out on his behalf by the ruler, thereby liberating his people from oppression and servitude. A few centuries later the laws of 'Ur-Nammu'[10] in Sumerian set the pattern for later laws: in having a prologue containing historical and religious background, and in giving a selection of rulings, phrased in the form: 'If a man does this, that shall be the consequence.' The tradition of writing down laws in a certain way was, therefore, established at this early date.

The Code of Eshnunna was written in the nineteenth century, about a generation before the more famous Code of Hammurabi of Babylon. It was a time when the kingdom of Eshnunna became very powerful, especially under Naram-Sin who ruled Assyria. His influence reached into Syria, Anatolia, and the Mediterranean,[11] and his power seems to have been more extensive than that of Hammurabi, particularly in the West. Laws from Eshnunna have been compared with the biblical Covenant Code for the alternating arrangement of some civil and penal cases; but the most striking parallel for content comes in one specific law about a goring ox:

If an ox gored and killed an(other) ox, both ox owners shall divide the price of the live ox and the carcase of the dead ox.   (LE 53)

And if one man's ox harms another's so that it dies, the owners must sell the live ox and share the price of it . . . they shall also share the dead animal.   (Exod. 21: 35)

Around 1800 BC Hammurabi proclaimed that Anum and Enlil had named him, the pious ruler, to proclaim justice in the land, 'to eliminate the evil and the wicked, so that the strong should not oppress the weak . . . to give justice to the orphan and the widow'. He also stated that 'the wronged man shall stand before the inscribed stela and read its precious ordinances'. The text emphasizes the king himself rather than a god as the actual lawgiver, and has a prologue which refers to historical events of the time.

Hammurabi's individual laws are formulated in the third person in two ways: 'If a man does this, that shall be the consequence' and 'He that does this, shall endure that consequence.'

After the laws, the text ends with curses and blessings, so there are three parts to the text. Divine authorization and social purpose existed in Mesopotamia from this early period, and in these respects the Babylonian laws are comparable to the biblical laws:

It is he (Yahweh) who sees justice done for the orphan and the widow, who loves the stranger and gives him food and clothing.   (Deut. 10: 18)

You must not be harsh with the widow or the orphan. (Exod. 22: 21)

Three groups of laws in the Hebrew Bible have been compared with cuneiform texts: the Covenant Code (Exod. 20: 23–23: 19), the Decalogue in Exod. 20: 1–17 and the laws in Deuteronomy. As with many parts of the Bible their dates are not certainly fixed, some scholars tending to a period during the early monarchy (tenth–ninth century BC), others to the eighth and seventh century or even later. How much the original text has been altered by later additions is also disputed.

The laws in the Covenant Code are formulated either in the second person in two ways: 'If you do this, that shall be the consequence' and 'You shall/ shall not do this'; or in the third person in two ways: 'If a man does this, that shall be the consequence' and 'He that does this, shall endure that consequence.' In Hammurabi's Code penalties are varied, in part according to the type of offence and the class of persons involved. Death, physical punishment, monetary fines, and restitution are all found, but in one section a series of laws gives penalties by retaliation, closely comparable with Exod. 21: 24–5:

If a man destroyed another man's eye, they shall destroy his eye.   (KH 196)

If he broke a man's bone, they shall break his bone.   (KH 198)

If a man knocked out a man's tooth, they shall knock out his tooth.   (KH 200)

If a man struck the cheek of a man who is older than he, he shall be struck with 60 lashes with a whip in the assembly.   (KH 202)[12]

---

[10] Perhaps promulgated by king Shulgi rather than Ur-Nammu.   [11] See Ch. IV, p. 87.

[12] The intervening laws KH 197, 199, 201 deal with similar cases where the two parties are not of equal status.

You shall give life for life, eye for eye, tooth for tooth, hand for hand, foot for foot, burn for burn, wound for wound, stroke for stroke.

Not only is the principle identical, but eye, tooth, and stroke occur in the same order.

The Decalogue laws in Exodus 20 are preceded by a prologue in which God identifies himself against a historical background: 'I am Yahweh your God who brought you out of the land of Egypt' and Moses as his agent. This is comparable to Hammurabi's prologue: 'When the sublime god Anum . . . assigned to Marduk . . . universal power . . . and they pronounced the name of Babylon and made it the most powerful in the world . . . they named me, Hammurabi, the pious prince, to eliminate the evil and the wicked.' Both the Decalogue laws and the laws of Hammurabi are followed by an epilogue in which the words are written down and then read to the people.

Proverbs and wisdom dialogues may underlie many of the apparent links between biblical and cuneiform law. A particular resemblance to the Ten Commandments with their second person formulation 'Thou shalt not kill' is normally found in Sumerian and Babylonian 'wisdom' literature. It occurs in the *Instructions of Shuruppak*, a composition which is known in Sumerian from the mid-third millennium BC, and at Emar towards the end of the Late Bronze Age, around the time of the Exodus. It was translated into Akkadian before the neo-Assyrian period. 'My son, let me give thee instructions . . . Do not neglect my instruction! . . . Do not steal anything . . . Do not pick a quarrel . . . Do not tell lies . . . Do not swear . . .' These injunctions are interspersed among others that have no biblical overtones, such as: 'Do not place a house too close to a public square, for it is taboo . . . Do not drive away a debtor, for that man may turn hostile to you . . . Do not break the side of the sweet reeds in the garden.'

The laws in Deuteronomy are preceded by a declaration that states the several purposes of the laws. Among them is the insistence that God 'is never partial, never to be bribed. It is he who sees justice done.' The laws conclude with a long series of curses and blessings (27: 15–30: 20), and a subsequent passage (32: 1) invokes heaven and earth as divine witnesses. Expressly stated is that the laws must be read periodically (31: 10–13). Each of these biblical codes thus consists of three parts, as does the Code of Hammurabi; and social purpose and a passage of curses and blessings figure in both.

Various specific instances of similarity among laws can be added, as follows.

THE COVENANT RITUAL

The Bible presents the laws of Israel as a covenant or treaty drawn up between God and his people by an intermediary. Hittite influence through treaties and loyalty oaths has been invoked to explain similarities in the invocation of heaven and earth as witnesses, and the curse-and-blessing element, which characterize biblical laws. The same themes occur in Aramaic and Assyrian treaties of the early Iron Age; and other kinds of text contain them, including monumental royal inscriptions. Egypt too used such forms in its treaties with rulers of western Asia. All treaty texts and loyalty oaths contain prohibition clauses expressed in second person formulation, such as: 'You shall not hold an assembly to adjure one another and give the kingship to one of you.'

A ritual is described in cuneiform texts from Mari and Tell al-Rimah in northern Iraq, dating from the time of Hammurabi. Animals were cut in half and two parties contracted a treaty or alliance by passing between the halves. Some of the vocabulary used is west Semitic, perhaps because the ritual was widespread among Amorite peoples in upper Mesopotamia, different groups using different wording. Genesis 15: 9–18 describes a ritual for making a covenant or agreement between Yahweh and Abraham. Abraham cut in half several animals, and a 'smoking furnace and a firebrand' passed between the halves. Jeremiah 34: 18–19 refers also to the ritual in which a calf is cut in half and men walk between the halves to conclude their covenant.

In Mesopotamia the covenant ritual cemented an agreement between men although they acted with the approval of their gods and invoked their support. The biblical ritual, however, cemented an agreement between man and god.

SORCERY

Sorcery is a capital offence in several Mesopotamian laws and in a law in Exodus.

If a man accused a man of sorcery but could not prove it, the accused man shall . . . jump into the River. If the River overwhelms him, his accuser shall take his house.   (KH 2)
They shall kill the person who performs sorcery.   (M. Ass. laws 47)

You shall not allow a sorceress to live.   (Exod. 22: 18)
Any man or woman who is a necromancer or magician must be put to death.   (Lev. 20: 27)

LEVIRATE MARRIAGE

According to Deut. 25: 5–10 a man whose married brother died without leaving children inherited the widow, and he begot children through her on behalf of his dead brother, a custom known as levirate marriage. The Middle Assyrian laws which were written or compiled around the fourteenth–twelfth centuries describe a similar practice in which a father-in-law can give the wife of a deceased son to another son, if the woman has not yet produced children. Cuneiform law and practice indicate some variations upon the theme throughout the different regions and periods, but in general it is accepted that a form of levirate marriage was practised in the Near East before the Iron Age.

DEBT RELEASE

In Leviticus 25: 10 the jubilee year is ordained once every fifty years. One of its provisions is release from debt: 'You will declare this fiftieth year sacred and proclaim the liberation of all the inhabitants of the land. This is to be a jubilee for you; each of you will return to his ancestral home, each to his own clan.' The word used for 'liberty' in Hebrew, *derōr*, is also found in Babylonian and Assyrian texts going back to around 2000 BC, *andurārum* and *durāru*. The Sumerian equivalent to the term is found even earlier, in texts of Urukagina king of Lagash. The cuneiform texts that use the word refer to periodic royal edicts which cancel the debts of citizens, debts which often resulted in enslavement. The amnesty is not of regular occurrence but appears to be intermittent, dependent on the king's decision. Often it was proclaimed soon after the accession of a new king, or after many years of a long rule. The difference in Palestine is that debt release was regular, linked to the agricultural practice of letting land lie fallow, and it did not depend upon a king's decision.

The word for justice in Babylonia, *mīšārum*, was sometimes linked to edicts of debt-release as well as to writing down laws, and it is cognate with the Hebrew word *mēšārīm*. The word seems to have a similar range of meaning in both languages.

THE SABBATH

Mesopotamians used the word *šapattu*, which is related to the modern words 'Sabbath' and 'sabbatical', but they applied it only to the lunar month, to mean the fifteenth day of the month when the moon was full, 'the day of peace of heart'. This was the moon's least dangerous phase between rising up from the Underworld, which was inhabited by potentially vindictive ghosts, and descending back into it. Such regular contact with the spirit world brought a periodic need for appeasement; only on the fifteenth day could one relax. These beliefs affected the days on which business could be carried out, as we know both from hemerologies (manuals which set out which days were auspicious for particular activities) and from the marked absence of cuneiform business records on certain dates. In biblical Hebrew the phrase 'new moon or Sabbath' seems to imply that the Sabbath could refer to a phase of the moon, and Amos 8: 5 implies that business was not carried out on those Sabbath days because the moon was full. However, a different use of the word is found in the fourth Commandment given in Exod. 20: 8–9, which is derived from the Creation according to Genesis 2: 2–3, where it meant one day of rest after six days of labour: 'Remember the Sabbath day and keep it holy. For six days you shall labour and do all your work. But the seventh day is a Sabbath for Yahweh your God. You shall do no work that day.' The chapter in Leviticus which defines the jubilee year gives a third definition to the Sabbath as the seventh year in which the fields will lie fallow.

For six years you shall sow your field, for six years you shall prune your vine and gather its produce. But in the seventh year the land is to have its rest, a sabbath for Yahweh. You must not sow your field or prune your vine. (Lev. 25: 3–4)

Essentially, therefore, the biblical word applied to a period of rest, and was flexible both in duration and in frequency; nowadays the Sabbath means one day of the week, but 'sabbatical' has a less regular timing and duration, and it has lost its association with the phases of the moon.

After Hammurabi's time no new collection of laws is known from Babylonia for more than 1200 years, but in Anatolia around 1600 BC were written the Hittite cuneiform laws. They have closer links with some biblical laws than do the laws of Babylonia on the subject of sexual matters such as bestiality.

Although the ancient collections of cuneiform laws are called 'codes', they are not codes in the modern sense of the word, for they do not collect systematically all possible cases, and they omit large areas of need. The reason for the order in which the laws are arranged in the composition is still a mystery, for they seem haphazard and incoherent in many places. Some scholars think that they represent an entirely academic exercise, barely related to everyday needs, whereas others think they were definitely functional and legislative. Some think the laws present reforms of existing practice, and others that they restate current practice, giving only sporadic examples. Some think the different codes present an ethical progression, for example from physical to financial penalties; whereas others think the variety of penalty represents actual options; indeed, alternative penalties are expressly allowed in an Assyrian contract, and likewise in the Twelve Tables which comprise the earliest Roman Law—itself probably based on ancient Near Eastern precedents. These problems affect our understanding of the biblical laws and the nature of their links with cuneiform codes.

Whether or not the cuneiform laws were first put together as an academic exercise, Babylonian scribes were certainly trained using manuals that listed legal phrases. For many centuries Hammurabi's Code was a text studied and set as an exercise for trainee scribes in schools, probably abroad as well as within Mesopotamia. A thousand years after Hammurabi died, excerpts from the prologue and epilogue to his laws were used in the text of a treaty between Babylon and Assyria. The Code of Eshnunna did not, as far as we know, persist in the same way, perhaps because Hammurabi conquered Eshnunna. However, its laws regulating the affairs of traders in way-stations[13] mean that some provisions would have been known and enforced beyond the kingdom itself, and may have persisted.

Prophecy and Pseudo-Prophecy

Cuneiform prophecies probably all stem from royal archives and have been found grouped into two sep-

arate periods. Earliest is the text of an oracle from the goddess Nanay in Uruk. Slightly later, to the time of Hammurabi of Babylon, belong oracles of various male and female deities from Mari on the middle Euphrates, and one oracle of the goddess Kitītum from Eshnunna. These oracles are all addressed to kings. Some are reported in, or written as, letters, others were collected together as a group on a single document. Occasionally they accompanied acts of divination by examining entrails, but this was not always the case. The language is often metaphorical and sometimes proverbial. Various words are used to describe the men and women whose utterances were accepted as the word of a deity: in a Mari text the word *nābûm* is applied to members of the semi-nomadic Hanean tribe, and it is also found in a twelfth-century text from Emar. It is cognate with the Hebrew *nābīʾ* 'prophet'.

The pre-exilic oracles in 2 Sam. 7: 4–17 and 1 Kings 11: 31–9 are addressed to the king. They are announced in a clear opening formula, such as: 'Thus saith the Lord of Hosts.' They confirm God's support for the ruler and his people as long as they are faithful, but remind that he will wreak revenge for apostasy. The style is rhetorical, and occasionally uses metaphorical language. The oracles are often grouped together within the text. All these features are matched in cuneiform oracles from Hammurabi's time.

In the seventh century BC a group of prophecies is recorded which had been uttered mainly by women associated with the oracle of Ishtar of Arbela. The utterances were focused upon specific situations facing the Assyrian king, whether Esarhaddon or Ashurbanipal. As with biblical prophecies they announce the deity that speaks, and often reassure with the expression 'Fear not'.

> Esarhaddon, king of the lands,
> Fear not! . . .
> I am Ishtar of Arbela.
> I wait to deliver your
> enemies to you.
> I am Ishtar of Arbela.
> I go in front of you and
> behind you. Fear not!

I am Yahweh. I will free you of the burdens which the Egyptians lay on you.   (Ex. 6: 6)

---

[13] The *bīt naptarim* has only recently been identified as a caravanserai.

I, Yahweh, who am the first and shall be with the last . . . Do not be afraid, for I am with you . . . I uphold you with my victorious right hand.   (Isaiah 41: 4 and 10)

Both the earlier and the Assyrian cuneiform oracles contain descriptive proverbial and metaphorical expressions, as do the biblical ones.

In Mesopotamia a different kind of prophecy is recorded in dreams. They are sometimes recounted in threes for confirmation, and contain apocalyptic descriptions of another world. Chief among them are the dreams of Enkidu and of Gilgamesh in the standard version of the *Epic of Gilgamesh*; and in the late Assyrian *Crown Prince's Vision of the Underworld*; also in an inscription of Nabonidus (sixth century BC) who has a vision during the night of Marduk appearing in glory. The profession of the dream interpreter, *šā'ilu*, goes back at least to the time of Hammurabi. These are terrifying apparitions for which the closest parallels are found in Ezekiel 1 and Daniel 2, both set in an explicitly Mesopotamian milieu. Gilgamesh's mother gives an interpretation of one of his dreams which can be compared quite closely with the interpretation of the vision in Daniel 11.

> (It means)
> A strong partner shall come to you,
> One who can save the life of a friend.
> He will be the most powerful in the land,
> His strength will be as great as Anu's sky bolt.
>
> (Gilgamesh ii)

(It means) Three more kings are going to arise in Persia. A fourth will come and be richer than all the others. And when, thanks to his wealth, he has grown powerful, he will challenge all the kingdoms of Javan.   (Dan. 11: 2–4)

The oracles against the nations in Ezekiel 21 and 24–32 have been compared with the poem *Erra and Ishum* for style and content: in both works the god declares in his fury that he will slay the just and the unjust alike, will lay waste the whole country, will hand everyone over to barbaric men, will let blood flow within the city, will destroy trees and dry up rivers.

A type of text sometimes described as pseudo-prophecy is known from the second millennium onwards in Mesopotamia, and in Egypt too. It makes cryptic 'predictions' of past events, divested of clear historical detail, and it links them to predictions for present and future time. The purpose seems to be to refer to fulfilled, reliable predictions from the past and link them to new predictions for the future and so give the latter credibility and authority.[14] One part of the format is based upon the kind of statement known from Akkadian and Hittite manuals of divination; for example:

> (If the 'Palace Gate'[15] is normal,
> And a second one lies on the right,)
> A rebel prince will arise.

Another characteristic feature, which pseudo-prophecy has in common with simple prophecy, is the interpretation of dreams, a Babylonian practice based in part upon manuals written for the professional instruction of dream-interpreters and diviners. Daniel 8: 23–5 and 11, and parts of the Book of Enoch contain elements characteristic of this genre, as well as other, more apocalyptic aspects.[16]

Whereas simple prophecy seems to have been made known to the public, pseudo-prophetic and apocalyptic texts were restricted. For instance, the Babylonian *Dynastic Prophecy*, written in the Seleucid period, has a colophon enjoining the reader to preserve secrecy and to restrict knowledge of the text to the initiated.

Tours of heaven and hell are one characteristic of apocalyptic texts. Tours of hell are described in the dream reports in the *Epic of Gilgamesh*, *Ishtar's Descent to the Underworld*, and the *Crown Prince's Vision of the Underworld*; and ascents to heaven are described in the *Legend of Etana* and the *Myth of Adapa*. In Jewish apocalyptic writings, tours of heaven and hell are often guided by an angel, as for example in the Book of Enoch and in the Testament of Levi. Both Daniel and Qumran Enoch give a more schematized view of world history as a sequence of distinct eras than is found in any cuneiform composition. They contain the concept of the end of time, when God's hidden purpose will finally be revealed throughout the world. No cuneiform text alludes to such a universal concept, or connects pseudo-prophecy to descriptions of the cosmos by means of tours of heaven and hell.

---

[14] Compare the triple prophecy for past, present, and future by the witches in Shakespeare's *Macbeth*.

[15] The 'Palace Gate' describes the umbilical fissure on the liver.
[16] See also Ch. II, p. 43.

Wisdom Literature

In Mesopotamia a tradition of writing wisdom literature began in Sumerian cuneiform in the third millennium and developed into a high art in Akkadian during the second millennium. Proverbs, fables, and longer works which explore the theme of man's duties and relationship to the gods are classed as wisdom writings, and were used in the education of princes, sages, and courtiers. Two major works which were composed in the late second millennium have been dated with rare precision. In the *Poem of the Righteous Sufferer* (known after its opening words as *Ludlul bēl nēmeqi*) a courtier named Šubši-mešrê-Šakkan tells how he suffered undeserved misfortune but was eventually restored to favour by Marduk. He was a high state official known to have served under a Kassite king around 1292 BC. Since the theme of unfair fate seems to have been a popular one at an earlier date, he probably adapted earlier material such as was found in Akkadian at Ugarit; there too Marduk the god of Babylon is the saviour. Scholars have compared the Book of Job with *Ludlul* for its theme of undeserved suffering and eventual redemption, and with the Babylonian *Theodicy* for other similarities. The *Theodicy* is a dialogue between a sufferer and his friend which contains the name of the author, Saggil-kēnam-ubbib, a man recently discovered to be the sage of Nebuchadnezzar I (1124–1103). These details confirm that such compositions belong in court circles rather than temples, and enable us to date the works accurately.

Wisdom, sages, and scribal arts in Mesopotamia were closely connected; for instance, the *Legend of Etana* was supposed to have been composed by a sage. From at least 2000 BC scribes (who would eventually become doctors, incantation priests, and courtiers) not only dutifully learned and copied proverbs and myths on to exercise tablets, but also studied the great lexical lists, such as the one now known as HAR.*ra* = *hubullu*.[17] In it objects were listed by category, beginning with trees (tablet 3), including animals and reptiles (tablets 13 and 14), plants (tablet 17), and fish together with birds (tablet 18). Nouns are mostly given without any addition, but in another, botanical lexical list the unidentified plant *kakkussu* is 'of the wall'. Early versions of the lists vary in order and content, and they were used abroad by adding a translation of each word.

Solomon, who reigned in the tenth century, was credited with 'wisdom': as well as composing proverbs and songs 'he could talk about plants, from the cedar in Lebanon to the hyssop growing on the wall; and he could talk of animals and birds and reptiles and fish' (1 Kings 5: 13–14). Solomon's knowledge, therefore, echoes mainstream Babylonian texts studied by scribes in Mesopotamia and beyond. He acquired his wisdom 'from the countries of the East and from Egypt', and recent scholars are inclined to agree that Assyria and Babylonia contributed more than Egypt in this respect.

Wisdom passages in the *Epic of Gilgamesh* are contained particularly in the speeches of the divine ale-wife Siduri, an independent woman who has her own house, and who is called the Ishtar of wisdom in a cuneiform text. Parallels have been noted between passages in Ecclesiastes and in *Gilgamesh*, of which the following is especially noteworthy:

> So, Gilgamesh, let your stomach be full
> Day and night enjoy yourself in every way,
> Every day arrange for pleasures,
> Day and night, dance and play,
> Wear fresh clothes.
> Keep your head washed; bathe in water
> Appreciate the child who holds your hand
> Let your wife enjoy herself in your lap,
> For this is the work of [mankind].

(*Gilgamesh Epic*, Old Babylonian version 10. 3. 6–14)

Go eat your bread with joy
And drink your wine with a glad heart, for what you do, God has approved beforehand.
Wear white all the time,
Do not stint your head of oil.
Spend your life with the woman you love, through all the fleeting days of the life that God has given you under the sun.

(Ecclesiastes 9: 7–9)

Like Siduri in the *Epic of Gilgamesh*, biblical Wisdom (Proverbs 1, 3, 8, and 9 especially) is personified as an attractive, independent woman with her own house.

A second connection between the two compositions is the proverb in tablet 5 of the *Epic of Gilgamesh*, which compares the strength of two people to a

---

[17] This is the first line of the list; *hubullu* means a loan, and HAR.ra is its equivalent in Sumerian.

double-stranded cord, both being much stronger than when they are single. A very similar proverb is found in Ecclesiastes 4: 9–12.

Like Mesopotamian goddesses, biblical Wisdom sings her own praises in a genre which seems to be reserved exclusively for female divinities. Her 'seven pillars' may contain a reinterpretation of an allusion to the Seven Sages of Mesopotamian tradition, for which the original sense was probably:

> Wisdom has built her house,
> The Seven have set its foundations
>
> (Proverbs 9: 1)

and in Proverbs 8: 30 she is called a craftsman-sage, using the Akkadian word *ummânu* 'sage, master-craftsman' as a loan into Hebrew; she is present, like Mami with Enki/Ea, alongside Yahweh at the Creation: 'I was by his side, a master-craftsman.' This close connection between wisdom and creation is common in Mesopotamian writings; the creator of mankind in the *Epic of Atrahasis* is the goddess Mami, always called 'wise' in that work, and her role in creation is also explicit in the *Theodicy*, stanza 26.

It has sometimes been claimed that the Babylonians did not personify abstract concepts in the way that Wisdom is personified in the Bible. This is not so, for deities such as Mīšarum 'Justice', Kittum 'Righteousness', Hasīsu and Hasīsatu (both 'Wisdom') are abstract nouns in origin.

Psalms, Lamentations, and The Song of Songs

Cuneiform Akkadian psalms and prayers of praise and of lamentation correspond to the main types of Hebrew psalms. For instance, Psalm 51, which is classified as a penitential or lament psalm, bears especially close resemblances to Akkadian *šu-ila* ('hand-raising') prayers. Comparisons have been drawn on several levels: the overall structure of the composition is the same, with address, lament, prayer, and thanksgiving in that order, comprising the whole; and the literary qualities in many respects of phrasing and imagery are alike. Even the theological ideas expressed in Hebrew and in Akkadian seem to be virtually identical, although the Akkadian texts often refer to more than one deity.

A particular feature for comparison is the acrostic. Babylonian literature has acrostics formed by syllabic signs, of which examples are found in hymns and prayers to the gods as well as in the Babylonian *Theodicy*. In this composition an acrostic accompanies the stanza form, giving the syllables of the author's name at the beginnings of the lines, the author being a sage, just as in earlier, Sumerian compositions the name of the first sage Oannes was used, barely concealed in the opening line. Concealed information has a serious purpose in leading the initiated reader to the original, semi-divine source of inspiration. Several psalms in the Bible incorporate alphabetic acrostics, for instance 119 in which each group of eight verses begins with a successive letter of the alphabet. Acrostics are also found elsewhere, for instance, in Lamentations 1–4.

In Sumerian literature the lamentation over the destruction of a city was popular in the late third millennium BC, and was commonly selected for school exercises in the time of Hammurabi, a few centuries later. The biblical Book of Lamentations, which bewails the fall of Jerusalem, has a similar form and many comparable expressions.

Early Mesopotamian literature contains several different kinds of text in which each part of the deity's body is compared to precious plants and timbers, stones and metals, ointments and perfumes, food and drinks, beautiful birds and animals, and natural beauty-spots. Some of the texts are love lyrics which may perhaps be related to the Sacred Marriage ceremony; an Assyrian love song records a dialogue between Nabu and Tashmetum in which the god calls her thighs a gazelle, her ankle-bones an apple of Siman, and her heels obsidian. Other love poems of this type appear to have a different context: the Sumerian *Message of Lu-dingira to his Mother* seems to refer to a filial relationship, and the esoteric *God Description* texts appear to be simply lists. The biblical *Song of Songs* uses the imagery of the bride and bridegroom, perhaps personifying the temple in Jerusalem and Yahweh within it as the Sumerian temple hymns praise the attributes of temples and their gods. The *Song of Songs* and its Mesopotamian antecedents lie behind the description of God's body in the mystical *Shi'ur Qomah*, one of the main texts for Jewish mysticism in late Antiquity and the Middle Ages. The awesome appearance of the deity in those texts was called Shekhinah. This word is not found in the Bible, but its cognates *šiknu* and *šikittu* occur in Babylonian omens and arcane religious texts.[18]

Historical Writing

Various forms of historical writing in Akkadian developed during the late third and the second millennium. Many so-called historical inscriptions incorporated other types of composition such as itineraries, oracles and dreams, tribute lists, and descriptions of building works. Royal annals described campaigns to the glory of the reigning king and the gods who helped and directed him; this type of text was written for Hittite and Assyrian kings, but apparently not for Babylonian rulers. There is a detailed personal account of how Esarhaddon, who was not his father's eldest son, justified his accession, and it has been compared with two Hittite accounts and with the narrative in 2 Sam. and 1 Kings 1–2. On the other hand, national chronicles simply gave a terse and dispassionate record of major events.

Some books of the Bible such as Samuel, Kings, and Chronicles are chiefly devoted to historical narrative. They contain passages which conform to types of text found as separate works in cuneiform. Some of these types are easy to pick out, such as letters (e.g. 1 Kgs. 21: 9–10; 2 Kgs. 5: 6 and 10: 2–3, 6) and lists of officials (e.g. 2 Sam. 23: 8–39; 1 Kgs. 4: 1–19). Other genres are court annals (e.g. 2 Sam. 8; 1 Kgs. 9: 10–28). Of the many references to royal annals in the books of Kings, 2 Kings 16: 19 may be cited as typical: 'The rest of the history of Ahaz, his entire career, is not all this recorded in the Book of the Annals of the Kings of Judah?'

In addition to these, there are passages which consist of public or royal addresses. Such are the speech of Sennacherib's cup-bearer at the siege of Jerusalem reported verbatim in 2 Kings 18: 17–18, Moses' speech to the people of Israel in Deut. 31–3, and David's dying speech to Solomon in 1 Kings 2: 1–9. Speeches of this type are sometimes found in Assyrian and Babylonian royal inscriptions and royal epics.

Genealogies are found both in cuneiform and in biblical texts. In Sumerian and Akkadian they occur from the third millennium onwards, sometimes in king-lists and in rituals for deceased ancestors, sometimes in the recital of royal titles which introduces a long inscription. A ritual in which the names of deceased royal ancestors are recited is also found at Ugarit, and has been compared with the Mesopotamian ritual known as *kispum*, in which a man recites the names of his ancestors in chronological order, inviting them to partake as spirits in a meal and to confer blessings upon his life, and his reign if he is a king: presumably such a recital was a part of purely oral tradition for lowlier families and illiterate tribesmen. Genesis 4: 17–26 and 1 Chron. 1–9 are genealogies incorporated into more-or-less relevant historical narrative.

Itineraries seem to have originated in administrative records concerned with trading expeditions. In cuneiform they are known from the third millennium BC onwards, with a particularly fine example from the Old Babylonian period, and a recently found Middle Assyrian example dated to the reign of Tukulti-Ninurta I (1244–1208) from the Habur river valley. Sometimes they are woven into royal inscriptions which recount the campaigns of Assyrian kings. In the Bible they are incorporated into narratives such as in Num. 21: 12–20; 33: 1–49; and Deut. 10: 6–7.

Some Assyrian accounts of royal campaigns are arranged in a geographical rather than a chronological order. From the unusually wide range of texts which we have for the expeditions of Sennacherib it has been possible to demonstrate that a king had to qualify for the top titles 'king of the four quarters' (after successful campaigns to roughly the four compass points) and 'king of the universe' (after seven victorious expeditions, the word 'universe' being equated with the number seven in several cuneiform texts). A comparable pattern may be seen in the oracles against foreign nations in the books of Amos, Ezekiel, and Zephaniah, in which Yahweh prophesies that he will defeat enemies on all sides of Judah. These victories seem to echo the Assyrian groupings and perhaps imply that Yahweh's title as the Lord of Hosts claims universal recognition.

The New Year, the Day of Atonement, and the Scapegoat Ritual

The Babylonians and Assyrians celebrated the Spring New Year with a festival marked by several important events. Foreign emissaries came to renew their

---

[18] See below, p. 77.

oaths of loyalty to the reigning monarch, and so witnessed the pageantry. A huge statue of the national god Bel, riding in his golden chariot, was conducted through the city along a processional route, through the city gate and into open country where the temple of the New Year's festival stood surrounded by a garden. There a ceremony of sacred marriage took place. The *Epic of Creation* was recited or performed during some of the proceedings, and the gods fixed or outlined the destinies for the coming year. Not only in Babylon could these festivities be viewed: similar ceremonies took place at other times of the year in other cities, including Uruk, Ashur, Arbela, and Harran; and they persisted into the time of the Roman empire.[19]

The Jews who established seats of learning in Babylonia during the early centuries of the Christian era were concerned to perform their festivals correctly according to a proper calendar. To guide them they compiled in the Babylonian Talmud a treatise known as *Rosh Hashanah* 'Beginning of the Year', in which they recognized four different dates for the New Year. The first day of Nisan, which falls at the spring equinox, was 'for kings and festivals' and therefore for counting regnal years. The first day of Tishri, which falls at the autumn equinox, was regarded by many as the time when the world was created, rather than in Nisan.

Babylonian religious customs appear to have influenced the Jewish ceremonies for the New Year of Tishri. Of course, in Israel the ritual was not a royal one, and perhaps this explains why it was not celebrated in the same month as the royal New Year ceremony in Babylon, traditionally held in Nisan. Rather as fates were fixed for the coming year by writing on the Tablet of Destinies and sealing with the Seal of Destinies in Mesopotamian ritual, so the Babylonian Talmud recorded that three books were opened in heaven at the New Year in Tishri upon which were inscribed judgements of the wicked, the righteous, and the intermediate, as all creatures passed before God. In a more general sense, 'From the beginning of the year sentence is passed as to what shall be up to the end of it.' The divine presence, the *shekhinah*, proceeded apparently in ten stages through the different parts of the temple before departing, and a later homily written for the New Year festival, perhaps around 700 AD, tells that 'these

ten days are the days of special grace when the *shekhinah* is near.' How early those practices go back in Hebrew ritual is unknown.

The Palestinian Talmud, which mainly took shape early in the fifth century AD, and which carried less authority in Judaism than the Babylonian Talmud, refers to the New Year of Tishri in similar terms:

Some authorities teach: all of them are judged on Rosh Hashanah, and the [divine] sentence of each one is sealed on Rosh Hashanah. Other authorities teach: all of them are judged on Rosh Hashanah, and the [divine] sentence of each one is sealed on Yom Kippur.

Since the Day of Atonement, Yom Kippur, ended the ten days of ceremonies for the New Year, the ritual duty of cleansing or purifying the temple took place on that day. The task was fraught with peril and could be carried out only by the High Priest, mainly by sprinkling and wiping with the blood of animals. Comparable is a Seleucid ritual text about the New Year festival in Babylon, which describes how the shrine of Nabu in Bel's temple was purified on the fifth day with blood: an exorcist rubbed or smeared the room with the carcase of a decapitated sheep. The Akkadian verb used, *kuppuru*, is cognate with Hebrew *kippēr*.

According to Leviticus 16: 5 ff. the scapegoat ritual of atonement was to be carried out each year on the tenth day of the seventh month. Aaron was required to select one of two goats by lot, to lay hands on the head of one, confessing the sins of Israel as he did so, and to drive it into the desert. The Hebrew text names Azazel, presumably a demon, as the divinity to whom the scapegoat was dedicated, the other goat being sacrificed to Yahweh. Azazel, a Semitic name, has recently been found in an Akkadian text found at Alalakh in Syria, dating to around 1700 BC, and is found also in a slightly later Hurrian text; the milieu is west Semitic and Hurrian rather than central Mesopotamian. Cuneiform sources in the Akkadian (at Ugarit), Hittite and Hurrian languages record rituals for removing impurity, especially plagues, in a comparable way, by transferring pollution to a substitute. Rituals of averting harm by substitution are known from Mesopotamia, chiefly in connection with the king and eclipses of the moon; and many Akkadian terms are used in Hittite rituals in general. From Anatolia the scapegoat ritual eventually travelled

---

[19] See Ch. II, pp. 49–53 and Ch. VIII, pp. 163–4.

to Marseilles, where it was performed in the cult of Apollo Apotropaios.

Assyrian and Babylonian Cults and Deities in Israel

The Assyrians and Babylonians did not deliberately introduce the cults of their gods into conquered lands, although vassal rulers were obliged to swear oaths of loyalty by the gods of the overlords as well as by their own indigenous deities. Presumably the deportees from Babylonia and Assyria who were settled in Palestine, and the officials who were posted there as administrators, would have brought their own gods and rituals with them. Pagan deities such as Ba'al and Asherah who were occasionally condemned or banned by Hebrew kings were Canaanite/Phoenician gods whose cults must mainly have been established in Palestine before the Hebrews entered the country. For instance Sheger, who is a moon-god as a bull-calf with horns, is found at Ebla, Mari, and Emar, spanning a period from c.2300–1100 BC, and is named in Exodus 13: 12, Deut. 7: 12 and 28: 4, 18, 51, in company with the goddess Ashtaroth, although in translation the pagan names are curiously disguised as 'offspring of cattle and of sheep'.

Sumerian myths, recorded from early in the second millennium, show that a variety of traditions was attached to the name of Dumuzi. He was a shepherd; he was a legendary Sumerian king who became a god; he was one of the gatekeepers of heaven. Various different modes of death are ascribed to him by these different traditions, and the myth of *Ishtar's Descent to the Underworld* tells why annual weeping was part of the cult of Dumuzi, marking his seasonal return from the earth to the Underworld. An Assyrian letter of the seventh century refers to Dumuzi lying in state to the accompaniment of wailing, in all the chief cities of Assyria concurrently. According to Ezekiel 8: 14 women wept for Tammuz (which is a variation on the name of the Sumerian god Dumuzi, translated into Latin in the Vulgate as Adonis) at the north gate of the Temple in Jerusalem in the sixth century. A Greek papyrus of the third century BC shows that the festival of Adonis with lying in state

was also celebrated in Egypt. Lucian of Samsat on the upper Euphrates refers to the annual wailing for Tammuz in the second century AD. So the practice which Ezekiel mentions came from Mesopotamia, was widespread, and continued for centuries. The fourth month of the standard Babylonian calendar is named Dumuzi, and the name still lives on in an Arabic month name for July. According to Ibn Wahšiya (c. AD 900) the Sabians of Harran continued to wail for Tammuz in the Middle Ages; and the holy book of the Mandaeans known as the *Ginza* specifically warns against participation in Tammuz festivals.

One of the names of the Sumerian hunter-god Ninurta was Sakkut in his capacity as 'bronze-holder of heaven'. His name may be found as Sakkuth in Amos 5: 26 together with Kaiwan (Kiyyun), which seems to be a form of the Babylonian name Kayyamān for the planet 'Saturn'. Amos specifies that this form of apostasy was a reason for God's punishment, which consisted of allowing the Exile to take place. Sakkut and Kiyyun are found at Qumran in the *Damascus Document*, although their pagan nature there is not overt.[20]

Tantalizing glimpses of Mesopotamian background can be gained from several biblical writings of the eighth century onwards. For example, in Isaiah 14: 13 'I will climb up to the heavens; and higher than the stars of God I will set my throne' reflects Babylonian cosmology in which the heaven of the stars was the nearest of three heavens, a scheme perhaps shared by Canaanite and Phoenician tradition. The name of Bildad in the Book of Job may be a form of Apil-Adad, also known as Apladad, literally 'son of Adad'. He was the god of 'Ana and Kannu'[21] on the middle Euphrates, whose oracle was well respected in the early first millennium; his importance continued into the Hellenistic period, where he is known from Greek inscriptions at Dura-Europos. The Akkadian demon Lilith is named in Isaiah 34: 14.[22] The 'cherubim' which 'stood on the right side of the house when the man went in' and by the throne of God in Ezekiel 10: 14 are known in Akkadian as *kurību*, a generic term meaning 'blessed' which refers to the winged, guardian spirits of the kinds that stood to left and right of monumental entrances at Assyrian courts.

[20] See Ch. II, p. 43 for other Babylonian material at Qumran.
[21] Perhaps the same as Kanneh in Ezekiel 27: 23. See also

Ch. V, p. 121.
[22] See Ch. VII, p. 156.

They were composite creatures with attributes from bulls, lions, men, and eagle's wings, and they were made of gold, silver, copper, and stone. Gigantic in architectural positions, they were used also in miniature for decorative fixtures on pieces of furniture, both in Canaan, Phoenicia, and Egypt, as well as in Mesopotamia. They have come down to us in the word cherubs, which now denote the cheerful winged toddlers who adorn so much art in Christian Europe.

Conclusion

During the Bronze Age the inhabitants of Palestine used the writing techniques and training that had originally developed in Mesopotamia. At that time methods of translation evolved to convert text from one language to another in cuneiform script. When the Hebrews settled in cities they began to use an alphabetic script to record their national literature, adapting older forms of composition, and converting pagan rituals to their special social and religious requirements.

Jerusalem contained literate men in the Amarna period who could read and write Akkadian, and who had been trained with gems of Mesopotamian literature. In the Early Iron Age the city kept records such as royal annals, according to clear statements in the Bible, and was continuously inhabited while the gradual change took place from cuneiform to alphabetic writing. Although the few clay tablets found in many Bronze Age cities in Palestine deliver clear evidence, in quantity they are not impressive. This deficiency may be explained in part with reference to writing materials other than durable clay. Archives from the Hittites, from Ugarit and from Emar, all in the Late Bronze Age, contain frequent reference to wooden writing boards which had a surface prepared from a mixture of wax and orpiment, suitable for inscribing both cuneiform and linear alphabetic scripts. In Anatolia and Syria–Palestine, where good timbers were readily available, these writing boards were commonly used, but they survive only exceptionally: in a well at Nimrud in Assyria, and in the cargo of a ship wrecked off the coast of Turkey. The transition from cuneiform to Hebrew in Palestine is therefore likely to have taken place upon a medium that has perished, and goes far towards explaining why so little clay material has been unearthed.

An unbroken tradition of scribal activity explains why so many general comparisons can be made between Akkadian and biblical literature. Proverbs, encyclopaedic lists, and excerpts from longer works presumably remained in the curriculum for training scribes, and were also used in oracles and incantations, for which the authority of ancient tradition was required. In other genres adaptation and evolution were quick to modify the inheritance. We have noted a cluster of echoes from legends about Sargon of Agade, who lived in the Early Bronze Age, in Genesis, Exodus, and 2 Samuel. They can be related to much later, Late Bronze Age pedagogic practices known from El-Amarna and Hattusa, where Egyptian and Hittite trainee scribes used those same legends for exercises.

Early in the Iron Age scribes for cuneiform and for alphabetic Aramaic worked side by side as they are shown on neo-Assyrian relief sculpture. The eighth-century statue from Tell Fekherye shows an easy paraphrase of Aramaic with Akkadian, and it was simple for Sennacherib's chief cup-bearer to address the besieged citizens of Jerusalem in Aramaic or Hebrew, basing his speech upon a written text. To suppose a wide gulf between cuneiform and the alphabetic scripts, or between Akkadian and Hebrew among educated men, is mistaken.

By the time of the Exile many Assyrians and Babylonians had lived in Palestine as administrators, deportees and traders, and many Hebrews lived in Mesopotamia, so various forms of cultural contact continued. In the following centuries significant strands of Judaism developed in rabbinic academies in Mesopotamia, where pagan practices and traditional academic institutions continued to flourish, sometimes under the patronage of foreign kings, well into the period of Roman imperialism.

Signs of influence can be found in many parts of the Bible. The training of scribes is the key to many of the resemblances between Mesopotamian texts and biblical passages. When the Hebrews created their unique literature and institutions they used for some of the building blocks the ancient traditions which emanated from their older, wealthier, and more powerful neighbours in the East.

FURTHER READING

MÜLLER, H.-P. (ed.), *Babylonien und Israel: historische, religiöse und sprachliche Beziehungen* (Darmstadt, 1991).

HUGHES, J., *Secrets of the Times*, Journal of the Society for Old Testament Studies, Supplement Series 66 (Sheffield, 1990).

SAGGS, H. W. F., *The Encounter with the Divine in Mesopotamia and Israel* (London, 1978).

1. Historical Background

ALT, A., 'Die Rolle Samarias bei der Entstehung des Judentums', *Kleine Schriften*, ii (Munich, 1933), 316–37.

BIRAN, A., and NAVEH, J., 'The Tell Dan Inscription: A New Fragment', *Israel Exploration Journal* 45 (1995), 1–18.

BONECHI, M., 'Relations amicales syro-palestiniennes: Mari et Ḫaṣor au XVIII siècle av. J. C.', in J.-M. Durand (ed.), *Florilegium marianum*, Mémoires de NABU 1, Recueil d'études en l'honneur de Michel Fleury (Paris, 1992).

BORGER, R., and TADMOR, H., 'Zwei Beiträge zur alttestamentlichen Wissenschaft aufgrund der Inschriften Tiglathpilasars III', *ZAW* 94 (1982), 244–50.

COGAN, M., and TADMOR, H., *II Kings: A New Translation with Introduction and Commentary*, Anchor Bible (New York, 1988).

DALLEY, S., 'Foreign Chariotry and Cavalry in the Armies of Tiglath-Pileser and Sargon II', *Iraq* 47 (1985), 31–48.

—— 'Yahweh in Hamath in the 8th Century BC: Cuneiform Material and Historical Deductions', *Vetus Testamentum* 40 (1990), 21–32.

EDZARD, D.-O., 'Amarna und die Archive seiner Korrespondenten zwischen Ugarit und Gaza', in J. Amitai (ed.), *Biblical Archaeology Today* (Jerusalem 1985), 248–59.

HAYES, J. H., and MILLER, J. M. (eds.), *Israelite and Judaean History* (London, 1977).

HOROWITZ, W., and SHAFFER, A., 'A Fragment of a Letter from Hazor', *Israel Exploration Journal* 42 (1992), 165–6.

KINGSLEY, P., 'Ezekiel by the Grand Canal: Between Jewish and Babylonian Tradition', *Journal of the Royal Asiatic Society* 3 (1992), 339–46.

KLENGEL, H., *Syria, 3000 to 300 BC* (Berlin, 1992).

KOCHAVI, M., et al. 'Aphek-Antipatris 1974–1977, The Inscriptions', *Tel Aviv* 2–5 (1975–8).

LABAT, R., *La Caractère religieuse de la royauté assyro-babylonienne* (Paris, 1939), esp. part 3, 'Le Roi representant les dieux sur la terre', and ch. 3 'La Guerre sainte'.

LEMAIRE, A., and JOANNÈS, F., 'Premières monnaies avec signes cunéiformes', *Nouvelles Assyriologiques Brèves et Utilitaires*, no. 95 (1994).

MCCARTER, P. K., 'The Patriarchal Age', in H. Shanks (ed.), *Ancient Israel* (Washington, DC, 1988), 1–30.

MALAMAT, A., *Mari and the Early Israelite Experience*; Schweich Lectures 1984 (Oxford, 1989).

MOORE, M. S., *The Balaam Traditions: Their Character and Development*, Society of Biblical Literature, Dissertation Series 113 (Scholars Press, Atlanta, 1990).

NA'AMAN, N., and ZADOK, R., 'Sargon II's Deportations to Israel and Philistia', *JCS* 40 (1988), 36–46.

NAVEH, J., 'Writing and Scripts in Philistia', *Israel Exploration Journal* 35 (1985), 8–21.

ODED, B., *Mass Deportations and Deportees in the Neo-Assyrian Empire* (Wiesbaden, 1979).

PIETERSMA, A., 'Jannes and Jambres', *Anchor Bible Dictionary* (New York, 1992).

REICH, R., 'The Identification of the "sealed kāru of Egypt"', *Israel Exploration Journal* 34 (1984), 32–8.

SWEENEY, M. A., 'Sargon's Threat against Jerusalem in Isaiah 10: 27–32', *Biblica* 75 (1994), 457–70.

WEIPPERT, M., 'Heilige Krieg in Israel und Assyrien', *ZAW* 84 (1972), 469–93.

2. Babylonian Traditions in Genesis and Exodus

ABOU ASSAF, A., BORDREUIL, P., and MILLARD, A. R., *La Statue de Tell Fekheryé* (Paris, 1982) with redating by A. Spycket, *Revue d'Assyriologie* 79 (1985), 67–8, and H. Sader, *Les États araméens en Syrie* (Beirut, 1987), 23–9.

AFANAS'EVA, V. K., 'Das sumerische Sargon-Epos', *Altorientalische Forschungen* 14 (1987), 237–46.

ALSTER, B., 'A Note on the Uriah Letter in the Sumerian Sargon Legend', *Zeitschrift für Assyriologie* 77 (1987), 169–73.

ARNAUD, D., *Recherches d'Aštata/Emar VI/4*, no. 767 (Paris, 1987), with M. Civil, *Aula Orientalis* 7 (1989), 7.

BAILEY, L. R., *Noah, the Person and the Story in History and Tradition* (Columbia, 1989).

BEYER, K., *Die aramäische Texte vom Toten Meer*, Ergänzungsband (Göttingen, 1994), 119–21.

BONECHI, M., and CATAGNOTI, A., 'Le Volcan Kawkab, Nagar et problèmes connexes', *NABU*, no. 65 (1992).

CLIFFORD, R. J., *Creation Accounts in the Ancient Near East and in the Bible*, Catholic Biblical Quarterly Monograph Series 26 (Washington, DC, 1994).

COHEN, S., *Enmerkar and the Lord of Aratta* (Ann Arbor Microfilms, 1980), lines 141–55 with commentary.

COOPER, J. S., 'Sargon and Joseph: Dreams come True', in A. Kort and S. Morschauser (eds.), *Biblical and Related Studies Presented to Samuel Iwry* (Eisenbrauns, 1985), 33–40.

DAVILA, J. R., 'Shinar', *Anchor Bible Dictionary*, v (New York, 1992), s.v.

DURAND, J.-M., 'Le Mythologème du combat entre le dieu de l'orage et la mer', *MARI* 7 (1993), 41–62.

EMERTON, J. A., 'Some False Clues in the Study of Genesis 14', *Vetus Testamentum* 21 (1971), 24–47.

FOSTER, B., *Before the Muses*, i (Ann Arbor, 1993), 282–9, for a translation of the so-called Kedor-Laomer texts.

GURNEY, O. R., 'A Note on the Babel of Tongues', *AfO* 25 (1974–7), 170.

HOFFNER, H., 'Second Millennium Antecedents to the Hebrew 'ōb', *Journal of Biblical Literature* 86 (1967), 385–401, and the *Chicago Assyrian Dictionary* s.v. apu B.

KRAMER, S., and MAIER, J., *Enki the Crafty God* (Oxford, 1989), 88, and chapter 'Sumerian Literature and the Bible', 154–9.

MULLEN, E. T., *The Assembly of the Gods*, Harvard Semitic Monographs 24 (Scholars Press, 1980).

SETERS, J. VAN, *Abraham in History and Tradition* (New Haven and London, 1975).

SOLLBERGER, E., and Kupper, J.-R., *Inscriptions royales sumériennes et akkadiennes* (Paris, 1971).

THOMPSON, T. L., *The Historicity of the Patriarchal Narratives* (Berlin and New York, 1974), ch. 9.

TOORN, K. VAN DER, 'The Nature of the biblical Teraphim in the Light of the Cuneiform Evidence', *Catholic biblical Quarterly* 52 (1990), 203–22.

—— and Horst, P. W. VAN DER, 'Nimrod before and after the Bible', *Harvard Theological Review* 83 (1990), 1–30.

Ünal, A., 'Das Motiv der Kindesaussetzung in den altanatolische Literaturen', in K. Hecker and W. Sommerfeld (eds.), *Keilschriftliche Literaturen*, ausgewählte Vorträge der XXXII rencontre assyriologique internationale (Berlin, 1986), 129–36.

VANDERKAM, J. C., *Enoch and the Growth of an Apocalyptic Tradition* (Washington DC, 1984).

VANSTIPHOUT, H., 'Another Attempt at the "Spell of Nudimmud"', *Revue d'Assyriologie* 88 (1994), 135–54.

3. Cuneiform Laws and biblical Parallels

ALSTER, B., *The Instructions of Shuruppak*, Mesopotamia 2 (Copenhagen, 1974); and see also C. Wilcke, 'Philologische Bemerkungen zum *Rat des Šuruppag* und Versuch einer neuen Übersetzung', *Zeitschrift für Assyriologie* 68 (1978), 196–232.

CHARPIN, D., 'L'Andurârum à Mari', *MARI* 6 (1990), 253–70.

Chicago Assyrian Dictionary s.v. andurārum, durāru, and šapattu.

FENSHAM, F. C., 'Malediction and Benediction in Ancient Near Eastern Vassal Treaties and the Old Testament', *ZAW* 74 (1962), 1–9.

—— 'Common Trends in Curses of the Near Eastern Treaties and Kudurru Inscriptions Compared with Maledictions of Amos and Isaiah', *ZAW* 75 (1963), 155–75.

GELLER, M. J., 'The Shurpu Incantations and Leviticus V 1–5', *Journal of Semitic Studies* 25 (1980), 181–92.

GREENGUS, S., 'Filling Gaps: Laws Found in Babylonia and in the Mishna but Absent in the Hebrew Bible', *Maarav* 7 (1991), 149–71.

—— 'Biblical and Ancient Near Eastern Law', *Anchor Bible Dictionary*, iv (1992), 242–52.

HELD, M., 'Philological Notes on the Covenant Rituals', *Bulletin of the American Schools of Oriental Research* 200 (1979), 32–7.

LEEMANS, W. F., 'Quelques considérations à propos d'une étude récente du droit du Proche-Orient ancien', *Bibliotheca Orientalis* 48 (1991), 409–37.

LEVY, J., 'The biblical Institution of Deror in the Light of Akkadian Documents', *Eretz Israel* 5 (1958), 21–31.

LOEWENSTAMM, S., *The Laws of Adultery and Murder in biblical and Mesopotamian Law*, Alte Orient und Altes Testament 204 (Neukirchen-Vluyn, 1980), 146–53.

McCARTHY, D. J., *Treaty and Covenant: A Study in Form in the Ancient Oriental Documents and in the Old Testament*, 2nd edn. (Rome, 1978).

NICHOLSON, E. W., *God and his People: Covenant and Theology in the Old Testament* (Oxford, 1986), esp. ch. 3.

OTTO, E., *Rechtsgeschichte der Redaktionen im Kodex Eshnunna und im 'Bundesbuch'*, Orbis Biblicus et Orientalis 85 (Göttingen, 1989).

PAUL, S., *Studies in the Book of the Covenant in the Light of Cuneiform and biblical Law*, Vetus Testament suppl. 18 (1970).

SKAIST, A., 'Levirat', in *RlA* vi (1980–3), 605–8.

WEINFELD, M., *Deuteronomy and the Deuteronomic School* (Oxford, 1972).

WESTBROOK, R., *Studies in biblical and Cuneiform Law*, Cahiers de la Revue Biblique 26 (Paris, 1988), with the review of J. N. Postgate, *Vetus Testamentum* 42 (1992), 431–2.

—— 'Cuneiform Law Codes and the Origins of Legislation'. *Zeitschrift für Assyriologie* 79/2 (1989), 201–22.

YARON, R., *The Laws of Eshnunna*, 2nd edn. (Magnes Press and Brill, 1988).

4. Prophecy and Pseudo-Prophecy

BODI, D., *The Book of Ezekiel and the Poem of Erra*, Orbis Biblicus et Orientalis 104 (Freiburg and Göttingen, 1991).

BORGER, R., 'Gottesbrief', *RlA* iii (1957–71), 575–6.

COLLINS, J. J., *The Apocalyptic Imagination. An Introduction to the Jewish Matrix of Christianity* (New York, 1987), esp. 14–22.

DURAND, J.-M., *Archives épistolaires de Mari*, i: 1 (= *Archives Royales de Mari* xxvi) (Paris, 1988), 421–54.

ELLIS, M. DE J., 'The Goddess Kititum Speaks', *MARI* 5 (Paris, 1987), 235–66.

FLEMING, D., 'Nābû and Munabbiātu: Two New Syrian Religious Personnel', *Journal of the American Oriental Society* 113 (1993), 175–83.

KVANVIG, H. S., *Roots of Apocalyptic* (Neukirchener Verlag, 1988).

LAMBERT, W. G., *The Background of Jewish Apocalyptic*, Ethel M. Wood lecture of 1977 (Athlone Press, 1978).

MALAMAT, A., *Mari and the Early Israelite Experience*, Schweich Lectures for 1984 (Oxford, 1989).

PRITCHARD, J. B. (ed.), 'An Old Babylonian Oracle from Uruk', *Ancient Near Eastern Texts Relating to the Old Testament*, 3rd edn. (Princeton, 1969), 604.

SHERWIN-WHITE, S., 'Seleucid Babylonia', in A. Kuhrt and S. Sherwin-White (eds.), *Hellenism in the East* (Duckworth, 1987), 10–14 (new translation of the Dynastic prophecy with evaluation of its historical background).

VANDERKAM, J. C., *Enoch and the Growth of an Apocalyptic Tradition* (Washington, DC, 1984).

WEIPPERT, M., 'Assyrische Prophetien der Zeit Asarhaddons und Assurbanipals', in F.-M. Fales (ed.), *Assyrian Royal Inscriptions: New Horizons* (Rome, 1981), 71–116.

5. Wisdom Literature

ALT, A., 'Die Weisheit Salomos', *Theologische Literaturzeitung* 76 (1951), 139–44.

DAY, J., 'Foreign semitic influence on the Wisdom of Israel and its appropriation in the Book of Proverbs', in J. Day, R. E. Gordon, and H. G. M. Williamson (eds.), *Wisdom in Ancient Israel, Essays in Honour of J. A. Emerton* (Cambridge, 1995), 55–70.

DELL, K., *The Book of Job as Sceptical Literature*, ZAW Beiheft 197 (1991).

GREENFIELD, J., 'The Seven Pillars of Wisdom (Prov. 9: 1) —A mistranslation', *Jewish Quarterly Review*, M. Held memorial volume, 76 (1985), 13–20.

LIVINGSTONE, A., *Court Poetry and Literary Miscellanea*, State Archives of Assyria iii, nos. 37 and 47 (Helsinki, 1989).

LORETZ, O., *Qoheleth und der Alte Orient* (Freiburg, 1964).

WHYBRAY, R. N., *The Book of Proverbs*, Cambridge Bible Commentary (Cambridge, 1972).

6. Psalms, Lamentations, and the Song of Songs

COOPER, J. S., 'New Cuneiform Parallels to the Song of Songs', *Journal of biblical Literature* 90 (1971), 157–62.

CUMMING, C. G., *The Assyrian and Hebrew Hymns of Praise* (Columbia, 1934).

DALGLEISH, E. R., *Psalm 51 in the Light of Ancient Near Eastern Patternism* (Leiden, 1962).

FINKEL, I., ''Adad-apla-iddina, Esagil-kin-apli and the series SA.GIG', in E. Leichty, M. de J. Ellis, and P. Gerardi (eds.), *A Scientific Humanist: Festschrift for A. Sachs* (Philadelphia, 1988), 143–60.

HILLERS, D., 'Lamentations', in the *Anchor Bible Dictionary*.

MATSUSHIMA, E., 'Le Rituel hiérogamique de Nabû', *Acta Sumerologica* 9 (1987), 131–75.

SOLL, W. M., 'Babylonian and biblical Acrostics', *Biblica* 69 (1988), 305–23.

STARR, I., *The Rituals of the Diviner*, Bibliotheca Mesopotamica 12 (Malibu 1983), 53, for the link between the *shekhinah* and Akkadian.

WIDENGREN, G., *The Accadian and Hebrew Psalms of Lamentation* (Uppsala, 1936).

7. Historical Writing

EDZARD, D.-O., 'Itinerare', *RlA* v (1976–80).

GRAYSON, A. K., *Assyrian and Babylonian Chronicles*, Texts from Cuneiform Sources (Locust Valley, New York, 1975).

GRAYSON, A. K., *Assyrian Royal Inscriptions* (Wiesbaden, 1976), vols. i and ii.

ISHIDA, T., 'The Succession Narrative and Esarhaddon's Apology: A Comparison', in M. Cogan and I. Eph'al (eds.), *Ah, Assyria . . . , Studies Presented to H. Tadmor* (Jerusalem, 1991), 166–73.

LIVERANI, M., 'Assyrische Propheteien', in F. M. Fales (ed.), *Assyrian Royal Inscriptions, New Horizons* (Rome, 1981).

MACHINIST, P., 'Assyria and its Image in the First Isaiah', *Journal of the American Oriental Society* 103 (1983), 719–37.

MALAMAT, A., 'King Lists of the Old Babylonian Period and biblical Genealogies', *Journal of the American Oriental Society* 88 (1968), 163–73.

MASON, R., *Zephaniah, Habakkuk, Joel*, Old Testament Guides (Sheffield, 1994).

METTINGER, T. N., 'YHWH Sabaoth—The Heavenly King on the Cherubim Throne', in T. Ishida (ed.), *Studies in the period of David and Solomon* (Tokyo, 1982), 109–38.

RÖLLIG, W., 'Ein Itinerar aus Dur-Katlimmu', *Damaszener Mitteilungen* 1 (1983), 279–84.

WILSON, R. R., *Genealogy and History in the biblical World* (Yale, 1977).

WOUDE, A. S. VAN DER (ed.), *The World of the Old Testament* (Grand Rapids, Mich., 1989).

8. New Year, Day of Atonement and Scapegoat Ritual

EPSTEIN, I. (trans.), *The Babylonian Talmud*, Mo'ed VII (London, 1938).

GOLDMAN, E. A. (trans.), *The Talmud of the Land of Israel* (Chicago, 1988), vol. xvi.

JANOWSKI, B., and WILHELM, G., 'Der Bock, der die Sünden hinausträgt', in B. Janowski, K. Koch, and G. Wilhelm (eds.), *Religionsgeschichtliche Beziehungen zwischen Kleinasien, Nordsyrien und dem Alten Testament*. Orbis Biblicus et Orientalis 129 (Freiburg and Göttingen, 1993).

Jewish Encyclopaedia s.v. Atonement, 281b.

PROPERZIO, P., 'New Light on the Cults of Artemis and Apollo in Marseilles', in R. F. Sutton (ed.), *Daidalikon, Studies in memory of R. V. Schroder* (Ill., 1989).

STRACK, H. L., *Introduction to the Talmud and Midrash*, 6th edn. (New York, 1959).

WRIGHT, D. P., 'Day of Atonement', *Anchor Bible Dictionary* (1992).

9. Assyrian and Babylonian Cults and Deities in Israel

COGAN, M., *Imperialism and Religion: Assyria, Judah and Israel in the Eighth and Seventh Centuries B. C. E.*, Society of Biblical Literature, Monograph Series 19 (Missoula, 1974).

DALLEY, S., and TEISSIER, B., 'Tablets from the Vicinity of Emar and elsewhere', *Iraq* 54 (1992), esp. 90–1.

DAY, J., *Molech* (Cambridge, 1989), 79–80.

HANDY, L. K., 'Tammuz', in *Anchor Bible Dictionary* (1992).

HOFFNER, H., 'Second Millennium Antecedents to the Hebrew 'ôb', *Journal of Biblical Literature* 86 (1967), 385–401 (and *Chicago Assyrian Dictionary* s.v. apu B).

LIPIŃSKI, E., 'Apladad', *Orientalia* 45 (1976), 53–74 with A. Cavigneaux and B. Ismail, 'Die Statthalter von Suhu und Mari im 8 Jh.v.Chr.', *Baghdader Mitteilungen* 21 (1990), 321–456.

IV

MESOPOTAMIAN CONTACT AND INFLUENCE IN THE GREEK WORLD

1. *To the Persian Conquest*

STEPHANIE DALLEY AND A. T. REYES

Introduction

HARDLY TWO OR THREE DAYS HAD PASSED BEFORE I went up to Homer the poet, when we were both at leisure, and questioned him about everything. 'Above all,' said I, 'where do you come from? The point is being investigated even yet at home.' 'I am not unaware', said he, 'that some think me a Chian, some a Smyrnaean, and many a Kolophonian. As a matter of fact, I am a Babylonian, and among my fellow countrymen, my name was not Homer, but Tigranes. Later on, when I was a hostage (*homeros*) among the Greeks, I changed my name.'[1]

In identifying Homer as a Babylonian, the author Lucian, writing from Samsat in modern Turkey in the second century AD, had satirical purposes in mind. In his time ancient Mesopotamian culture, recognized by the Greeks as older and more venerable than their own, could still be traced in the temples and academic institutions of old cities between the Tigris and the Euphrates, notably at Babylon, Borsippa, Uruk, Ashur, and Harran, and was emerging with new vigour at Hatra, Palmyra, and Apamea-on-Orontes.[2] To many people the culture of Mesopotamia seemed even older than that of Egypt. In the words of Michael Psellos, citing the philosopher Chaeremon, who had taught the emperor Nero, 'The Chaldaeans present themselves as the teachers of the Egyptians, whereas the Egyptians boast that it was the Chaldaeans who became their disciples . . . I found that the wisdom of the Chaldaeans is older than the one zealously

practised among the Egyptians.'[3] Thus, it seemed to many of Lucian's contemporaries that the origins of much that appeared Hellenic—even Homer's epics, the most 'Greek' of all Greek poetry—actually lay in 'Babylon', a convenient term denoting the homeland of Assyrian and Babylonian civilization. Until quite recently scholars who knew little of the evidence from Near Eastern literature and history were inclined to dismiss all such statements by late Classical writers as unfounded, for they thought all traces of Babylonian civilization had long since disappeared.

There is, however, greater validity to calling Homer a Babylonian than Lucian, tongue-in-cheek, had implied. As the study of cuneiform texts has progressed, scholars have found more and more similarities between Mesopotamian epic literature, particularly between the *Epic of Gilgamesh*, and the *Iliad* and *Odyssey*, to the point where a new attempt is needed to explain how the likenesses came about. Opinions are still divided as to whether some kind of literary archetypes, inevitable manifestations of national pride at certain stages of social evolution, can account for clusters of similarities, or whether complex modes of diffusion provide a preferable model. Contact, mainly indirect, between Mesopotamia and the Aegean world had already had a long history prior to 730 BC, the approximate *floruit* of Homer, and written sources from the Near East indicate that these two areas were known to each other long

---

[1] Lucian, *Verae Historiae* 2. 20 (trans. Harmon).
[2] See Ch. II, pp. 49–52; Ch. VII, pp. 151–5.

[3] *FGrH* 618 F 7. On Chaeremon's judgement, see P. van der Horst, *Chaeremon of Alexandria* (Leiden, 1984).

before the Greek 'orientalizing period' of the seventh century, when Hellenic culture is generally admitted to have fallen most heavily under Near Eastern influence. Contacts of several kinds persisted through the Persian wars, into Hellenistic times and afterwards, during the Roman empire. There was not simply one 'orientalizing' period; there were several.

This chapter traces the successive periods of Mesopotamian contact and influence from the third millennium up to the conquest of Babylon by Cyrus II in 539 BC, and tries to identify where the main areas of interaction lay. It begins by looking at the general area of the Aegean and east Mediterranean which was regarded as Greek in the Classical period, but which in the Bronze Age included, for instance, the non-Greek Minoans of Crete. It considers how the Hittites conveyed certain Babylonian academic traditions from Mesopotamia to the coastal cities of western Anatolia. After the Greeks adopted the alphabet and used it to record the remarkable wealth of their literary creativity, it becomes possible to outline more precisely the aspects of Hellenic culture which seem to resemble those known from much earlier in Mesopotamia. By comparing similar artistic themes on material objects one may reinforce the likelihood that certain types of literary themes were diffused from Mesopotamia to the Aegean and Greece.

Chapter 5 will show that these themes were then transmitted to Rome and its empire. Far from having been supplanted by the glory that was Greece, key aspects of Mesopotamian culture survived the death of cuneiform writing and continued to flourish into the third century AD. So we must now look to see whether late Greek texts that claim Mesopotamian ancestry are in fact as untrustworthy as was previously assumed. Cuneiform texts have shown how the accretion of literary material over centuries was periodically recomposed into a new and fairly coherent form, and how the manifest inclusion of ancient material, still recognizable when it is embedded in newer contexts, was regarded as a strength, not a sign of literary incompetence. It implies no diminution of the Classical achievement to show that elements of Greek and Roman culture drew upon very ancient

religious, technical, and literary traditions from Mesopotamia. Rather, the transfer and adoption of these elements took place precisely because of a high degree of intellectual, political, and economic sophistication among the recipients.

From the Third Millennium to *c.*1500 BC

This long period encompasses the pre-palatial and early palatial periods of Crete and Greece,[4] during which people gradually concentrated in ever larger settlements. This development eventually created a demand for a system of recording accounts, the centralized storage of produce, and luxury goods.

During the Early Helladic period (*c.*3000–2000 BC) there appeared in Greece and Anatolia roughly conical, clay stamps, usually with a circular base incised with simple geometrical patterns. They may well be related to the accounting tokens which were in widespread use in southern Mesopotamia, the Susiana plain, and the upper Euphrates river valley. If, as was long ago suggested, the conical stamps in Greece indicate 'the survival of a tradition which passed from the east . . . several centuries before',[5] they are antecedents for a system of accounting which was needed in palace-centred economies, and they were probably triggered by knowledge passed on by traders who worked between the Near East in general and the east Mediterranean.

At Sippar on the Euphrates and in two graves at Ashur on the middle Tigris have been found copper or bronze 'belly button' pans, each with a raised central boss, raised concentric rings and a long handle. They are related to a plainer type of 'frying-pan' commonly found in the cities of lower Mesopotamia. The pans with boss and rings have been found widely in north-western Anatolia, including at Troy in level IIg.[6] Dated between about 2500 and 2250 BC, they are clear evidence for specialized goods from Mesopotamia reaching a distant region which would later be populated by Greek-speaking people.

---

[4] Greek-speaking people arrived in Greece at an unknown time before 1600 BC, but the Minoans in Crete were not Greek-speakers.

[5] J. Boardman, *Greek Gems and Finger Rings* (London, 1970), 21.

[6] P. Calmeyer, 'Das Grab eines altassyrischen Kaufmanns', *Iraq* 39 (1977), 87–97; E. Klengel-Brandt, 'Trade and Exchange: The Old Assyrian period', in P. O. Harper (ed.), *Assyrian Origins, Discoveries at Ashur on the Tigris* (New York, 1995), 45–6 with bibliography.

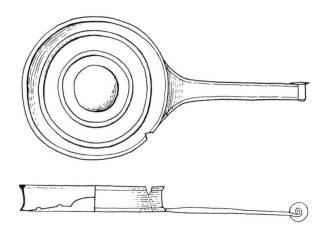

36. Bronze belly-button pan from a grave in Ashur, length 0.52 m. Similar pans come from the Troad.

There are two inscriptions with the name of Naram-Sin, king of Eshnunna and Assyria, which have been found in the east Mediterranean. One of them is said to have been discovered around 1894, on a piece of white stone, on the island of Kythera, although it is now lost: 'To the god Mishar of Dur-Rimush, his lord, Naram-Sin the son of Ipiq-Adad, has offered this for his life.'[7] From Kourion in Cyprus comes a seal inscribed with the name of a servant of the same Naram-Sin.[8] This is king Naram-Sin, who not only ruled Eshnunna around 1950 BC, but also was king of Assyria.[9] He took the supreme title 'king of the four world quarters' which implies extensive conquests, and he was deified during his lifetime. His conquests would have given Eshnunna access to trade in north Syria and Anatolia, and contact between Naram-Sin and the Aegean world may have been effected through these areas. But since it is possible that both items came westwards as heirlooms much later, they constitute unreliable evidence for this period.

Nevertheless, Greek tradition would remember that the island of Kythera had strong eastern connections: Herodotos reported that the cult of Kytheran Aphrodite was 'Assyrian';[10] and Pausanias traced the

route by which her cult had travelled: 'Among men, it fell first to the Assyrians to worship Ourania (Aphrodite), and after the Assyrians to the Paphians of Cyprus and to those of the Phoenicians living around Ashkelon in Palestine; and the Kytherans, having learned from the Phoenicians, worship her.'[11]

A number of cylinder seals has been found in the Aegean with devices cut in Old Babylonian (early second millennium) or Mittanian (mid-second millennium) styles. They come from Mycenaean sites in Greece, and Minoan sites in Crete.[12] Although such seals travelled widely and their designs were often re-cut in the Levant, nevertheless they made Mesopotamian iconography available in the Aegean.

Firm written evidence for contact with Minoan Crete comes mainly from Mesopotamian sites and consists of references to Cretans in cuneiform tablets from a royal archive at Mari on the middle Euphrates, dating to around 1800 BC. The texts record the transfer of Cretan goods to palaces at Mari and Babylon. Cretan drinking vessels and weaponry, often encrusted with gemstones and inlaid with precious metals, were received at Mari. One text tells of Cretan shoes sent to Hammurabi king of Babylon; another records that a Cretan boat (or a model of one) was built at Mari. A third mentions an overseer of Cretan merchants at Ugarit who worked with an interpreter and participated in the trade between Mesopotamia and the Aegean.[13] The presence of Cretan goods at Ugarit has been confirmed by excavations there. In central Anatolia the many Assyrian trading colonies known from texts found at Kanesh lasted until at least 1800 BC, and it is probable that Assyrians maintained similar colonies in northern Syria.[14] Similarities between the administrative systems which are indicated by sealings on locking devices at Karahüyük near Konya and Phaistos in Crete may be due to influence from Assyrian trade.[15]

[7] D. R. Frayne, *Royal Inscriptions of Mesopotamia: Old Babylonian Period*, iv (Toronto 1990), 554 no. 2, with full bibliography.

[8] Ibid. 554–5 no. 2001.

[9] D. Charpin, 'Données nouvelles sur la chronologie des souverains d'Ešnunna' in J.-M. Durand and J.-R. Kupper (eds.), *Miscellanea Babylonica: Mélanges offerts à M. Birot* (Paris 1985), 51–66.

[10] Herodotos 1. 105, 131, 199; cf. Nonnos 3. 111. Discussed by P. Cartledge, *Sparta and Lakonia: A Regional History 1300–362 BC* (London, 1979), 122–3.   [11] 1. 14. 7; cf. Pausanias 3. 23. 1.

[12] J. S. Smith, 'Cylinder Seals in the Aegean', MA thesis, Bryn

Mawr College (Pennsylvania 1989); I. Pini, 'Mitanni-Rollsiegel des "Common Style" aus Griechenland', *Praehistorische Zeitschrift* 58 (1983), 114–26.

[13] References and details are given by E. H. Cline, *Sailing the Wine-Dark Sea* (Oxford, 1994), 126–8.

[14] M. T. Larsen, *The Old Assyrian City-State and its Colonies* (Copenhagen, 1976).

[15] J. Weingarten, 'The Sealing Structure of Karahöyük and Some Administrative Links with Phaistos on Crete', *Oriens Antiquus* 29 (1990), 63–95.

37. A. An Old Assyrian cuneiform
Akkadian clay tablet from Kültepe;
B. A Linear B Mycenaean Greek clay
tablet, from Knossos.

A

B

The evidence that cuneiform writing on clay was used in the Levant, for instance at Byblos and Alalakh, makes it possible that Linear A, the still-undeciphered predecessor of Linear B (a script used to write Mycenaean Greek), was developed in Crete under Near Eastern influence during this time. Assyrian traders used a simplified version of Akkadian cuneiform writing, employing about 68 signs, mostly with simple syllabic values, writing from left to right on clay tablets, usually with rulings to separate the lines. Linear A was likewise written on clay tablets from left to right with line rulings, employing about 100 signs, mostly with simple syllabic values. As in Mesopotamia, Syria, and Anatolia, Linear A and Linear B clay tablets were sun-dried. These writing methods may have spread from Mesopotamia to Crete and to the Mycenaean Greeks. The argument for this influence rests largely on our knowledge that sealing and writing began earlier in Mesopotamia than in the Aegean, as did the cities and palaces that required them.

The Late Bronze Age (c.1500–1100 BC)

During the first part of this period the palaces of Crete and Greece were at their height, with their own artistic skills and traditions in architecture, pottery, lapidary art, and metalwork, none of which shows dependence upon Mesopotamian types. Evidence for influence of other kinds is, however, discernible in written sources. By this time the use of Akkadian cuneiform writing for international agreements was spreading from Mesopotamia throughout the whole of the Near East including Egypt.

North Syria continued to be important to the peoples of the east Mediterranean for gaining access to the centres of power in Mesopotamia. A thirteenth-century Akkadian text from the archives at Ugarit refers explicitly to the trade with Crete: 'From the present day, Ammistamru, son of Niqmepa, king of Ugarit, exempts Sinaranu, son of Siginu. . . . His ship is exempt when it arrives from Crete. He has to bring his presents to the king . . .'. Mycenaean pottery

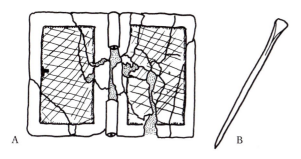

38. A. Writing board of boxwood with ivory hinges, fourteenth century BC, from shipwreck at Ulu Burun; B. Copper stylus from Hattusa, of similar date.

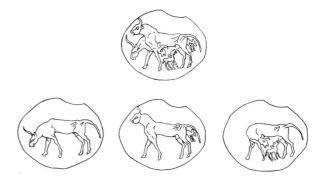

39. Minoan-style seal found at Tell Brak in north-east Syria.

vessels have been found mainly on coastal sites in Syria and Palestine but seldom inland or in eastern Anatolia.[16] A shipwreck, dated to the late fourteenth or early thirteenth centuries, at Ulu Burun near Kaş in southern Turkey, gives some indication of the international contacts possible, for it carried Mesopotamian, Egyptian, Syrian, Palestinian, Cypriot, and Aegean materials.[17] However, non-perishable artefacts potentially from Mesopotamia found in Greece and the Aegean are all small objects such as beads, pendants, plaques, and cylinder seals, which may have reached the Aegean indirectly through Cypriot or Levantine intermediaries. This is indicated in particular by a cache of cylinder seals found in a palatial Mycenaean building in Boiotian Thebes, dated *c*.1220 BC. Although their engraved designs are Mesopotamian, several were re-cut in a local Cypriot style, suggesting that Cyprus was an important link in a network that reached from Mesopotamia to the Greek mainland, but they exerted very little influence upon local designs.[18] Instead we may discern the influence of Cretan art upon wall-painting in western Asia, for instance at Alalakh and Mari. From Tell Brak in Syria comes a lens-shaped seal with a device certainly in-

fluenced in shape and motif by Late Minoan glyptic style, showing, almost as a cartoon, a cow in three successive stages of its life: grazing, giving birth, and suckling its young.[19]

Recently new Hittite texts have clarified long-standing problems in identifying the coastal cities of western Anatolia. A treaty which the Hittite king Tudhaliya IV concluded with his vassal Sausga-muwa who ruled the kingdom of Amurru in Syria in the second half of the thirteenth century, forbade: 'traffic between Ahhiyawa and Assyria via the harbours of Amurru.' Many scholars now accept that 'Ahhiyawa' is a form of the word Achaea, meaning the Achaean or Mycenaean Greek world, or a part of it.[20] If so, the treaty demonstrates that trade between Assyria and the Mycenaean world was important, substantial, and regular, and the Mycenaeans were not simply exchanging products sporadically with coastal towns in the Levant. Herodotos' claim that Phoenicians in the Bronze Age carried Egyptian and 'Assyrian' cargo to Greece, especially to Argos, cannot be faulted in essentials.[21] The clay tablets inscribed in Linear B use words loaned from Akkadian for reed, 'sesame' (linseed) oil, which was the main oil crop of lower

[16] For the Levant and Transjordan, see A. Leonard, *An Index to the Late Bronze Age Aegean Pottery from Syria-Palestine* (Jonsered, 1994); id., 'The Significance of the Mycenaean Pottery found East of the Jordan River', *Studies in the History and Archaeology of Jordan* 3 (1987), 261–6. For Anatolia, N. Özgüç, *Maşat Hüyük* ii (Ankara, 1982), 102–3, but perhaps following the withdrawal of Hittite power there, according to Cline.

[17] G. F. Bass *et al.*, 'The Bronze Age Shipwreck at Ulu Burun: 1986 Campaign', *AJ Arch.* 93 (1989), 1–29.

[18] E. Porada *et al.*, 'The Cylinder Seals Found at Thebes in Boiotia', *AfO* 28 (1981–2), 1–78.

[19] R. B. K. Amiran, 'A Seal from Brak: Expression of Consecutive Movements in Late Minoan Clyptic', *Iraq* 18 (1956),

57–9.

[20] T. R. Bryce, 'Ahhiyawans and Mycenaeans: An Anatolian Viewpoint', *Oxford Journal of Archaeology* 8 (1989), 297–310; O. R. Gurney, 'Hittite Geography Thirty Years On', in H. Otten *et al.* (eds.), *Hittite and Other Anatolian and Near Eastern Studies in Honour of Sedat Alp* (Ankara, 1992), 213–21.

[21] 1. 1; cf. the assessment of the Trojan War and the Assyrian Empire given by the Athenian in Plato, *Laws* 3. 685c: 'Troy was a portion of the Assyrian Empire.' Homer notes that Priam's allies at Troy used a variety of languages (*Iliad* 2. 803–4; 4. 437–8; 10. 420), and Roman authors imagined Akkadian to have been among them: M. J. Dewar, 'Nero on the Disappearing Tigris', *CQ* 41 (1991), 269–72.

40. A. Rock sculpture near Smyrna (Izmir), showing Hittite-style king of Mira and traces of Luwian hieroglyphs, thirteenth century BC; B. Silver boss from the seal of the same king, inscribed in Akkadian cuneiform and Luwian hieroglyphs.

A

B

Mesopotamia, cumin, gold, and tunic.[22] A remarkably large number of words used later in alphabetic Greek for weights, measures, and trading commodities are Semitic words. Although they are not all necessarily Akkadian (east Semitic)—some cannot be distinguished from Canaanite or Phoenician (west Semitic)—they show that early Greeks met, and were influenced by, the established Semitic trading communities to the east.[23]

The seal of a scribe with a Luwian hieroglyphic inscription has recently been found at Troy. Luwian at this period was also written in cuneiform which scribes would have learned from Mesopotamian manuals, so the presence of Luwian this far west is significant when combined with the following evidence. A rock relief which overlooks the Karabel pass near Smyrna shows a ruler who dressed as a Hittite king and wrote Luwian in hieroglyphs. He was probably a vassal of Tudhaliya IV and has been identified as Tarkaššanawa king of Mira, who had his silver-bossed royal seal inscribed both in Luwian

hieroglyphs and in Akkadian cuneiform. He ruled a country which is now thought to lie north of the Maeander river and thus controlled the main road from the heartland of Anatolia westwards to Miletos.[24] Miletos has been identified in the Linear B tablets from Pylos and in cuneiform Hittite texts;[25] craftswomen from Miletos had worked in Pylos, far away on the west coast of mainland Greece, and a brother of the Mycenaean king at Pylos had lived at Miletos, although by the time of Tudhaliya IV the Mycenaeans may have lost control of the city.

The Amarna letters, written in cuneiform yet found in Egypt, have long shown that close links existed between the kingdoms of Babylonia, Assyria, Anatolia, Cyprus, and Egypt. Messengers travelled frequently between the various capitals; royal marriages took place; and many prestigious gifts were exchanged. As our understanding of Hittite geography has progressed, so has the extent of relationships recorded in those letters widened. The range is confirmed by letters and official records found in the Hittite cap-

---

[22] The words for Asia and Europe which have come down to us through Greek may also be Akkadian in origin, and referred originally to the coming out, *asiu*, and the going in, *erēbu*, of the sun; they may have come into Greek at this or at a later period.

[23] H. Zimmern, *Akkadische Fremdwörter als Beweis für babylonischen Kultureinfluss* (Leipzig, 1915); E. Masson, *Recherches sur les plus anciens emprunts sémitiques en grec* (Paris, 1967); M. Astour,

Hellenosemitica: An Ethnical and Cultural Study in West Semitic Impact on Mycenaean Greece, (2nd. edn., Leiden, 1967).

[24] Gurney, 'Hittite Geography: Thirty Years On'. We thank J. D. Hawkins for imparting his readings of the name (forthcoming in *Anatolian Studies*).

[25] K. Gödecken, 'A Contribution to the Early History of Miletus', in E. French and K. Wardle (eds.), *Problems in Greek Prehistory*, (Bristol, 1988), 307–15.

ital Hattusa. When the Pharaoh wrote in cuneiform to Tarhunda-radu, king of Arzawa, we can deduce that a scribe whose training had included Akkadian *belles lettres* was in regular attendance at each court, even if Tarhunda-radu's scribe said Hittite was easier for him than Akkadian.[26] Apasas, the capital city of Arzawa, has now been identified with reasonable certainty as Ephesos, one of the great coastal cities of Ionia.[27] Whether Ahhiyawan and Arzawan kings received letters in Hittite or Akkadian, scribes who had learned from the traditional Mesopotamian cuneiform syllabus were present at their courts. The association between Akkadian and Hittite writing is so close that early Hittite royal inscriptions had traditionally been recorded both in Akkadian and in Hittite cuneiform. Therefore the letters bring clear evidence for the knowledge of Akkadian manuals to the western coast of Anatolia. We know from the tablets found at El-Amarna that the scribes who wrote and translated letters from abroad were conversant with traditional works of literature such as the myth of Adapa and the myth of Nergal and Ereshkigal. At Hattusa the *Epic of Gilgamesh*, in three different languages, and legends of the kings of Agade, were well known to the scribes.

With such knowledge resident in every palace whose ruler aspired to international relations, it is plain that the influence of Babylonian academic traditions was present at the very centres of Mycenaean Greek power. Other experts followed. A letter from the Pharaoh asked a Cypriot king to send to Egypt a specialist in bird-augury, a practice which had developed in Mesopotamia and was adopted by the Hittites, eventually to be codified in written manuals such as *Šumma ālu*.[28]

Homer wrote about the war at Troy in the *Iliad* using geographical and personal names which seem to correspond to names in Hittite texts: not only is Ahhiyawa probably Achaea, but Tawagalawa may be Eteokles, and Alaksandu of Wilusa may be Alexander (Paris) of Ilion. Whether or not all these equations are correct, it is certain that this period was an exceptional one in Mesopotamia for several reasons. In Assyria Tukulti-Ninurta I (*c.*1244–1208) ruled so effectively that he conquered the mountain people

north-west of Assyria, and so became an immediate neighbour of the Hittites who were ruled at that time by Tudhaliya IV. He also conquered Babylon and took back to his capital as highly prized booty many literary texts. This act reflects his interest in literature which is known for another reason, that he had composed a famous epic in a Babylonian literary dialect depicting himself as a great warrior-hero and his battles as heroic deeds influenced by the will of the gods.[29] Fine speeches, deep emotions, similes from nature, and vivid descriptions of battle characterize an exceptional composition. The legendary quality of these two great contemporary rulers may be related to the garbled names of Nimrod and Tidal in Genesis 10 and 14.

It has become customary to describe as a Dark Age the times that ended the Bronze Age in the twelfth century, during which the people of the east Mediterranean, Anatolia, and the Levant lost virtually all knowledge of their ancestry. But recent archaeological evidence from Tyre, Tiryns, Lefkandi in Euboia, and Perati (where the great silver mines at Laurion continued to be worked) and textual evidence from Emar, Malatya, and Carchemish on the Euphrates, show that this was not so. International trade continued to a lesser extent, old customs remained in use, and dynastic succession persisted; times were hard at Emar, but people still bought and sold, recording their activities on clay tablets. Hattusa was thoroughly destroyed by enemy action; Ugarit was chiefly ruined by an earthquake; but many Near Eastern cities such as Akku, Tyre, Sidon, Byblos, Carchemish, Harran, and Malatya managed to maintain their traditional way of life despite undoubted hardships.

By the end of the Late Bronze Age there is evidence not just for trade between areas in the Aegean and Mesopotamian spheres of influence, but for much more. Kings of the great cities in western Anatolia had direct contact with Mesopotamian cuneiform traditions when they corresponded with Hittite, Levantine, and Egyptian powers, and a knowledge of Mesopotamian literature was available at all those royal courts in written form, not just as an oral tradition. Just as religious elements in Minoan and Mycenaean

---

[26] W. L. Moran, *The Amarna letters* (Baltimore, 1992), nos. 31 and 32.

[27] I. Singer, 'Western Anatolia in the Thirteenth Century BC according to the Hittite Sources', *Anatolian Studies* 33 (1983),

205–17.

[28] Moran, *The Amarna Letters*, 107 no. 35.

[29] B. R. Foster, *Before the Muses* (CDL Press, Bethesda, Md., 1993), i. 209–29.

society tended to survive into the Iron Age,[30] so both Mycenaean and Near Eastern elements in the poetry of Homer and Hesiod may have had their genesis in the Bronze Age. Long before the seventh century, Mesopotamian culture began to influence Greek-speaking people.

The Early Iron Age (c.1100–900 BC)

It is difficult to define the extent of relations between Greece and Mesopotamia at the beginning of the Early Iron Age because political disruptions in the Greek world and the Near East dislocated Mycenaean, Anatolian, and Levantine links in the trading networks that had extended from Mesopotamia to the east Mediterranean. However, new avenues of communication between Greeks and Mesopotamians may have been created as a result of the collapse of the Mycenaean and Hittite palaces and subsequent migrations into Cyprus and the Levant. Hittite traditions continued to some extent in the neo-Hittite states of north Syria and Cilicia, although they were written down in Luwian hieroglyphs and in Aramaic linear alphabetic script, rather than in cuneiform.

There are no contemporary documents to guide us. Cuneiform sources which date to this time do not refer to any Greeks, and in any case they do not match the earlier wealth of records from Mari, Ugarit, and Emar. In Greece the practice of writing, which had presumably been limited to a scribal class within the Mycenaean palaces, seems to have died out, although it continued in Cyprus. In later times Cypriots and Anatolians could claim kinship with the Assyrians on the basis of a presumed descent from the Bronze Age kings, but these literary references do not necessarily document historical relations.[31]

Archaeological excavations have, nevertheless, established a framework within which to view this period. By the second half of the eleventh century BC the Phoenicians, heirs to the coastal Canaanites,

had re-established trading networks between the Greek mainland and the Near East, and coastal disruptions within this network were less severe than was once thought. This brought the Greeks into contact with the alphabetic writing of the Phoenicians which they eventually adopted, and with the script came scribes with methods of academic training established long ago in Mesopotamia.[32] The new network, like its Bronze Age precursor, reached Mesopotamia, for this was the heyday of the great kings of the Middle Assyrian period, notably Tiglath-pileser I (1115–1077) who campaigned in Anatolia around the upper Euphrates, and reached Phoenician maritime cities in the Levant, receiving gifts from the rulers of Byblos, Sidon, and Egypt. Assyria expanded its empire westward under Ashur-dan II (932–912) and his successors, and negotiations for treaties and other obligations were conducted initially in Akkadian with interpreters. The fabulous palaces and courts of the Assyrian kings created a vast demand for specialized goods and since Greeks, most notably Euboians, were among those commercially active in the Levant at this time,[33] it cannot be doubted that they were aware of the wares, intellectual and material, that Mesopotamia offered.

Archaeological evidence links the Euboians specifically with Mesopotamia or Mesopotamian-inspired trade. A tomb dating to the tenth century at Lefkandi in Euboia contained among its other grave-goods a gold necklace with a finely granulated pendant-attachment, 'exactly matched by ones from Babylonia belonging to around 2000 BC',[34] so it may have arrived in Euboia long before, although equally good parallels exist between this type of necklace and ones from Syria, whence the example from Lefkandi may have come. The shape of the three-armed gold earrings with mulberry decorations is also known to have derived ultimately from Assyria, although the type was used in north Syria as well.[35] Also telling, despite its modest appearance, is a single protogeo-

---

[30] M. P. Nilsson, *The Minoan-Mycenaean Religion and its Survival in Greek Religion* (2nd edn., Lund, 1950).

[31] e.g. Hyginus, *Fabulae* 58, 242, 270.

[32] J. Naveh, *Early History of the Alphabet: An Introduction to West Semitic Epigraphy and Palaeography* (2nd edn., Jerusalem, 1987); id., 'Semitic Epigraphy and the Antiquity of the Greek Alphabet', *Kadmos* 30 (1991), 143–52; B. B. Powell, *Homer and the Origin of the Greek Alphabet* (Cambridge, 1991).

[33] M. Popham, 'An Engraved Near Eastern Bronze Bowl

from Lefkandi', *Oxford Journal of Archaeology* 14 (1995), 103–7; P. Courbin, 'Fragments d'amphores protogéometriques à Bassit (Syrie)', *Hesperia* 62 (1993), 95–113.

[34] M. R. Popham, 'Lefkandi and the Greek Dark Age', in B. Cunliffe (ed.), *Origins: The Roots of European Civilisation* (London, 1987), 75.

[35] C. Kardara, 'Hermata, Triglena Moroenta', *AJ Arch.* 65 (1961), 62–4 for the type.

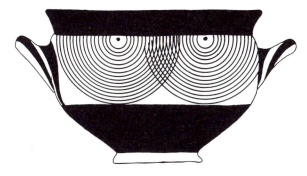

43. Euboian cup painted with pendant semicircles. Pottery of this type has been found at Nineveh in the Nabu temple as well as at Tyre and in Galilee.

41. Gold necklace from Lefkandi.

42. Gold jewellery from Lefkandi, showing Mesopotamian elements of design and technique.

metric sherd from the site of the temple of Nabu in Nineveh,[36] belonging to a typically Euboian cup decorated with a series of semicircles hanging from the lip.

In the Late Bronze Age the people known as Danuna in an Amarna letter, and as the Denyen in Egyptian accounts of the Sea Peoples, came from Adana in Cilicia. A bilingual inscription from Kara-tepe, north-east of Adana, dating perhaps to the mid-eighth century BC, refers to the 'house' (dynasty) of Mopsos in alphabetic Phoenician and in Luwian hieroglyphs. The name Mopsos was a common one, found both in Linear B and in Hittite texts, and can-not be used to infer that Cilicia had a population of Greek speakers from before the Dark Age. However, some Mycenaean and Iron Age Greek pottery has been found on major Cilician sites; Luwian hiero-glyphic writing persisted there through the Late Bronze Age into the eighth century; and later, Ion-ians were almost certainly present in that area in the time of Ashurbanipal.[37] Historical links between the Danaoi-Greeks in the *Iliad* and Danuna in Near Eastern texts, or between the Homeric seer Mopsos and the Cilician house of Mopsos, although often passionately proposed, are now considered to be unlikely.[38]

Cilicia, with its great cities at Adana, Tarsos, Mersin, and Kelenderis, flourished from the Bronze Age through the time of hardship into the Iron Age. It has still

[36] Birmingham City Museum 1989, A 343. See R. Campbell Thompson and R. W. Hutchinson, *The Excavations on the Temple of Nabu at Nineveh* (Oxford, 1929 (= *Archaeologia* 79 (1929)), 137).

[37] See § 5.

[38] J. Vanschoonwinkel, 'Mopsos: légendes et réalité', *Hethitica* 10 (1990), 185–211.

hardly been explored, but cylinder seals in the Adana museum tell a tale of multinational dealings. Extending in date from the late third millennium to the Achaemenid period, they are designed in Mesopotamian, Levantine, Cappadocian, and Syrian styles in which are mingled Egyptian and Cypriot motifs.[39]

The Neo-Assyrian Period
(c.900–612 BC)

Akkadian words that refer to 'Ionians' first appear in cuneiform texts at this time.[40] In Greek texts, however, the neo-Assyrian empire is documented only from later periods. In them the Greek words *Assurios* and *Assurie* reflect an awareness that the Assyrians were important players in the arena of politics and economics in the Near East. The terms could be used not only as generic ones for the Near East or any Near Easterner, but also as specific ones denoting Assyria (*Assurie*) and Assyrian origin (*Assurios*).[41] Greek writers (Herodotos is a notable exception) could use the terms *Assurios* and *Assurie* interchangeably with *Surios* (Syrian) and *Surie* (Syria). Arvad in Phoenicia was known as the 'Assyrian harbour'; the Mediterranean coast could be referred to as 'Assyrian' territory.[42]

Intensified interaction resulted directly from the expansion of the neo-Assyrian empire from the tenth and ninth centuries onwards under kings who regulated trade through the Levant and Cilicia. With the westward campaign of Tiglath-pileser III in 734, firm trading links were established with the Mediterranean.[43] Just as their predecessors had done in Anatolia, Assyrian kings established trading colonies in the mer-

cantile cities of the West.[44] Business letters written in Luwian and records in Aramaic are known from Ashur in Late Assyrian contexts, which implies that merchants in Mesopotamia were multilingual, and that scribes who were also translators were available.[45]

Apparent above all at this time is the mobility between different regions and the varied contacts stimulated by trade, warfare and diplomacy. The Greeks could not have failed to have come into contact with Assyrians, not least in their capacities as customs officials in charge of harbours in Phoenicia and elsewhere. The coastal sites of Tell Sukas, Ras el-Basit, and Al-Mina, all with a Greek population (whether permanent or transient), were adjacent to the Assyrian provinces of Kinalua and Simirra. When Greek pottery begins to appear at Hamath in the late ninth or early eighth century, its rulers had just abandoned their traditional alliance with Damascus and come to terms with Assyria.[46] A group of craftsmen based at Guzana (Tell Halaf) was exporting ivories and bronzes both to the palaces at Nimrud and to wealthy patrons in Athens by the third quarter of the ninth century.[47] Dor, at which late eighth-century Greek pottery has been found, became the capital of the Assyrian province for the Carmel and Sharon coasts. In archaeological terms the material evidence for an Assyrian presence in the Levant is limited but still apparent: seals, architecture, and 'palace wares'[48] have been recovered, and would have become familiar to Greek Levantines.

Traditionally historians and archaeologists have interpreted contact between Greeks and Assyrians as antagonistic. They explain the paucity of Greek archaeological material in the Levant as a result of west-

[39] O. Tunça, *Catalogue des sceaux-cylindres du Musée régional d'Adana, Syro-Mesopotamian Studies* 3: 1 (Malibu, 1979).

[40] J. Brinkman, 'The Akkadian Words for "Ionia" and "Ionian"'' in R. F. Sutton (ed.), *Daidalikon: Studies in Memory of Raymond V. Schoder, SJ* (Wauconda, Ill., 1989), 53–7.

[41] T. Nöldeke, 'Assurios, Surios, Suros', *Hermes* 5 (1871), 443–68; J. A. Tvedtnes, 'The Origin of the Name "Syria"', *JNES* 40 (1981), 139–40; R. N. Frye, 'Assyria and Syria: Synonyms', *JNES* 51 (1992), 281–5.

[42] M. Elat, 'Phoenician Overland Trade within the Mesopotamian Empire', in M. Cogan and I. Eph'al (eds.), *Ah, Assyria . . . Studies in Assyrian History and Ancient Near Eastern Historiography Presented to Hayim Tadmor* (Jerusalem, 1991), 27. See e.g. *ANET*, 533–4 §§ 15–8 (Treaty of Esarhaddon with Ba'al of Tyre).

[43] H. W. F. Saggs, 'The Nimrud Letters, 1952—Part II', Iraq 17 (1955), 127–30 (ND 2715) = J. N. Postgate, *Taxation and Conscription in the Assyrian Empire* (Rome, 1974), 390–2.

[44] Elat, 'Phoenician Overland Trade', 21–35.

[45] O. Pederson, *Archives and Libraries in the City of Assur* II (Uppsala, 1986), 98.

[46] P. J. Riis and M.-L. Buhl, *Hama* ii: 2 (Copenhagen, 1990), 186 no. 673 (krater fragments); S. Parpola, 'Appendix I: A Letter from Marduk-Apla-Usur of Anah to Rudamu/Urtamis, King of Hamath', 257–65 in the same volume.

[47] G. Herrmann, 'The Nimrud Ivories I: The Flame and Frond School', *Iraq* 51 (1989), 89–109, assigning a bronze bowl from the Kerameikos cemetery in Athens to this group. On the date of the bowl, see G. Markoe, *Phoenician Bronze and Silver Bowls from Cyprus and the Mediterranean* (Berkeley, 1985), 153.

[48] See e.g. C.-M. Bennett, 'Some Reflections on Neo-Assyrian Influence in Transjordan', in R. Moorey and P. Parr (eds.), *Archaeology in the Levant* (Warminster, 1978), 168–71; R. Amiran, *Ancient Pottery in the Holy Land* (Jerusalem, 1969), 291; H. Tadmor and M. Tadmor, 'The Seal of Belu-Ašaredu, Majordomo', *Yediot* 31 (1967), 68–79.

ward incursions in the ninth century by Ashurnasirpal II and Shalmaneser III who, they argue, discouraged trade. This picture obscures a variety of relationships and draws its inspiration from two common images, neither one valid. The first is the traditional one of the Assyrian war machine relentlessly antagonizing its neighbours, a one-dimensional view now largely superseded. The second is likewise traditional, and presents the Greeks as a seafaring, democratic power, at odds with eastern tyranny. But at this time Greek city-states were ruled by tyrants or kings, and were not united as a seafaring power.

However, some references to Greeks in the fragmentary cuneiform sources involve piratical raids some-where along the Levantine coast resulting in forceful action by Assyrian soldiers. The Akkadian terms used to identify Greeks in these texts are ^kur^*yamnaya* and ^kur^*yaman*, both cognate with Ionia, *m* being often pronounced *w*. Many of the cuneiform references that document conflict between Greeks and Assyrians date to the time of Sargon II in the late eighth century, and most may refer to a single campaign;[49] they cannot, therefore, confirm that conflict in general characterized the relationship between Assyrians and Greeks. Nor does the tale of Yamani, who usurped the throne of the Philistine city Ashdod and was removed in a revolt assisted by Sargon, add to the picture, for the name Yamani, often reckoned to be Greek, is a good Semitic one still used in Arabic, and is distinguishable from the Akkadian word for 'Ionian'.

After Sennacherib sent an army into Cilicia in 696 to quell a rebellion, Berossos says that he rebuilt Tarsos 'in the image of Babylon'.[50] The theme of building to replicate Babylon occurs in Assyrian texts, which suggests Berossos used sources based on original records.[51] Sennacherib installed in a new temple an Assyrian statue of Sandon god of Tarsos, equated since Hittite times with Marduk god of Babylon. Roman coins from Tarsos show that it was still worshipped in the time of Hadrian, and the locals did not tear it down when the Assyrians left. The cult still flourished in St Paul's lifetime. The cuneiform sources make clear that Sennacherib was more concerned to maintain the flow of tribute into Assyria than to curtail the activities of Greeks along the southern coast of Anatolia. Excavations at Tarsos do not contradict this, since there are no perceptible breaks in the archaeological sequence.[52]

The Greeks also remembered that Sennacherib left a statue of himself on the battlefield as a memorial of victory, and he ordered that an account of his courage and heroic deeds be inscribed in 'Chaldaean' script for future times. Whether or not the king is correctly named, the statue was presumably one of the well-known stelai set up around the empire to mark Assyrian interests. This may have been the same stele reported centuries later by eyewitnesses as having been installed by 'Sardanapalos',[53] a corruption in Greek of the royal names Esarhaddon and Ashurbanipal, which stood for a legendary conflation of several Assyrian kings. Strabo describes the stele as carved with a stone figure whose fingers on the right hand are shown 'snapping together', and gives a Greek version of its inscription in Assyrian letters:

Sardanapalos the son of Anakyndaraxes built Anchiale and Tarsos in one day. Eat, drink, be merry, because all things else are not worth *this*!

meaning a snap of the fingers.[54] Diodoros Sikelos, who gives another version of the inscription, says that the Chaldaean inscription was translated into Greek.[55]

With Sardanapalos came those other legendary Assyrian figures who would populate Greek historical writing: Semiramis, Ninos, and Ninyas. Semiramis combines the name and historical figure of Sammuramat, wife of Shamshi-Adad V (823–811) and mother of Adad-nirari III (c.810–783) with Naqia the mother of Esarhaddon.[56] Strabo tells[57] how Semiramis' fame was so widespread that monuments in Asia Minor and Iran were ascribed to her,[58] and this is confirmed by the discovery in Anatolia of a stele on which Sammu-

[49] On the possibility that Nimrud letter no. 69 dates to the time of Sargon II, rather than Tiglath-pileser III, see H. J. Katzenstein, *The History of Tyre* (Jerusalem, 1973), 232.

[50] Berossos, *FGrH* 680 F 7c; Abydenos, *FGrH* 685 F 5; cf. Hellanikos *FGrH* 4 F 63 on Sardanapalos and Tarsos.

[51] S. Dalley, 'Tarsus in the Image of Babylon', in *Proceedings of the Fourth Anatolian Iron Ages Symposium* (held in May 1997). (forthcoming).

[52] G. M. A. Hanfmann, 'The Iron Age Pottery of Tarsus', in H. Goldman (ed.), *Excavations at Gözlü Küle, Tarsus*, iii (Princeton, 1963), 159.

[53] e.g. Polybius 8. 10. 3.

[54] Strabo 14. 5. 9.

[55] 2. 23. 3. (from Aristoboulos, *FGrH* 139 F 9); cf. Cicero, *Tusculan Disputations* 5. 101.

[56] But note the very different etymology suggested by M. Weinfeld, 'Semiramis: Her Name and Her Origin', in *Ah, Assyria . . .*, 99–103.

[57] 16. 1. 2.

[58] Note e.g. Antipater of Sidon, *Palatine Anthology* 7. 748 on 'a vast stone mound of Assyrian Semiramis' with J. Ebert, 'Das Literaten-Epigramm aus Halikarnass', *Philologus* 130 (1986), 37–43.

A

44. A. Stele of the Assyrian king Shamshi-Adad V pointing his finger. Height 2.18 m.; B. Stele of Sammu-ramat found in Turkey. Height 1.40 m.

B

ramat recounted her own deeds in cuneiform.[59] She was therefore a genuine historical character. Ninos was the eponymous founder of Nineveh and later of Nineveh-in-Caria, Aphrodisias, and the legendary descendants of Semiramis and Ninos were Ninyas and Sardanapalos, whose links with genuine historical events at the Assyrian court are described in the following chapter.[60]

Greek mercenaries may have served in the Assyrian army, as they certainly did in Israel, Judah, and Egypt. A late Greek chronicler mentions that Pythagoras the mathematician served as a mercenary in the Assyrian army,[61] but since he is thought to have lived in the sixth century BC the specifically Assyrian connection cannot be taken at face value.[62] Later Greeks recognized, as modern scholars have done, Mesopotamian elements in his scientific knowledge and sought a rational explanation which need not be historically correct. Consequently some writers said that the Persian king Cambyses captured Pythagoras in Egypt and brought him to Babylon, others that he studied with the 'Assyrian' Zaratos. This is normally taken to be a Hellenized form for the Iranian wise man Zoroaster, although an Akkadian name such as Zer-iddin with a Greek ending -*os* cannot necessarily be ruled out.[63]

Some Greeks provided tribute directly to Assyria. An inscription of Esarhaddon records the following:[64] 'All the kings of the midst of the sea, from the land of Cyprus (and) the land of "Ionia" to the land of Tarsisi, bowed down at my feet. I received their heavy tribute.' This almost certainly meant that Greek kings or high dignitaries travelled to pay homage to Esarhaddon in person, and so observed the royal court in Nineveh at first hand. Bilingual texts would have recorded their obligations. Esarhaddon listed the names of the Cypriot kings, and they are mainly Greek.[65]

Assyria did not dominate the Greek world in a political or military sense, but profited by receiving goods which it regarded as tribute. This tributary relationship is confirmed by a fragmentary cuneiform text from the time of Ashurbanipal (668–627) which records as a tribute-paying area a place ia-⌈ma⌉-na between Cilicia and Malatya; the restoration is very probable and implies that the area contained resident Greeks.[66] Tarsos in Cilicia headed an Assyrian province in the late eighth century. Such a relationship would have required a translation service to make a record of agreements and obligations for each party to keep. When Gyges of Lydia sent a messenger to Ashurbanipal in Nineveh, the Assyrian king recorded with some surprise: 'There was no interpreter for his language. His language was different, and his words were not understood.' We now know that the Lydians spoke an Indo-European language which is not close to Luwian, Lycian, or Hittite.

Greeks and Mesopotamians met in Syria and the Levant. Excavations have shown that northern coastal Syria was cosmopolitan partly because it provided, via the Orontes River, a convenient way to enter Mesopotamia. The attention paid to that area by archaeologists, especially the town of Al-Mina, should not, however, obscure the importance of other harbours further south,[67] for until early this century ports along the coastline of Syria and Palestine functioned as feeding stations into the different trading routes that led to Mesopotamia.[68]

They also met in Egypt. There were temples in Egypt dedicated to Mesopotamian deities.[69] Greeks established a trading post at Naukratis in the Nile Delta, in the same way that Tiglath-pileser III and Sargon II had set up trading posts along the borders of Egypt. At Elephantine on the upper Nile the Aramaic-speaking peoples had begun to acquire

[59] V. Donbaz, 'Two Neo-Assyrian Stelae in the Antakya and Karanmaraş Museums', *Annual Review of the Royal Inscriptions of Mesopotamia Project* (1990) 5–24.

[60] *RE*, Suppl. vii, *s. v.*, 'Ninos', 'Ninyas', 'Semiramis'; E. A. Speiser, 'In Search of Nimrod', *Eretz-Israel* 5 (1958), 32–6 favoured an identification of Ninos with Tukulti-Ninurta I.

[61] Abydenos *FGrH* 685 F 5.

[62] For a summary of the traditions, see K. Freeman, *The Pre-Socratic Philosophers* (Oxford, 1946), 73–83.

[63] e.g. Alexander Polyhistor *FGrH* 273 F 94; Hippolytos, *Refutation* I. 2. 12; cf. Cicero, *De Finibus* 5. 29. 87. For an early dating of Zoroaster see P. Kingsley, 'The Greek Origin of the Sixth-Century Dating of Zoroaster', *Bulletin of the Schools for Oriental and African Studies* 53 (1990), 245–65; and compare

'Zardan' as the name of the Buddha's Chaldaean teacher, Ch. II, p. 39 above.

[64] R. Borger, *Die Inschriften Asarhaddons Königs von Assyrien* (Graz, 1956), 86: 10–11.

[65] A. T. Reyes, *Archaic Cyprus* (Oxford, 1994), 49–60 for the texts.

[66] E. Forrer, *Die Provinzeinteilung des assyrischen Reiches* (Leipzig, 1920), 53, rev. 3: 8.

[67] J. Boardman, *The Greeks Overseas*, (rev. edn., London, 1980), 34–109, for Al-Mina; see also M. Y. Treister, 'North Syrian Metalworkers in Archaic and Greek Settlements?', *Oxford Journal of Archaeology* 14 (1995), 159–78.

[68] E. Wirth, *Syrien* (Darmstadt, 1971), 331–60.

[69] e.g. J. C. L. Gibson, *Textbook of Syrian Semitic Inscriptions*, ii (Oxford, 1975), 125–32, for a temple of Nabu.

Assyrian habits: names, epistolary styles, and technical legal terms are adopted from Mesopotamia.[70]

They also met in Anatolia. If it is correct to equate king Midas of Phrygia, who consulted the oracle at Delphi, with Mita king of Mushki cited in inscriptions of Sargon II, we may see once again a network of political connections extending from Greece to Assyria, linked by the exchange of messengers and translators.[71]

Berossos[72] mentions a tradition that Sennacherib 'built a temple at Athens and erected bronze statues upon which he engraved his own exploits'.[73] The contents of this passage are usually dismissed as unlikely, but the allusion to bronze statues calls to mind the handful of bronzes of probably Mesopotamian origin dedicated in Greek temples at Athens, Delphi, Olympia, Rhodes, and Samos.[74] Some were originally attachments to furniture or vessels; others may have been votive statuettes. One group from the temple of Hera at Samos represents votives standing next to dogs, and these are related to the worship of Gula, the Babylonian goddess of healing whose symbol is the dog. Dog burials in Samos and elsewhere in the eastern Mediterranean are comparable with a tenth-century dog cemetery excavated near a sanctuary-site of Gula at Isin in Mesopotamia.[75] From Samos too comes a corroded figure of the *mušhuššu*-dragon, originally associated with the god of Eshnunna but later appropriated by Marduk the city god of Babylon and then adopted by the Assyrian god Ashur after the sack of Babylon by Sennacherib in 689 BC.[76] These items suggest particularly close connections between Mesopotamia and Samos. The annual cult procession on Samos in which the image of Hera was bathed and clothed is certainly Near Eastern in character, recalling the *akītu*-festival of the New Year in Babylon.

Mesopotamian cylinder seals have also been found at these Greek temple sites. Assyrian textiles too, it has long been suspected, made their way to Greece and inspired particular decorative motifs such as the lotus and palmette chain on East Greek vases. On Corinthian pottery floral motifs, rosettes, and lions have been pointed out as descendants of Assyrian motifs, and the shape of the Protocorinthian alabastron may have been derived from the repertoire of Assyrian ceramic shapes.[77] At Tarsos an authentic Assyrian jar and a jar imitating Assyrian glazed ware were found, the latter perhaps manufactured in a Greek centre such as Rhodes, although 'it is possible that other factories were active in Syria and Phoenicia.'[78] Gold jewellery from mainland Greece and Ionia reflects clear Mesopotamian influence, and represents the late flowering of a tradition of craftsmanship that had persisted from Early Dynastic times.[79]

We turn now from information about trade and political interchange to evidence that Mesopotamia had a cultural effect upon the Greek world. Here we find influence in religious practices, magic, art, literature, and music. Scholars have often noted resemblances, but the difficulty still remains to pinpoint exactly when, where, and how each practice was transmitted. The presence of itinerant craftsmen, seers and singers has been inferred from a passage in the *Odyssey*:

No man of his own accord goes out to bring in a stranger from elsewhere, unless that stranger be master of some craft, a prophet or one who cures diseases, a worker in wood, or again an inspired bard, delighting men with his song. The wide world over, men such as these are welcome guests.[80]

[70] F. M. Fales, 'La Tradition assyrienne à Elephantine d'Égypte: nouvelles données et perspectives', *Transeuphratène* 9 (1995), 119–30.

[71] Herodotos I. 14, and J. D. Hawkins, 'Mita', in *RlA* viii (1995).

[72] See Ch. II § 5.

[73] Berossos, *FGrH* 680 F 7(31) (vol. 3C1).

[74] J. Curtis, 'Mesopotamian Bronzes from Greek Sites: The Workshops of Origin', *Iraq* 56 (1994), 1–25 with refs.

[75] L. P. Day, 'Dog Burials in the Greek World', *AJ Arch.* 88 (1984), 32; J. Boessneck, 'Die Hundeskelette von Isan Bahriyat (Isin) aus der Zeit um 1000 v. Chr.', in B. Hrouda *et al.* (eds.), *Isin-Isan Bahriyat i: Die Ergebnisse der Ausgrabungen 1973–1974* (Munich, 1977), 97–109. Medical practices in the Greek word involving dogs may have been derived indirectly from Hittite

practice; see B. J. Collins, 'The Puppy in Hittite Ritual', *JCS* 42 (1990), 211–26 with S. H. Lonsdale, 'Attitudes Towards Animals in Ancient Greece', *Greece and Rome* 26 (1979), 146–59.

[76] Curtis, 'Mesopotamian Bronzes from Greek Sites', 8, 11, fig. 20; F. A. M. Wiggermann, 'Tišpak, His Seal, and the Dragon Mušhuššu', in O. M. C. Haex *et al.* (eds.), *To the Euphrates and Beyond. Archaeological Studies in honour of Maurits N. van Loon* (Rotterdam and Brookfield, 1989), 117–34.

[77] H. Payne, *Necrocorinthia* (Oxford, 1931) 19, 67–8, 142, 270.

[78] Hanfmann, 'The Iron Age Pottery of Tarsus', 252, figs. 85, 136, no. 1118 and 1119.

[79] K. R. Maxwell-Hyslop, 'The Ur Jewellery', *Iraq* 22 (1960), 105–15.

[80] 17. 383–5 (trans. Shewring).

45. A. Bronze *mušhuššu*-dragon from Samos, height 0.105 m.; B. Bronze figurine of Pazuzu from Assyria, seventh century BC, height 0.146 m.; C. Egyptian figure of Bes; D. Bes on a cylinder seal from Ugarit, Late Bronze Age.

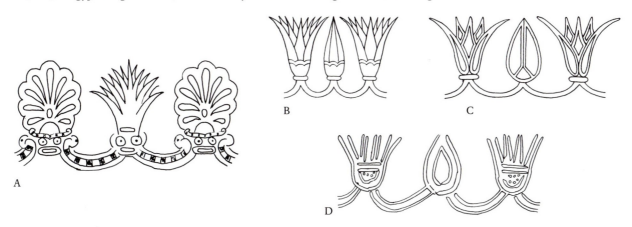

46. Lotus and bud motif: A. Wall painting from the palace of Tukulti-Ninurta I; B. Motif on a threshold slab of Sennacherib, *c.*700 BC; C. Painted decoration on a Corinthian vase, *c.*700 BC; D. Incised decoration on Urartian bronze.

47. Striding, roaring lions: A. Babylonian terracotta plaque, early second millennium BC; B. Painted decoration on a Corinthian aryballos vase; C. Column base from palace of Sennacherib at Nineveh as shown on a sculpture of Ashurbanipal.

Travellers such as these would have transmitted aspects of Mesopotamian culture to the Greeks.[81] However, there is no certainty that works containing Mesopotamian teachings could be consulted in the libraries maintained by Greek tyrants, notably Peisistratos of Athens and Polykrates of Samos,[82] although the archaeological evidence discussed above indicates especially strong ties between Mesopotamia and Samos.

Certain magic and religious rituals probably derive from Mesopotamian ones. Among them are purification rites for individuals and the use of a scapegoat; the practice of burying foundation deposits beneath a building; and various forms of sympathetic magic whereby effigies were used to substitute for the intended victims, or to represent the effects of particular spells;[83] divination by 'lekanomancy', or the examination of liquids poured out on a dish (Greek *lekane*, a word which is cognate with Akkadian *lahannu* and Aramaic *laqnu*); and extispicy, or the inspection of entrails in a sacrificial animal. The last-named practice spread as far as Italy together with the direct translation of Babylonian technical terms. Tatian, a theologian of the second century AD and himself an Assyrian, asserted categorically that Greeks had learnt the art of divination through sacrifice via Cyprus.[84] These rituals go back to the early second millennium in Akkadian texts and had spread from Mesopotamia to Palestine and to the Hittites. From Ephesos comes a Greek inscription on a piece of limestone, dated around the sixth century, recording bird omens: 'If (a particular bird) flying from right to left disappears from view, (the omen is) favourable . . . If, flying from left to right, it disappears on a straight course, unfavourable.'[85] This kind of omen is known from Mesopotamia more than a thousand years earlier, such as: 'If many eagles keep flying over a city, the city will be besieged.'[86] Such omens in cuneiform were col-lected and incorporated into the great Babylonian manual of omens *Šumma ālu*, and would have been used by itinerant seers as well as at the Assyrian court. Both for Greeks and for Babylonians the kind of bird was significant, eagles and herons being especially noteworthy. This 'un-Greek' Greek text appears to be a translation or paraphrase of an older one which ultimately derived from Mesopotamia. It shows that such works, written in Greek, were available. An inscription recounting the oath taken by Greek settlers at the foundation of a colony at Kyrene shows how closely cuneiform and Greek texts can be compared for magical practices:

. . . they moulded wax images and burnt them while they uttered the following imprecation, all of them, having come together, men and women, boys and girls: 'May he, who does not abide by this agreement but transgresses it, melt away and dissolve like the images, himself, his seed, and his progeny.'[87]

Similar spells are known from the Assyrian incantation series *Maqlû*, written on tablets of the neo-Assyrian period: 'Just as these figurines melt, run, and flow away, so may sorcerer and sorceress melt, run, and flow away.'[88] Because certain religious, ritualistic, and magical types of expression were shared, it is not surprising that the accompanying imagery has features in common. Correspondences between particular Mesopotamian divinities or demons and Greek ones are not coincidental, and are occasionally supported by a Greek word which is a phonetic rendering of an Akkadian one. For example, there are connections between the Greek god of medicine Asklepios, who sometimes appeared in dreams as a dog, and was sometimes pictured with a dog, and Gula the Babylonian goddess of healing whose symbol was a dog. Her title *azugallatu* is rendered in Greek as *asgelatas* (note the change of gender).[89] The

[81] W. Burkert, *The Orientalizing Revolution: Near Eastern Influence on Greek Culture in the Early Archaic Period* (Cambridge, Mass., 1992), 1–8.

[82] Athenaios 1.3 a; Aulus Gellius 7. 17. 1; C. Wendel, *Die griechisch-römische Buchbeschreibung verglichen mit der des vorderen Orients* (Halle, 1949), 18–23 for speculation on a Milesian library.

[83] For love spells, see J. C. Petropoulos, 'Sappho the Sorceress', *ZPE* 97 (1993), 43–56.

[84] Tatian, *Oratio ad Graecos* 1. 1 (ed. Whittaker).

[85] C. Börker and R. Merkelbach, *Inschriften griechischer Städte aus Kleinasien, Band 15, Die Inschriften von Ephesos, Teil 5*, no. 1678 (Bonn, 1980).

[86] D. B. Weisberg, 'An Old Babylonian Forerunner to Šumma Ālu', *Hebrew Union College Annual* 40–1 (1969–70), 87–105. See Ch. VI § 2.

[87] R. Meiggs and D. M. Lewis, *Greek Historical Inscriptions*, no. 5 (rev. edn., Oxford, 1989), 5–9, for the translation, A. J. Graham, *Colony and Mother City in Ancient Greece* (Manchester, 1964), 226.

[88] Maqlû 2.146–57; translation from D. R. Hillers, *Treaty Curses and the Old Testament Prophets* (Rome, 1964), 21. See also T. Abusch, 'The Ritual Tablet and Rubrics of Maqlû: Toward the History of the Series', in *Ah, Assyria . . .* , 233–53.

[89] Burkert, *Orientalizing Revolution*, 75–9.

names of the Greek spirits Gello and Lamia transcribe the Akkadian *gallu* and *lamaštu*.[90]

Purely iconographic transmission has been observed. The giant Humbaba, who appears in the *Epic of Gilgamesh*, has been associated with a series of masks that appear in Tiryns and Sparta, as well as the Levant, Cyprus, and Egypt. They were probably hung outside houses above doorways according to Mesopotamian and Phoenician custom.[91] The wrinkled, grimacing face contributed to the development of the standard representation of the Gorgon in Greek art, perhaps influenced also by the iconography of the Mesopotamian *pazuzu*-demon.[92] A Greek sculpture from Selinunte in Sicily is one example of how Perseus, like Gilgamesh, is occasionally depicted slaying a Humbaba-like figure representing Medusa (again note the change of gender). The name of the Egyptian Bes figure, with whom the Greek masks have also been connected, is now recognized as an Akkadian word meaning 'dwarf', and may have entered Egyptian iconography from Mesopotamia in the Amarna period.[93] One-eyed monsters like the Cyclops Polyphemos appear on Mesopotamian seals,[94] and the nine-headed hydra killed by Herakles resembles many-headed creatures known in Mesopotamian myth and art, his series of labours in literature being comparable with the series of deeds of the Sumerian god Ninurta in early cuneiform texts, deeds later appropriated by the god Nergal.[95]

It is not surprising that some Mesopotamian traits and borrowings are embedded within early Greek poetry in both form and content. Wandering divines could also be wandering singers, since Greeks thought song was a prophetic gift bestowed by the gods. Some literary works were sung; their introductions, 'I shall sing', both in Babylonian and in Greek, show that this was so; even the bawdy subject-matter and style of the Mesopotamian *aluzinnu*-entertainers and of the Greek iambic poets are very similar.[96] Epic elements in Homeric poetry with Mesopotamian antecedents include extended similes, alternation between divine and human settings, the importance of dreams and prophecies, the use of long speeches with formulaic passages, and the humorous portrayal of argumentative gods. Close comparisons have been made between Gilgamesh and Achilles, between the episode in which the hero laments the death of his friend and companion Enkidu, and the killing of Patroklos.[97] The catalogue of Zeus' lovers in the same epic may depend on a similar catalogue of Ishtar's lovers in the sixth tablet of *Gilgamesh*, and the metamorphosis of the latter may reflect an early belief in the transmigration of souls.[98] Just as excerpts from the *Epic of Gilgamesh* were used in magical incantations, so were extracts from the *Iliad* used in the Greek magical papyri. The Greek epic *Kypria* (a title suggesting the importance of Cyprus in the transmission of Mesopotamian myth) begins with the motif that the gods planned to reduce human population,[99] which is the underlying theme of the *Epic of Atrahasis*, written in cuneiform in the Middle Bronze Age but still popular in the Assyrian period. The *Epic of Atrahasis* also has clear antecedents for Poseidon's description of the division of the world among the gods by lot in the *Iliad*.[100] The legend of Etana bears a resemblance to the story of Ganymede, known already to the poet of the *Iliad*, in that both were carried up to heaven by an eagle.[101]

The *Works and Days* and the *Theogony* of Hesiod also display elements derived from Mesopotamian poetry, not surprisingly since the poet's father came from Kyme on the west coast of Anatolia. Like several Sumerian and Babylonian accounts of creation in which a succession of gods is born from Sky and Earth, Hesiod's poems tell of successive divine generations springing from Ouranos and Gaia. In the *Works and Days* Hesiod passes on agricultural advice, a tradition of instructional poetry

[90] D. R. West, 'Gello and Lamia: Two Hellenic Daemons of Semitic Origin', *Ugarit-Forschungen* 23 (1991), 359–68.

[91] C. Faraone, *Talismans and Trojan Horses: Guardian Statues in Ancient Greek Myth and Ritual* (Oxford, 1992).

[92] J. B. Carter, 'The Masks of Ortheia', *AJ Arch.* 91 (1987), 355–83.

[93] F. A. M. Wiggermann, 'Mischwesen B', *RlA* viii. 254.

[94] M. Knox, 'Polyphemos and his Near Eastern Relations', *JHS* 99 (1979), 164–5.

[95] C. Bonnet and C. Jourdain-Annequin (eds.), *Heracles* (Rome, 1992).

[96] M. L. West, 'Some Oriental Motifs in Archilochus', *ZPE* 102 (1994), 1–5.

[97] Extensive comparisons are made in M. L. West, *The East Face of Helicon* (Oxford, 1997).   [98] *Iliad* 14. 313–28.

[99] *Kypria*, frag. 1 (ed. M. Davies, *Epicorum graecorum fragmenta*, Göttingen, 1988).

[100] 15. 185–95.   [101] 5. 265–7; 20. 231–5.

48. A. Gilgamesh and Enkidu slay
Humbaba, shown on a cylinder seal;
B. Middle Bronze Age stone head of
Humbaba from temple at Tell al-
Rimah; C. Bronze band of decoration
from a shield from Olympia; D. Perseus
and the Gorgon, sculpture from
Selinunte in Sicily, 575–550 BC.

with predecessors in Sumerian and Akkadian literature.[102] The poem also identifies appropriate and inappropriate actions for particular days, a type of literature which already had a long history in Mesopotamia.[103]

Written proverbs and animal fables also have Near Eastern precursors which are a thousand years earlier in cuneiform, and there are dicta common to Mesopotamian writings and the works of early Greek lyric poets. Thus the advice of Shamshi-Adad I (c.1813–1781) to his son recalls a Greek proverb known to Archilochos:

[102] M. L. West (ed.), *Hesiod: Works and Days* (Oxford, 1978), 3–30.
[103] R. Labat, 'Hemerologien', *RlA* iv (1972–5). Hesiod was also credited with a work on astronomy: H. Diels and W. Kranz

(eds.), *Die Fragmente der Vorsokratiker* no. 4 (Berlin, 1951), 38, and is connected with a bird omen at Nineveh, Hes. fr.364. Cf. Aristotle, *Historia Animalium* 601ᵇ3.

The bitch in her haste gave birth to blind ones.
The bitch in haste bears blind ones.[104]

Compare too a proverb cited in an Assyrian letter with one allegedly quoted by the fifth-century Spartan general Lysander to his troops:

The man who seized the tail of a lion sank in the river. / He who seized the tail of a fox was saved[105]

For where the lion-skin does not reach, there the fox-skin must be attached.[106]

Aesop's use and popularizing of the animal fable comes from Mesopotamian tradition, and is closely associated with Ahiqar, whose connections with the late Assyrian court are discussed in Chapter VII. Likewise the beast fables of other Greek authors, such as Semonides of Amorgos, stem from the East.[107]

It was not only their themes that singers in Mesopotamia and Greece had in common. Certain Greek musical instruments also have Mesopotamian origins, including the lyre, harp, lute, drum, and cymbals, all with their analogues in the modern recital hall. The so-called Pythagorean system of tuning was formalized and written down in Mesopotamia in the Middle Bronze Age, and presumably travelled to Greece with the relevant instruments.[108] But cuneiform evidence does not yet substantiate the assertion of Iamblichos that musical proportion was a Babylonian discovery which reached Greece through Pythagoras.[109]

The Greeks also believed that their mathematical knowledge derived from Babylonian sources. Herodotos is at pains to argue that, in his view, the Greek system of mathematical survey and land-measurement derived from Egypt rather than Mesopotamia, as others had presumably suggested.[110] Since the works of the most famous pre-Euclidean Greek mathematicians have not survived extant, the Greek debt to Mesopotamian mathematics cannot be assessed

adequately. It may, however, be assumed that, by the sixth century, Thales and Pythagoras knew the essential elements of Babylonian mathematics, as a result of having travelled in Mesopotamia or Egypt. Many key mathematical texts in cuneiform were compiled before 612 BC, often using much older sources.

With the fall of Nineveh in 612 BC, there is no need to suppose a diminution in contacts between the Greek world and Mesopotamia. Herodotos thought that the seat of power was transferred deliberately from Nineveh to Babylon without a change of dynasty. As far as we can tell, the successors to the neo-Assyrian empire built upon foundations laid by their predecessors.

The Neo-Babylonian Period (612–539 BC)

Written sources in Akkadian and Greek continue to document regular traffic between Mesopotamians and Greeks, although no royal accounts of campaigns survive in Akkadian for this period. The brother of the lyric poet Alkaios of Lesbos served as a soldier in the Babylonian army during Nebuchadnezzar's siege of Ashkelon in 604 BC;[111] no doubt there were other Greek mercenaries. Cuneiform sources record local traders in Babylon importing bronze, iron, and purple wool, all described as having come from 'Ionia'.[112] Among craftsmen living at Babylon are 'Ionian' carpenters and one whose profession is not understood; since none of their names seems to be satisfactorily rendered into Greek, it has been suggested that these 'Ionians' were Anatolians from western Asia Minor or Cilicia, both areas with significant Hellenic associations. The combination of a non-Greek name with the ethnic description 'the Ionian' may indicate descent from a mixed marriage.[113]

[104] W. L. Moran, 'An Assyriological Gloss on the New Archilochus Fragment', *Harvard Studies in Classical Philology* 82 (1978), 17–19.   [105] Plutarch, *Lysander* 7. 4.

[106] B. Alster, 'An Akkadian Animal Proverb and the Assyrian Letter ABL 555', *JCS* 41 (1989), 187–93.

[107] B. E. Perry, *Aesopica: A Series of Texts relating to Aesop or Ascribed to him or Closely Connected with the Literary Tradition that Bears his Name* (Urbana, Ill., 1952); H. Lloyd-Jones, *Females of the Species* (London, 1975).

[108] O. R. Gurney, 'Babylonian Music Again', *Iraq* 56 (1994), 101–6.

[109] *In Nicomachi arithmeticam introductionem* 118. 23.

[110] 2.109. J. Høyrup, '*Dynamis*, the Babylonians and Theaetetus

147c—148 d 7', *Historia Mathematica* 17 (1990), 63–86; and 'Subscientific Mathematics: Undercurrents and Missing Links in the Mathematical Technology of the Hellenistic and Roman World', *Filosofi og videnskabsteori pa Roskilde Universitetscenter*, 3. Raekke: Preprints og Reprints no. 3 (1990).

[111] D. L. Page, *Sappho and Alcaeus* (Oxford, 1955) 223–4 for the fragments and argument.

[112] A. L. Oppenheim, 'Essay on Overland Trade in the First Millennium BC', *JCS* 21 (1967), 236–54. Much later, the Edict of Diocletian shows that Miletos produced purple dye.

[113] Cf. J. N. Coldstream, 'Mixed Marriages at the Frontiers of the Early Greek World', *Oxford Journal of Archaeology* 12 (1993), 89–107.

If the Greek tradition that the lawgiver Solon travelled outside Athens for ten years is true,[114] he may have become conversant with Mesopotamian traditions abroad. This would explain why his annulment of debts in Athens in the early sixth century is so similar to Mesopotamian practice. Although there are Levantine parallels for such an edict, the practice is essentially a Mesopotamian one, known from the Middle Bronze Age and revived in neo-Assyrian times.[115] At this period Babylonian scribes were still trained using Hammurabi's law code as a set text. Around the same time in Crete the law code of Gortyn was recorded on a public stone monument, and it echoes in both format and contents laws from the time of Hammurabi. In particular, for its themes dealing with marriage, property and adoption, in its references to lawcourts, witnesses, oaths taken before a deity, and in being written on stone for public viewing, it suggests a Mesopotamian inheritance. For example, the following law reads like an adaptation of a Babylonian law:

If a man died leaving children, should the wife so desire, she may remarry holding her own property and whatever her (first) husband might have given her according to what is written in the presence of three free, adult witnesses.[116]

As before, Greeks encountered Mesopotamians throughout the east Mediterranean. A cuneiform text dated to 568/7 records a battle between an Egyptian army under Amasis, whose allies probably included Greeks from Kyrene and Cyprus, and a Babylonian force under Nebuchadnezzar.[117] The Pharaoh Apries (589–570), who favoured Greek mercenaries within his army, was an ally of Nebuchadnezzar II by 567 BC.[118] Herodotos writes that in Anatolia 'Labynetos of Babylon', a son of Nebuchadnezzar II, mediated between the Lydians and the Medes in a battle that took place in 585 BC.[119] Similarly, Kroisos of Lydia (560–547), perhaps the grandson of Gyges, made alli-ances with both Spartans and Babylonians against Persia.[120] Such alliances, as before, required the service of translators to deal with foreign messengers and to enable written agreements to be drawn up and oaths recorded. It was not unusual for Mesopotamians to be found in Anatolia, for Samsat and Malatya, both on the upper Euphrates, were major Assyrian administrative centres; and Nabonidus, the last Chaldaean king of Babylon, rebuilt the temple of the moon-god in Harran.

Among pre-Socratic Ionian philosophers said to have been especially acquainted with Babylonian culture were Thales and Anaximander of Miletos,[121] Pythagoras of Samos, Pherekydes of Syros,[122] and Kleostratos of Tenedos.[123] The fame of Thales was particularly widespread, even in later Antiquity among Arab chroniclers, since he had predicted an eclipse in a battle between the Lydians and Medes.[124] Anaximander 'invented' the shadow-clock (gnomon) long used in Babylon as an aid to practical astronomy, and set up a sundial in or near Sparta.[125] His map of the world may have resembled the cuneiform world map of the late eighth or early seventh century,[126] for when Herodotos ridiculed Greek map-makers who 'show Ocean running like a river round a perfectly circular earth', he was unaware that they were following Mesopotamian tradition.[127] The assumption was widespread in Antiquity that the knowledge and training of the earliest Greek philosophers derived from so-called 'Chaldaean' wise men, and their east Greek origins make transmission likely: east Greek ports, notably Miletos and Samos, Smyrna and Ephesos, as well as Cilician cities, must have been centres for the dissemination of Mesopotamian influence in addition to Cyprus, Rhodes, and Crete. Translation was commonplace: the trilingual inscription from Xanthos shows Aramaic, Greek, and Lycian versions of a text side by side, and the Assyrian palace sculptures show scribes working side by side writing Akkadian and

---

[114] e.g. Plutarch, *Solon* 25. 5.

[115] J. N. Postgate, *Early Mesopotamia* (London, 1992), 195; F. R. Kraus, *Königliche Verfügungen in altbabylonische Zeit* (Leiden, 1984); N. Lemche, 'Andurarum and Mišarum: Comments on the Problem of Social Edicts and their Applications in the Near East', *JNES* 38 (1979), 11–22.

[116] R. F. Willetts, *The Lawcode of Gortyn* (Berlin 1967).

[117] A. T. Reyes, *Archaic Cyprus* (Oxford, 1994), 75 for the text.

[118] A. Leahy, 'The Earliest Dated Monument of Amasis and the End of the Reign of Apries', *Journal of Egyptian Archaeology* 74 (1988), 183–99.

[119] 1. 74; W. Röllig, 'Erwägungen zu neuen Stelen König Nabonids', *Zeitschrift für Assyriologie* 56 (1964), 239.

[120] Herodotos 1. 69. 3; 77. 2; 3. 47. 1–2.

[121] e.g. Herodotos 2. 109; Diogenes Laertios 2. 1–2

[122] e.g. Josephos, *Contra Apionem* 1. 2.

[123] e.g. Pliny, *Natural History* 2. 31

[124] Herodotos 1. 74, J. N. Mattock, 'Islam', in K. J. Dover (ed.), *Perceptions of the Ancient Greeks* (Oxford, 1992), 92.

[125] Diogenes Laertios 2. 1. See Ch. VI § 1b.

[126] See Ch. VIII, p. 177.

[127] 4. 36. 2. W. Horowitz, 'The Babylonian Map of the World', *Iraq* 50 (1988), 147–65.

Aramaic versions of a single text. In such places some parts of scribal training must have been carried out in two languages and two alphabets, or two writing systems, as they had been in the Late Bronze Age even before alphabets were adopted.[128]

Nebuchadnezzar became a famous legendary figure to later Greeks, but the legends developed largely under the influence of biblical rather than Mesopotamian tradition. As a result of his fame, a Greek source used by Josephos attributed to him a reputation as a builder, responsible for the massive circuit walls of Babylon and the 'Hanging Gardens', one of the seven wonders of the world. In fact an earlier Assyrian tradition had become confused and attributed wrongly to Babylon.[129] It is remarkable that more stories about the Assyrians than about the Babylonians were known to the Greeks, and this may imply that contacts were closer in the seventh than in the early sixth century.

Babylon fell to Cyrus II, king of Persia, in 539 BC. By the early fifth century, Greeks were at war with Persia. Such overt hostilities, it might be thought, would have curtailed contact with Mesopotamia. But that, as the following chapter shows, was not the case.

---

[128] See Ch. VII, pp. 141–2.
[129] S. Dalley, 'Nineveh, Babylon and the Hanging Gardens: Cuneiform and Classical Sources Reconciled', *Iraq* 56 (1994), 45–58.

FURTHER READING

1. Introduction

BOTTÉRO, J., *Mesopotamia* (Chicago, 1987), 26–40.
CAH² et al.
HOLZHEY, K., *Assur und Babel in der Kenntnis der griechisch-römischen Welt* (Freising and Munich, 1921).
WEST, M. L., *The East Face of Helicon* (Oxford, 1997).

2. From the Third Millennium to c.1500 BC

CLINE, E. H., *Sailing the Wine-Dark Sea: International Trade and the Late Bronze Age Aegean* (BAR International Series 591, Oxford, 1994).
DICKINSON, O. T. P., *The Aegean Bronze Age* (Cambridge, 1994).
HUXLEY, G. L., 'Kythera and the Minoan Maritime Economy', in Academica Belgica, Istituto per la Civiltà Fenicia e Punica, *Atti del Convegno Internazionale 'Moventi Precoloniali nel Mediterraneo Antico'* (Rome, 1988), 65–71.
KLENGEL, H., 'Near-Eastern Trade and the Emergence of Interaction with Crete in the Third Millennium BC', *Studi Micenei ed Egeo-Anatolici* 24 (1984), 7–19.
PETRUSO, K. M., *Keos 8: Ayia Irini: The Balance Weights* (Mainz, 1992).
SCHMANDT-BESSERAT, D., *Before Writing* (Austin, Tex., 1992).

3. The Late Bronze Age (c.1500–1100 BC)

BECKMAN, G. M., 'Mesopotamians and Mesopotamian Learning at Hattusa', *JCS* 35 (1983), 97–114.
CARTLEDGE, P., *Sparta and Lakonia: A Regional History 1300–362 BC* (London, 1979).
CHADWICK, J., *The Mycenaean World* (Cambridge, 1976).
CLINE, E. H., *Sailing the Wine-Dark Sea* (Oxford, 1994).

DAVIES, A. M., 'The Linguistic Evidence', in G. Cadogan (ed.), *The End of the Early Bronze Age in the Aegean* (Leiden, 1986), 93–123.
DUHOUX, Y., 'Les Contacts entre Mycéniens et barbares d'après le vocabulaire du Linéaire B', *Minos* 23 (1988), 75–83.
GURNEY, O. R., 'Hittite Geography: Thirty Years on', in H. Otten et al. (eds.), *Hittite and other Anatolian and Near Eastern Studies in Honour of Sedat Alp* (Ankara, 1992), 213–21.
JANSEN, H. G., 'Troy: Legend and Reality', in J. M. Sasson (ed.), *The Civilizations of the Ancient Near East* (New York, 1995), ii. 1121–34.
HANKEY, V., 'Egypt, the Aegean, and the Levant', *Egyptian Archaeology* 3 (1993), 27–9.
LAMBROU-PHILLIPSON, C., *Hellenorientalia* (Goteborg, 1990).
LAROCHE, E., 'Luwier, Luwisch, Lu(w)iya', *RlA* vi (1987–90), 181–4.
MACQUEEN, J. G., 'The History of the Hittite Empire: An Overview', in J. M. Sasson (ed.), *Civilizations of the Ancient Near East* (New York, 1995), ii. 1085–106.
MORAN, W. L., *The Amarna Letters* (Baltimore, 1992).
VAN DEN HOUT, T. P. J., 'Khattushili III, king of the Hittites', in J. M. Sasson (ed.), *The Civilizations of the Ancient Near East* (New York, 1995), ii. 1107–20.

4. The Early Iron Age (c.1100–900 BC)

CROWLEY, J. L., *The Aegean and the East* (Jonsered, 1989).
DOTHAN, T., and DOTHAN, M., *People of the Sea: The Search for the Philistines* (New York, 1992).
HAWKINS, J. D., 'Karkamish and Karatepe: Neo-Hittite City-States in North Syria', in J. M. Sasson et al, (ed.), *Civilizations of the Ancient Near East* (New York, 1995), ii. 1295–307.

IKEDA, Y., 'Assyrian Kings and the Mediterranean Sea: The Twelfth to Ninth Centuries BC', *Abr-Nahrain* 23 (1984–5), 23–31.

KANTOR, H. J., *The Aegean and the Orient in the Second Millennium* BC (Bloomington, Ind., 1947).

KAPLAN, P., 'The Development of Goldwork at Lefkandi on the Island of Euboia from the Eleventh to the Ninth Centuries BC', M.Phil. thesis, Oxford University (Oxford, 1990).

KOPCKE, G., and TOKUMARU, I. (eds.), *Greece Between East and West: Tenth to Eighth Centuries BC* (Mainz, 1992).

NEGBI, O., 'Early Phoenician Presence in the Mediterranean Islands', *AJ Arch.* 96 (1992), 599–615.

STEVENSON-SMITH, W., *Interconnections in the Ancient Near East* (New Haven and London, 1965).

5. The Neo-Assyrian Period (*c.*900–612 BC)

BARNETT, R. D., 'Oriental Influences on Archaic Greece', in *The Aegean and the Near East: Studies Presented to Hetty Goldman* (Locust Valley, NY, 1956), 212–38.

BURKERT, W., 'Homerstudien und Orient', in J. Latacz (ed.), *Zweihundert Jahre Homer-Forschung: Rückblick und Ausblick* (Stuttgart and Leipzig, 1991), 155–81.

FARAONE, C., 'Molten Wax, Spilt Wine, and Mutilated Animals: Sympathetic Magic in Near Eastern and Early Greek Oath Ceremonies', *JHS* 113 (1993), 60–80.

GERMAIN, G., *Genèse de l'Odyssée* (Paris, 1954)

GRESSETH, G. K., 'The Gilgamesh Epic and Homer', *CJ* 70 (1975), 1–18.

GUNTER, A. C., 'Models of the Orient in the Art History of the Orientalizing Period', in H. Sancisi-Weerdenburg and H. W. Drijvers (eds.), *Achaemenid History, V: The Roots of the European Tradition* (Leiden, 1990), 131–47.

GURALNICK, E., 'East to West: Near Eastern Artifacts from Greek Sites', in D. Charpin and F. Joannès (eds.), *La Circulation des biens, des personnes et des idées dans le Proche-Orient ancien* (Paris, 1992), 327–40.

HELM, P. R., '"Greeks" in the Neo-Assyrian Levant and "Assyria" in Early Greek Writers', Ph.D. thesis, University of Pennsylvania (Philadelphia, 1980; Ann Arbor microfilms).

KOENEN, L., 'Greece, the Near East, and Egypt: Cyclic Destruction in Hesiod' *Transactions of the American Philosophical Association* 124 (1994), 1–34.

LIVERANI, M., 'The Trade Network of Tyre According to Ezekiel 27', in M. Cogan and I. Eph'al (eds.), *Ah, Assyria, . . . Studies in Assyrian History and Ancient Near Eastern Historiography Presented to Hayim Tadmor* (Jerusalem, 1991), 65–79.

MORRIS, S. P., *Daidalos and the Origins of Greek Art* (Princeton, 1992).

ODED, B., *Mass Deportation and Deportees in the Neo-Assyrian Empire* (Wiesbaden, 1979).

PENGLASE, C., *Greek Myths and Mesopotamia* (London, 1994).

PURCELL, N., 'Mobility and the Polis', in O. Murray and S. Price (eds.), *The Greek City* (Oxford, 1990), 29–58.

UNGNAD, A., *Gilgamesch-Epos und Odysee* (Breslau, 1923), repr. in K. Oberhuber (ed.), *Das Gilgamesch-Epos* (Wege der Forschung 215, Darmstadt 1977), 104–37.

WALCOT, P., *Hesiod and the Near East* (Cardiff, 1966).

WEST, D. R., 'Some Minoan and Hellenic Goddesses of Semitic Origin', *Ugarit-Forschungen* 23 (1991), 369–81.

WEST, M. L., 'The Ascription of Fables to Aesop in Archaic and Classical Greece', in *La Fable* (Fondation Hardt, Geneva, 1984), 105–36.

—— 'The Rise of the Greek Epic', *JHS* 108 (1988), 151–72.

—— *Ancient Greek Music* (Oxford, 1992).

—— 'The Date of the Iliad', *MH* 52 (1995), 203–19.

WILLIAMS, R. J., 'The Literary History of a Mesopotamian Fable', *Phoenix* 10 (1956), 70–7.

6. The Neo-Babylonian Period

BURKERT, W., 'Iranisches bei Anaximandros', *Rheinisches Museum für Philologie* 106 (1963), 97–134.

—— *Lore and Science in Ancient Pythagoreanism* (Cambridge, Mass., 1972).

—— 'Orientalische und griechische Weltmodelle von Assur bis Anaximandros', *Wiener Studien* 107/8 (1994/5), 179–86.

DILKE, O. A. W., *Greek and Roman Maps* (London, 1985).

FRAME, G., *Babylonia, 689–627 BC: A Political History* (Istanbul and Leiden, 1992).

HOROWITZ, W., 'The Babylonian Map of the World', *Iraq* 50 (1988), 147–65.

KIRK, G. S., *et al.*, *The Presocratic Philosophers* (2d edn., Cambridge, 1983).

RÖLLIG, W., 'Landkarten', *RlA* vi (Berlin, 1980–3).

SACK, R. H., *Images of Nebuchadnezzar* (Selinsgrove, 1991).

WEST, M. L., 'Ab Ovo, Orpheus, Sanchuniathon and the Origins of the Ionian World Model', *CQ* 44 (1994), 289–307.

V

MESOPOTAMIAN CONTACT AND INFLUENCE IN THE GREEK WORLD

2. Persia, Alexander, and Rome

STEPHANIE DALLEY AND A. T. REYES

The Achaemenid Period (539–330 BC)

IN THE ACHAEMENID PERIOD THE NATURE OF the evidence for contact and influence between the Greek and Mesopotamian worlds changes. Contemporary Greek histories and records survive, making it possible to document more fully interaction throughout the Near East and Mesopotamia from a Greek point of view. To this interaction the Persian Wars posed no obstacles. Archaeological excavations have found no discernible break in the material records of relevant sites in Cilicia or along the Levant, and written sources show that the overland routes from the Mediterranean into Mesopotamia and Iran remained open.[1] During this period of over two hundred years, indigenous Babylonian religion and literature, far from being overlaid by Persian practices, actually flourished with royal patronage, and were widely admired for their antiquity and sophistication. Élitist education in cuneiform continued to produce scholars, although their achievements are hard to trace because archaeologists have not yet found a large library of this period, and because individual scholars were still not acknowledged by name as they

were in Greece. This was to begin to change when Alexander reached Babylon.

The range of Greek areas potentially in contact with Mesopotamia may be gauged by the mints of Greek coins found in Babylonia. These include: Aegina, Aspendos, Athens, Chios, Corinth, Kelenderis, Kyzikos, Lycia, Macedonia, Miletos, Nagidos, Samos, and the Troad.[2] Greeks and Mesopotamians continued to meet in Anatolia, Egypt, and in places further east such as Babylon and Susa, where they worked side by side within the Persian administrative system;[3] at the latter site a bronze model of a knucklebone was found which had previously been dedicated at the temple of Apollo at Didyma.[4] The Persian king regularly spent time in Babylon, where he acted in accordance with local custom,[5] and it is often here that Classical sources report meetings between him and the Greeks, where the latter would have had the opportunity to view Babylonian buildings, customs, and works of art. The busy Royal Road ran overland through Sardis, past Babylon and onwards to Susa and Pasargadae, but there were other routes too: the Athenian general Konon 'sailed into Cilicia and from there, having travelled to Thapsakos (perhaps

[1] Herodotos 6. 24; 6. 70; 7. 3; 7. 6; A. Yardeni, 'Maritime Trade and Royal Accountancy in an Erased Customs Account from 475 BCE on the Ahiqar Scroll from Elephantine', *Bulletin of the American Schools for Oriental Research* 293 (1994), 67–78.

[2] For coin hoards from Mesopotamia, J. Elayi and A. G. Elayi, *Trésors de monnaies phéniciennes et circulation monétaire* (Paris, 1993), 268–77.

[3] D. M. Lewis, *Sparta and Persia* (Leiden, 1977); Herodotos 5. 52–4 on the road from Sardis to Susa.

[4] J. Boardman, *The Greeks Overseas* (rev. edn. London, 1980), 108.

[5] A. Kuhrt, 'Usurpation, Conquest, and Ceremonial: From Babylon to Persia', in D. Cannadine and S. Price (eds.), *Rituals of Royalty: Power and Ceremonial in Traditional Societies* (Cambridge, 1987) 20–55. Note Xenophon, *Cyropaedia* 4. 4. 10 in which Cyrus tells the conquered peoples that 'nothing different whatsoever will happen to you' and 8. 6. 22 stating that the king spent seven months of the year at Babylon.

49. Bronze knucklebone dedicated
to Apollo at Didyma, found at Susa.
Height 0.23 m. Weight c. 200 lb.

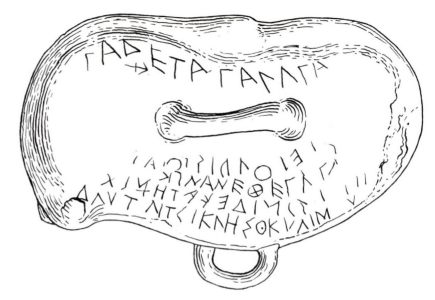

Mas'oudiye) in Syria, sailed down the Euphrates river into Babylon'.[6] Mass deportation by Persian kings brought Greeks to live in Mesopotamia: to Susa, to Ampe near the Tigris after the sack of Miletos in 496, and to 'Arderikka, in the land of Kissia', 60 kilometres north of Susa.[7] Perhaps more influential were Greek mercenaries such as those who fought with Xenophon and returned home with tales of foreign cities.

A few cuneiform inscriptions mention Greeks and Mesopotamians together, but in general the Babylonian sources are less informative than the Greek. A text mentions payments in which Ionians in Sippar are involved.[8] The Foundation Charters of Susa note that cedar, brought from the west, was transported via Babylon to Susa by Ionians among others, presumably living or stationed in Babylon.[9] The Charters also record that Babylonian and Ionian artisans worked at the palace in charge of baked bricks,[10] implying the use of mathematics in calculating brickwork, which the Babylonians had developed to a sophisticated level about two thousand years earlier.[11] Since by that time Aramaic was the *lingua franca* of

the whole of the Near East, some forms of Mesopotamian learning would have been available in Aramaic. About Babylonians in Greek cities we have no comparable evidence.

Since the Persian king adopted the paraphernalia of his imperial predecessors, Greeks would have identified certain practices or objects as Persian rather than Mesopotamian. Artistic motifs taken over by the Persians were adopted by Greek artists who, in assimilating Persian styles, were in fact perpetuating old, Mesopotamian imagery.[12] For example, a group of seals cut in a Graeco-Persian style adopts devices that already had a long history in Assyrian and Babylonian art.[13] Fashionable affectations used by Greeks of this time included parasols[14] and an over-garment called an *ependutes* (literally a pull-over).[15] These the Greeks thought of as Persian, whereas in fact the former had been adopted from the ceremonial trappings of the Assyrian monarch, while the latter was probably Babylonian in origin. Aischylos could speak of the Persian king driving a 'Syrian' chariot and the image he has in mind derives from the famous Assyrian motif, adopted by the Persians, showing the king

[6] Diodoros 14. 81. 4.

[7] Herodotos 6. 20 and 119. 3–4.

[8] J. Brinkman, 'The Akkadian Words for "Ionia" and "Ionian"', in R. F. Sutton (ed.), *Daidalikon*, (Wauconda Ill., 1989), 63; R. Zadok, 'On Some Foreign Population Groups in First-Millennium Babylonia', *Tel Aviv* 6 (1979), 169.

[9] W. J. Vogelsang, *The Rise and Organisation of the Achaemenid Empire* (Leiden, 1992), 132–4.

[10] V. Scheil, 'Inscriptions des Achéménides à Suse', in *Mémoires de la Mission Archéologique de Perse*, xxi (Paris, 1929), 8–9, ll. 37–8; ibid. xxiv (Paris, 1933), III, ll. 45–6.

[11] M. A. Powell, 'Masse und Gewichte', *RlA* vii (1987–90), 490–1.

[12] M. C. Miller, 'Perserie: The Arts of the East in Fifth-Century Athens', Ph.D thesis, Harvard University (Cambridge, Mass., 1985).

[13] J. Boardman, 'Pyramidal Stamp Seals in the Persian Empire', *Iran* 8 (1970), 19–45.

[14] M. C. Miller, 'The Parasol: An Oriental Status-Symbol in Late Archaic and Classical Athens', *JHS* 112 (1992), 91–105.

[15] M. C. Miller, 'The *Ependytes* in Classical Athens', *Hesperia* 58 (1989), 313–29.

50. Mesopotamian themes on Greek seals.

pursuing his quarry in a chariot.[16] Babylonian textiles reached the Greek mainland as they may have done earlier, conveying Mesopotamian designs as well as contributing to the reputation of Mesopotamia for finery and extravagance.[17]

One result of the Persians conquering Babylon was that the Greeks saw the Persian empire as the natural inheritor of Mesopotamian traditions, and in trying to understand Persia they looked to its predecessors in the Assyrian and Babylonian empires. Herodotos, whose promised work on Assyrian history is not extant, was not the first Greek student of Assyriology, for Hekataios of Miletos certainly referred to the geography of Mesopotamia and incorporated genealogies in his writings, rather in the style of Mesopotamian king-lists.[18] Hellanikos of Lesbos, Charon of Lampsakos, Xanthos of Lydia, and Dionysios of Miletos, whatever their precise chronological relationships to Herodotos, also wrote works touching on Assyrian and Babylonian history, of which no text survives.

Despite the regularity of contact over the previous centuries, the terms Syrian, Assyrian, Babylonian, or Chaldaean were still used either for their specific meaning or else as generic words for any Near Easterner. This confusion would persist in Classical literature through Roman times into modern usage,

but the Greeks are only partly to blame, for the last Chaldaean king of Babylon had left inscriptions at Harran which implied that kings of Assyria and Babylon came from a single dynasty. Thus Herodotos tended to use the terms Assyrian and Babylonian synonymously. When Classical writers speak of Assyrian letters, they are thought to refer, except in a few instances, to the Aramaic script rather than to cuneiform writing.[19] The distinction between (Persian) Magi and Chaldaean Sages was frequently confused too, since the word Magi could be used to mean any eastern priest—magician.

Although there are inaccuracies in Herodotos' report on Babylon and Babylonian customs, much has eventually been confirmed by cuneiform sources.[20] His stories, despite their Hellenic veneer, contain authentic Mesopotamian material. For example, he is accused of never having visited Babylon, since he describes the city as square, rather than as the irregular quadrilateral that is clear from the archaeological excavations there. But Esarhaddon too describes Babylon as a square in a cuneiform inscription, so Herodotos may simply have followed archival tradition here.[21] In the episode recounting Darius' recapture of Babylon he records the taunt of a Babylonian soldier against the Persians: 'for you will take us at the time when mules give birth.' This phrase reflects

[16] Aesch. *Pers.* 84. The same image is at work in 52–4, describing the Babylonians in Xerxes' army.

[17] Athenaios 2. 48b; Pliny, *Natural History* 8. 48; note also Athenaios 15. 692c–d on the luxury of Babylonian perfume.

[18] S. West, 'Herodotus' Portrait of Hecataeus', *JHS* 111 (1991), 144–60.

[19] R. Schmitt, 'Assyria Grammata und Ähnliche: Was wussten die Griechen von Keilschrift und Keilschriften?', in C. W. Müller *et al.* (eds.), *Zum Umgang mit Fremden Sprachen in der Griechisch-Römischen Antike* (Stuttgart, 1992), 21–35. Cf. Herodotos 4. 87, where the phrase refers to Persian cuneiform.

[20] e.g. J. MacGinnis, 'Ctesias and the Fall of Nineveh', *Illinois Classical Studies* 13 (1988), 37–41; S. Dalley, 'Nineveh, Babylon and the Hanging Gardens: Cuneiform and Classical Sources Reconciled', *Iraq* 56 (1994), 45–58; but see R. Rollinger, *Herodots babylonischer Logos* (Innsbruck, 1993), with D. Fehling, *Herodotos and his 'Sources'* (Leeds, 1989), for a different view. Cf. W. K. Pritchett, *The Liar School of Herodotos* (Gieben, Amsterdam, 1993), and Dalley's review of Rollinger in *Orientalistische Literaturzeitung*, 91 (1996), 526–31.

[21] A. R. George, *Babylonian Topographical Texts* (Leuven, 1992), 345 with refs.

the type of birth-omen found in the Akkadian manual *Šumma izbu*:

> If a ewe gives birth to a lion, and it has no right eye, the city will be taken by means of a breach.[22]

His account of how girls had to prostitute themselves for Mylitta once in their lifetime has been substantiated in cuneiform texts.[23] He was mainly concerned with recent history and with recounting those features alien to the Greeks: geography, building traditions, court legends, and strange customs. Irrelevant to his purposes were those features of life and literature that the Greeks and Babylonians had in common. In his time even the recent past had passed into legend, and semi-fictional compositions such as the *Cyropaedia* of Xenophon and the biblical book of Esther were becoming fashionable alongside other court narratives in Aramaic.[24] His account of the Assyrian queens Semiramis and Nitokris (Naqia),[25] and his description of Babylon with its splendid walls, gates, and temples, were formative for the view of Mesopotamia that later writers held.[26]

Ktesias, a Greek doctor living in the Persian court around 390 BC, elaborated on Herodotos' description and tales of Babylonia in the *Persika*.[27] Although he had visited Mesopotamia, his embellishments were often over-imaginative—but so popular that his version of the histories of Ninos, Sardanapalos, and Semiramis became a source of inspiration for later Greek romances and novels. However, recent studies show that he too elaborated upon genuine Assyrian sources, as is shown in the following section. Another genuine theme from Mesopotamian literature is told by Herodotos and taken up in the *Persika* in telling of the origin of Cyrus. It reproduced elements of the folklore concerning Sargon of Agade, abandoned by his parents in a basket of rushes, later to become a gardener and subsequently king.[28] Echoes from Mesopotamian literature have been noted (or disputed) in the works of other Greek authors: for instance,

Aischylos has been thought to have assimilated the cunning nature of Ea into his version of Prometheus.[29]

Later Classical tradition continued to ascribe a Mesopotamian education to Greek scientists and philosophers. It is difficult to see what motives they would have had for claiming such influence if it had not existed, since they were proud of their own traditions and had successfully begun a new vogue for individual, instant authorship and personal writing. The naming of contemporary authors contrasts with the anonymity of ancient Near Eastern literature, which was composed by compilation and redaction and ascribed in many cases to the Seven Sages. Demokritos of Abdera (*fl.* 430 BC), was said to have received instruction from 'Chaldaean Magi' who were left behind at the house of Demokritos' father when Xerxes retreated from Greece in 480 BC; others thought that Demokritos travelled to Babylon in order to learn from the Chaldaeans.[30] He allegedly wrote learned works on Babylonian 'sacred writing' and 'Chaldaean theory', as well as a book on 'Babylonian ethics' which he had copied from the 'pillar of Akikaros', a reference to the sayings of Ahiqar the Assyrian sage. We know that the fame of Ahiqar as a sage had reached Greece by the end of the fourth century, since Theophrastos, a pupil of Aristotle, wrote a work named after Ahiqar.[31]

Definitely reliable as evidence that some Babylonian literature had now reached Greece in translation comes from the work of Damaskios, a Syrian Neoplatonist philosopher of the fifth to sixth century AD.[32] According to him, Eudemos of Rhodes, working in Athens under Aristotle, collected information about Chaldaean beliefs which were incorporated into his *History of Astronomy*. It was probably this work which included an account of the Babylonian *Epic of Creation*,[33] giving the correct names for the Babylonian deities with the occasional mistake that is recognizable as a misreading of a Greek alphabetic letter. A generation, therefore, before the work of

[22] E. Leichty, *The Omen Series Šumma Izbu* no. 35 (Locust Valley, NY, 1970), 76.

[23] G. Wilhelm, 'Marginalien zu Herodot Klio 199', in T. Abusch (ed.), *Lingering over Words, Studies in Near Eastern Literature presented to W. L. Moran* (Atlanta, 1990), 505–24; S. Dalley, 'NIN.LÍL = Mullissu: The Treaty of Barga'yah and Herodotus' Mylitta', *Revue d'Assyriologie* 73 (1979), 73.   [24] See Ch. VII, pp. 146–9.

[25] H. Lewy, 'Nitokris-Naqi'a', *JNES* II (1952), 264–86.

[26] e.g. Aristophanes, *Birds* 552; Dionysios of Halikarnassos 4. 25. 3; Seneca, *Dialogues* 2. 6. 8.

[27] F. W. König, *Die Persika des Ktesias von Knidos* (Graz, 1972);

N. Wilson, *Photius: The Bibliotheca* (London, 1994); J. M. Bigwood, 'Diodorus and Ctesias', *Phoenix* 34 (1980), 195–207; J. Boncquet, 'Ctesias' Assyrian King-List and his Chronology of Mesopotamian History', *Ancient Society* 21 (1990), 5–16.

[28] R. Drews, 'Sargon, Cyrus and Mesopotamian Folk History', *JNES* 33 (1974) 387–93; B. Lewis, *The Sargon Legend* (Cambridge, Mass., 1980).

[29] S. R. West, 'Prometheus Orientalized', *MH* 51 (1994), 129–49.

[30] Diogenes Laertios 9. 34–5.   [31] Ibid. 5. 50.

[32] L. G. Westerink and J. Combès, *Damascius. Traité des premiers principes* (Paris, 1986–91).   [33] See Ch. VIII, p. 164.

Berossos on Babylon became available to the Greeks, Mesopotamian myth and cosmology were being disseminated and studied within the Athenian academy and philosophical schools. According to Simplikios (sixth century AD) Kallisthenes sent to Greece, upon Aristotle's request, 'records of Babylonian observations'.[34] Since such records were normally kept in cuneiform, a translation service from Akkadian to Greek is implied. By this time many records were kept both in Akkadian and in Aramaic within Mesopotamia, and the trilingual inscription from Xanthos in Lycia shows that there were Anatolian cities where Greek and Aramaic were set side by side on public monuments.[35] When Eudoxos of Knidos (c.390–340 BC), a pupil of Plato, stated categorically that Chaldaean horoscopes and predictions were least to be believed,[36] presumably he had read them, and the Greek texts *Brontologia* and *Selenodromia*, on omens derived from thunder and the moon respectively, seem to have been translations from Assyrian originals[37] and were no doubt taken seriously. Therefore the tale that Plato met a Chaldaean astrologer just before he died in 347 BC is not altogether improbable.[38] Pausanias noted: 'But I know that the Chaldaeans and the Magi of India first said that the soul of man is immortal, and by them both the rest of the Greeks and, not least, Plato the son of Ariston, were persuaded.'[39]

When Alexander the Great entered Babylon in 331 BC, therefore, he represented as much the culmination of a process as the beginning of a new era. His choice of Babylon as capital symbolized Hellenic recognition of the place Mesopotamia held in world esteem, and the enormous prestige that accrued to associations with Babylonia and Assyria, especially their writings.

Alexander and his Successors in Babylon (330–c.128 BC)

With Alexander's march to Babylon and the subsequent rule of the Seleucids there, frequent contact

between Greeks and Mesopotamians is self-evident. Greek interest manifested itself in more intense antiquarian research on the history and geography of the area. The poet Kallimachos presumably discussed the Tigris and Euphrates in his work *The Rivers of the World*,[40] and Theophrastos' scientific studies would benefit from the wider knowledge of botanical and geological materials and from the collation of Babylonian works on plants and stones made by colleagues of Aristotle. Alexander's conquests, his avid collecting of knowledge, and his reception of foreign emissaries in Babylonia, brought for the first time a direct national link between Greece and Babylonia. His travels gave rise to the *Alexander Romance* in which episodes from Babylonian epic are mingled with Greek material.[41]

Alexander and the Seleucid kings took part in the customary Babylonian royal rituals, ensuring that these were still kept and studied under royal patronage. The Greek overlords adopted a Mesopotamian style of kingship and participated in the New Year festival (which was actually celebrated at different times of the year in different cities)[42] with its recital of the Babylonian *Epic of Creation*. That Assyrian place-names persisted is reported by the Roman historian Ammianus who noted that although Seleukos Nikator established many cities along the Euphrates, 'nevertheless, they have not lost their first names, which the original settlers gave them·in the Assyrian tongue',[43] and local Greek inscriptions, in giving the new, Greek names, obscure the continuity of tradition. A notable example is Palmyra, known by that name to Greeks and modern tourists, but as Tadmor to Babylonians, Aramaic-speakers, and Arabs. Alexander and the Seleucids maintained the old names of months, cities, and temples in Babylonia, exactly as the Achaemenid kings had done. They made no attempt to turn Babylon, Borsippa, Nippur, or Uruk into Greek cities (*poleis*), but allowed them to continue as before. A large library containing literary and religious texts on cuneiform tablets has been

[34] Kallisthenes, *FGrH* 124 T 3.

[35] See Figs. 68–9 in Ch. VII.

[36] Cicero, *De Divinatione* 2. 42. 87.

[37] C. Bezold and F. Böll, *Reflexe astrologische Keilinschriften bei griechischen Schriftstellern* (Heidelberg, 1911), and Ch. V below.

[38] S. Mekler (ed.), *Academicorum Philosophorum Index Herculanensis* (Berlin, 1902) 13, col. 3: 36, cited in J. Kerschensteiner, *Platon und der Orient* (Stuttgart, 1945), 195, with commentary. Cf. Seneca, *Epistula* 58. 31; Cicero, *De Finibus* 5. 29. 87; Strabo 17. 1. 29; aspects of Babylonian astronomy and astrology may also have been learnt

in Egypt: cf. Ps.-Plato, *Epinomis* 987a; Aristotle, *De Caelo* 292a; *Palatine Anthology* 9. 80 (Leonidas of Alexandria). See also J. Høyrup, 'Dynamis, the Babylonians, and Theaetetos 147c7–148d7', *Historia Mathematica* 17 (1990), 201–22.   [39] 4. 32. 4.

[40] R. Pfeiffer (ed.), *Callimachus* (Oxford, 1949), 351 no. 457–9 for fragments.

[41] See Ch. VIII, pp. 170–1.

[42] G. Çagirgan and W. G. Lambert, 'The Late Babylonian *Kislimu* Ritual for Esagil', *JCS* 43–5 (1991–3), 71–88.

[43] Ammianus Marcellinus 14. 8. 6.

51. Clay tablet with both sides inscribed in Greek, giving a phonetic transcription of a cuneiform text.

52. Graeco-Babylonian tablet giving a Babylonian incantation against evil spirits, with a phonetic transcription in Greek.

recovered from Uruk, and shows that academic pursuits of a traditional kind continued with no sign that they were losing their vigour. From now onwards the names of famous Babylonian scholars appear tantalizingly in the writings of Greek and Roman authors.

Alexander put Harpalos in charge of the treasury in Babylon, and the Ionian Kallinikos is named as a 'herald' in charge of revenues at the temple of Bel in Babylon in 314 BC, a temple post probably taken over from the Achaemenid bureaucracy which had conducted its business in Aramaic and Akkadian.[44] Aristotle records that Antimenes of Rhodes, an official at Babylon in charge of roadways, even revived an old law that had fallen into disuse when he reinstated a tithe on all imports; presumably some publicity for this dictate was required in Aramaic, and a

written record in cuneiform.[45] These instances demonstrate that ethnic Greeks held high administrative positions in Babylon itself under a local style of administration in which the use of two or more languages was normal. Traditional methods of keeping records—*bullae*, clay tablets—continued in a few spheres of activity, even though parchment and papyrus were available and very commonly used. Babylonian scribes by now were accustomed to writing both in cuneiform on clay and in Aramaic or Greek on papyrus or parchment. So-called Graeco-Babylonian tablets are known with cuneiform on one side and Greek transcriptions on the other, inscribed with texts which all seem to be school exercises for learning to write one or the other language. They show the closest link between Babylonian and Greek traditions of

[44] M. W. Stolper, *Late Achaemenid, Early Macedonian, and Early Seleucid Records of Deposit and Related Texts* (Naples, 1993), 82–6

with commentary.

[45] Aristotle, *Oeconomica* 2. 2. 34.

learning,[46] reflecting the start of a major shift towards Greek as the cultural language of instruction, rather than any Near Eastern language. This shift may be related to political developments under the Seleucids, in which complex legal transactions began to be documented in Greek in addition to cuneiform and Aramaic.[47]

It was in Egypt rather than Mesopotamia, however, that one of Alexander's successors, Ptolemy Philadelphos, had Babylonian works as well as Egyptian ones translated into Greek, presumably for library use, making them available to Greeks on a regular basis at the famous library in Alexandria.[48]

Alexander may even have introduced Mesopotamian practices into other areas. Plutarch records the curious story that Alexander promoted a gardener called Abdalonymos to the kingship of Paphos in Cyprus.[49] The story presumably derives from a garbled understanding of the royal substitution ritual whereby a man substituted for the king until a period of danger had passed. The most famous instance of this is recorded in a Babylonian chronicle, for the king, Erra-Imitti, accidentally died, and the substitute, Enlil-bani, who likewise happened to be a gardener, became the real king in his stead.[50] Other forms of contact represent a continuation of older practices; even towards the end of the Seleucid period Mesopotamian designs were making their way into Greece. For instance, at Olympia Antiochos Epiphanes (175–164 BC) dedicated a woollen curtain adorned with Assyrian weavings and dyed Phoenician purple, probably following a standard procedure for Near Eastern kings by dedicating luxury items in Greek sanctuaries.[51]

Among Greeks a source for Babylonian history and customs was the *Babyloniaka* of Berossos, a genuine figure whose legendary life is still debatable in its details: he is said to have established a school of Chaldaean astronomy on Kos; he was reported as the father of the Babylonian Sibyl, and the Athenians are said to have set up a golden statue of him on

account of his abilities as a sage.[52] Berossos wrote that he made use of temple records, and the few extant fragments of his work bear out this claim. Some scholars claim to have identified among the shreds some of the hallmarks of Hellenistic ethnographic style, but this is not certain, for there are elements in that style that can now be traced among the writings of neo-Assyrian kings. Berossos' description of the Creation parallels the Babylonian *Epic of Creation*, and he recounts the story of the Flood, although not the version we know which names the survivor of the Flood as Ut-napishtim. For in preserving the name Xisuthros at that point in the story, he reflects the Sumerian name Ziusudra, as does Lucian in his adaptation of the Flood story.[53] Among influential figures who later studied the *Babyloniaka* were Apollodoros of Athens (170–110 BC), a pupil of Diogenes of Babylon;[54] the Roman antiquarian and bibliophile Varro (82–37 BC), who wrote a work on astronomy dependent on Mesopotamian materials;[55] Juba (46 BC–AD 23), king of Numidia, who wrote a two-volume work on Assyria;[56] and the philosopher Seneca (4 BC–AD 65).[57]

How much traditional types of Mesopotamian literature had an effect upon Greek composition at this time is still unknown, for traces of possible influence are hard to date. Satire, acrostics, and pastoral poems, all of which had had long lives in Mesopotamia, find their way into Hellenistic literature. The following passage, from the Sumerian tale of Dumuzi, may be compared with any Hellenistic bucolic poem of unrequited love:

> O my sister, let the shepherd marry thee,
> O maid Inanna, why art thou unwilling?
> His fat is good, his milk is good,
> The shepherd, everything his hand touches is bright,
> O Inanna, let the shepherd Dumuzi marry thee,
> O thou who . . . , why art thou unwilling?[58]

Contest literature, in which two protagonists put rival points of view, and antiphonal responses in which one

[46] S. M. Maul, 'Neues zu den "Graeco-Babyloniaca"', *Zeitschrift für Assyriologie* 81 (1991), 87–107.

[47] L. T. Doty, *Cuneiform Archives from Hellenistic Uruk*, Ph.D. thesis, Yale University (New Haven, 1977), 327–33 with comments in Stolper, *Late Achaemenid . . .* , 62.

[48] Synkellos, *Ecloga Chronographica* 516 (ed. A. A. Mosshammer, Leipzig, 1984), doubted in A. Momigliano, *Alien Wisdom* (Cambridge, 1975), 145.   [49] Plutarch, *Moralia* 340c–e.

[50] ANET 266–7 (The 'Sargon Chronicle'). .

[51] Pausanias 5. 12. 4; cf. Herodotos I. 14; 46–56; 8:35 on Gyges, Kroisos, and Midas.

[52] Pliny, *Natural History* 7. 37.

[53] Corrupted to Skythea, see H. W. Attridge and R. A. Oden, *The Syrian Goddess* (Missoula, 1976), 18–19 § 12.

[54] Synkellos, *Ecloga Chronographica* 71 (ed. Mosshammer, 1984).

[55] St Augustine, *City of God* 21. 8; for Mesopotamian elements in Varro's treatises, note N. Sallmann (ed.), *Censorinus: De Die Natali Liber* (Leipzig, 1983), a 4th-cent. AD work heavily dependent on Varro as a source.   [56] Tatian, *Oratio ad Graecos* 36.

[57] *Naturales Quaestiones* 3. 29.

[58] ANET 41. Cf. e.g. Theokritos 6; 11.

53. Inscription in Greek and (a longer version in) Aramaic, from the Piraeus, dedicated to Nergal by the priest Yatan-Bel.

ΑΣΕΓΤΕΣΥΜΣΕΛΗΜΟΥΣΙΔΩΝΙΑ

singer or chorus responds to another, already observable in the *Iliad* (1. 604) and *Odyssey* (24. 60), have very early antecedents in Mesopotamia. The apparent proliferation of these genres at this time reflects the close relationships between east and west.

We know from Pliny[59] and Strabo[60] that Nippur and Uruk as well as Babylon continued to produce world-class scholars from academies of learning, most notably Diogenes 'of Babylon' the Stoic.[61] The very fact that he became head of the Stoic school in Athens and then received acclamation in Rome implies that he represented a prestigious tradition of travelling scholars from Mesopotamia. Now that key astronomical texts in cuneiform have at last been edited, there is no doubt that the Babylonians continued to study the subject in their academies, still writing down their observations in cuneiform, not only during the period of Seleucid rule, but also long after Greek rule had departed from Mesopotamia. Greek astronomers such as Hipparchos and Ptolemy took over certain aspects of Babylonian astronomy, and they could have done so either from translations made in Mesopotamia or from texts available in Egypt, written in Greek. Strabo mentions Kidenas, Nabourianos, and Seleukos as famous Chaldaean astronomers of the time; among men with Greek names mentioned by the sources as students of Chaldaeans are Apollonios of Myndos and Artemidoros of Parium. Sudines and Zachalias are also mentioned by Pliny

as famous scholars.[62] Kastor of Rhodes, in the first half of the first century BC, wrote a volume on Babylon that was widely consulted, and he had knowledge of Babylonian Venus-observations.[63] Sometimes a high-ranking Babylonian took a second, Greek name for himself or his son; this is usually difficult to demonstrate from the Babylonian cuneiform texts that survive; it is much better attested in Egypt where Greek texts are preserved.[64] Therefore it is not always clear which of these scholars with Greek names were Babylonian and which were Greek by family or place of origin.

Chaldaean sages were travelling extensively, as they had done for centuries. An inscription from Thessalian Larisa mentions Antipater, a Chaldaean astronomer from Hierapolis-Membidj (significantly also called Nineveh)[65] in Syria. The Roman architect Vitruvius identified him as a disciple of Berossos.[66] Attalos I of Pergamon was said to have consulted the Chaldaean scholar Sudines.[67] Particularly important is a bilingual Phoenician and Greek inscription from the Piraeus in Athens, dated to around the third century BC, which gives the name Yatan-Bel (the element Bel being Babylonian) to the head of the priests of the Babylonian god Nergal.[68] That these holy men living abroad had an effect on Greek practices may be seen in the mention of Ereshkigal, Mesopotamian goddess of the Underworld, on several Greek magical papyri from Egypt. In these papyri, she is most often

[59] *Natural History* 6. 123; 7. 56. 193; 37. 60. 169. See also R. J. van der Spek, 'Nippur, Sippar, and Larsa in the Hellenistic Periods', in M. de Jong Ellis (ed.), *Nippur at the Centennial* (Philadelphia, 1992), 235–60. Pliny's assertions that scholars 'from Babylon' actually came from Seleukeia, and that Babylon was ruined, are incorrect, as shown in Ch. II.   [60] Strabo 16. 1. 6.

[61] See Ch. II, pp. 45–9.

[62] *Natural History* 37. 60. 169; cf. 30. 2. 4–5 mentioning Arabantiphokos of Babylon and Tarmoendas of Assyria; Athenaios 5. 222a on Herodikos of Babylon.

[63] See Ch. VI, pp. 133–4.

[64] S. Sherwin-White, 'Aristeas Ardibelteios', *ZPE* 50 (1983), 209–21; cf. *Inscriptiones Graecae* 12. 715 on Phanodemos, described as a 'Babylonian' on a 3rd-cent. BC inscription, who became *prox-*

enos (a guest of the state) on the Greek island of Andros. See also S. M. Sherwin-White, 'A Greek Ostrakon from Babylon of the Early Third Century BC', *ZPE* 37 (1982), 51–70.

[65] Philostratos, *Life of Apollonios* 1. 18–20; Ammianus Marcellinus 14. 8. 7.

[66] Vitruvius, *De Architectura* 9. 6. 2; G. W. Bowersock, 'Antipater Chaldeus', *CQ* 33 (1983), 491.

[67] Polyainos, *Strategemata* 4. 20. W. Heubner, 'Zum Planetenfragment des Sudines (P. Gen. inv. 203)', *ZPE* 73 (1988), 33–42; 'Nachtrag zum Planetenfragment des Sudines (P. Gen. inv. 203)', *ZPE* 74 (1989), 109–10.

[68] See M. G. G. Amadasi, 'Influence directe de la Mésopotamie sur les inscriptions en Phénicien', in H.-J. Nissen (ed.), *Mesopotamien und seine Nachbarn* (Berlin, 1978), 388.

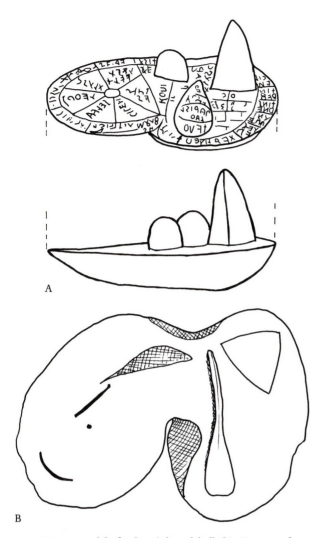

55. Altar dedicated in Aramaic and Greek to Bel of Tadmor (Palmyra), found on the island of Kos.

54. A. Bronze model of a sheep's liver, labelled in Etruscan, from Piacenza, Italy; B. Terracotta model of a sheep's liver, found near Rome.

found in association with the name Neboutosoualeth, presumably derived in part from the name Nabu.[69] By the late fourth century BC models of livers were being made near Rome for recording omens,[70] in a style derived from Mesopotamia which had come to Italy through Greeks and Etruscans. With them came the translation of Akkadian technical terms.[71] The Hippocratic corpus contains prognostic texts concerning childbirth and illness that bear similarities to Akkadian ones, though the latter are couched as conditional sentences, the former as factual observations.

Resemblances have also been noted between Greek and Mesopotamian pharmacological lore, both in content and formulation.[72]

There is evidence that people could enter and worship in the various temples of the Near East regardless of their own particular ethnic background. Architecturally there was no rigid distinction, for traditional styles persisted.[73] Even at Seleukeia-on-Tigris and Ai Khanum in Afghanistan which were essentially Greek foundations, ground plans suggest conventional Mesopotamian structures were still being built. Greek deities were directly associated or equated with Semitic ones from this period and on into Roman times, as there was already very little difference in the forms of sacrifices, in the outward appearance of divine statues, and in the attributes of deities. Warrior gods rode in chariots and hurled thunderbolts whether they were Greek or Semitic. Bilingual inscriptions from Palmyra in particular demonstrate a close association between Jupiter or Zeus and Bel, Nabu and Apollo, Nanay and Artemis, giving alternative names according to the language of the inscription.[74] At Hatra the sun-god was Shamash

[69] H. D. Betz (ed.), *The Greek Magical Papyri in Translation*, i, 2nd edn. (Chicago, 1992), e.g. 65, 89, 93, 126, 232.

[70] L. B. van der Meer, 'Iecur Placentinum and the Orientation of the Etruscan Haruspex', *BABesch* 54 (1979), 49–64; R. D. Biggs and J.-W. Meyer, 'Lebermodelle', *RlA* vi (1980–3).

[71] See Ch. I, pp. 10–12 and Figs. 29–31.

[72] R. Labat, *Traité Akkadien de diagnostics et pronostics médicaux* (Paris, 1951).

[73] S. Downey, *Mesopotamian Architecture* (Princeton, 1988).

[74] Strabo 16. 1. 7; *LIMC* s.v. 'Bel'.

in Aramaic and Helios in Greek; and a nude Herakles in Graeco-Roman style is labelled Nergal.[75] Aphlad at Dura-Europos is the Assyrian god Apil-Adad in Roman clothes; Mesopotamia and Euphrates, personified on the mosaics at Mas'oudiye are Roman in style and costume.[76] At Borsippa, Hierapolis-Membidj, Seleukeia, Palmyra, and Dura, Nabu was equated with Apollo.[77] A cuneiform tablet of Seleucid date, found in the area around the archive building at Seleukeia, records that a man with a Greek name made a dedication to Nergal, and Greek graffiti were scratched on the temple of Bel at Dura while it was still in use.[78] Greek slaves could be dedicated within Babylonian temples.[79] On a stele found on the island of Kos a bilingual inscription in Greek and Palmyrene records a dedication to Bel.[80] Nergal is also seen on the fifth-century coinage of Cilicia, the reverse showing Ares perhaps because he, like Nergal, was associated with war.[81] Nimrod 'the mighty hunter', named in Genesis 10: 8–9 as the founder of Babylon, Uruk, and Akkad, and associated with Ninurta the patron god of hunting in Mesopotamia, was assimilated with the Greek hunter Orion in later Antiquity.[82] Such close associations have sometimes been interpreted as showing how the strength of Hellenism in the Near East overwhelmed local beliefs, but the same evidence may alternatively be seen to reflect the desire of Greeks to link their gods to older and more venerable traditions than their own.

Rome and Mesopotamia (c.128 BC onwards)

Pompey made a Roman colony of western Syria in 64 BC, and then the ambitious Crassus failed to penetrate further east when he was totally defeated in 53 BC by Parthians and their allies at Harran, now pronounced Carrhae. In the following year a Pal-

myrene shrine was dedicated to Bel at Dura-Europos. Despite repeated incursions by Roman emperors, central Mesopotamia was never successfully incorporated into the Roman empire. Mesopotamian learning, however, had long since been present in Rome itself, and cults of Bel enjoyed new life in the Near East.

Such an outstanding event was the visit of Diogenes of Babylon to Rome in 155/6 BC that it was remembered more than a century later.[83] It inspired among Romans an interest in Mesopotamia which was subsequently reinforced by intermittent events that brought the two countries into direct contact. Trajan marched down the Euphrates to Ktesiphon in AD 116 and claimed to have conquered Adiabene, the kingdom on the middle Tigris which included Arbela, seat of Ishtar's famous temple and oracle. But Trajan's success was short-lived, and is barely discernible in material or intellectual terms within the main part of Mesopotamia. Hadrian visited Palmyra around 130/1. Troops under Lucius Verus attacked Seleukeia-on-Tigris, and sacked it in 165, capturing Ktesiphon; Septimius Severus, whose future as emperor was foretold by the oracle of Bel at Apamea-on-Orontes, campaigned in Mesopotamia in 195 and captured Ktesiphon in 198. Twice he tried to capture the Arab city of Hatra, because it enjoyed great fame for the wealth of the sun-god Shamash-Bel, stored in his temple Esagila which was named after the still flourishing temple of Marduk-Bel in Babylon.[84] The cult of Bel from Palmyra was installed in Rome in 273/4, following Aurelian's victory over Zenobia,[85] and Carus, with the young Diocletian in his entourage, captured Seleukeia and Ktesiphon in 283. Between Hadrian and Diocletian 'Mesopotamia was four times lost and four times recovered', and no lasting settlement or administration interfered with religious and intellectual life in the great cities of the central area. As if to mask this unsatisfactory state of affairs, many Roman writers referred to Mesopotamia when

[75] S. Downey, *The Heracles Sculpture* = C. B. Wells (ed.), *The Excavations at Dura-Europus, Final Report III*, Part I, Fascicle I (New Haven, 1969); *LIMC* s.v. 'Helios (in peripheria orientali)'.

[76] *LIMC* s.v. 'Aphlad', 'Euphrates' and 'Mesopotamia'.

[77] *LIMC* s.v. 'Nabu' for refs.; cf. Strabo 16. 1. 7.

[78] Downey, 54, 105–10.

[79] J. Oelsner, 'Griechen in Babylonien und die einheimischen Tempel in hellenistischer Zeit', in D. Charpin and F. Joannès (eds.), *La Circulation des biens, des personnes et des idées dans le Proche-Orient ancien* (Paris, 1992), 341–50.

[80] G. Levi della Vida, 'Une Bilingue gréco-palmyrenienne à

Cos', *Mélanges Syriens offerts à M. René Dussaud*, ii (Paris, 1939), 883–6.

[81] C. M. Kraay, *Archaic and Classical Greek Coins*, pl. 60 no. 1035 (London, 1976), 281.

[82] K. Van der Toorn and P. W. Van der Horst, 'Nimrod Before and After the Bible', *Harvard Theological Review* 83 (1990), 11.

[83] Cicero, *De Oratore* 2. 155–60; *Tusculan Disputations* 4. 5.

[84] Dio 75. 12. 2.

[85] Zosimos 1. 61, (1)–2, translated in M. H. Dodgeon and S. N. C. Lieu (eds.), *The Roman Eastern Frontier and the Persian Wars (AD 226–363)* (London, 1991), 107.

they meant the very northern part in the foothills of the Taurus mountains where Rome did indeed have a permanent presence: this restricted area was the Roman province of 'Mesopotamia' following the successes of Septimius Severus.

Until recently scholars have not expected to find any remnants of Babylonian traditions lurking among the evidence for Mesopotamia in the Roman period, and have claimed that a kind of historical amnesia separated the indigenous population from an awareness that cultural progress and achievement had been continuous for the past three millennia. Chapters II, VII, and VIII of this volume attempt to rectify this: for Babylon, Borsippa, Ashur, Arbela, there is clear evidence of continuity from texts, art, and architecture, although cuneiform was no longer used. New centres of worship modelled upon the older ones come to the forefront at Palmyra, Apamea-on-Orontes, and Hatra, where oriental paganism successfully resisted the advance of Christianity for centuries. Both Aramaic and Classical sources show that academic life continued to flourish in Babylonia. Roman penetration did have a marked effect upon Levantine cities, but the interior, beyond the mountains of Amanus, Lebanon, and Anti-Lebanon, was much less affected, and would have seemed remote and exotic to Romans in Italy.

Roman rulers relied on scholarly studies in trying to comprehend the extent of foreign regions. Pliny writes that Augustus commissioned a study of eastern lands from the geographer Dionysios of Charax on the lower Tigris.[86] Alexander Polyhistor, who arrived in Rome as a captive after fighting against Rome as a Near Eastern mercenary, became famous by compiling histories of all the countries of the east for Roman patrons, and his prolific output included a Chaldaean history.[87] Strabo devoted Book 16 of his *Geography* to Assyria and provided a conspectus of information about Babylon accumulated by his predecessors. Diodoros Sikelos began his huge history of the world with an account of Near Eastern tradi-

tions, giving colourful details about Nineveh and Babylon. Among ancient travellers and geographers, it became conventional to claim to have wandered as far as Mesopotamia. Often Roman ethnographers simply translated the Greek texts into Latin, but Greek continued to be the written language of educated men in the eastern part of the empire, and was seldom replaced by Latin there. Many of the so-called 'Greek' ethnographers, geographers, and antiquarians from this time onwards, writing in Greek, are in fact Near Eastern or Anatolian, taking up the mantle of earlier Ionians from Miletos, Halikarnassos, and the eastern islands: Strabo was from Amaseia in eastern Anatolia, Lucian from Samsat on the Euphrates, Alexander Polyhistor from Miletos, and Arrian from Bithynia in north-west Asia Minor.

Certain aspects of Babylonian tradition which had taken a hold upon the people were not favoured officially, although 'Chaldaean' astrologers and prophets, repeatedly expelled from Rome,[88] could still find favour in exalted circles.[89] The general Sulla consulted them, and Plutarch reports that a 'Chaldaean', 'after looking Sulla intently in the face, and studying carefully the movements of his mind and body . . . declared that this man must of necessity become the greatest in the world'.[90] This art of divination through inspection of a subject's physiognomy is well attested as a Mesopotamian practice which had been formulated in standard Akkadian manuals.[91]

Cicero, despite his suspicion of Chaldaean divination and astrology,[92] translated into Latin the *Phaenomena*, a work on astronomy by Aratos of Soloi in Cilicia (*c*.315–245 BC), itself a rough translation of a prose work by Eudoxos of Knidos, and a source of inspiration for the Roman poets Lucretius and Vergil.[93] The Roman philosopher and astronomer L. Tarutius Firmanus, a contemporary of Cicero, may have used Mesopotamian records in working out the dates of particular events.[94] Lucretius had consulted Berossos on the causes of the light and phases of the moon, as had the architect Vitruvius.[95] *Astronomica*, a long

---

[86] *Natural History* 6. 31. 141; Pliny possibly intended 'Isidoros of Charax'.   [87] *FGrH* 273 F 19(a)39.

[88] e.g. Valerius Maximus 1. 3. 3. See, in general, B. W. Jones, *The Emperor Domitian* (London and New York, 1992), 119–24; and Livy 39. 16. 5–3 on attempts by Roman praetors to discourage religious superstition during the Hannibalic Wars by confiscating particular books; Aulus Gellius 14. 1 for a debate over the value of Chaldaean astrology.

[89] e.g. Plutarch, *Marius* 42. 4.

[90] Plutarch, *Sulla* 5. 5. 6 (trans. Perrin).

[91] F. R. Kraus, *Texte zur babylonischen Physiognomatik* (Berlin, 1939).   [92] *De Divinatione* 2. 98.

[93] Cicero, *De Natura Deorum* 2. 41; *ad Atticum* 2. 1. 11; for a translation of Aratos, see G. R. Mair (ed.), *Callimachus, Lycophron, Aratus* (London and New York, 1921), 357–473.

[94] *De Divinatione* 2. 98; Plutarch, *Romulus* 12. 5.

[95] Lucretius, *De Rerum Natura* 5. 727–8; Vitruvius, *De Architectura* 9. 2. 1.

poem in five books, written by Marcus Manilius in the reigns of Augustus and Tiberius, represents astrological interests.[96]

The philosophers of Apamea-on-Orontes were particularly concerned to explain the underlying science behind Chaldaean beliefs which were especially important to the Stoics. The interest in astrology of Posidonios, praised by Strabo as 'a master philosopher and a candidate for first honours among learned men',[97] and the Stoic school lent a certain respectability to Chaldaean astrology.[98] A priest of Bel at Apamea-on-Orontes headed an Epicurean school there, giving useful evidence that priests and philosophers were not necessarily distinct.[99] The scholar Ptolemy (c. AD 100–78) was well informed about Chaldaean learning, presumably because detailed works were available to him in Alexandria and among the many scholars in upper Egypt at Akhmim.[100]

The Greek novel, which arose mainly in Hellenized cities in Anatolia, may owe a genuine debt to Assyria. The legendary figures of Ninos and Semiramis are the main characters of the *Ninos Romance*, the oldest Greek novel extant, now dated around the first century BC. The startlingly new theme of romantic royal love seems to have evolved out of a royal inscription of Sennacherib, only recently discovered, in which the king records for posterity his love for his wife Tashmetum-sharrat:

And for Tashmetum-sharrat the queen, my beloved wife, whose form the Great Goddess has made more beautiful than any other women, I have had a palace of love, joy and pleasure built. At the command of Ashur, father of the gods and queen Ishtar may we both live long in this palace and enjoy happiness to the full.[101]

This is the palace in Nineveh beside which the famous Hanging Gardens were constructed, and she is the queen for whom the gardens were built. Early in the seventh century BC this favourite queen was soon ousted by the redoubtable Naqia whose own son Esarhaddon came to the throne after Sennacherib

was murdered by two of his other sons. Nikolaos of Damascus relates a story about 'Semiramis' in which two sons from her first marriage planned to kill her, in order to stop her son Ninyas becoming king. Recent work shows that in this tale 'Semiramis' represents Sennacherib (note the change of gender) and Ninyas represents Esarhaddon.[102] There is no doubt, therefore, that Greek themes about Assyrian royal lovers go back to authentic cuneiform material. Themes from the same episode were used in the tale relating the life of Ahiqar, for in the latter is named the officer Nabu-shum-ishkun, who took part in the attempted murder according to the clear testimony of a contemporary Assyrian royal letter.[103]

In the *Ninos Romance*, now known only from fragments, no genuine historical kernel can be discerned beyond the use of the name Semiramis for the heroine. Ninos is described as king of Assyria, Semiramis as his cousin. The two characters provide an exotic tale of love, marriage, adversity, and separation around the Mediterranean. Babylon became popular as a setting in the novels: the denouement of the romance of *Chaereas and Kallirhoe*, for example, takes place there. The Greek novel is also linked, in part, to the development of the historical romance, of which the best known is the *Alexander Romance* with its themes from Akkadian mythology and its final scene of Alexander's death in Babylon.[104]

Illustrating their popularity within Greek legend and romance, Ninos and Semiramis flourished in art. They are both portrayed on a sculptured panel from the basilica at Aphrodisias in Caria, dating probably to the third century AD. The Assyrian royal couple are shown on a floor-mosaic dated to c. AD 200, from Antioch-on-Orontes, and a similar mosaic from Alexandretta explicitly names Ninos, whose reputation as a conqueror was widespread.[105] According to Lucian a statue of Semiramis stood on the right-hand side of the entrance to the temple of the Syrian goddess at Hierapolis-Membidj, where Babylonians were still to be found at the shrine, and another statue of her

[96] G. P. Goold (ed.), *Manilius: Astronomica* (Cambridge, Mass., and London, 1977). Note also Propertius 4. 1B (ed. Goold) for a poem purporting to be a prophecy from one 'Horos', trained by 'Horops of Babylon'.

[97] 2. 3. 5.   [98] Note Diodoros 2. 29. 4.

[99] J. P. Rey-Coquais, 'Inscriptions grecques d'Apamée', *Annales archéologiques de la Syrie* 23 (1973), 66–8. Panaetios (c.185–109 BC, a Stoic pupil of Diogenes of Babylon, served as a priest of Poseidon in Rhodes.

[100] H.-J. Thissen, *Der verkommene Harfenspieler* (Vienna, 1992), 80–3. See also Ch. VI, pp. 134–5.

[101] R. Borger, 'König Sanherib's Eheglück', *Annual Review of the Royal Inscriptions of Mesopotamia project* 6 (1988), 5–11.

[102] S. Zawadzki, 'Oriental and Greek Tradition about the Death of Sennacherib', *State Archives of Assyria Bulletin* iv: 1 (1990), 69–72.

[103] See Ch. VII, p. 147.   [104] See Ch. VIII, pp. 170–1.

[105] Cf. St Augustine, *The City of God* 4. 6.

56. Sculptures of Semiramis and Ninos from the Basilica at Aphrodisias on the Maeander River, second half of the third century AD. Height 0.98 m.

in the same temple stood in the interior, next to other mythic or legendary figures, and these were presumably still to be seen in the third century when Membidj was still a flourishing centre of paganism with regular worship and festivals.[106] Such figures appeared, of course, in Greek or Roman dress according to the fashion of the time, and are therefore recognizable only from captions. At Palmyra a scene from the Babylonian *Epic of Creation* appears on the frieze of the great temple of Bel, which was built with money given largely by merchants from the city of Babylon.[107] Because it is not inscribed, it was at first thought to illustrate the battle between Zeus and Typhon, for the style is Classical and the gods wear Roman military dress. The frieze, together with the date of foundation, probably implies that the Babylonian New Year festival was celebrated there in the time of Zenobia, with the *Epic of Creation* perhaps recited in Aramaic.[108]

Old Mesopotamian names and themes were sometimes perpetuated in Greek and Roman accounts. The Greek rhetorician Aelian (*c.* AD 170–235) who taught at Rome wrote *On the Characteristics of Animals* in which the baby Gilgamos, clearly a Hellenic form for Gilgamesh, was hurled from a tower, and being saved by an eagle, was brought up by a gardener, and eventually became king of Babylon.[109] Elements from the *Legend of Sargon's Birth*, which Cyrus II also used, can be recognized in the story. Ovid may have relied on Babylonian material for elements of the 'Oriental' tales in Book 4 of the *Metamorphoses*; for instance, Father Orchamus in the story of Leucothoe presumably personifies Uruk under a Roman name.[110] Suetonius was evidently aware of the Mesopotamian belief that culture was brought by the Seven Sages who rose up from the sea as half-carp, half-man.[111] In his day the soldiers who went to Mesopotamia may have seen such figures as monumental sculpture, at the Fish Gate to the Nabu temple at Nimrud, or similar decoration on the temple of Nabu which still flourished at Borsippa, to complement Berossos' description of the first sage in the *Babyloniaka*: 'Its entire body was that of a fish, but a human head had grown beneath the head of the fish, and human feet likewise had grown from the fish's tail. It also had a human voice.'

A set of texts known as Chaldaean or Assyrian oracles, from which Porphyry and later Neoplatonists drew inspiration, was known to philosophers and

[106] *Dea Syria* 39–40; L. Goldschmidt, *Babylonian Talmud* (Leipzig, 1913), vii, Avoda zarah fo. 11b.

[107] *Corpus Inscriptionum Semiticarum* 2. 3915 (AD 24); M. Gawlikowski, 'Palmyra as a Trading Centre', *Iraq* 56 (1994), 27–33. On the popularity of Palmyrene names using 'Bel' or 'Nabu' as an element, see P. Hiersimoni, 'Who's Who at Palmyra: An Overview', *Orientalia Lovanensia Periodica* 25 (1994), 89–98.

[108] See Ch. II, pp. 49–50.

[109] *De Natura Animalium* 12. 21; B. Lewis, *The Sargon Legend* (1980).

[110] P. Perdrizet, 'Légendes babyloniennes dans les *Metamorphoses* d'Ovide', *Revue de l'Histoire des Religions* 105 (1932), 193–228.

[111] *RE* s.v. Telchines 10, quoting the Byzantine epitome of his work *On Words of Insult*.

57. An Assyrian sage as a fish-man, drawn from a stone sculpture which stood at a doorway inside the temple of Ninurta at Nimrud from the ninth century onwards (Suetonius knew of this tradition). Height 2.4 m.

59. Syrian storm-god Adad from Til Barsip, installed c.900 BC together with several other similar monuments. Height (as restored) 3.03 m.

58. Statuette of Nabu playing the lyre, from Dura-Europos. Height 0.33 m.

60. Sculpture in relief of Adad from Dura-Europos. 0.45 × 0.24 m.

Christian writers from at least the third century.[112] That these oracles derived from Mesopotamian ones has been denied by scholars who were not aware that Babylonian and Assyrian cults with oracles still flourished in the Roman period. Proklos, who died in AD 484, said in connection with the Chaldaean Oracles that the 'Once Transcendent' was Ad and the 'Twice Transcendent' was Adad, thereby playing upon the Akkadian (east Semitic) form of the Storm-god's name, whose pre-eminence in north Syria (at Aleppo and Guzana, for instance) entitled him to claim the epithet Bel. This hints at a Syrian origin for the Chaldaean Oracles. That Adad was still venerated under this name is known from a stone plaque found in a temple at Dura-Europos.[113] Its inscription in Greek recorded that, 'Adad-iabos . . . erected this foundation of the sanctuary of Aphlad . . . god of 'Ana on the Euphrates', thus identifying the temple as that of the Assyrian god Apil-Adad 'Son of Adad' whose importance is now underlined by a series of long cuneiform inscriptions found at 'Ana, dating to the eighth century BC.[114] The name of the dedicant in the Greek inscription shows that the cult of Adad persisted too. North of Aleppo, at Killiz, an altar dedicated in Greek to Bel shows that the cult of Bel was not restricted to Apamea and Palmyra. The two bulls that flank the scene of sacrifice are traditional attributes of the Storm-god, and so Bel in this case is almost certainly Adad. These pieces of evidence show that Babylonian cults were flourishing not just in lower Mesopotamia where Roman influence was negligible, but also in north Syria, where it was firmly established.

Both at Palmyra and at Apamea-on-Orontes, Bel 'the giver of fortune' was known internationally for his reliable oracles, and his fame was recognized as far away as southern France.[115] The oracle of Sin at Harran presumably continued into the Islamic period, for the city remained a major centre of paganism in early Christian times.[116] At Arbela the famous oracle of neo-Assyrian times may have persisted until very late, for a priest of Sharbel (the goddess Issar-Bel of Arbela) was not converted to Christianity until the fourth century AD.[117] Egyptian religious texts invoking 'Hermes' and known as the *Corpus Hermeticum* were widely influential in the development of the theosophical system known as Gnosticism, which served as a rival to early Christianity within the Roman Empire. They have sometimes been thought to have an ill-defined basis in Mesopotamian lore, for which transmission through Palmyra, Apamea, and Harran can now be suggested.[118]

Dream-books, which list instructions for understanding dreams, have antecedents in cuneiform manuals, especially from Uruk, that give guidance on interpretation according to systematic rules. They became popular during this period, with the *Oneirokritika* of Artemidoros of Lydia (second century AD), which appeared in five books, and was consulted frequently.[119] Centuries earlier, Cicero's learned friend Nigidius Figulus, whose works included a volume on thunder-omens that perpetuated Mesopotamian tradition, may also have written an account of dream interpretation.[120] As a genre, dream-books had a long life: they remained popular in Byzantine times and eventually influenced Freud's *Interpretation of Dreams*.[121]

It cannot be doubted, therefore, that many forms of Babylonian worship and ritual persisted into late Antiquity. Ammianus wrote that, at Nineveh in AD 337, the Sassanian Persian kings 'offered sacrifice in the middle of the bridge over the Anzaba, and finding the omens favourable crossed with great confidence'.[122] The reference to sacrifices has been dismissed as a literary construct, since these 'are in fact no part of Persian ritual'.[123] It may be better, however, to take the statement as confirmation that

---

[112] R. Majercik, *The Chaldaean Oracles* (Leiden, 1989).

[113] M. Rostovtzeff, *The Excavations at Dura Europos, fifth season* (New Haven, 1934) 111–15.

[114] A. Cavigneaux and B. K. Ismail, 'Die Statthalter von Suhu und Mari im 8 Jh. v.Chr', *Baghdader Mitteilungen* 21 (1990), 321–456.

[115] See Ch. II, p. 51.   [116] See Ch. VII, pp. 152–3.

[117] P. Bedjan, *Acta Martyrum et Sanctorum*, iv (Paris and Leipzig, 1890–1907; repr. Hildesheim 1968), 133, discussed by P. Peeters, 'Passionaire d'Adiabène', *Analecta Bollandiana* 43 (1925), 261–304. On the late history of Arbela, see, in general, J. M. Fiey, *Assyrie chrétienne* (Beirut, 1965).

[118] B. P. Copenhaver, *Hermetica* (Cambridge, 1992), pp. xxxiii and lii.

[119] R. J. White, *The Interpretation of Dreams* (Park Ridge, NJ, 1975) for a translation. See also A. H. M. Kessels, 'Ancient Systems of Dream-Classification', *Mnemosyne* 22 (1969), 389–424.

[120] A. Swoboda (ed.), *P. Nigidii Figuli Operum Reliquiae* (Amsterdam, 1964) fragments 80–105.

[121] S. R. F. Price, 'The Future of Dreams: From Freud to Artemidorus', *Past and Present* 113 (1986), 3–37; P. Athanassiadi, 'Dreams, Theurgy, and Freelance Divination: The Testimony of Iamblichus', *Journal of Roman Studies* 83 (1993), 115–30.

[122] Ammianus Marcellinus 18. 7. 1.

[123] J. Matthews, *The Roman Empire of Ammianus* (London, 1989), 49.

62. Basalt altar showing a priest sacrificing to Bel, first–third century AD, from Killiz, north of Aleppo. 0.60 × 0.75 m.

61. Stone plaque of the god Aphlad from Dura-Europos, AD 54. 0.51 × 0.31 m.

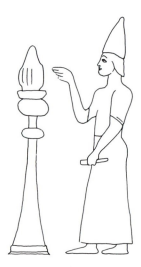

63. Assyrian priest on the Balawat gates of Shalmaneser III (ninth century BC).

64. Chaldaean priest, from wall painting in Temple of Bel, Dura-Europos. Hat and robe are white.

Mesopotamian ritual continued at Nineveh as in other Assyrian cities.

Mesopotamian products, as might be expected, appeared on the Roman market, which implies that trade flourished as before. Pliny notes:

Babylon . . . made famous the weaving of different colours and gave this process its name . . . Metellus Scipio includes among the charges laid against Capito that Babylonian throw-over covers for couches were sold for 800,000 sesterces, when not long ago in Nero's principate, these cost four million.[124]

---

[124] *Natural History* 8. 196. On the reputation of Mesopotamian textiles, see Lucretius 4. 1029, 1123; Nonnos 40. 303.

Indeed, the drop in price implies that those goods were more common than before. The anonymous author of the *Periplus of the Erythraean Sea* adds that the *kaunakes*[125] was a type of heavy cloak developed by the Babylonians, which proved so useful that it was adopted from India to Italy.[126] The edict of the emperor Diocletian on maximum prices in Rome records the importation of Babylonian sandals, belts, and chest straps.[127] Silk passed through Mesopotamia and Palmyra on its long journey to the West. Less pleasant was an epidemic that swept Rome in the late second century AD, affecting Syria, Athens, and the western Mediterranean; it was popularly believed to have begun in Babylonia and was transmitted into Italy and elsewhere by Roman soldiers on campaign.[128]

In late Antiquity, therefore, Mesopotamia continued to exert its cultural influence. Julian the Apostate, who became emperor of Rome in AD 355, deliberately designed his march into Persia to include a viewing of the temple of the moon-god Sin at Harran, and he named his horse Babylonius.[129] St Augustine of Hippo, writing in the fourth century AD, described Ninos, king of Assyria, as the first empire builder, and acknowledged that 'that kingdom lasted so long, that the Roman empire has not equalled its duration'.[130] That its influence lasted far longer than its temporal power, Clement of Alexandria had already seen in the second century AD. As part of an exhortation designed to prove that Christianity was superior to pagan philosophies, he wrote:

I know your teachers, even if you should wish to conceal them: you learn geometry from Egyptians, astronomy from Babylonians; your spells for health you take from Thracians, and the Assyrians have educated you in many ways . . .[131]

[125] The name may derive from the late Babylonian word *gunnaku*. B. Hemmerdinger, 'De la méconnaissance de quelques étymologies grecques', *Glotta* 48 (1970), 50–1. Note also *Corpus Inscriptionum Latinarum* 6. 9431 on a Babylonian dealer in eastern furs at Rome.   [126] *Periplus* 6. 2. 35.

[127] 9. 17, 23; 10. 8a, 10. E. R. Graser, 'The Edict of Diocletian on Maximum Prices', in T. Frank (ed.), *Rome and Italy of the Empire* (Baltimore, 1940), for a translation.

[128] *Historia Augusta*, 'Verus' 8. 1–2; Ammianus Marcellinus 23. 6. 24.

[129] Ammianus Marcellinus 23. 3. 6.   [130] *City of God* 4. 6.

[131] *Protreptikos Logos* 6. 60.

FURTHER READING

*CAH*²

1. The Achaemenid Period

BAIGENT, M., *From the Omens of Babylon* (Harmondsworth, 1994), 177.

CUMONT, F., *Astrology and Religion among the Greeks and Romans* (London, 1912).

DREWS, R., 'Assyria in Classical Universal Histories', *Historia* 14 (1965), 129–42.

—— *The Greek Accounts of Eastern History* (Cambridge, Mass., 1972).

FESTUGIÈRE, A. J., 'Platon et l'Orient', *Revue Philologique* 21 (1947), 5–45.

KEYSER, P. T., 'Alchemy in the Ancient World', *Illinois Classical Studies* 15 (1990), 353–78.

KOSTER, W. J. W., *Le Mythe de Platon, de Zarathustra, et des Chaldéens* (Leiden, 1951).

KUHRT, A., 'Assyrian and Babylonian Traditions in Classical Authors: A Critical Synthesis', in H.-J. Nissen and J. Renger (eds.), *Mesopotamien und seine Nachbarn* (Berlin, 1978), 539–53.

—— 'Survey of Written Sources Available for the History of Babylonia under the later Achaemenids', *Achaemenid History*, i: *Sources, Structures, and Synthesis* (Leiden, 1987), 147–57.

—— 'Achaemenid Babylonia: Sources and Problems', *Achaemenid History*, iv: *Centre and Periphery* (Leiden, 1990) 177–94.

ROOT, M. C., *The King and Kingship in Achaemenid Art* (Leiden, 1979).

SANCISI-WEERDENBURG, H., et al. (eds.), *Achaemenid History*, viii: *Continuity and Change* (Leiden, 1994).

2. Alexander and his Successors in Babylon

DREWS, R., 'The Babylonian Chronicles and Berossus', *Iraq* 37 (1975), 39–55.

GLOTZ, D., *Studien zur altorientalischen und griechischen Heilkunde, Therapie, Arzneibereitung, Rezeptstruktur* (Wiesbaden, 1974).

GOOSSENS, G., *Hierapolis de Syrie* (Louvain, 1943).

GRIFFIN, J., 'Theocritus, The Iliad, and the East', *American Journal of Philology* 113 (1992), 189–211.

KUHRT, A., and SHERWIN-WHITE, S., 'Aspects of Seleucid Royal Ideology: The Cylinder of Antiochus I from Borsippa', *JHS* 11 (1991), 71–86.

—— *From Samarkhand to Sardis* (London, 1993).

KUHRT, A., and SHERWIN-WHITE, S. (eds.), *Hellenism in the East* (London, 1987).

McEWAN, C. W., *The Oriental Origin of Hellenistic Kingship* (Chicago, 1934).

OELSNER, J., *Materialen zur babylonischen Gesellschaft und Kultur in hellenistischer Zeit* (Budapest, 1986).

VATTIONI, F., 'I Matematici Caldei di Strabone', *Annali Istituto Orientale Napoli* 7–8 (1985–6), 123–31.

WAERDEN, B. L. VAN DER, *Die 'Agypter' und die 'Chaldäer'* (Berlin, Heidelberg, and New York, 1972).

WEST, M. L., 'Near Eastern Material in Hellenistic and Roman Literature', *Harvard Studies in Classical Philology* 73 (1969), 113–34.

3. Rome and Mesopotamia

BARB, A. A., 'The Survival of Magic Arts', in A. Momigliano (ed.), *The Conflict between Paganism and Christianity in the Fourth Century AD* (Oxford, 1963), 100–25.

BERTINELLI, M. G. A., 'I Romani oltre l'Eufrate nel II Secolo d. C. (le province di Assiria, di Mesopotamia, e di Osroene)', *ANRW* 2. 9. 1 (1976), 3–45.

BOWIE, E. L., and HARRISON, S. J., 'The Romance of the Novel', *Journal of Roman Studies* 83 (1993), 159–78.

COLLEDGE, M. A. R., *The Parthian Period* (Leiden, 1986).

CORNA, D. DEL, 'I Sogni e la Loro Interpretazione nell'età dell'Impero', *ANRW* 2. 16. 2. (1978), 1605–18.

DALLEY, S. M., 'Bel at Palmyra and Elsewhere in the Roman Period', *ARAM* (forthcoming, 1997/8).

HÄGG, T., *The Novel in Antiquity* (Oxford, 1983).

OPPENHEIM, A. L., *The Interpretation of Dreams* (Philadelphia, 1956).

POTTER, D., *Prophets and Emperors: Human and Divine Authority from Augustus to Theodosius* (Cambridge, Mass., and London, 1994).

RAWSON, E., *Intellectual Life in the Late Roman Republic* (London, 1985).

REARDON, B. P., *Collected Ancient Greek Novels* (Berkeley, 1989).

SCHMIDT-COLINET, A., *Palmyra. Kulturbegegnung im Grenzbereich* (Mainz, 1995).

VI

LEGACIES IN ASTRONOMY AND CELESTIAL OMENS

D AVID P INGREE

Introduction

C ELESTIAL PHENOMENA THAT WERE REGARDED as ominous in Mesopotamian culture fall into three broad categories: meteorological (for example thunder, lightning, rainbows, and cloud formations), optical (for example halos, coronas, parhelia, flashes, and variations in the colour and brilliance of stellar light), and, for the want of a better term, astronomical (for example eclipses; first and last visibilities of the Moon, the planets, and certain constellations; retrogressions of the planets; and conjunctions of the planets and the Moon with each other and with the fixed stars). Most of these omens are preserved for us in the cuneiform tablets of the series *Enūma Anu Enlil*, and in the numerous texts derived from or parallel to the series.[1] The omens are formulated as a protasis which describes phenomena in a conditional clause, and an apodosis which states the inferred impending event, for example, 'If Jupiter approaches the Crook, the harvest of Akkad will prosper.'

This series and its parallels are primarily known —as yet imperfectly—in the form to which they had evolved by the seventh century BC. But it is clear from the survival of some Old Babylonian texts and some translations into Hittite and Elamite made in the second millennium BC that at least some of the omens, primarily solar and lunar, were current in that millennium. References to lunar eclipses associated with historical events around the end of the Early

Dynastic period push the date when this phenomenon was regarded as ominous back even further, to the last three centuries of the third millennium BC. Tablets of solar and lunar omens in Akkadian have been discovered in Syria (at Alalakh, Emar, and Qatna), in Anatolia (at Boghazköy), and in Elam (at Susa). They were copied in the second millennium, which shows that this science of celestial omens spread rapidly to the neighbouring cultures under Mesopotamian influence.

Analyses of some of the stellar and planetary omens demonstrate that they also go back earlier, in part to the Old Babylonian period, in part to the last few centuries of the second millennium BC, and in part to about the eighth century BC. Serious misunderstandings of many of the optical and astronomical phenomena mentioned in *Enūma Anu Enlil* are displayed by the compilers of and commentators on the neo-Assyrian tablets preserved in Ashurbanipal's library of the seventh century BC. They indicate that there was a break in the tradition of observing and interpreting celestial phenomena; this presumably occurred in the Kassite period, dated c.1651–1157 BC.

Embedded within the neo-Assyrian versions of *Enūma Anu Enlil* are some of the first evidences that mathematics were applied to the prediction of astronomical phenomena—an application that depends on the fundamental recognition that some of these phenomena are periodic. That that recognition was already made in the Old Babylonian period is proved

---

This is a revision and expansion of an article published in H.-J. Nissen and J. Renger (eds.), *Mesopotamien und seine Nachbarn*, 2 vols. (Berlin, 1982), ii 613–31.

[1] For an attempt at a history of *Enūma Anu Enlil* and a biblio-

graphy of the most recent work on it see D. Pingree, 'Mesopotamian Celestial Omens', in J. D. North (ed.), *General History of Astronomy*, vol. i A (forthcoming).

by an Old Babylonian tablet containing a linear zig-zag scheme[2] applied to a water-clock.[3] This involves the variation in the length of daylight over a solar year, a variation which is also dealt with mathematically in Tablet 14 of *Enūma Anu Enlil*.[4] Similarly the so-called *Astrolabes*, which are cuneiform texts apparently of the late or immediately post-Kassite period, display a linear zig-zag scheme for determining the length of daylight.[5] The earliest evidence that the phenomena of a planet were recognized as periodic is found in omens 22–33 of Tablet 63 of *Enūma Anu Enlil*;[6] those omens are based on the 'mean' intervals between the first and last visibilities of Venus. The cuneiform text known as MUL.APIN, whose title means 'the constellation of the Plough', is a compilation of astronomical material, including catalogues of stars and constellations, written in the period between 1000 and 700 BC. The second of its two tablets treats in greater detail rough schemes for predicting heliacal risings and settings of the planets,[7] lengths of daylight measured by a water-clock,[8] gnomon[9]-shadows,[10] and intercalations.[11] Several contemporary or slightly later texts represent the level of astronomical knowledge that is apparent in MUL.APIN; others represent innovations, as, for instance, a table based on seasonal hours of which, as in Egyptian timekeeping, there are twenty-four in a nychthemeron;[12]

and a star-catalogue, the so-called GU-text, in which the stars are arranged in 'strings' that lie along declination circles and thus measure right-ascensions or time-intervals.[13] This latter text employs the stars of the zenith (*ziqpu*), which are also separated by given right-ascensional differences.[14]

The use of the nineteen-year intercalation cycle by some astronomers may go back as far as the mid-eighth century in Babylon,[15] though the date of its acceptance as the basis for the civil calendar is far from clear.[16] In any case, this fundamental cycle, which is embedded in the late antique and medieval Jewish and Christian liturgical calendars,[17] some versions of which survive today, was widely known in the Achaemenid period (539–331 BC). At the same time the first serious attempts to devise mathematical models for predicting lunar and planetary phenomena began;[18] these attempts eventually culminated, in about 300 BC, in the systems used for computing the astronomical tables, *Ephemerides*, of the Seleucid and Parthian periods.[19]

In the Achaemenid and later periods the applications of celestial omens were expanded further. Among the more interesting of these are the use of such omens at the time of a nativity to determine the course and character of the native's[20] life,[21] or at the time of a year-beginning to determine the nature

---

[2] A linear zig-zag scheme is the name now given to one arithmetical method used by the Babylonians to represent deviations from the mean solar, lunar, and planetary movements. The tablet to which this refers is of the Old Babylonian period; systems A and B, discussed below, date from the Seleucid period and later.

[3] H. Hunger and D. Pingree, MUL.APIN. *An Astronomical Compendium in Cuneiform*, AfO 24 (Horn, 1989), 163–4.

[4] F. N. H. Al-Rawi and A. R. George, 'Enūma Anu Enlil XIV and other early Astronomical Tables', AfO 38/9 (1991–2), 52–73.

[5] C. B. F. Walker and H. Hunger, 'Zwölfmaldrei', *Mitteilungen der Deutsch-Orient Gesellschaft* 109 (1977), 27–34.

[6] BPO i.   [7] MUL.APIN (see n. 3) II i 38–67, and pp. 146–50.

[8] MUL.APIN II ii 43–iii 15, and p. 154.

[9] The gnomon is a pointer of a certain length that casts a shadow on a suitably marked surface; the time of the day can be read from this shadow.

[10] MUL.APIN II ii 21–42, and pp. 153–4.

[11] MUL.APIN II i 9–24 and A i–ii 20, and pp. 152–3.

[12] E. Reiner and D. Pingree, 'A Neo-Babylonian Report on Seasonal Hours', AfO 25 (1974–7), 50–5.

[13] D. Pingree and C. Walker, 'A Babylonian Star-Catalogue: BM 78161', in *A Scientific Humanist: Studies in Honor of Abraham Sachs* (Philadelphia, 1989), 313–22; for a different interpretation of this tablet see J. Koch, 'Der Sternenkatalog BM 78161', *Die Welt des Orients* 23 (1992), 39–67.

[14] J. Schaumberger, 'Die *Ziqpu*-Gestirne nach neuen Keilschrifttexten', *Zeitschrift für Assyriologie* 50 (1952), 214–29.

[15] This conjecture is based on the existence of lists of eclipse possibilities arranged in periods of 18 years, starting with the first

year of Nabu-naṣir (Nabonassar) in 747 BC, and on Ptolemy's correct conversion of an eclipse-triple in years 1 and 2 of Marduk-apla-iddin (Mardokempad), that is in 721/720 BC, into the Egyptian calendar. Both of these facts suggest that the Astronomical Diaries began to be kept in Babylon in the first year of Nabu-naṣir, and that the intercalations used by the astronomers who made the observations were regulated by the 19-year cycle so that the lists of possible eclipse dates would serve as an index to the Diaries, and so that Ptolemy could convert the dates in the Diaries into Egyptian dates with confidence.

[16] The usually accepted date is 384 BC, based on the data in R. A. Parker and W. H. Dubberstein, *Babylonian Chronology* (Providence, 1956); but, as has been pointed out by C. Walker, much of that data is derived not from documents dated in the civil calendar, but from astronomical tables that necessarily utilize the 19-year cycle.

[17] O. Neugebauer, *Ethiopic Astronomy and Computus* (Vienna, 1979).

[18] See e.g. O. Neugebauer and A. Sachs, 'Some Atypical Astronomical Cuneiform Texts', JCS 21 (1967), 183–218; and 22 (1969), 92–113; cf. HAMA 547–55. For the predictions of the 7th cent. see Pingree, 'Mesopotamian Celestial Omens'.

[19] The fundamental publication remains O. Neugebauer, *Astronomical Cuneiform Texts*, (hereafter abbreviated to ACT) 3 vols. (London, 1955); cf. HAMA, 347–540.

[20] 'Native' is the term for the person to whom the omens of nativity are applied.

[21] A. J. Sachs, 'Babylonian Horoscopes', JCS 6 (1952), 49–75; F. Rochberg-Halton, 'Babylonian Horoscopes and their Sources', *Orientalia* NS 58 (1989), 102–23; and eadem, 'TCL 6 13: Mixed

of the coming year;[22] and specific relationships were developed between the zodiacal signs and the planets on the one hand and various categories of terrestrial objects and human activities on the other.[23] Related to some of these themes are the associations, accumulated over centuries, between celestial and terrestrial events on a monthly basis which were incorporated in the *Astronomical Diaries*.[24] Those which we have at present were written in Babylon between 652 and 47 BC.

Roughly corresponding to the last three stages in the evolution of Mesopotamian astral omens and mathematical astronomy are three periods when these sciences were transmitted, in their contemporary forms, to other cultures, where they were usually modified so as better to suit the needs of the recipient civilizations. These periods are the neo-Assyrian, the Achaemenid, and the Hellenistic, each of which will be discussed separately. In the following brief survey there is only a rough indication of the technical character of the transmitted material; in most cases the publications referred to in the notes will supply the details.

The Neo-Assyrian Period
(*c*.1000–612 BC)

A. INDIA

Evidence for extensive contact between the Harappan civilization and Mesopotamia towards the end of the third millennium BC is overwhelmingly convincing. However, the interpretation of the inscriptions on Harappan seals as recording, in a Dravidian language, an astral religion related to an alleged counterpart in Mesopotamia[25] is too hypothetical and unsubstantiated for us to consider it further.

The influence of the astronomy of MUL.APIN upon Vedic texts composed between shortly before 1000 and about 500 BC can be clearly discerned in a number of respects.[26] There are, first of all, some similarities between the lists of the 18 constellations in the path of the Moon given in MUL.APIN[27] and the lists of 27 or 28 constellations (naksatras) found in three early Vedic texts.[28] These include the fact that both lists begin with the Pleiades, a choice motivated in the Mesopotamian tradition by the importance of the Pleiades (MUL.MUL) in intercalation rules, but one having no particular rationale within the Indian tradition; and the fact that deities are associated with the constellations in Mesopotamia in accordance with a theory that the constellations are the manifestations of those gods and goddesses, while the association of deities with the constellations in India seems totally arbitrary and unexpected. However, the fact remains that the two lists are not identical, so that whatever influence the Indians received from Mesopotamia, it does not suffice to explain the whole of what they did in response; this is generally true of all transmissions of knowledge from one culture to another. There is always a need for adjustments that will make the foreign ideas fit in better with those of the recipient culture.

In MUL.APIN an ideal year of 360 days divided into twelve equal months of 30 days each is employed for certain purposes.[29] This same ideal year is referred to in a late hymn of the *Rgveda*[30] and in the *Atharvaveda*.[31] Again, it serves a specific purpose in the Babylonian tradition, but is only an ornament of learning in the Indian. Similarly, in the real lunar calendar, intercalary months had been added by the Babylonians since the Old Babylonian period to cause the seasonal festivals to fall in months bearing specific names. Such intercalary months are first referred to in India in a

Traditions in Late Babylonian Astrology', *Zeitschrift für Assyriologie* 77 (1987), 207–28. An edition of all known nativity omens will soon be published by F. Rochberg-Halton.

[22] e.g. H. Hunger, *Spätbabylonische Texte aus Uruk* (Berlin, 1976), 95–9 (no. 93). The beginnings of such a technique can be traced to *Enūma Anu Enlil, BPO* ii. 78–9 (XVIII 14–16)) and to the second tablet of MUL.APIN II B 1–2, p. 150.

[23] E. F. Weidner, *Gestirn-Darstellungen auf babylonischen Tontafeln* (Vienna, 1967); and E. Reiner, *Babylonian Astral Magic* (Philadelphia, 1995), 94–5.

[24] A. Sachs and H. Hunger, *Astronomical Diaries and Related Texts from Babylon*, i–ii (Vienna, 1988–9).

[25] See, in particular, the various writings of A. Parpola on this subject, e.g. *The Sky-Garment* (Helsinki, 1985); and *Deciphering the Indus Script* (Cambridge, 1994).

[26] D. Pingree, 'MUL.APIN and Vedic Astronomy', DUMU-E₂-DUB-BA-A, *Studies in Honor of Åke W. Sjöberg* (Philadelphia, 1989), 439–45.

[27] MUL.APIN I 31–9 and p. 144.

[28] *Taittirīyasamhitā*, ed. A. Y. Dhupakara, 2nd edn (Pāradī, 1957), IV 4, 10; *Taittirīyabrāhmana*, ed. N. S. Godabole, as *Ānandāśrama Sanskrit Series* 37, 3 vols., 3rd edn. (Poona, 1979), I 5 and III 1; and *Atharvavedasamhitā*, ed. R. Roth and W. D. Whitney, 2nd edn. rev. M. Lindenau (Berlin, 1924), XIX 7, 2–5. For the possible identifications of these constellations see D. Pingree and P. Morrissey, 'On the Identification of the *Yogatārās* of the Indian *Naksatras*', *Journal for the History of Astronomy* 20 (1989), 99–119.

[29] e.g. MUL.APIN I ii 36–iii 12, and pp. 139–40.

[30] *Rgvedasamhitā*, ed. F. M. Müller, repr. as *Kāśī Sanskrit Series* 167, 3rd edn., 2 vols., (Vārānasī, 1965), I 164, 11.

[31] *Atharvaveda* IV 35, 4.

late hymn of the *Ṛgveda*.[32] This reflects the situation in the *Taittirīyasaṃhitā* which gives to the twelve months seasonally appropriate names like 'Hot', 'Cloudy', and 'Sweet', and also mentions an intercalary month whose function must have been to keep those month-names accurate.[33]

In the ideal calendar of MUL.APIN the critical points of the solar year—namely, the equinoxes and solstices—were placed on the fifteenth day of months I, IV, VII, and X, that is, on the nights of their full moons. In Yajurvedic texts the months are normally counted from the night of the full moon (*pūrṇimānta*) and this appears to be the older practice in the Vedic liturgical calendar even though it was recognized that the month might also be counted, as in Mesopotamia, from the night of the new moon (*amānta*).[34] One of the significances of the full moon night is that the year begins on such a night, but the choice of the full moon on which the year begins depends on the weather rather than on the dates of the equinoxes or solstices.[35]

However, in the later liturgical calendar recorded in a Vedic text[36] the months are reckoned from the new moon as in Mesopotamia and intercalation is employed by adding an extra month before the first month of the year, a practice also followed in the Babylonian calendar. This Vedic text also described the motion of the rising-point of the Sun north and south along the eastern horizon between the solstices;[37] the same phenomenon is described in similar detail in MUL.APIN.[38]

Finally, MUL.APIN associates each of the cardinal directions with a constellation: north with Ursa Maior (MAR.GÍD.DA 'wagon'), south with Piscis Austrinus (KU₆ 'fish'), west with Scorpius (GÍR.TAB 'scorpion') and east with Perseus (ŠU.GI 'old man') and the Pleiades (MUL.MUL *zappu* 'bristle').[39] In another Vedic text it is stated that the Pleiades (Kṛttikāḥ) rise to the east, and Ursa Maior (Saptarṣayaḥ) to the north.[40] Since all of this astronomical information from the tradition of MUL.APIN must have reached India through Iran, it is tempting to connect these associations of the stars and the cardinal directions with the concept of stars as generals of the directions found in the Pahlavī *Bundahishn*: Sirius (Tishtrya) is the general of the east, alpha Scorpii (Sadwēs) of the south, alpha Lyrae (Wanand) of the west, and (as in Mesopotamia and India) Ursa Maior (Haftōreng) of the north.[41]

Omens have probably always been regarded by Indians, as they have been by others, as a means of knowing the future.[42] There are, for instance, various references in the *Ṛgveda*[43] and in the *Atharvaveda*[44] to an ominous bird (*śakuna*). But the earliest attempts to list and classify omens and to provide their ritual countermeasures (*śānti*) occur in two places. The first is in the *Kauśikasūtra*[45] of the *Atharvaveda*; the other is the common source,[46] now lost, of the *Adbhutabrāhmaṇa* (which is adhyāya VI or V of the *Saḍviṃśabrāhmaṇa*), the *Āśvalāyanagṛhyapariśiṣṭa*, and the *Adbhutaśānti* of the *Atharvavedapariśiṣṭa*.[47] The omens in the latter are without apodoses, so that it is impossible to find exact parallels to them in the cuneiform omen series; but often the same phenomena occur as ominous. The *śānti* rituals for pacification, which are still important in Indian religious life, may well have been inspired by the Mesopotamian *namburbi* rituals that were performed in order to avert the impending harm for which omens had given warning.[48]

[32] *Ṛgveda* I 25, 8.

[33] *Taittirīyasaṃhitā* I 4, 14 and IV 4, 11.

[34] See e.g. *Taittirīyasaṃhitā* VII 5, 6.

[35] Ibid. VII 4, 8.

[36] *Kauṣītakibrāhmaṇa*, ed. G. V. Ojhā, Ānandāśrama Sanskrit Series 65, 2nd edn. (Poona, 1977), 19, 2.

[37] *Kauṣītakibrāhmaṇa* 19, 3.

[38] MUL.APIN II i 11–13 and 17–18, and pp. 150–2.

[39] MUL.APIN II i 68–70, and p. 152.

[40] *Śatapathabrāhmaṇa*, ed. V. Ś. Gauḍa and C. Ś. Caudharī, 3 vols. (Kāśī, 1937–40), 2, 1, 2, 3–4.

[41] W. B. Henning, 'An Astronomical Chapter of the Bundahishn', *Journal of the Royal Asiatic Society* (1942), 229–48, esp. 231.

[42] Concerning omen literature in India see D. Pingree, *Jyotiḥśāstra* (Wiesbaden, 1981), 67–80.

[43] *Ṛgveda* II 42–43 and X 165.

[44] *Atharvaveda* VI 27–29 and VII 64.

[45] M. Bloomfield, 'The Kauçika-sūtra of the Atharva-veda', *Journal of the American Oriental Society* 14 (1890), i–lxviii and 1–416, XIII = kandikās 93–136.

[46] N. Tsuji, 'On the Formation of the Adbhuta-Brāhmaṇa', *Annals of the Bhandarkar Oriental Research Institute* 48–9, (1968), 173–8.

[47] *Saḍviṃśabrāhmaṇa* with the *Vedārthaprakāśa* of Sāyaṇa, ed. B. R. Sharma, Kendriya Sanskrit Vidyapeetha Series 9 (Tirupati, 1967); the *Āśvalāyanagṛhyapariśiṣṭa*, ed. as Ānandāśrama Sanskrit Series 105, (Poona, 1937), IV 11–22; and the *Adbhutaśānti* of the *Atharvavedapariśiṣṭa*, see G. M. Bolling and J. von Negelein, *The Pariśiṣṭas of the Atharvaveda*, 2 vols. (Leipzig, 1909–10), pariśiṣṭa LXVII.

[48] E. Ebeling, 'Beiträge zur Kenntnis der Beschwörungsserie Namburbi', *Revue d'Assyriologie* 48 (1954), 1–15, 76–85, 130–41, and 178–191; 49 (1955), 32–41, 137–48, and 178–92; and 50 (1956), 22–33, and 86–94; and R. Caplice, 'Namburbi Texts in the British Museum', *Orientalia* NS 34 (1965), 105–31; 36 (1967), 1–38 and 273–98; 39 (1970), 111–51; and 40 (1971), 133–83.

B. GREECE

The earliest Greek text to display the influence of the Mesopotamian astronomy of the tradition of MUL.APIN is Homer's *Iliad*. The most persuasive echo is in the description of Achilles' shield as it was fashioned by Hephaistos:[49]

> On it he fashioned the earth, the heaven, and the sea,
> The unwearying Sun and the full Moon,
> On it all the signs with which heaven is wreathed,
> The Pleiades, the Hyades, and the might of Orion
> And the Bear which they call by the name Wagon,
> Which circles around it (heaven) and keeps an eye on Orion,
> Alone not sharing in the bathings of the Ocean.

In the first line earth, heaven, and sea correspond to the three Mesopotamian gods Enlil, Anu, and Ea, after whom the three 'paths' of the first star catalogue in MUL.APIN are named.[50] In the second line is given the situation of the common omens 'If on the fourteenth day the Moon and the Sun are seen together' and 'If the Moon and the Sun are in balance';[51] with the Moon in Libra or in Aries it was used as an intercalation criterion in MUL.APIN.[52] In the third line are mentioned the ominous constellations[53] in the sky, a reference to *Enūma Anu Enlil* Tablets 50 and 51,[54] some of whose constellation omens are found in MUL.APIN.[55] The fourth line mentions three constellations that are named in precisely this order in the Old Babylonian *Prayer to the Gods of the Night*,[56] namely MUL.MUL the Pleiades, *is lê* 'jaw of an ox', and SIPA.ZI.ANA 'true shepherd of Anu', and they are listed in this order in section B of *Astrolabe B* as stars of the Path of Ea.[57] In the fifth line we are informed that Ursa (Maior) is called 'Wagon', as it is in the cuneiform texts; and in the sixth and seventh lines that it circles about the sky and does not set. This reminds us not only of its position as the first of the circumpolar stars in the first star catalogue in MUL.APIN,[58]

but also of a comment on Tablet 50 of *Enūma Anu Enlil*: 'The Wagon stands all year, namely, it circles around.'[59]

In the *Odyssey* the division of the night into three parts[60] is perhaps influenced by the Mesopotamian division of the night into three watches. The *Odyssey* also mentions the turning-points (*tropai*) of the Sun, seen from the island called Syrie.[61] This probably refers to the kind of observations, described in MUL.APIN, of how the rising point of the Sun moves along the eastern horizon between the two solstices, as we have noted previously in connection with a Vedic description.

The agricultural calendar found in Hesiod's *Works and Days* is governed by the heliacal risings and settings and the culminations of certain constellations and individual stars.[62] Although this may have been inspired by the Mesopotamian tradition, precise correspondences are lacking.[63] What we can remark is that the five constellations or stars named by Hesiod are all familiar to the Mesopotamians; for the Pleiades are MUL.MUL, Sirius is KAK.SI.SA 'straight arrow', Arcturus is ŠUDUN 'yoke', Orion SIPA.ZI.ANA and the Hyades *is lê*.

On an island which is called by the doxographers either Syros or Syra, and which may be the island of Syriē where the *Odyssey* had located the observations of the solstices, lived one Pherekydes in the early sixth century BC. Diogenes Laertios claimed that his instrument for observing the turning-points of the Sun on the horizon, *hēliotropion*, was still preserved on Syros.[64] Pherekydes' contemporary, Thales of Miletos, is claimed to have predicted a solar eclipse on the occasion of a battle between Kyaxares the Mede and Alyattes the Lydian, and this eclipse is often identified with one that occurred on 28 May 585 BC. Aetios, a doxographer who wrote *c.* AD 110, is the first writer known to us to have stated that Thales understood the cause of a solar eclipse correctly.[65] More recent

---

[49] *Iliad* 18. 483–9 (and cf. *Od.* 5. 272–7); see O. Wenskus, *Astronomische Zeitangaben von Homer bis Theophrast* (Stuttgart, 1990), 35–8.

[50] MUL.APIN I i 1–ii 35, and pp. 137–9; see also *BPO* ii. 17–18.

[51] DIŠ UD.14.KAM 30 *u* 20 KI *ahameš* IGI.MEŠ; and DIŠ 30 *u* 20 *šitqulu*. These two omens are found frequently in, e.g. H. Hunger, *Astrological Reports to Assyrian Kings*, State Archives of Assyria 8 (Helsinki, 1992).

[52] MUL.APIN II i 14–15 and 19–21, and p. 151.

[53] Greek *teirea*.   [54] *BPO* ii.

[55] MUL.APIN II iii 16–iv 12, and pp. 145–6; cf, also MUL.APIN II i 25–31.

[56] A. L. Oppenheim, 'A New Prayer to the "Gods of the Night"',

Analecta Biblica 12 (1959), 282–301; cf. also *BPO* ii. 2–3.

[57] Section B of the text gives a more elaborate list than the other Astrolabe lists. *BPO* ii. 5.   [58] MUL.APIN I i 15–22, and p. 137.

[59] *BPO* ii, III 28 c on pp. 42–3.

[60] *Od.* 12. 312 and 14. 483; see Wenskus, *Astronomische Zeitangaben*, p. 33 n. 82.

[61] *Od.* 15. 403–4; see Wenskus, *Astronomische Zeitangaben*, 38–9.

[62] *Works and Days* 381–640.

[63] Wenskus, *Astronomische Zeitangaben*, 41–50.

[64] *Lives of the Philosophers* I. 119 = Diels-Kranz⁷ i. 44. 8; see also Wenskus, *Astronomische Zeitangaben*, 39–40.

[65] Aetius 2. 24. 1 = Diels-Kranz⁷ i. 78. 22–4.

scholars have claimed that Thales used Babylonian astronomy to make this prediction despite the fact that it was beyond the capability of Babylonian astronomy at that date to do so with confidence, though the Babylonians could indicate on which days at the end of a month or months to look for a solar eclipse.[66] I suspect that Thales actually made his prediction on the basis of Babylonian omens, in many of which the apodosis contains the prediction of a solar eclipse.[67] In support of this hypothesis is the fact that a Mesopotamian observer would have been able to choose the month in which to look, but our oldest teller of this tale, Herodotos,[68] claims that Thales predicted only the year, not the month, in which day would be changed into night.

In any case, Thales' younger contemporary, Anaximander, seems also to have used omens (presumably Babylonian) to predict an earthquake and volcanic eruption in Sparta.[69] He also is said to have first introduced the gnomon into Greece,[70] though he shares this claim with his pupil, Anaximenes.[71] The gnomon was, of course, well known in Mesopotamia; for example the second tablet of MUL.APIN contains a table of shadows derived from a gnomon.[72] And it is therefore truthfully that Herodotos reports that the Greeks learned of the hemispherical sundial (*polos*), the gnomon and the twelve parts of the day (the twelve *bēru*) from the Babylonians.[73]

The Achaemenid Period (538–331 BC)

A. INDIA

Probably in the late fifth century BC there was composed by Lagadha[74] in north-western India (presumably in the kingdom called Gandhāra by the Achaemenids) a manual for determining the (mean) times for performing those Vedic sacrifices which are bound to the seasons, to the months, or to a specific time of day; these are the obligatory sacrifices (*nitya*) or certain oblations (*haviryajna*) incumbent on all members of higher *varṇas* (*dvijas*).[75] This manual[76] is the first work on mathematical astronomy in India, and is almost entirely dependent on Mesopotamian sources of the seventh and sixth centuries BC as transmitted to India through an Achaemenid intermediary.[77] This text includes a description of an outflowing water-clock such as those attested in the Mesopotamian *Astrolabes*, in MUL.APIN[78] and in other cuneiform texts.[79] The amount of water that is poured into the water-clock for each period of daylight is determined by a characteristically Babylonian linear zig-zag function, as is the length of daylight itself; the latter function is based on the ratio 3 : 2 of the longest to the shortest day in the year, which ratio is Babylonian in origin and unsuitable for latitudes in most of India. Other Sanskrit texts of a slightly later period[80] but probably going back to Achaemenid sources, describe gnomons whose noon-shadows are also computed by Babylonian linear zig-zag functions; the Achaemenid sources are probably not directly reflected in the shadow-table of the Pahlavī *Shāyast ne shāyast*, which rather may be derived from an Indian prototype.[81] Finally, Lagadha's intercalation cycle of five years certainly owes its use of *tithis* (here, as in the cuneiform texts, a *tithi* is a thirtieth of a mean synodic month) to Babylonia and also, most likely, the idea of representing the relationship of the solar year to the synodic month in a mathematical form. But its year-length of 365 days perhaps comes from Iran, where this Egyptian parameter may have been adapted by the Achaemenids.[82]

[66] S. Parpola, *Letters from Assyrian and Babylonian Scholars*, State Archives of Assyria 10 (Helsinki, 1993), 34–5 (nos. 45 and 46) and 130–1 (no. 170); and see Hunger, *Reports*, 219 (no. 382).

[67] See e.g. *BPO* ii, XVIII 9 (pp. 78–9); F. Rochberg-Halton, *Aspects of Babylonian Celestial Divination: The Lunar Eclipse Tablets of Enūma Anu Enlil*, *AfO* 22 (Horn, 1988), 88 (XVI 18); 141 (XVIII A 27'); 162 (XIX I iv 4'); 169 (XIX III 5); 186 (XX I 2, B 9); 188 (XX II 9); etc.

[68] *Histories* 1. 74 = Diels-Kranz⁷ i. 74. 20–1.

[69] Cicero, *On Divination* 1. 50. 112 = Diels-Kranz⁷ i. 82. 23–6.

[70] Diogenes Laertios, *Lives of the Philosophers* 2. 1 = Diels-Kranz⁷ i. 81. 13–14; Eusebios, *Praeparatio evangelica* 10. 14. 11 = Diels-Kranz⁷ i. 82. 14–16; and Sudas s.v. Anaximandros = Diels-Kranz⁷ i. 82. 9.

[71] Pliny, *Natural History* 2. 187 = Diels-Kranz⁷ i. 93. 36–9.

[72] MUL.APIN II ii 21–42, and pp. 153–4.

[73] *Histories* 2. 109.   [74] *CESS* A5, 538a–543a.

[75] The *brāhmaṇas*, for instance, were members of a high *varṇa*.

A 'caste' (*jāti*) is not a *varṇa*, but a group which may or may not belong to a *varṇa*.

[76] The *Jyotiṣavedāṅga*, as preserved in the recension used by Ṛgvedīya Brāhmaṇas.

[77] D. Pingree, 'The Mesopotamian Origin of Early Indian Mathematical Astronomy', *Journal for the History of Astronomy* 4 (1973), 1–12.   [78] MUL.APIN II ii 43–iii 15, and p. 154.

[79] O. Neugebauer, 'The Water Clock in Babylonian Astronomy', *Isis* 37 (1947), 37–43.

[80] The *Arthaśāstra* of Kautilya and the *Śārdūlakarnāvadāna*; *Arthaśāstra*, ed. R. P. Kangle, 3 vols. (Bombay, 1960–5), II 20, 39–42; *Śārdūlakarnāvadāna*, ed. S. Mukhopadhyaya, (Santiniketan, 1954), 54–5 and 100–3.

[81] Translated into English by E. W. West, *Sacred Books of the East*, v (Oxford, 1880), 397–400.

[82] S. H. Taqizadeh, *Old Iranian Calendars* (London, 1938).

At the same time as this level of mathematical astronomy together with the water-clock and the gnomon was introduced into India, many of the omens of *Šumma ālu* (one of the chief Babylonian manuals of non-astronomical omens) and of *Enūma Anu Enlil* were transmitted into India, also through Iran. In a sermon entitled the *Brahmajālasutta*, which the Buddha delivered in the Pāli language in the fifth century BC, various activities engaged in by mendicants (*Śramaṇas*) and *Brāhmaṇas* in exchange for food are condemned, including the interpretation of omens.[83] In this sermon the Buddha lists the terrestrial phenomena that are ominous in almost precisely the same order as they occur in *Šumma ālu*. He catalogues the general topics of the protases of *Enūma Anu Enlil*, including some technical terms which echo their Mesopotamian equivalents: lunar eclipses, solar eclipses, observations of the stars (probably meant to include both constellations and planets), the Moon's and the Sun's going on their paths, their going off their paths (= changing their KI.GUB), the stars going on their paths (i.e. of Enlil, Anu, and Ea), the falling of meteors and shooting stars, the 'burning of the directions' (= IZI.AN.NE), earthquakes, thunder, and the risings, the settings, the brightness, and the dimness of the Moon, the Sun, and the stars.[84] Despite the Buddha's condemnation of these omens here (at least when they are interpreted for profit), in a later Buddhist story of about the first century AD[85] an outcaste displays a knowledge of the Babylonian mathematical astronomy of Lagadha and others, and of astral and terrestrial omens similar to those of *Enūma Anu Enlil* and of *Šumma ālu*, and this knowledge is used to establish that the outcaste is equal to a *Brāhmaṇa*.

Through this and related texts[86] Buddhism spread these Indian adaptations of Mesopotamian science to Central Asia, presumably beginning with the missionaries whom king Aśoka dispatched to that area in the middle of the third century BC. A local tradition of astral omens related to *Enūma Anu Enlil* developed in this region either from the Buddhists, or from remnants of Achaemenid lore, or from a combination of both. This development permitted the Chinese writer of the *Records of the Grand Historian*, composed shortly after 100 BC, to record omens from the region of the Oxus that are strikingly similar to some found on cuneiform tablets.[87] This tradition of celestial omens continued into medieval Sogdian.

The oldest complete collection of Mesopotamian-inspired omens that we have in Sanskrit is the vast *Gargasaṃhitā*. It was composed in about AD 100 on a basis of earlier material, and it represents an extensive Indianization of the phenomena which are included in the protases and of the predictions which are made in the apodoses. These changes are still apparent in the *Book of the Zodiac* that, in the relevant parts, was transmitted to the Mandaeans through Sassanian Iran.[88] The *Gargasaṃhitā* assembles omens from both *Šumma ālu* and *Enūma Anu Enlil*. Some sections of it that I have examined in manuscript (the work has not yet been edited or printed), for instance the chapter on Venus's motion,[89] indicate many cases of indisputable derivation from the older cuneiform texts, though frequently, even allowing for local Indian modification, in a more elaborate form. This suggests that the Sanskrit text and its many derivatives may preserve a stage in the development of Mesopotamian omens in the two or three centuries following the reign of Ashurbanipal, a period for which no Akkadian documents have yet been uncovered. These conclusions must remain tentative until the texts of the *Gargasaṃhitā* and of *Šumma ālu* and the rest of *Enūma Anu Enlil* are established, and their precise relationships are analysed in detail. But the *Gargasaṃhitā* and associated omen texts in Sanskrit[90]

[83] The sermon is preserved in the *Dīghanikāya*, ed. T. W. Rhys Davids, 3 vols. (London, 1899–1921), i. 1, 21–7; see D. Pingree, 'Mesopotamian Omens in Sanskrit', in D. Charpin and F. Joannès (eds.), *La Circulation des biens, des personnes et des idées dans le Proche-Orient ancien* (Paris, 1992), 375–9.

[84] See Ch. II, p. 39 for evidence that the Buddha's father had scholars versed in Chaldaean astronomy at his court.

[85] The *Śārdūlakarṇāvadana* (see n. 80).

[86] See e.g. D. Pingree, 'Astronomy and Astrology in India and Iran', *Isis* 54 (1963), 229–46, esp. 240–1.

[87] The *Shih-Chi*, written by Ssu-Ma Chi'en; see C. Bezold, 'Sze-ma Ts'ien und die babylonische Astrologie', *Ostasiatische Zeitschrift* 8 (1919), 42; see for further suggestions regarding Baby-

lonian influence on early Chinese astral omens J. Needham, *Science and Civilization in China*, ii (Cambridge, 1956), 353–4.

[88] See *CESS* A2, 116a–117b; A3, 29b; A4, 78a; and A5, 78b for Garga; and E. S. Drower, *The Book of the Zodiac* (London, 1949).

[89] D. Pingree, 'Venus Omens in India and Babylon', in F. Rochberg Halton (ed.), *Language, Literature and History*, American Oriental Society 67 (New Haven, 1987), 293–315.

[90] The *Paitāmahasiddhānta* of the *Viṣṇudharmottarapurāṇa*, *CESS* A4, 259a; the *Bṛhatsaṃhitā* of Varāhamihira, *CESS* A5, 564b–571a; with its commentary by Bhaṭṭotpala, *CESS* A4, 270b–272a, and A5, 246a–246b; and the *Bhadrabāhusaṃhitā* of Bhadrabāhu, *CESS* A4, 285a–286a, and A5, 250a–250b.

contain mathematical schemes for the motions of the planets, which are based (as are some cuneiform texts of the late Achaemenid period)[91] on the divisions of periods of visibility, invisibility, and retrogressions into smaller arcs and times, and their variation according to the longitude at which the period begins.[92] This shows that these Sanskrit texts do have their origins in Achaemenid Mesopotamia. They also provide us with the first mathematical models for the planets in India and with new information concerning the stage of development reached in planetary theory in Babylon, immediately preceding the brilliant achievement of the Seleucid period.

B. EGYPT

For our knowledge of celestial omens in Achaemenid Egypt we depend on one demotic papyrus written in the late second or early third century AD.[93] The first part of this text, on eclipse omens, is clearly datable to the Achaemenid period, and contains not only omens paralleled by those in the Moon and Sun sections of *Enūma Anu Enlil*, though modified for their application to Egyptian society, but also, it appears, a discussion of the Babylonian 18-year eclipse cycle. The date of the second part, on lunar omens, is not so clear, and may be post-Achaemenid; but the phenomena described in the protases can in general be matched with phenomena mentioned in the Moon section of *Enūma Anu Enlil*. Whether the omens from the Moon, Sun, and Storm-god sections described in Greek under the Ptolemies, which I will discuss later, are derived from a transmission during the Achaemenid or from one during the Hellenistic period has yet to be determined.

Also ambiguous is the date at which the programme of observation carried out by one Harkhebi

was introduced into Egypt, though it seems likely that it was sometime while the Achaemenids ruled that land. Harkhebi's activities are described in an inscription of the early third century BC on a statue of the astronomer found at Tell Faraoun.[94] The account mainly describes observations of phenomena related to those mentioned in MUL.APIN: the risings and settings of stars that are ominous, the presence of Venus in its (Babylonian) exaltation-sign Pisces, the culminations of the stars, the motion of (the rising-point of) the Sun to the north and to the south, and the determination of the length of daylight; to these he adds the prediction of the heliacal rising of Sirius, something which the Babylonians had started doing as early as the late seventh century BC.[95]

It was probably in the late Achaemenid period, in the middle of the fourth century BC, that Egyptian astronomers devised their own intercalation cycle of 25 years of 365 days each.[96] It is plausible to suggest that, like Lagadha in India and like Kleostratos of Tenedos, Oinopides of Chios, and Meton of Athens in Greece, the Egyptian astronomers were inspired by Babylonian models of the intercalation cycle.

C. GREECE

During the Achaemenid period the earliest Greek astronomers to imitate the Babylonians were observers of the turning-points of the Sun and inventors of intercalation cycles of 8 years (Kleostratos and Eudoxos), of 19 years as in Mesopotamia (Meton), and of 59 years (Oenopides). Also imitative of Mesopotamian star-lore was a calendar indicating the dates of star phenomena associated with changes in the weather (*parapegma*) constructed by Euktemon and Meton.[97] It is not unreasonable to consider Heraklitos'

[91] See e.g. O. Neugebauer and A. Sachs, 'Some Atypical Astronomical Cuneiform Texts I', *JCS* 21 (1967), 183–218, esp. 192–8 (Text C: Mars, Venus) and 209–10 (Text F: Saturn); and 'Some Atypical Astronomical Cuneiform Texts II', *JCS* 22 (1969), 92–113, esp. 93–4 (Text H: Mars); A. Aaboe, J. P. Britton, J. A. Henderson, O. Neugebauer, and A. J. Sachs, *Saros Cycle Dates and Related Babylonian Astronomical Texts* (Philadelphia, 1991), 35–43 (Text M: Mercury); and J. P. Britton and C. B. F. Walker, 'A 4th Century Babylonian Model for Venus: BM 33552', *Centaurus* 34 (1991), 97–118. Similar schemes are found occasionally among the Procedure Texts in *ACT* ii. 362–444, e.g. in no. 812 §§ 11–29 (Venus) on pp. 396–403; see also A. Aaboe and P. Huber, 'A Text Concerning Subdivisions of the Synodic Motion of Venus from Babylon: BM

37151', in M. de J. Ellis (ed.), *Essays on the Ancient Near East: Studies in Memory of Jacob Joel Finkelstein* (Hamden, Conn., 1977), 1–4.

[92] See, besides the article cited in note 85, D. Pingree, 'Babylonian Planetary Theory in Sanskrit Omen Texts', in J. L. Bergren and B. R. Goldstein (eds.), *From Ancient Omens to Statistical Mechanics, Essays on the Exact Sciences Presented to Asger Aaboe* (Copenhagen, 1987), 91–9.

[93] R. A. Parker, *A Vienna Demotic Papyrus on Eclipse- and Lunar Omina* (Providence, RI, 1959).   [94] *EAT* iii. 214–16.

[95] *HAMA* 542.   [96] *EAT* iii. 220–5.

[97] See A. C. Bowen and B. R. Goldstein, 'Meton of Athens and Astronomy in the Late Fifth Century B.C.', in E. Leichty *et al.* (eds.), *A Scientific Humanist* (Philadelphia, 1988), 39–81.

obscure statements concerning the Moon to be a part of this concern with intercalation cycles.[98]

By the late fifth and early fourth century BC other elements of contemporary Babylonian astronomy begin to appear in Greek texts. Plato in particular is aware of the periodicity of celestial phenomena and of the relative velocities of the planets;[99] some believe that he was also aware of the Babylonian division of the ecliptic into twelve equal parts.[100] Even if he were not, his pupil Eudoxos was. Indeed, one source claims that Eudoxos brought 'the Assyrian sphere' to Greece.[101] Though the Assyrians (and the Babylonians) did not construct celestial spheres, the statement is true in the sense that Eudoxos described a large number of constellations of which many were originally conceived in Mesopotamia. Eudoxos also places the solstices and equinoxes in the middles of the zodiacal signs Aries, Cancer, Libra, and Capricorn,[102] seeming to continue the tradition of MUL.APIN where they were located in the middles of the first, fourth, seventh, and tenth months. Another of Plato's pupils, Philip of Opus, was the first to name the planets in Greek, relying apparently on the 'barbarians' of Egypt and Syria.[103] The Greek gods whom he thus associated with the planets are clearly intended to correspond to the planetary deities of the Babylonians. It was probably only in the third century BC, however, that the Babylonian division of the zodiac into 360 degrees and their use of sexagesimal fractions were introduced into Greek astronomy.[104] Finally, there is evidence that Eudoxos was already aware of Babylonian nativity omens or hemerologies;[105] in the early Hellenistic period Theophrastos[106] praised the Chaldaeans for the predictions concerning 'the lives and deaths of individuals' and in the second decade of the third century BC Berossos on the island of Kos was successfully teaching the Babylonian form of genethlialogy.[107]

The Hellenistic Period and Thereafter (331 BC onwards)

A. THE WEST

In Ptolemaic Egypt in about the middle of the second century BC someone composed a treatise in Greek on astral omens and attributed it to Petosiris.[108] The fragments of this work, and similar fragments ascribed to the 'ancient Egyptians', are late reworkings of texts that were certainly influenced by Mesopotamian omens. It is not clear whether that influence came from Egyptian adaptations of the Achaemenid period or, as seems more likely, from Greek versions made in the second century. They are preserved in the *Effects (of Astral Phenomena)* (*Apotelesmatika*) composed by Hephaistion of Thebes in *c.* AD 415 and in the *On Signs* (*Peri sēmaiōn*) compiled by John of Lydia in about 550. These texts utilize lunar and solar eclipses and comets as the main ominous phenomena, but supplement them with wind-directions, shooting stars, halos, thunder, lightning, and rain. All of these are features of *Enūma Anu Enlil*, although the Greek tradition on comets is far more elaborate than that which is found in cuneiform. Some similar omens are given by Ptolemy.[109] The close affinities of these omens and those in other Greek texts of the Roman period with *Enūma Anu Enlil* were pointed out long ago by Bezold and Boll, for both form and content;[110] as more is known of the Akkadian texts more parallels become apparent. A large body of astral omen literature descends from this material, in Greek and Latin as well as in Aramaic, Hebrew, Syriac, Arabic, and Persian.

As just one example we may consider the *Apocalypse of Daniel*, of which we have a Greek translation of an Arabic text made by Alexius of Byzantium in 1245.[111]

---

[98] W. Burkert, 'Heraclitus and the Moon: The New Fragments in *P.Oxy.* 3710', *Illinois Classical Studies* 18 (1993), 49–55.

[99] Plato, *Republic* 529a–530b and 616b–617d; and *Timaeus* 39b–d and 40a–b.

[100] They depend on *Phaedrus* 246e–247c, which certainly does not refer directly to the zodiacal signs.

[101] An anonymous commentator on Aratos states this; see F. Lasserre, *Die Fragmente des Eudoxos von Knidos* (F. 2) (Berlin, 1966), 39.   [102] Ibid. (FF. 65–78) 52–6.

[103] Philip of Opus, *Epinomis* 986e–987d.   [104] *HAMA* 590.

[105] Lasserre, *Die Fragmente des Eudoxos*, (F. 343) 119. The study and recording of omens which determine lucky and unlucky days. For evidence that Herodotos quoted a Babylonian omen,

see Ch. V, p. 110.

[106] Proclus, *In Platonis Timaeum*, ed. E. Diehl, iii (Leipzig 1906), 151.

[107] Vitruvius, *On Architecture* 9. 6. 2. Genethlialogy is natal astrology.

[108] Concerning the several works attributed to this author and their contents, see D. Pingree s.v. Petosiris in *Dictionary of Scientific Biography*, x (New York, 1974), 547–9.

[109] Ptolemy, *Apotelesmatika* 2. 9. 18 and 2. 14.

[110] C. Bezold and F. Boll, *Reflexe astrologischer Keilinschriften bei griechischen Schriftstellern* (Heidelberg, 1911).

[111] *Catalogus Codicum Astrologorum Graecorum* 8, 3, (Brussels, 1912), 171–9.

The omens interpreted in this text include solar and lunar eclipses, halos around the two luminaries, new moons, comets, falling stars, rainbows, flashes of light, the reddening of the sky, thunder, lightning, rain, hail, and earthquakes—in other words, material from all parts of *Enūma Anu Enlil* including Moon, Sun, and Storm-god, but not Ishtar. Alexius informs us that the Arabic original that he turned into Greek had been translated itself from Greek in the 660s. Indeed, three versions of an apocalyptic prophecy of Daniel are available in Arabic.[112] The longest of them is stated to have been translated from Syriac and to be based on Dhū al-Qarnayn (Alexander the Great), Balaʿam, Andronikos,[113] Ptolemy, Hermes, and ʿUzayr (Ezra) or ʿAzīz the Scribe. And, indeed, a Syriac version of the *Apocalypse of Daniel* is extant.[114] Much remains to be done to clarify the interrelationships of all these texts, which are written in virtually every language of Europe and the Near East.

More momentous for mankind was the Greek invention of horoscopic astrology, probably in Egypt around 100 BC. It was made on the basis of Aristotelian physics, Hellenistic planetary theory and such elements of Mesopotamian astral science as the exaltation-signs of the planets, the dodecatemoria,[115] trine aspect,[116] and the benefic or malefic characters of the planets.[117] Some specific methods of computation that had been developed in Mesopotamia were also incorporated into Greek astrology. These include the computation of the date of the native's conception, found exemplified in several of the cuneiform 'proto-horoscopes' and attributed by the Greeks to Petosiris,[118] Epigenes,[119] and Zoroaster;[120] the Babylonian rising times according to System A for Babylon applied to the computation of the length of the native's life by Berossos, while Hypsikles' adaptation of System A for the latitude of Alexandria was used for the same purpose by Epigenes, and Petosiris used System A adapted for the latitude of Ancona; others employed System B.[121] System A was transmitted with Greek astrology to India in the second century AD and was recorded in Syriac by George, bishop of the Arabs, in the early eighth century. The scheme of lengths of moonlight on the thirty nights of a synodic month, which is found on Tablet 14 of *Enūma Anu Enlil*, occurs in modified forms twice in Pliny,[122] in Vettius Valens' *Anthologies*,[123] and in the *Geoponika* of Cassianus Bassus, who ascribes it to Zoroaster.[124] The spread of Greek astrology throughout the world has carried with it these traces of Babylonian science.

In about 300 BC the Babylonian lunar theory known as System B was formulated in columns which are labelled alphabetically by modern scholars, each column having characteristic, recognizable contents. The whole ephemerides belonging to this system were translated into Greek, as we now know from a papyrus fragment which preserves Column G; it can only be used in conjunction with the other columns of a System B ephemeris.[125] This papyrus can be dated to the second or third century AD. But System B was probably known earlier in Greek since its period relations and those of the Babylonian 18-year eclipse cycle form the basis of mean motions of the moon, its apogee, and its node recorded by Hipparchos in the mid-second century BC.[126] These parameters, slightly modified by Ptolemy, were adopted in the *Almagest* (c. AD 150) and thereby spread throughout Eurasia. The lunar and other astronomical theories of the Babylonian astronomers Kidenas, Naburianos,

[112] F. Sezgin, *Geschichte des arabischen Schrifttums*, vii (Leiden, 1979), 312–17.

[113] This work is also noticed in Syriac. A. Mingana, 'Some Early Judaeo-Christian Documents in the John Rylands Library', *Bulletin of the John Rylands Library* 4 (1917–18), 50–118; and E. A. Wallis Budge, *The Syriac Book of Medicines*, ii (London, 1913), 521 and 654.

[114] G. Furlani, 'Di una raccolta di trattati astrologici', *Rivista degli studi orientali* 7 (1916–18), 885–9, and 'Astrologisches aus syrischen Handschriften', *Zeitschrift der Deutschen Morgenländischen Gesellschaft* 75 (1921), 122–8, esp. 122–5.

[115] Dodecatemoria are twelfths of the zodiacal signs.

[116] Trine aspect: the aspect of two heavenly bodies which are 120 degrees (one-third of the zodiac) distant from each other.

[117] D. Pingree, 'Astrology', in J. North (ed.), *General History of Astronomy* (forthcoming).

[118] E. Riess, 'Nechepsonis et Petosiridis fragmenta magica', (F. 14) *Philologus*, Suppl. 6 (1892), 325–94, esp. 357–8.

[119] Censorinus, *De die natali*, 7. 5–6.

[120] J. Bidez and F. Cumont, *Les Mages hellénisés*, 2 vols. (Paris, 1938), ii. 161–2 (O 14).   [121] *HAMA* 712–24.

[122] Pliny, *Natural History* 2. 58 and 18. 324.

[123] Valens, *Anthologies* 1. 12. 1–6.

[124] Bidez and Cumont, *Les Mages hellénisés*, ii. 174–7 (O 39).

[125] O. Neugebauer, 'A Babylonian Lunar Ephemeris from Roman Egypt', in *A Scientific Humanist* (Philadelphia, 1988), 301–4.

[126] *HAMA* 309–12; see also for this and some of what follows, A. Jones, 'The Adaptation of Babylonian Methods in Greek Numerical Astronomy', *Isis* 82 (1991), 441–53, and id., 'Evidence for Babylonian Arithmetical Schemes in Greek Astronomy', in H. D. Galter (ed.), *Die Rolle der Astronomie in den Kulturen Mesopotamiens* (Graz, 1993), 77–94.

and Sudines are discussed by Posidonios,[127] Strabo,[128] Pliny,[129] Vettius Valens,[130] and an early third-century commentator on Ptolemy's *Handy Tables*.[131] Ptolemy in the *Almagest* was able to use ten Babylonian observations of lunar eclipses dated between 721 and 382 BC;[132] these were presumably all found in the cuneiform *Astronomical Diaries*. The Babylonian 18-year eclipse cycle, the so-called 'Saros', was tripled by Hipparchos to form the *exeligmos* of 54 years,[133] from which Geminus in the late first century AD derived a linear zig-zag function of lunar velocity.[134] Secondary functions for finding the movements in lunar longitude based on such a velocity function are found in Sanskrit texts of Greek origin.[135]

Extrapolating from the *Astronomical Diaries* the Babylonians compiled what we now call *Goal Year Texts* in order to predict astronomical events for the coming year. Those texts give clearly the periodic character of planetary movements. Ptolemy claims that the Babylonian goal-year periods are the basis for his mean daily motions of the five planets.[136] These goal-year periods were known to pseudo-Heliodoros, whose work is incorporated into the early seventh-century *Treasures* of Rhetorius of Egypt,[137] and they form the basis for a set of planetary tables constructed by al-Zarqālī at Toledo in the eleventh century,[138] following, he claims, the tables of Ammonios. This Ammonios must be Heliodoros' brother of that name who is known to have constructed astronomical tables.[139] There exist various translations of al-Zarqālī's tables into Spanish and Latin, as well as new tables using the goal-year periods in several languages, for example those of Profatius the Jew dated around 1300.[140] In India, planetary tables based on the Babylonian goal-year periods were produced, but substituting 142 synodic periods in 227 years for Venus instead of the normal Babylonian 5 synodic periods in 8 years, by Haridatta in 1638,[141] and by Trivikrama in 1704.[142] Both men wrote in Rājasthāna where they probably learned of the goal-year periods from one of the Sanskrit translations of Persian astronomical works. These texts belong to the Ptolemaic tradition and the translations were made in the early seventeenth century, as was, for instance, the *Yantraśiromani* composed by Viśrāma in 1615.[143] However, a local tradition of these goal-year periods may have survived in India from the fourth or fifth century; for fragments of Chinese astronomical tables of the twelfth and thirteenth centuries, and of Uighur astronomical tables of the fourteenth century, from Central Asia seem to be based on the goal-year periods, although they use the Indian constellations to measure longitudes.[144]

The long period-relations of the planets that underlie the Babylonian planetary *Ephemerides* of the Seleucid and Parthian periods were apparently known to John of Lydia in the middle of the sixth century,[145] and certainly to Rhetorius in the early seventh.[146] From Rhetorius descends the Byzantine tradition represented by Theophilos of Edessa in the eighth century[147] and

[127] F. Lasserre, 'Abrégé inédit du commentaire de Posidonios au Timée de Platon (PGen.inv.203)', in *Protagora, Antifonte, Posidonio, Aristotele*, (Florence, 1986), 71–127; and W. Hübner, 'Zum Planetenfragment des Sudines (PGen.inv.203)', *ZPE* 73 (1988), 33–42 and 109–110.   [128] Strabo, *Geography* 16. 1. 6.

[129] Pliny, *Natural History* 2. 39.

[130] Valens, *Anthologies* 9. 12. 10 (ed. Pingree, 1986); see also App. XXIII.

[131] A. Jones, *Ptolemy's First Commentator* (Philadelphia, 1990), 3. 6.   [132] *HAMA* 77–9, 81–2, 104, and 317–19.

[133] The exeligmos is a period of 669 months, at the end of which the cycle of eclipses repeats for the third time; it eliminates the $\frac{1}{3}$ day left over in a single eclipse cycle of $6585\frac{1}{3}$ days.

[134] *HAMA* 602–3.

[135] O. Neugebauer and D. Pingree, *The Pañcasiddhāntikā of Varāhamihira*, 2 vols. (Copenhagen, 1970–1), II 2–6 and vol. ii 16–22; and III 5–8 and vol. ii 26–8; and *CESS* A5, 564a–564b.

[136] *HAMA* 150–2.

[137] *HAMA* 1051–2. I am preparing an edition of Rhetorius' immense compilation, in which this material occupies 6. 2.

[138] J. M. Millás Vallicroza, *Estudios sobre Azarquiel* (Madrid and Granada, 1943–50), 72–237 and 378–94; see M. Boutelle, 'The Almanac of Azarquiel', *Centaurus* 12 (1967), 12–19.

[139] *HAMA* 1037. Rhetorius 6. 2 refers to Ammonios' *Kanōn* as a different text from the one ascribed to Heliodoros.

[140] J. Boffito and C. Melzi d'Eril, *Almanach Dantis Aligherii* (Florence, 1908); for Profatius' use of the *Toledan Tables* see G. J. Toomer, 'Prophatius Judaeus and the Toledan Tables', *Isis* 64 (1973), 351–5.

[141] D. Pingree, *Sanskrit Astronomical Tables in the United States* (Philadelphia, 1968), 55b–59b, and id., *Sanskrit Astronomical Tables in England* (Madras, 1973), 141–2.

[142] Pingree, *Sanskrit Astronomical Tables in the USA*, 64b–66a; and *CESS* A3, 92b–93b; A4, 105a; and A5, 131b.

[143] Viśrāma, *Yantraśiromani*, ed. K. K. Raikva, *The Yantrarāja of Mahendra Sūri* (Mumbayī, 1936), 83–117, I 92; see also *CESS* A5, 659b.

[144] Prof. Michio Yano of Kyoto has discovered the Chinese tables; for those in Uighur see G. R. Rachmati, *Türkische Turfan-Texte*, vii (Berlin, 1937), 9–11.

[145] John Lydus, *On Months* 3. 16, but this paragraph is preserved only in one manuscript.

[146] Rhetorius, *Treasures* 5. 51.

[147] Theophilus, *On Initiatives*, to be included in my forthcoming edition.

Michael Psellos in the eleventh.[148] The rich Arabic tradition begins with Māshā'allāh's borrowing the information from his colleague Theophilos.[149] These same periods appear in the Sanskrit *siddhānta* of Vasiṣṭha,[150] who clearly derived them from a Greek source translated into Sanskrit in the third or fourth century.

Another technique for computing planetary positions was developed from Mesopotamian prototypes by Greek and Egyptian astronomers in the early Roman period in Egypt. It consisted of tabulating the dates and longitudes of the Greek-letter phenomena[151] (as in the Babylonian *Ephemerides*) or one of them, and sometimes the dates of the planets' entries into the zodiacal signs (as in the Babylonian *Almanacs*), and then providing schemes that fill in the gaps in longitude and time between the phases. Parts of such systems survive in Demotic[152] and in Greek papyri.[153] Similar schemes are found in Sanskrit, but derived from a Greek source of the first century AD.[154]

Traces of Babylonian influence have been discerned in the reports of Greek observations of the fixed stars in the early third century BC.[155] In the next century Hipparchos used polar longitudes and co-declinations as his co-ordinate system for them.[156] He may have been influenced by a Babylonian use of an equivalent for right-ascensional differences in their culminations, as reflected in the *Zenith-star lists* and in the GU-text which lists meridian lines, 'strings'.[157] Hipparchos' practice probably lies behind the Indian choice of polar co-ordinates for the chief stars of the constellations.[158] Finally, Hipparchos' alignments of

fixed stars preserved by Ptolemy in the introduction to his star-catalogue[159] seem related conceptually at least to those in the cuneiform *Space-Intervals* (*dalbana-dalbana*) text which lists stars with reference to the intervals between them.[160]

I conclude this brief survey of the impact of Mesopotamian astral sciences on other civilizations by a brief consideration of the history of a very simple Babylonian lunar period-relation: nine anomalistic months equal 248 days.[161] Several cuneiform tablets of the last two centuries BC contain tables based on this period-relation; three Greek papyri, a reference by Geminus, a statement by Hipparchos quoted by Ptolemy, and several references in the *Anthologies* of Vettius Valens prove that the period-relation was known to Greek astronomers at least from the time of Hipparchos. Hipparchos himself, however, seems to have been the discoverer of a second period-relation: 110 anomalistic months equal 3,031 days. These period-relations appear in Indian texts, both together and separately.[162] The two period-relations supplemented by a third (449 anomalistic months equal 12,372 days, which is equivalent to four 3,031-day periods plus one 248-day period) were used as the basis of the *vākya*-system[163] for the Moon in South India shortly after AD 1000, while *vākya*-systems for the planets were constructed from the Babylonian period-relations given by Varāhamihira from the *Vasiṣṭhasiddhānta*. Finally, several Arabic compendia of astronomical tables (*zījes*) present descriptions of the Uighur calendar which indicate that the Uighurs, whom we have already seen to have used the goal-

[148] Michael Psellus, *Didaskalia pantodapē* 161; see also his fragmentary letter in P. Tannery, *Mémoires scientifiques*, iv (Paris, 1920), 264–5.

[149] E. S. Kennedy and D. Pingree, *The Astrological History of Māshā'allāh* (Cambridge, Mass., 1971), 132.

[150] The *Vasiṣṭasiddhānta*, summarized by Varāhamihira in his *Pañcasiddhāntikā* XVII 1–60 and vol. ii. 109–26.

[151] Greek letters are used to denote the first and last visibility of a planet in the east and in the west, as well as the stationary points of a planet in the east and in the west, and the acronychal rising of the superior planets.

[152] *EAT* iii. 225–41, and *HAMA* 789–92.

[153] See the articles by Jones cited in n. 126, and his forthcoming publication of astronomical papyri from Oxyrhynchus.

[154] In the *Yavanajātaka*, composed by Sphujidhvaja in 269 or 270: D. Pingree, *The Yavanajātaka of Sphujidhvaja*, Harvard Oriental Series 48, 2 vols. (Cambridge, Mass., 1978), LXXIX 35–51 and vol. ii. 410–14; and in the *Pauliśasiddhānta* as summarized by Varāhamihira, *Pañcasiddhāntikā* XVII 64–80, and vol. ii. 126–8; see *CESS* A4, 233a, and A5, 224b.

[155] B. R. Goldstein and A. C. Bowen, 'On Early Hellenistic Astronomy: Timocharis and the First Callippic Calendar', *Centaurus* 32 (1989), 272–93.

[156] *HAMA* 277–80.   [157] See above, nn. 13 and 14.

[158] The yogatārās of the nakṣatras. See the article by Pingree and Morrissey cited in n. 28.

[159] Ptolemy, *Almagest* 7. 1.

[160] C. B. F. Walker and J. Koch, 'The Dalbanna Text', *Die Welt des Orients*, 26 (1995), 27–85.

[161] A. Jones, 'The Development and Transmission of 248-day Schemes for Lunar Motion in Ancient Astronomy', *Archive for the History of the Exact Sciences* 29 (1983), 1–36.

[162] Both in the *Vasiṣṭhasiddhānta*; the first period-relation underlies the rule in the *Pauliśasiddhānta* and the second is used by the *Romakasiddhānta*; all three are known from their summaries in the *Pañcasiddhāntika* of Varāhamihira. For the *Romakasiddhānta* see *CESS* A5, 517b.

[163] This is a system of computation based on the use of successively smaller period-relations to determine lunar and planetary positions.

year periods for the planets, also used the 248-day period for the Moon.

The Babylonian legacy, then, permeates the divination, astrology, and astronomy of Eurasia from the beginning of the last millennium BC, and was the basis for much of what was done in Greece, in India, in Sassanian Iran, in Byzantium, in Syria, in Islam, in Central Asia, and in Western Europe. Even when local cultures imposed changes and improvements, the Babylonian identification of significant phenomena, and the parameters and structures of their mathem-

atical models, provide convincing evidence of their presence. These valuable 'trace-elements' allow us to reconstruct a true picture of the complex interchanges of scientific ideas that have characterized the history of Eurasia for at least the past 3,000 years. Much remains to be done since there remain immense quantities of tablets, papyri, and other manuscripts to be read and understood. I hope this brief survey will inspire others to join in the search for Babylon beyond the borders of Babylonia.

FURTHER READING

NORTH, J. , *The Fontana History of Astronomy and Cosmology* (London, 1994).

WALKER, C. (ed.), *Astronomy before the Telescope* (London, 1996).

VII

THE LEGACY OF BABYLON AND NINEVEH IN ARAMAIC SOURCES

Alison Salvesen

Aramaic and Syriac: Background

MOST PEOPLE, IF THEY KNOW ANYTHING about Aramaic, will rightly associate it with the language of Jesus. Those familiar with the Old Testament may recall that it was used much earlier by the Jews following their exile to Babylon (after 586 BC) and that parts of the Books of Daniel and Ezra are written in Aramaic, not Hebrew. Aramaic and its descendant Syriac still have an important function today in respectively the Jewish and Eastern Christian liturgies. But who were the original speakers of Aramaic, the Aramaeans?

The Aramaeans are somewhat unusual in having had a culture that survived their political independence and national existence, and a language that outlasted all of these, being spoken and written by groups quite unrelated to the original Aramaeans, and still used by a dwindling number of small communities in the Near East. Therefore the significance of Aramaic is out of all proportion to the political importance of the original Aramaeans.

The Aramaeans' emergence historically occurs at the end of the twelfth century BC, when they appear as a semi-nomadic people. But the first reference is in Assyrian royal inscriptions, in a fourteenth-century cuneiform text which mentions the 'fields of the Aramaeans'. In the time of the Assyrian king Tiglath-pileser I (1115–1077), the large number of Aramaeans migrating to the upper and middle regions of the Euphrates led to instability in the area. Assisted by the power vacuum of the time, the Hittite and Egyptian empires being in decline, the Aramaeans were able to gain control of inland Syria and the middle

Euphrates. There were nomadic raids on north-west Babylonia, where the Chaldaeans also appeared in the ninth century: though these people are often found in alliance with the Aramaeans against the Assyrians and popularly associated with them, they are probably unrelated to them.

The Aramaeans founded kingdoms in what corresponds roughly to inland Syria in the present day. In the south and central regions these were Zobah, Bit-Rehob, Maʿakah, Geshur, Damascus, Hamath: Bit-Agusi, Bit-Halupe and Bit-Adini on the middle Euphrates: Bit-Zamani on the upper Tigris: and Bit-Bahiani in northern Mesopotamia. (The tribal origin of these states is illustrated by some of these names, Bit meaning 'house' or 'clan'.) The tenth to eighth centuries BC marked the zenith of the Aramaeans' political fortunes, reflected in the many references to them in the Old Testament Books of Kings: the Israelite and Judaean monarchs had both friendly and hostile relations with Aram of Damascus, Aram-Zobah and Aram-Beth- (Bit-) Rehob.

By the ninth century, however, the Assyrians were recovering and were gradually able to incorporate the Aramaean kingdoms into the Assyrian system of provinces. The imperial policy of deporting groups of conquered peoples from their homes and resettling them further east brought large numbers of Aramaic speakers into the heart of the Assyrian Empire. In Babylonia Aramaean tribes had been settling since the early eleventh century, and their language noticeably influenced local usage. Thus the end of the Aramaeans' political independence was the beginning of their linguistic ascendancy, since Aramaic slowly began to be adopted as the chief language of first the Assyrian and then the Babylonian empire.

So Aramaic, originally the language of the Aramaeans alone, was to take on an importance out of all proportion to the number of its speakers. A Semitic language related to Hebrew, Akkadian, and Arabic, it was written like Hebrew and other west Semitic tongues using a consonantal alphabet. This means that vowels were not included in writing, though sometimes the presence of long vowels was indicated by a semiconsonant, an innovation of the Aramaeans: w for û or ô, y for î or ê, h or ' for final â. It was therefore far easier to write than Assyrian cuneiform which required a knowledge of hundreds of characters. For this reason, as the Aramaean kingdoms were broken up and their populations deported, the Assyrians began to adopt Aramaic as the medium of communication within the empire.

The period of transition from the use of Akkadian to Aramaic as the primary official language is illustrated by evidence from two monuments. First, the eighth-century statue of a man from Tell Fekherye provides a bilingual inscription, with neo-Assyrian on the front and Aramaic on the back, which may indicate that at this stage Aramaic was of secondary importance. A relief of Tiglath-pileser III (745–727) shows two scribes, one writing on clay, and the other on some sort of perishable material, presumably in Aramaic. This highlights the other advantage of Aramaic: it could be written on almost anything, whereas cuneiform demanded clay tablets or waxed boards. A common phenomenon in this time of transition was the attachment of Aramaic dockets or endorsements to cuneiform clay tablets, as a translated summary of their contents.

Another mark of close association is in words for professions, in which Aramaic mimics the *qaṭṭāl* pattern of formation commonly found for that type of noun in Akkadian.

Although the use of cuneiform writing continued into Seleucid times, Aramaic increasingly took over as the chancellery language in the neo-Babylonian empire (626–539) to facilitate communications, rather as English is used worldwide today even between non-English-speaking countries. For instance, in 2 Kings 18: 26, the ministers of King Hezekiah ask the Assyrian besiegers of Jerusalem to address them in Aramaic, which they understand, in order to prevent the Hebrew-speaking populace from being demoralized

65. Bilingual inscription in Akkadian and Aramaic on the statue of a local ruler from Tell Fekherye, north-east Syria.

by the Assyrians' threats. The incident took place in
701 BC. Although at this stage it was largely only those
in the upper echelons of society who spoke Aramaic,
it gradually became the vernacular language of many
different groups. In fact the population of Babylonia
was among the earliest to adopt it.

But it was the Achaemenid empire (539–330) which
particularly encouraged the use of Aramaic as a *lingua franca*, since the Iranian conquerors found its
script both simple and already widely used throughout their new territory. Educated people throughout
the region wrote in Aramaic, and their hastier writing style influenced the development of a more cur-
sive script. Though the use of Aramaic had eclipsed
Akkadian to a certain extent, it is important to note
that the Akkadian language had had a considerable impact on Aramaic. Its influence can be seen in
Aramaic phonology, morphology, and syntax, and it
provided many loan words, particularly in the area
of science, arts, religion, and law. Besides, Aramaic
writing itself was known in Greek, Egyptian, and
Jewish sources as 'Assyrian' script, since its development in the Assyrian period had not been forgotten.

Aramaic texts from the Achaemenid period have
been found in such far-flung places as Persepolis in
Persia, Elephantine in upper Egypt, and Daskyleion
in north-west Turkey. Most are from the fifth century BC. Excavations at Daskyleion have yielded *bullae* with cuneiform or Aramaic inscriptions, mainly
from the time of Xerxes, and from the same period
an Aramaic funerary inscription invoking the Babylonian gods Bel and Nebo to protect the tomb. At
Xanthos, on the south-west coast of Lycia, archaeologists discovered a trilingual inscription on a rectangular stele dating from the mid-fourth century BC.
Inscribed on the two wide faces of the stele are texts
in the indigenous languages of Lycian and Greek
which give the historical circumstances of the institution of a new cult set up near the sanctuary to Leto,
the mother of Apollo and Artemis. On the narrow
side facing the onlooker is the Aramaic text issued
by the satrap's chancellery, giving authorization to
the cult.

The great empire of the Mauryan kings in India,
built up by Ćandragupta in the time of Seleukos I,
was in contact with the Babylonian court. In 303
Ćandragupta made a treaty of alliance with Seleukos;
and his successor asked Antiochos I to send him
a sophist. The great king Aśoka, who converted to

66. Pair of scribes writing Akkadian on clay and Aramaic on
leather or papyrus for Tiglath-pileser III, eighth century BC.

67. Pair of scribes recording booty in Akkadian on a hinged writing board and in Aramaic on a scroll, shown on a sculpture of
Ashurbanipal, mid-seventh century BC.

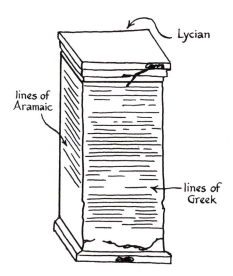

68. Trilingual inscription on an altar from Xanthos, south Turkey, in Aramaic, Greek, and Lycian.

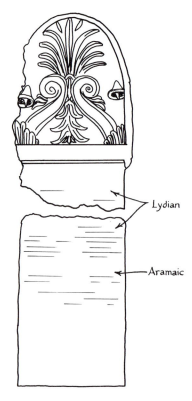

69. Marble anthemion from Sardis in west Turkey, inscribed in Lydian and Aramaic, 394 BC. Height 0.80 m.

Buddhism, put up inscriptions in Aramaic on rocks and pillars, most famously at Taxila, around 256 BC. Some of those found in Afghanistan are accompanied by a version in Greek or in Prakrit. Written Aramaic, therefore, was the chief language for international communication into which edicts composed in Prakrit were translated.

One of the most curious finds from the very end of this era is an exorcistic text from Seleucid Uruk, which is in Aramaic but written in cuneiform script. This text is very important both as a witness to the use of cuneiform at this late date and as a guide to the pronunciation of Aramaic in this region, since the vowels can be better represented in cuneiform syllabic writing than in Aramaic consonantal script.

Unfortunately, few official or purely literary Aramaic texts survived, simply because of the perishability of the materials on which the language could be written—parchment and papyrus—and those we do have were either carved on non-perishable media or were preserved by accidents of climate and geography, as with the Aramaic documents from the Dead Sea area and from Elephantine in Egypt. The Elephantine finds include a number of legal documents, in which the terminology has often been influenced by Babylonian and Assyrian formulae, as well as having links with Egyptian demotic legal style.

The influence of Aramaic as an international language slowly began to wane following the conquests of Alexander the Great in the Middle East in the late

70. Column capital from Sarnath near Benares on the River Ganges in India. Elements of the design predate Alexander. Aśoka added edicts in Aramaic, Greek, and Prakrit to such pillars in the third century BC.

71. Three shallow pottery bowls inscribed with incantations, two in Aramaic and one in Syriac. Similar bowls were also inscribed in Mandaean, Pahlavi, and Arabic. Babylonian gods were often invoked. Sassanian to early Islamic period. Diameters between 0.15 and 0.17 m.

fourth century. Greek tended to take its place as the *lingua franca* in the region. However, by that time Aramaic had become the vernacular language of several ethnic groups, including the Jewish population of Palestine. A large number of the Aramaic texts that remain are religious in nature, and for that reason were preserved through frequent copying and reverent safe-keeping. They include the treasured texts of Jews, Christians, and Mandaeans.[1] The Aramaic of this period, 300 BC–AD 600, varies in dialect and script. The Jews used what is known as Aramaic or 'Assyrian' square script, not only for Aramaic but also for

Hebrew, a practice that continues today. The types of Aramaic used by Jews in Palestine and Babylon differed. Christians used the dialect of the city of Edessa, Syriac, which became the Christian *lingua franca* of the Syro-Mesopotamian region rather as Latin was a means of communication for Christians in medieval Europe. Syriac script was semi-cursive and in time developed eastern and western forms. The Mandaeans' language was close to that of the Babylonian Jews, but was written in a script more akin to Syriac.

Apart from Aramaic's use by religious communities, it was the language of certain independent cities

[1] The Mandaeans are a Gnostic, non-Christian baptismal sect in Lower Mesopotamia.

and states during the Hellenistic period. These include Palmyra (Tadmor), the Parthian city of Hatra, and the Arabian state of Nabataea whose capital was Petra. Aramaic inscriptions from this period have also been discovered at Ashur.

Because of the role of Aramaic as the means of communication for government before it became the vernacular of many areas of Syria, Mesopotamia, and Palestine, it continued to transmit the earlier culture of the Assyrians and Babylonians, even though many of its users in the later period were monotheists or influenced by Hellenic culture. Incidental remarks in various Aramaic sources reveal the extent to which Mesopotamian religious ideas had spread abroad. For instance, an ostracon from the garrison at Elephantine wishes the writer's brother Haggai good health through the agency of Bel, Nebo, Shamash, and Nergal, and another Aramaic letter from the region refers to the existence of a temple of Nebo at Elephantine. Similar witnesses are found during the early Christian period. Most worthy of note are three parchment amulets written in Syriac for an Iranian client and dating from the sixth or seventh century AD, which reveal a highly syncretistic and eclectic approach to religion. Two commence with a Christian, Trinitarian, formula, but all three amulets then summon the aid of a variety of divine and celestial beings with Babylonian, Egyptian, and Mandaean connections, including Nebo, Bel, Shamish, Nergal, and Delibat—Ishtar of Dilbat, the morning star.

There are further examples of paganism surviving in magic and superstitious religion to a late date. Many exorcistic incantation bowls dating from just before the Islamic Conquests (mid-seventh century AD) were excavated at Nippur. Although most of them can be easily traced to the Christian, Jewish, or Mandaean communities by their differing scripts and the deities they invoke, one of them is in the form of an oracle of Nanay, Nirig (= Nergal), Sin, Shamash, and Bel against a spirit causing barrenness.[2] However, they are referred to as 'holy angels' rather than gods, also in contrast to the later Mandaean conception of them as the evil spirits of the seven planets. A similar attitude is found in an early Mandaean amulet which can still speak of 'Samish, Bel, and Nirig' as benevolent beings. The overlap between religion and astrology can be seen in borrowings such as Syriac 'āthaliyā and Mandaean tāliā, meaning 'eclipse', often referring to the dragon which in Mesopotamian thought caused eclipses by obscuring the moon by his head and tail. Both words are derived from Akkadian antalû, 'eclipse'. In addition, the Syriac term sām ḥayyē, 'medicine of life', used of Christ, is ultimately derived from the Akkadian phrase, šam balāti.

Dialogue Poetry

In addition to religious ideas, there are also themes, figures, and genres which survived from Assyrian and Babylonian culture and re-emerged in later literature, sometimes even influencing European writing.

Dialogue poetry is a long-lived genre that has strong roots in ancient Mesopotamia. Its main feature is a dispute, usually in poetic form, which takes place between two or more protagonists. They are often non-human, or personifications of abstract qualities. The subject is the relative merit of the protagonists, and this is argued out in debate form. The conclusion is either known already, achieved by clever argument, or decided by an outside authority. Most of these features are common to the earliest known forms which survive in cuneiform Sumerian dating from the beginning of the second millennium BC. They are also found two and a half millennia later, in Syriac, the Aramaic dialect of Edessa which became the literary language of Christians in the Near East. In addition, there are many poems of the medieval period in Hebrew, Arabic, Judaeo-Persian, Latin, and other languages, which ultimately derive from this same genre of dialogue poetry. The tenson of Spain and Provence is another related form.

The earliest dispute poems are in Sumerian, dating from the Old Babylonian period, and take place between natural rivals such as Summer and Winter, Cattle and Grain, Bird and Fish, Pickaxe and Plough, Tree and Reed, Silver and Copper, Upper and Lower Millstones, Heron and Turtle, Goose and Raven, Herdsman and Farmer. Some have survived complete and are up to 300 lines long, while others are fragmentary. In Akkadian from the Old Babylonian to neo-Assyrian periods we have debates between Tamarisk and Palm, Ox and Horse, Wheat and the

[2] J. Montgomery, Aramaic Incantation Bowls from Nippur (Philadelphia, 1913), no. 36.

Grain Goddess. The agricultural context is clearly apparent in the majority of these poems.

The basic structure in each case consists of an introduction to the presiding parties with a brief narrative, the matter of the dispute, and the dispute proper, where each protagonist praises himself and denigrates his opponent. At this point there may be some narrated action, and then the poem is rounded off by a third party. Sometimes there is reconciliation between the two sides. There are many exceptions to this pattern, but the debate sections are often similar. For instance, the structure of the Syriac dispute poems by St Ephrem the Syrian, writing in the fourth century, bears a strong resemblance to that of examples originating two millennia earlier.

But there is a missing link. There are few clear examples of the genre in Imperial Aramaic, where we would have expected to find them. This is no doubt because, in contrast to Sumerian and Akkadian examples preserved on cuneiform tablets, Aramaic tended to be written on perishable materials. However, some biblical passages have links with dialogue poetry: it has been suggested that Job's dialogues with his friends in the Book of Job may be based on a form containing shorter speeches against a single opponent—finally resolved, of course, by the Lord. Another example may be found in the dialogue of the lovers in the Song of Songs, or the argument of Wisdom and Folly in Proverbs 7–9.

In Aramaic itself the Book of Ahiqar refers to the bramble and the pomegranate in a way that may suggest an underlying dispute poem. In Jewish Aramaic, the Targums, or biblical paraphrases, often insert a dispute between Cain and Abel in Genesis 4: 8, and between Isaac and Ishmael in Genesis 22: 1. In these contexts, the dispute serves to explain the terse narrative and probably reflects the influence of the dialogue genre, rather than abbreviating a pre-existent dispute poem on the subject. There are more clear-cut disputes in the Targums, for example the Dispute of the Months at Exodus 12: 2 in some manuscripts, between Moses and the sea in Exodus 14: 29–31, and between the sea and the land over which of them should be made to keep the corpses of the drowned Egyptians. At Judges 5: 5 Mounts Tabor, Hermon, and Carmel argue over who should receive the Glorious Presence of God, but it is Sinai that is chosen. In Second Targum to Esther 7: 10, eleven or twelve trees discuss on which one of them the villain Haman is to be hanged. There is also a dispute of the Letters of the Alphabet as to whether Aleph or Beth should begin the first verse of the Bible.

In Middle Persian there is a poem called the Babylonian Tree, which resembles the earlier Akkadian poem the Tamarisk and the Date, but here the dispute is between the Date Palm and the Goat. It may date from the turn of the era.[3]

It is the Syriac poems, however, which provide the closest parallels with the Sumerian and Akkadian dispute poems. Their survival is due largely to their popularity which led to frequent and widespread copying. Some manuscripts contain only one side of the argument, and this suggests that they may have been performed as part of the church liturgy on certain occasions, with half the choir representing one protagonist and half the other.

The two main Syriac forms are the *drasha*, or dispute poem, and the *soghitha* (plural *soghyatha*), or dialogue poem. St Ephrem uses *drasha* form for a dispute between Death and Satan, between Death and Man, and between Virginity and Abstinence in marriage, and there are refrains which may serve a didactic purpose. (The argument between two different ways of life may owe a good deal to the Greek rhetorical school exercises and the diatribe of Stoic and Cynic moral preaching, as in the *Synkrisis Biōn* of Gregory of Nazianzus (AD 329–89).)

The *soghitha* form has some narrative elements, with dramatic but not always adversative dialogue. They are often anonymous compositions which elaborate on a biblical or theological theme. Alphabetic acrostics, where each stanza begins with a successive letter of the alphabet, are frequent, which may indicate a link with Jewish and biblical material since some Psalms have this feature, or else with the much earlier Babylonian syllabic acrostics of the thirteenth to twelfth centuries BC.[4] If performed in public, as they seem to have been, the *soghyatha* must have been close to religious drama. Often there are tragic overtones, as in the dialogue between Cain and Abel, or humorous ones, as in the *soghitha* of the Cherub and the Thief. In the latter the penitent thief who was crucified on Good Friday attempts to get into Paradise as promised by Christ, and the cherub

---

[3] See also Ch. VIII, p. 173.   [4] See Ch. III, p. 75.

stationed at the entrance at first refuses to let him pass. There are also dialogues between the Church and the Synagogue, between Body and Soul, and even between the theological opponents Nestorius and Cyril of Alexandria, a debate which is as fictional as the rest!

Wisdom Literature and Court Narratives

AHIQAR[5]

Wisdom literature was a very important genre in Antiquity all over the Middle East. Various collections of fables and maxims circulated, intended for the education of young men, especially those who aspired to civil office. Many examples of this ancient wisdom literature from the Near East survive, from passages in the *Epic of Gilgamesh*, through the biblical Book of Proverbs up to the sayings included in the twelfth-century Latin work *Disciplina Clericalis* of Pedro Alfonso. Given the enthusiasm in the ancient Near East for wise sayings and stories involving clever heroes, it is not surprising that one of its longest-lived tales should be about the sage Ahiqar, an Assyrian courtier.

There are many different versions of the story of Ahiqar, ranging from the tale of the vizier Haykar in the *Arabian Nights*, to the slave Aesop of the Greek Fables. Other texts in Syriac, Ethiopic, Armenian, Turkish, Georgian, Slavonic, Russian, Rumanian, and Serbian also exist, and there are allusions to the story in one of the Apocryphal writings of the Bible,[6] the Book of Tobit (see below). Most forms include one or two series of proverbs, said to have been uttered by Ahiqar in an effort to educate his recalcitrant nephew.

The basic form of the tale is as follows: Ahiqar is the counsellor of the Assyrian king Sennacherib, and therefore enjoys high status and influence, but to his great sadness he has been unable to father a son. He adopts his nephew Nadan and educates him as his successor. However, Nadan proves ungrateful, and unworthy of the opportunities offered to him. He makes a false accusation against Ahiqar to the king,

who is determined to execute his former minister, and sends an official named Nebosumiskun to kill Ahiqar. However, Nebosumiskun recognizes his victim as the man who once saved his own life when the king turned against him. So he hides Ahiqar and kills a slave in his stead. Since Ahiqar is thought to be dead, Pharaoh of Egypt uses the opportunity to test the king of Assyria by asking him to send a man who can perform an apparently impossible task in return for three years' worth of tribute from Egypt. If he fails the Assyrian king will have to pay his rival the same amount. In despair, the king mourns the death of the wise Ahiqar, and so Nebosumiskun is able to bring Ahiqar back to court. The king is delighted and sends Ahiqar to Egypt to carry out Pharaoh's task. Ahiqar is successful, and Pharaoh loses his claim for tribute. When Ahiqar returns to Assyria he punishes Nadan, and lectures him in a second set of proverbs. Nadan swells up and dies.

There was much dispute over the exact origins of the Ahiqar story, but these have now become clearer thanks to two archaeological discoveries in the twentieth century. The first was made at Elephantine in Egypt, where a fragmentary Aramaic papyrus was found. First published in 1911, it dates from the fifth century BC, and contains a simple version of the first part of the Ahiqar story, including references to the deities El, Shamash, and perhaps also Shamayn. Since the papyrus text is unlikely to represent the original manuscript of the story, the inference is that an Aramaic narrative of this sort underlies the many different versions that we know, later editors and translators being responsible for monotheizing the text. However, there are indications in the Aramaic that the story and the proverbs were once separate and have since been brought together, the narrative being in official Aramaic and the proverbs in a western dialect which predates it. Some have thought that the Aramaic Ahiqar story is itself a translation from Akkadian, but others believe that at least the proverbs were originally in Aramaic because of the wordplay between the words for 'arrow' and 'sin', which are similar in Aramaic.

The second archaeological discovery was of a clay cuneiform tablet at Warka/Uruk in a dig that took place in the winter of 1959/60. Although dated to the

---

[5] See also Ch. V, p. 118.
[6] Accepted by the Roman Catholic Church as part of the Bible but whose inspiration is rejected by other churches.

147th year of the Seleucid era (i.e. 165 BC), and therefore a late text, it gave part of a list of ancient kings and their wise men, *apkallu* or *ummânu*. The last complete entry names Esarhaddon and his *ummânu* 'Aba-Enlil-dari, whom the Ahlamu [Aramaeans] call Ahuqar.' This biographical information matches that of the Aramaic Ahiqar story, and offers several tantalizing possibilities: that Ahiqar may have been an historical figure at the Assyrian court; that the name Ahuqar/Ahiqar implies he was an Aramaean (hence the popularity of his story in Aramaic and Syriac); that his presence may have been due to the Queen Mother Naqiya, the Aramaean wife of Sennacherib and mother of Esarhaddon; and that the Ahiqar story may have had an Akkadian precursor. We also know from cuneiform sources that an official named Nabu-shum-ishkun served Sennacherib. Certainly the tale and the sets of proverbs that have been integrated into the narrative illustrate the symbiotic relationship between the Assyrians and Aramaeans, in terms of both culture and politics.

TOBIT

The story of Ahiqar was so well known that other writers felt at liberty to allude to it, and to bring in Ahiqar as a subordinate character in their own works. The Book of Tobit in the Apocrypha was probably written in Aramaic originally, and Aramaic fragments of the story were found among the Dead Sea Scrolls, but its full form survives only in Greek translation. It is the work of a Jew and tells of Tobit, an Israelite exiled to Nineveh under the Assyrian king Shalmaneser V (727–722). There Tobit angers his successor Sennacherib (705–681)[7] by burying executed Israelites: his property is confiscated and he runs away. Sennacherib is soon murdered by his sons, and Esarhaddon takes the throne (681–669). He appoints over the royal revenues Ahiqar, who is Tobit's brother's son and who petitions for Tobit's return to Nineveh. Ahiqar is described as 'chief cup-bearer, keeper of the privy seal, comptroller and treasurer' under Sennacherib and Esarhaddon. When Tobit is accidentally blinded by sparrow droppings Ahiqar looks after him for two years before going to Elymais. At the end of the story, when Tobit's son Tobias comes home with his bride and cures

his father's blindness, Ahiqar and Nadab (= Nadan)[8] come to see him.

These brief appearances of Ahiqar merely provide background to the main adventure involving Tobias, but it still seems a little daring of the author to hijack the character of Ahiqar and turn him into an Israelite, presumably with the intention of authenticating his own narrative. However, he may have been influenced by the figure of Joseph and perhaps also of Daniel (though the biblical Book of Daniel had not yet come into being), both of them Hebrews who held influential posts through their God-given wisdom.

As for the proverbs in Tobit (4: 4–21, 12: 6–11), these are Judaized too, though the recommendation to pour wine on the graves of the dead is far from biblical. The sayings in Tobit 4: 10, 12, 15, 17, 18 show some correspondence with those in the Syriac version of Ahiqar at 8: 41, 2: 5–6, 43, 10.

Finally, the filial piety of Tobias is contrasted strongly with the ingratitude of Nadan: at Tobit's death he reminds Tobias of what Nadan did to Ahiqar who brought him up, forcing him 'to hide in a living grave', and how Ahiqar survived to see God punish Nadan for what he had done by sending him into eternal darkness. Tobit even attributes Ahiqar's escape from Nadan's trap to his own almsgiving! The moral is drawn—charity brings escape from death, but wickedness leads to destruction. In this way the author of the Book of Tobit not only appropriated the character of Ahiqar but gave his story a thoroughly Jewish interpretation and colouring.

AESOP

The Ahiqar story was also a very strong influence on the Greek story of the ugly but clever slave Aesop. Many Greek writers from the time of Herodotos[9] onwards allude to the character, and the complete story of his life occurs in three recensions, the prototype of which probably goes back to the second century AD, though the tradition may date from the fifth century BC. Aesop was credited with wise fables, which often circulated independently of the Aesop narrative. The most developed and best-known form of the fables is that in Latin by Phaedrus in the first century AD, and this is the one that underlies the

---

[7] This chronology is based on that of the Old Testament, which misses out Sargon.

[8] B and N are readily miscopied in Aramaic script.

[9] 2. 134.

French version of La Fontaine in the seventeenth century.

The Life of Aesop describes the fortunes of a Thracian slave on the island of Samos, who outwits his enemies and masters, wins his freedom by interpreting an omen for the Samians, and is sent by them on an embassy to Kroisos of Lydia. He wins Kroisos' favour and writes fables for him.

Aesop then goes to the court of Lykurgos (or Lykeros), king of Babylon: this is where the Ahiqar story must have been inserted. The king is involved in riddle contests with other kings, and with Aesop's help he prevails. Aesop marries but has no children, so adopts the noble youth Ainos. Ainos turns out to be ungrateful and plots against his adoptive father, with the result that Lykurgos orders Aesop's execution for treachery. Aesop is secretly saved by the official Hermippos who conceals him in an empty tomb until a national crisis arises and Lykurgos regrets his action. Aesop is restored and Ainos' treachery unmasked, though Aesop forgives him and instructs him through wise proverbs. He also solves the crisis caused by the request of Nectanebo king of Egypt for a tower built in mid-air, and himself goes to Egypt to be the man able to answer any question whom Nectanebo challenged Lykurgos to provide. Some of the events in Egypt differ from those in the Ahiqar story, but Aesop eventually returns to Babylon laden with gifts.

At this point the story returns to the Greek form of the narrative, as Aesop goes back to Greece and is condemned to death on a false charge of sacrilege by the Delphians. He tries to plead for his life by telling fables, but is executed by being thrown off a cliff. When Delphi is subsequently smitten by plague, the citizens erect a monument in his memory and punishment is decreed for his murderers.

It has been argued that the middle part of the Aesop story, set in Babylon and Egypt, is not directly dependent on the Ahiqar story because the sets of fables are so different. Instead, it is said that Aesop and Ahiqar arose independently from the same eastern Mediterranean milieu in the sixth or fifth century BC. Given the very close parallels in the story lines, this is most unlikely, and it is far more probable that in each case different collections of favourite

proverbs and fables were tacked on at an appropriate moment in the narrative.

OTHER COURT NARRATIVES

The stories of Ahiqar and Tobit have their setting in the last two centuries of Assyrian rule, in the eighth/seventh centuries BC. Another story from the same background has recently come to light on a papyrus found in Egypt. The language is Aramaic, but it is written in Egyptian Demotic script. It tells of the confrontation between Ashurbanipal, king in Nineveh, and his brother Shamash-shum-ukin, king in Babylon, which culminates in the siege and capture of Babylon by Ashurbanipal and the death of his brother. It shows how popular tales from the Assyrian court must have been and how they found a keen audience in Egypt. Such popularity does not necessarily demand a Jewish component.

Stories centred around the courts of Nebuchadnezzar and Cyrus in Babylon a century or so later, all seem to feature Jews, especially the timeless sage Daniel.[10] The biblical Book of Daniel is quite a puzzle for scholars because it combines narrative and apocalyptic parts, and although it begins in Hebrew the middle section is in an updated form of the Aramaic used as an official medium of the Assyrian, neo-Babylonian, and Achaemenid empires. However, the change in genre does not coincide with the change in language.

The early part of the book concerns the fortunes of an observant Jewish exile in Babylon whose wisdom enables him to become a respected member of the royal court. When Nebuchadnezzar is troubled by a dream it is Daniel alone who can describe and interpret it, so the king makes him governor of Babylonia and head of his wise men. Daniel interprets a second troubling dream for Nebuchadnezzar, and warns him that it will be fulfilled if the king does not realize that it is God who confers human sovereignty. The king falls a victim to proud thoughts and so the divine threat comes to pass: Nebuchadnezzar loses his empire, he is driven from human society and becomes like a beast, eating grass like an ox and becoming drenched and bedraggled in appearance. After the allotted time of seven years has passed he

---

[10] See also Ch. III, p. 64 for the Book of Esther.

recovers his sanity and recognizes the sovereignty of the Most High God. His royal state is returned to him and he praises the King of Heaven (Daniel 4: 16–33).

The Book of Daniel as we have it represents a development of earlier traditions which was circulated in the early second century to encourage Jews persecuted by Antiochos Epiphanes, but some details such as the portrayal of Nebuchadnezzar can be traced a long way back. One clue can be found in the small Aramaic fragment found among the Dead Sea Scrolls at Qumran, the Prayer of Nabonidus. This text dates from the first century BC and it purports to be 'the words of the prayer which Nabonidus king of Babylon prayed when stricken by a terrible ulcer by the decree of God in Teman, for seven years'. The king says that he prayed to the gods of silver and gold, wood, stone, and clay, but it was only through God that he was forgiven. A Jewish diviner told him to 'recount and record in order to give honour to the name of God'.

This is of course reminiscent of Nebuchadnezzar's seven years of exile from human society and his consultation of Daniel concerning his dream, as described in the Bible. The name of the king has been changed, he speaks in the first person, and the order of events is slightly different. But the Qumran fragment and the Book of Daniel appear to have different elaborations of what is essentially a common tradition.

The historical Nabonidus did indeed spend a period of time away from Babylon, and lived principally in Tayma in Arabia for ten years (553–543 BC). In a stele he erected in Harran, he claims that at the behest of his god Sin, the king of the gods, he lived 'in seclusion of tracts far distant and secluded', and at the appointed time ten years later Sin said that he could return. However, there is no mention of madness or illness even in sources hostile to Nabonidus.

Not only is the Book of Daniel set in Babylon, but the story of Susanna and the tale of Bel and the Dragon (now relegated to the Apocrypha) also take place there. All the stories of the Daniel cycle in their present form were written in the Hellenistic period, at a considerable time after the events they purport to describe, and therefore some of the details are inaccurate from a historical point of view. This is particularly evident in another Apocryphal book, Judith, which depicts Nebuchadnezzar as king of Assyria rather than Babylon!

Balaam

In Numbers 22–4 the king of Moab in the time of Moses summons the diviner Balaam from Pethor to put a curse on the Israelites who are invading his land. On his way to fulfil his commission, he encounters an angel of Yahweh who insists that he speak only what God tells him to. As a result he finds it impossible to curse the Israelites and blesses them instead.

72. Balaam holding an astrolabe, from the Kennicott Bible. Drawn at Corunna, north-west Spain, completed AD 1476.

Other strands of the Old Testament tradition take a more negative view of Balaam, linking him to Israel's apostasy during the wanderings in the wilderness, and the later writers in the New Testament connect him with greed and sexual immorality rather than with divination.

Numbers 23: 7 and Deuteronomy 23: 4 suggest that Balaam came from northern Mesopotamia. Pethor, Balaam's home town, has been identified as Assyrian Pitru, which lies on a bend of the Euphrates south of Carchemish in Syria. During the Bronze Age its culture was predominantly Babylonian with much influence from Canaanites and Hittites. Extensive archives of tablets written in Babylonian cuneiform, dating to the twelfth century, have been excavated at Emar, to the south of Pitru along the river.

The antiquity of Balaam as a seer is attested independently of the Old Testament by an inscribed wall-plaster of the end of the eighth century excavated at Deir 'Alla in Palestine, a non-Israelite sanctuary. The text contains prophecies written in Aramaic and related to the Old Testament text. All these indications suggest that the biblical portrayal of Balaam is as a Mesopotamian diviner or *bārû*.[11]

Another figure in the Old Testament, Enoch, may also belong to a Mesopotamian milieu of divination. In the later, pseudepigraphical,[12] tradition of 1 Enoch, Enoch's role is developed into that of intermediary between heaven and earth. The earliest form of Book One of 1 Enoch, known as the 'Book of Watchers', was found in Aramaic among the Dead Sea Scrolls, and it begins with words and phrases taken from the biblical text about Balaam (Numbers 22).

Recently a considerable part of the *Apocryphon of Jannes and Jambres* has come to light. These are the two men who are named in 2 Timothy 3: 8 who resisted truth by withstanding Moses, a reference that does not quite correspond to the events described in Exodus 7: 11, where 'the wise men and sorcerers' of Egypt copy the miracles performed by Moses. They may also appear as 'Jannes [Jochanan] and his brother' in the *Damascus Document* found in the Cairo Geniza and at Qumran among the Dead Sea Scrolls where they are the evil counterparts of Moses and Aaron, and leaders of apostate Israel in Egypt.[13] This tradition is continued in medieval Jewish sources, where Jannes and Jambres lead the 'mixed multitude' out of Egypt and are the ones responsible for the worship of the Golden Calf. Pliny the Elder, writing in the first century AD, describes Moses, Jannes, and Jambres as magicians among the Jews, and Lucius Apuleius has a similar list the following century. Numenios of Apamea, writing in the second century AD, referred to them as Egyptian magicians and sacred scribes, but Jewish sources make them sons or assistants of Balaam, chiefs of the Chaldaeans who practised their magical expertise in Egypt.

Some scholars have suggested that the two magicians may be connected with the figures Harut and Marut in the Quran (in Surah 2, Al-Baqarah) where they are described as two angels in Babylon, to whom were revealed certain arts. The explanation of the commentators is that these two angels believed that if they became human they would propagate good conduct in the world, but when they did descend to earth, they were tempted and sinned and taught sorcery. They were punished by being suspended between earth and heaven, though the Arab writer al-Kisa'i (*c.*1200) says that they were hung upside down in a well in Babylon.

The *Apocryphon of Jannes and Jambres* also regards the two magicians as sons of Balaam. It has been recognized as belonging to a genre described as a magus legend, which shares many characteristics with the *Epic of Gilgamesh* and the *Tale of Buluqiya*.[14] Two themes in the Apocryphon can be linked with the *Epic of Gilgamesh*: of the intruder who enters Paradise and cuts down a tree; and of the unrepentant wise man who has sinned and who curses the prostitute at the time of his death.

It seems very likely, therefore, that Balaam has his origin in a Mesopotamian magician. The Near Eastern tradition that attributes two sorcerer sons, Jannes and Jambres, to Balaam may also go back to ancient Mesopotamia. Alternatively the three may have been associated by later Jewish tradition because all were magicians and also enemies of Israel and its true worship.

---

[11] See also Ch. III, p. 61.

[12] Pseudepigraphical works are those ascribed to a well-known figure in order to give them authority and authenticity.

[13] F. García Martínez, *The Dead Sea Scrolls Translated: The Qumran Texts in English* (Leiden, 1994), 36, 50.

[14] See Ch. VIII, pp. 171–2.

73. Statue of a god, perhaps the sun-god Shamash-Bel, from Temple V at Hatra. Height *c.*1.05 m.

74. Statue of Nanay from Hatra, inscribed in Aramaic, second–third century AD. Height 0.90 m.

Ashur and Hatra

The great cities in which the late cuneiform libraries, scholastic academies, and foreign overlords were based lay in the area of lower Mesopotamia that corresponds to Babylonia. By contrast in upper Mesopotamia in the impoverished cities of Assyria cuneiform writing was abandoned much earlier. It was replaced almost entirely by Aramaic; Greek influence was minimal. In Aramaic legal texts some terminology has been recognized as having Assyrian rather than Babylonian ancestry.

The city of Ashur suffered neglect for many centuries following the downfall of the Assyrian empire in 612 BC but its fortunes revived when Hatra was built only 50 kilometres to the west as a new foundation which became a major centre for Parthian kings. The early history of Hatra is unknown, and the earliest dated inscription of AD 97/8 may be two or three centuries later than the earliest monumental buildings. According to recent evidence Hatra was destroyed in AD 240 by the Sassanian king Ardashir. The city of Ashur seems to have gone into terminal decline at about the same time. There are many inscriptions at both Ashur and Hatra in Aramaic, dating from the Parthian era.

Two public buildings at Ashur are especially notewothy for the light they throw on the legacy of Assyria. Over the great temple of Ashur was built a new, Parthian-style temple with long halls (*iwans*)

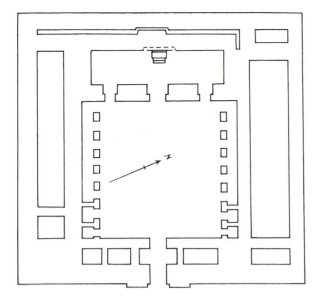

75. Parthian temple of the New Year festival at Ashur.

but it followed the alignment and orientation of the old temple. Aramaic votive inscriptions show that it was dedicated to Ashur and his consort Sherua,[15] a goddess who had vied with Mullissu ('Mylitta' in Herodotos) as spouse of the national god during the period of the Assyrian empire. Even more significant for continuity in ritual was the rebuilding of the temple of the New Year festival which stood outside the city walls. This shrine had been splendidly refurbished by Sennacherib early in the seventh century BC. The inhabitants of Ashur under Parthian rule rebuilt it according to the ancient plan, doing so because the ritual of its festival was still important.

At Hatra a deity named Issar-Bel on inscriptions was pre-eminent. This name, at first thought to be Ashur, is now firmly identified as belonging to a female deity, and can be related to earlier Assyrian Issar, a dialect form of Ishtar. The unexpected male epithet Bel may perhaps be connected to her role in the New Year rituals. In addition, the great temple at Hatra dedicated to the sun-god was called SGYL, i.e. Esagila, the name of Marduk's temple in Babylon.[16]

Other Babylonian and Assyrian gods were still worshipped in both cities. This implies the survival of ancient festivals and beliefs. Nabu is common in personal names: for instance at Ashur we find Nabû'aqeb, 'Nabu has protected'. Nergal is the subject of several

fine statues, sculptures, and dedications. The goddess Nanay is drawn and labelled on a potsherd, together with a god and a child as a family trinity. A stone statue of Nanay is labelled conveniently on the back.

Harran and Edessa

Just 50 kilometres apart, the cities of Edessa and Harran were rivals in Hellenistic times and under Islam in the medieval period. References to Harran date back to 2000 BC, and if ancient Edessa is to be identified with 'DM', a caravan station near Harran mentioned in eighteenth-century cuneiform itinerary lists, it too has a long history. Seleukos I Nikator founded a new city on the site of an older fortress there in 304 BC and named it Edessa, probably after the capital of Macedonia. But today the site of Harran is uninhabited, a circumstance that has facilitated archaeologists in their search for the city's history, while Edessa is now the town of Urfa in southern Turkey, about 65 kilometres north of the border with Syria.

In the early centuries AD the two cities represent a polarization in attitudes towards the new religion of Christianity. Edessa became the centre, if not the origin, of Syriac Christianity in Mesopotamia, while Harran remained steadfastly pagan, to the point that when a bishop was eventually appointed to the city in 361, he chose to reside in Edessa. At precisely the same time, when the Emperor Julian 'the Apostate' set out on his Persian campaign, he avoided Edessa simply because it was Christian, and went to Harran instead.[17] The Church historian Theodoret reported that Harran 'is a barbarous place, full of the thorns of paganism', and the pilgrim nun Aetheria would not visit it because there were so few Christians there, even in AD 384. The tenacity of ancient religious cults in Harran and the success of Christianity in Edessa can be explained to some extent by their different histories.

HARRAN

The name Harran is related to the Akkadian for 'caravan route', as it was on an important trade route.

---

[15] e.g. B. Aggoula, *Inscriptions et graffites araméens d'Assour* (Naples, 1985), no. 24.

[16] See B. Aggoula, *Inventaire des inscriptions hatréennes* (Paris,

1991), no. 107; also 191, 192, 225, 244, 245.

[17] Sozomen, *Hist, Eccl.* 6. 1. 1.

76. Stela of Nabonidus preserved in east entrance to Umayyad mosque at Harran.

It has links with the biblical narrative, as Abram is said to have migrated from Ur 'of the Chaldees' to Harran, and the names of his family recall place-names in the vicinity which are known from Assyrian cuneiform texts.[18]

Harran was also an important centre for the cult of the moon-god Sin. There are references to Harran among the Ebla tablets (*c.*2500 BC) and Mari tablets (1800 BC). The temple of Sin there, Ehulhul, was important enough to the Assyrian kings Shalmaneser III and Ashurbanipal to merit restoration. In the sixth century BC this temple was neglected for many years, but Nabonidus (555–539) eventually rebuilt it, on the instructions of Sin who appeared to him in a dream.

As for the city itself in the early period, Sargon II freed it of taxes, and it became the residence of the last Assyrian king around the time of the fall of Nineveh. A famous oracle was based there in Assyrian times.

In the Roman empire, Harran was known as Carrhae in accordance with its pronunciation at that date. It had ill-fated associations with three emperors, being the place where Crassus was defeated by the Parthians in 55 BC,[19] the scene of the assassination of Caracalla in AD 217 shortly after he had participated in the moon cult,[20] and a stop on Julian's disastrous expedition against the Persians in 363, the

halt having been made in order to sacrifice to the moon.[21]

Since the moon played a major role in Bedouin and Nabataean Arab religion, the pre-Roman rulers of Harran, who were of Arab stock, may have encouraged its cult. But it is clear from Greek and Latin writers that the cult of Sin continued to be of more than merely local importance in Harran well into the Christian period. In fact, on his expedition against the Byzantines in AD 549 the Persian emperor Khosroes granted Harran exemption from the tribute imposed on Edessa, on the grounds that the city was not Christian like his enemies, but 'of the old religion'.

Besides Sin, other divinities were worshipped there too. The emperor Theodosios had a temple of the sun destroyed in 382, which may have been located in Harran.[22] According to the anonymous Syriac work, the *Teaching of Addai*, which dates to the early fifth century, Harranians worshipped 'Bath Nikkal', i.e. the daughter of Ningal,[23] in addition to the sun and moon. The Syriac writer Isaac of Antioch says that Shamash, Sin, and Be'el-shamin were the divinities in Harran.[24] And Jacob of Sarug (451–521) mentions the deities of a number of cities, including Harran, whose gods he names as Bel-shamin, the Lord of the Heavens, perhaps to be identified with Sin; Bar-nemre, 'Son of the Shining One', perhaps Shamash, who is sometimes Sin's son in Mesopotamian mythology, or the Babylonian fire god Nusku, who was regarded as son of Sin at Harran, and may even have been identified as Nebo; Tar'atha, i.e. Atargatis, the Syrian Great Goddess; 'my lord with his dogs', a localized form of Nergal, ruler of the Underworld and brother of Sin; and Gadlat, an Arabian goddess. However, from the context in which this information appears it is clear that Jacob is speaking from a historical perspective, and his comments may not reflect the religious situation in Harran of his own time.[25]

SUMATAR HARABESI

From a reading of the Classical authors it seems likely that some of the major shrines for the Harranians were outside the city, so the findings at Sumatar

[18] See Ch. III, p. 68.   [19] Plutarch, *Life of Crassus*.
[20] Herodian 4. 13, Spartian 6. 4, Dio Cassius 8. 4.
[21] Ammianus Marcellinus 23. 3.
[22] Libanius, *Against the Priests*.
[23] However, some have suggested that the text should be read

'Beth Nikkal', 'house of Ningal'.
[24] *Opera Omnia* I, Hom, xi–xii, ed. Bickell. (Gissae, 1873).
[25] Memra on the Fall of the Idols, *Homiliae Selectae Mar Jacobi Sarugensis*, III, ed. P. Bedjan (Paris and Leipzig, 1907), pp. 797 f.

Harabesi may be of relevance. Sumatar Harabesi is a site 50 kilometres north-east of Harran, and 60 kilometres south-east of Edessa. The Syriac inscriptions found there date from AD 164/5, and include dedications to MR'LH', to be understood either as Marilaha, 'Lord God', or Marelahe, 'Lord of the gods'. The title may well be connected with the moon-god Sin because the site has yielded a number of moon symbols, for instance a pillar surmounted by a horned crescent. In addition, coins from Hatra had the inscription 'Sin MR'LH''. Segal equated Marilaha with Be'el-shamin, 'Lord of the Heavens', who was originally a west Semitic deity, the title then becoming a generic term for the supreme deity in any local pantheon. The name is also familiar from Jacob of Sarug's list of Harranian deities. On the other hand, the inscription could be read as Marelahe, 'Lord of the gods', the equivalent of the Akkadian title *Bēl-ilāni* which is applied to Sin in Nabonidus' inscriptions, but again was used for the chief divinity in local pantheons. The context in which MR'LH' appears in the Sumatar Harabesi inscriptions suggest that the god was seen as bestower of political power, a known function of the moon-god and reflected in Nabonidus' gratitude towards Sin in an earlier epoch.

The buildings excavated at Sumatar Harabesi are even more intriguing. There are eight groups of ruins, six of them consisting of a single building on top of a subterranean grotto with its entrance facing a central mount. The Syriac inscriptions and symbols of Sin mentioned above come from this site, and suggest that this was a cultic site dedicated to Sin in the mid- to late-second century AD.

There is some speculation that the buildings correspond to the Arab author al-Mas'udi's description of the temples of the Harranian Sabians who enjoyed the status of tolerated pagans under Muslim rule, and whose temples represented the seven planets as agents of the Supreme Being.[26] The religion was known as 'Chaldaean paganism' to the Arabs, which would indicate that the medieval cult of the Sabians was a development of the Harranian worship of Marilaha with an admixture of ancient Babylonian astrological religion, Hellenistic Hermetic ideas, and Indian influences. Animal sacrifices continued to play a part at the level of popular religion, but a more intellectual type of Sabianism was also known to Arab authors, where the Greek philosophical and Hermetic elements were paramount. This was no doubt the heritage of the Neoplatonic philosophers who seem to have taken refuge in Harran in the sixth century from the intolerant Christian orthodoxy of the Byzantine emperors. It was a Sabian of the ninth–tenth century, Thabit b. Qurra, who bore witness to the continuing failure of Christianity to influence the culture of Harran, when he stated that 'this blessed city has never been defiled with the error of Nazareth', and spoke proudly of the transmission of paganism by Harranians.

EDESSA

It is more than likely that many Edessenes journeyed to Sumatar Harabesi to practise pagan religious rites, and this would help to explain how Christianity could become strong within the city itself. But orthodox Christianity took some time to prevail there amongst the other religions such as paganism and Judaism, and sects that were variations on a Christian theme were influential at various times. Bardaisan (154–222) was a prominent Christian connected with Edessa, but what we know of his teachings is strongly marked by the influence of Mesopotamian astrology as well as by Hermeticism. Although Bardaisan rejected the idea that the planets exercised supreme control over the lives of individuals, the role of horoscopes in Bardaisanite cosmology was reduced, not eliminated. He still believed that astrological fate had an influence on human affairs, though its authority was ultimately derived from the Highest God and did not affect the exercise of moral choice. The fourth-century Christian poet Ephrem, who lived in Edessa for the last ten years of his life, said that Bardaisan saw the sun as Father of Life, the moon as Mother, and that he and his disciples descended into caves to sing hymns and expound their doctrine: again, there may be some connection to the caves at Sumatar Harabesi. Ephrem cannot be regarded as a very reliable source for Bardaisan's own teaching, but his observations may reflect in some measure the ideas of later followers. Certainly the notion that Fate and the stars played any part at all in life, even in a limited way, was anathema to orthodox Christianity,

---

[26] See Ch. VIII, p. 167.

which abhorred astrological practices and championed the doctrine of free will.

In spite of the *Teaching of Addai's* insistence that the population of Edessa largely converted to Christianity in the mid-first century AD, pagan theophoric names were still appearing in inscriptions and documents in the second century, such as Shamash-geram, Amath-Sin, Abad-Shamash, and Sharbel. In Edessa there was a gate called Beth Shemesh where once a temple to the sun had stood, and crescent moons and stars appeared on coins in the period of the monarchy which ended when Edessa finally became a Roman *colonia* in the mid-third century AD. From the same period there is a mosaic of Orpheus on the floor of a cave-tomb, which some scholars have connected with the god Nebo, who according to the *Apology of Pseudo-Melito*, ascribed to the late second century AD,[27] was identified with Orpheus at Hierapolis-Mabbug (Membidj), the city where the Syrian Great Goddess was worshipped. Other sources indicate the continuing importance of Nebo in the Christian period at Edessa. The son of Marduk/Bel, he was probably imported from Ashur and came to be regarded as the patron and protector of the city. He was linked with figures in other religious systems who were connected with wisdom: Hermes, Thoth, the Persian god Hoshang, Apollo, Enoch, Idris, and Orpheus. Bel is the other god who appears many times in Syriac sources and is a Babylonian deity.

The *Teaching of Addai* itself hints that the pagan cults continued, when it says that at the conversion of the city to Christianity the high places to Nebo and Bel were broken down, except for the great altar in the middle of the city.[28] The *Acts of the Martyr Sharbel* claim that in the fifteenth year of Trajan, Christians were made to sacrifice to Nebo and Bel in Edessa during the feast held on 8th Nisan. However, the historical reliability of this is unlikely.[29] Jacob of Sarug (died *c.*519) speaks of the worship of Nebo, Bel, 'and many others', although this may refer to the religious situation of the past.[30] But the rescript of the Emperor Theodosios in AD 382 grants the Edessenes permission to assemble in the pantheon, even though no sacrifice is permitted. The implication is that pagans

in Edessa were sufficiently influential to merit this concession. In the early fifth century the zealous bishop Rabbula destroyed some pagan shrines, and even at the end of the same century Joshua the Stylite reports the celebration of a spring festival. John of Ephesos records that in 579 Anatolios, the governor of Edessa, was caught in the act of secretly sacrificing to 'Zeus' in the city, and this may be an indication that the cult of Bel was continuing underground.[31]

So we can see that although the religious paths of Harran and Edessa diverged considerably in the early centuries AD, the cities were not completely polarized. Even some centuries after the Muslim conquest and subsequent widespread conversion to Islam, Assyrian–Babylonian concepts remained deeply embedded in Harranian religion, and had not been easily eradicated in Christian Edessa.

There is evidence that the situation was similar in other places in Mesopotamia in the early centuries of the Christian Era. It is particularly interesting when it is Christian sources that mention the continuation of the worship of ancient deities such as Nanay, whom the *Acts of the Martyrs of Karkha* say was still being worshipped by the inhabitants of Meisan.[32] The Syriac *Acts of Mar Ma'in*, describing events around the city of Dura-Europos, mention the cults of Nanay, Bel, and Nebo, and report that there was an altar to Nebo on a mountain top near the Euphrates where festivities took place. Another hagiographical text, the *Acts of Sharbel*, mentions a great spring festival linked to the cult of Bel. In the fifth century Isaac of Antioch speaks of the gods of the town of Beth Hur near Nisibis which was founded by Harran: 'Venus' i.e. Belti/Balthi, Gadlat, Shamash, and Sin.[33]

The Legacy in the Babylonian Talmud

The Babylonian Talmud is a compendium of legal discussions and decisions in Jewish Law which was committed to writing in Babylonia in the fifth century AD. The language is a mixture of Hebrew and Aramaic, and reflects the debates of the great rab-

[27] W. Cureton, *Spicilegium Syriacum* (London, 1855), 25, ll. 12–13.
[28] G. Howard, *The Teaching of Addai*, SBL Texts and Translations 16. Early Christian Literature Series 4. (Chico, Calif., 1981).
[29] W. Cureton, *Ancient Syriac Documents* (London and Edinburgh, 1864), 41–2.

[30] Memra on the Fall of the Idols, *Homiliae Selectae Mar Jacobi Sarugensis*, III pp. 797 f.   [31] *Hist. Eccl.* 3. 28.
[32] On the Persian Gulf, roughly present-day north Kuwait.
[33] Homilies on the conquest of Beth Hur by the Arabs (Bickell, pp. 167–70).

binical schools or *yeshivoth* which were centred around the lower Euphrates in Babylon, at Pumbedita and Sura in particular. Incidental details within the legal discussions and illustrative anecdotes reveal that Mesopotamian pagan practices and beliefs had persisted into this period.

Lecanomancy, or divination by dropping oil on water and interpreting the patterns that result, is a very ancient Mesopotamian practice. Passages in the Babylonian Talmud describe it, giving ritual instructions combined with hymns and prayers in a way attested in long-lived cuneiform manuals. The Aramaic text transformed the material for Judaic use, by turning Akkadian divine names into common names —for instance, Ea became Sea, and Sin, Shamash, and Marduk became three luminaries. Moreover, Jewish hymns and prayers were substituted for pagan ones.

Particular kinds of stones were specified in the Akkadian manuals, and they, like the deities, were made less specific in the Jewish adaptation. Both for healing and for divination the ancient Mesopotamians had developed a 'science' of stones, and their tradition remained prestigious throughout the Seleucid period when the Babylonian scholar Sudines was famous, and into the second century AD when Zachalias carried it on.[34]

Necromancy, particularly the practice of consulting a skull in order to contact a ghost, is well known in Assyrian texts. It is referred to in the Babylonian Talmud and the Mishnah, not always with approval, and the term used in the Hebrew Bible for a medium (*ba'alath 'ov*, 1 Samuel 28) is applied in some rabbinic literature equally to 'one who consults a skull'. Intermediate between cuneiform and Talmudic sources comes evidence from a skull found at Nippur and inscribed, apparently, with an exorcistic incantation, poorly preserved in Aramaic. It mentions Lilith, the female demon who was originally a Sumerian demon of the desolate steppe: Sumerian *lil* means 'wind'. Her various later derivatives attacked pregnant women and babies, and caused impotence in young men, and for this reason amulets were worn even by Jews and Christians to ward off her influence. The name Lilith occurs in Isaiah 34: 14, though this is variously translated by different versions, and the Hebrew word is derived from the Akkadian *lilītu*, the feminine form

of *lilu*. Many legends about her circulated in later Judaism, particularly the notion that she was Adam's first wife before Eve was formed from his rib, and she is also mentioned in the Talmud.[35]

The rabbis of Babylonian Judaism accepted the principles upon which Babylonian astrology and magic-science were based, but they differed over the degree to which Jews should practise them. Astronomy was uncontroversial, as it enabled the rabbis to intercalate the year and fix its festivals. The attitude to astrology was more equivocal. Some held that everybody had a *mazzāl* (Akk. *manzaltu*, 'position of a star'), a personal star which influenced his or her destiny. One rabbi even refused the headship of the prominent academy of Pumbeditha in Babylon, on the advice of an astrologer. But others denied that Jews were under the control of the heavenly bodies, holding that their lives were determined by their performance of *mitzvoth*, righteous acts that could avert even certain and astrologically predicted death.

The Jews were also aware of the Assyrian festivals of Kanuni and Mahur, which had given their names to months from at least 2000 BC in Assyria, in the forms *Kinūnum* and *Mahhur ili/muhur ilāni*. Similarly, at Hatra Kanun was still the name of a month in the second century AD, and continues to be used today in Syriac.

'AGGADIC MEASURES'

Rabbinic scholarship developed in the great Judaic schools of Mesopotamia as well as in Palestine. Over several centuries it formulated the so-called 'aggadic measures', a set of thirty-two rules for discovering the inner meanings of Scripture. They include cryptic techniques of letter substitution known as Athbash (e.g. A = Z, B = Y); puns, sound-play, and allegory; Notarikon, which involves taking parts of words as abbreviations for other words or as acronyms; Gematria, the substitution of numbers for letters (e.g. A = 1, B = 2, etc.), which gives Babel and Rome the same numerical value in Hebrew and thus equates the two 'evil empires' (compare Revelation 13: 18, where the number 666 is a cryptic allusion to Nero, being the numerological equivalent of his name). Similar methods were used by Greeks to interpret dreams and oracles.

---

[34] See also Ch. II, pp. 47–8.   [35] Nidd. 24b, BB. 73a, Shabb. 151b, 'Erub. 100b.

77. Church of Chaldaeans, who branched off from the Assyrian Church, in Aleppo, built in neo-Assyrian style.

Some of these hermeneutic techniques, especially Gematria and Notarikon, have now been recognized in Akkadian cuneiform texts of the Bronze Age (before *c.*1000 BC). Some can be dated as early as the third millennium BC, and they continue into the Iron Age. Gematria and Notarikon in their primitive forms can be traced back to the use of cuneiform writing, and to the bilingual (Sumerian/Akkadian) structure of that system. Such exegetical techniques certainly occur in cuneiform texts from the seventh or eighth centuries BC, and the method of numerological manipulation was known as *arû* in Assyria.

Although the terms Gematria and Notarikon are derived from Greek, it is unnecessary to assume that a Greek intermediary was responsible for the emergence of these techniques in Jewish hermeneutics. It is likely that both Jews and Greeks took over some of the 'aggadic measures' independently from Mesopotamian cuneiform, adapting them to their alphabetic scripts and developing them for their particular exegetical needs.

Syriac Views of the Assyrians

Christian authors writing in Syriac had a divided attitude to their heritage. On the one hand they rejected the traditional cults, whether the gods happened to be of Babylonian, Assyrian, Syrian, or Arab origin. In addition, Christians in the south of Mesopotamia felt no sense of continuity with the Babylonians,

and to them the term 'Chaldaean' was synonymous with 'astrologer'. But in the north the outlook was different, with Christians from Adiabene (Hadyab), Beth Garmai, Arbela (Irbil), and Karka de-Beth Selokh (Kirkuk) using the names Assyria and Assyrians (*Athor* and *Athoraye*) as geographical terms. For instance, in the late sixth century, an archdeacon from Arbela signed synodical documents for the metropolitan 'of the Assyrians'. On a more personal level, the legendary martyr Kardagh of the fourth century was said to be of the stock of the kingdom of the Assyrians, with Sennacherib on his mother's side, while the saints Behnam and his sister claimed direct descent from Sennacherib too. The Syriac *History of Karka de Beth Selokh* ascribes the city's foundation to 'King Sardana, son of Sanherib', i.e. Esarhaddon, son of Sennacherib, 'whose kingdom occupied a third of all the inhabited earth, and whom all the world feared'. It is claimed in the *History* that he was the king who responded to the preaching of Jonah in Nineveh by ordering a fast of repentance. In fact, the northern Syriac Christians were fascinated by the story of Jonah. Some works imply that the Ninevites, and therefore their Assyrian 'ancestors', were the first Gentile converts to Christianity, since Jonah is seen as prefiguring Christ. In the late sixth century, it was the metropolitan of Karka de Beth Selokh who introduced the Fast of the Ninevites into the church calendar of the Church of the East. This notion of a link between Christians living in northern Mesopotamia and the ancient Assyrians may go back to the account in 2

Kings 18: 9–12, where the king of Assyria deports many Israelites to cities in northern Mesopotamia. Similarly in 2 Kings 19: 36–7 Sennacherib's sons Adrammelech and Sharezer kill him as he worships in the temple of his god in Nineveh, and then flee to 'the land of Ararat', i.e. Armenia. The account is now partially substantiated by cuneiform texts of the early seventh century BC, where the son's name is given as Arda-Mulissi, which explains the forms in the Bible and Berossos, respectively Adramelech and Adramelos. From this event Jewish legends arose which relate that the fleeing sons released Jewish captives and became famous heroes. This legend was also used by the Armenians, and was chronicled by Michael the Syrian in the twelfth century.

Even today Syriac Christians originating from northern Iraq sometimes call their sons Sennacherib or Sargon, and consciously identify themselves with the past by calling themselves 'Assyrians' (*Athorayē*) rather than 'Syrians' (*Surāyē*). This was a nationalistic attitude fostered by Anglican missionaries to the Nestorian Church in the area during the nineteenth century and then encouraged by the British in the late 1940s. The identification supplies the need for a sense of nationhood, pride in the achievements of a powerful ancient civilization, and an ancestry connected with the Bible. The idea has now spread to some Syriac Christians of other denominations.

Conclusion

Babylonian and Assyrian civilization lived on in Aramaic culture in two main spheres of influence, the religious and the literary. In the Aramaic-speaking region of northern Mesopotamia, archaeological finds and comments in the works of Syriac writers demonstrate the longevity of ancient beliefs. Deities such as Sin and Nebo continued to be worshipped well into the Christian Era, alongside native Syrian and imported Hellenistic cults. Astrology and astronomy were particularly influential, perpetuated in worship as at Sumatar Harabesi and employed as a science by the Jews.

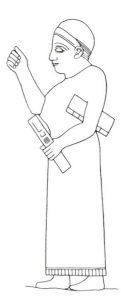

78. Scribe from Neirab in north Syria, sixth century BC. His hinged writing board was suitable for writing both Akkadian cuneiform and Aramaic.

Such traditions had been absorbed into Aramaic and Syriac from their Mesopotamian milieu. Aramaic had been used alongside Akkadian cuneiform at court for more than 150 years before it became the main language of the Achaemenid chancellery, and a thorough steeping in Mesopotamian genres led to the composition and popularity of Aramaic court narratives and dialogue poetry. Both Aramaic and Syriac were used while traditional Mesopotamian paganism flourished, hence the way in which pagan and astrological terms occasionally surface in Christian Syriac writing.

Much more must be lost to us because of the perishability of the materials on which Aramaic was so conveniently written. It is only when the process of copying and transmission was not disrupted (as in the case of the biblical material) or by some accident of climate (as with the Elephantine papyri) that clear evidence has survived. Even when literary forms and characters were Judaized or Christianized, for example Ahiqar as portrayed in the Book of Tobit, and Syriac dialogue poetry, their Babylonian and Akkadian antecedents are apparent.

FURTHER READING

1. Aramaic and Syriac: Background

ABOU ASSAF, A., BORDREUIL, P., and MILLARD, A. R., *La Statue de Tell Fekherye et son inscription bilingue assyro-araméenne* (Paris, 1982) [redated by Spycket and Sader, below].

AZARPAY, G., and KILMER, A., 'The Eclipse Dragon on an Arabic Frontispiece-Miniature', *Journal of the American Oriental Society* 98 (1978), 363–74.

BALKAN, K., 'Inscribed Bullae from Daskyleion-Ergili', *Anatolia* 4 (1959), 123–8.

BEYER, K., *The Aramaic Language* (English tr. J. F. Healey; Göttingen, 1986).

BONGARD-LEVIN, G. M., *Mauryan India* (English version, Calcutta, 1986).

BRINKMAN, J. A., *Prelude to Empire: Babylonian Society and Politics 747–626 B.C.* (Philadelphia, 1984), 12–14.

BROCK, S. P., 'Three Thousand Years of Aramaic Literature', *ARAM* 1 (1989), 11–23.

FALES, F. M., *Aramaic Epigraphs on Clay Tablets of the Neo-Assyrian Period = Studi semitici* NS 2 (Rome, 1986).

FURLANI, G., 'Tre trattati astrologici siriaci sulle eclissi solare e lunare', *Atti della Accademia Nazionale dei Lincei, Anno CCCXLIV Series VIII, Rendiconti, Classe di Scienze morali, storiche e filologiche*, 2 (1947), 569–606.

GARELLI, P., 'Importance et rôle des Araméens dans l'administration de l'empire assyrien', in H. Kühne, H.-J. Nissen, and J. Renger (eds.), *Mesopotamien und seine Nachbarn. Politische und Kulturelle Wechselbeziehungen im Alten Vorderasien vom 4. bis 1. Jahrtausend v. Chr.* (Berlin, 1982), 437–47.

GIGNOUX, P., *Incantations magiques syriaques* (Collection de la Revue des Études Juives; Louvain, 1987).

GORDON, C. H., 'The Aramaic Incantation in Cuneiform', *AfO* 12 (1937–9), 105–17.

GREENFIELD, J. C., 'Aramaic in the Achaemenian Empire', *Cambridge History of Iran* ii. 698–71.

—— 'Babylonian-Aramaic Relationship', in H. Kühne, H.-J. Nissen, and J. Renger (eds.), *Mesopotamien und seine Nachbarn. Politische und Kulturelle Wechselbeziehungen im Alten Vorderasien vom 4. bis 1. Jahrtausend v. Chr.* (Berlin, 1982), 471–82.

HEALEY, J. F., 'Ancient Aramaic Culture and the Bible', *ARAM* 1 (1989), 31–7.

KAUFMAN, S. A., *The Akkadian Influences on Aramaic* (Assyriological Studies 19; Chicago, 1974).

—— 'Languages (Aramaic)', *Anchor Bible Dictionary* iv. 173–8.

METZGER, H., et al., *Fouilles de Xanthos VI. La Stèle Trilingue du Létôon* (Paris, 1979).

MILLARD, A. R., 'Mesopotamia and the Bible', *ARAM* 1 (1989), 24–30.

MONTGOMERY, J., *Aramaic Incantation Bowls from Nippur* (Philadelphia, 1913).

NAVEH, J., 'Aramaic Script', *Anchor Bible Dictionary* i. 342–5.

NAVEH, J., and SHAKED, SH., *Amulets and Magic Bowls: Aramaic Incantations of Late Antiquity* (Jerusalem, 1985).

OATES, J., 'The Arameans', *CAH*[2] iii: 2. 184–6.

OELSNER, J., *Materialen zur babylonischen Gesellschaft und Kultur in hellenistischer Zeit* (Budapest, 1986).

POSTGATE, N., 'Ancient Assyria—A Multi Racial State', *ARAM* 1 (1989), 1–10.

SADER, H., *Les États araméens de Syrie* (Beirut, 1987), 23–9.

SPYCKET, A., 'La Statue bilingue de Tell Fekheriyé' *Revue d'Assyriologie* 79 (1985), 67–68.

STOL, M., 'The Moon as Seen by the Babylonians', in D. J. W. Meijer (ed.), *Natural Phenomena, their Meaning, Depiction and Description in the Ancient Near East* (Amsterdam and New York, 1992), 245–76.

TADMOR, H., 'The Aramaization of Assyria: Aspects of Western Impact', in Kühne, H., Nissen, H.-J., and Renger, J. (eds.), *Mesopotamien und seine Nachbarn. Politische und Kulturelle Wechselbeziehungen im Alten Vorderasien vom 4. bis 1. Jahrtausend v. Chr.* (Berlin, 1982), 449–70.

WIDENGREN, G., 'Aramaica et Syriaca', in *Hommages à André Dupont-Sommer* (Paris, 1971), 221–31.

YARON, R., 'Aramaic Deeds of Conveyance', *Biblica* 41 (1960), 248–74, 379–94.

2. Dialogue Poetry

BROCK, S. P., 'Dramatic Dialogue Poems', in H. J. W. Drijvers et al. (eds.), *IV Symposium Syriacum* (Orientalia Christiana Analecta 229; Rome, 1987), 135–47.

GORDON, E. I., 'A New Look at the Wisdom of Sumer and Akkad', *Bibliotheca Orientalis* 17 (1960), 122–52, esp. 144–7.

LAMBERT, W. G., *Babylonian Wisdom Literature* (Oxford, 1960), ch. 7.

MURRAY, R., 'Aramaic and Syriac Dispute-Poems and their Connections' [presented at the Aramaic conference, London, 1991].

REININK, G. J., and VANSTIPHOUT, H. L. J. (eds.), *Dispute and Dialogue Poems in the Ancient and Medieval Near East* (Leuven, 1991).

VANSTIPHOUT, H. L. J., 'The Mesopotamian Debate Poems: A General Presentation. Part I', *Acta Sumerologica* 12 (1990), 271–318; 'Part II', 14 (1992), 339–67.

3. Wisdom Literature and Court Narratives: Ahiqar and Tobit

Introductory Reading

CHARLES, R. H., *The Apocrypha and Pseudepigrapha of the Old Testament in English*, ii (Oxford, 1913), 715–84.

CONYBEARE, F. C., HARRIS, J. R., and SMITH LEWIS, A., *The Story of Ahikar from the Syriac, Arabic, Armenian, Ethiopic, Greek and Slavonic Versions* (London, 1898).

GARCÍA MARTINEZ, F., *The Dead Sea Scrolls Translated: The Qumran Texts in English* (Leiden, 1994), 293–9.

JONES, J. R., and KELLER, J. E., *The Scholar's Guide: A Translation of the Twelfth Century* Disciplina Clericalis *of Pedro Alfonso* (Toronto, 1969).

LINDENBERGER, J. M., 'Ahiqar', in J. H. Charlesworth (ed.), *The Old Testament Pseudepigrapha* (London, 1985) ii. 479–507.

MOORE, C. A., 'Tobit, the Book of', *Anchor Bible Dictionary* (New York, 1992) vi. 585–94.

SCHÜRER, E., *The History of the Jewish People in the Age of Jesus Christ* (rev. edn., ed. G. Vermes, F. Millar, and M. Goodman; Edinburgh, 1986) iii: 1, 232–9.

More Specialized Reading

CAZELLES, H., 'Le Personnage d'Achior dans le livre de Judith', *Recherche de science religieuse* 39 (1951), 125–37, 324–7.

COWLEY, A. E., *Aramaic Papyri of the Fifth Century B.C.* (Oxford, 1923), 204–48.

GREENFIELD, J. C., 'Ahiqar in the Book of Tobit', in J. Doré, P. Grelot, and M. Carrez (eds.), *De la Torah au Messie* (Paris, 1981), 329–36.

GRELOT, P., 'Histoire et sagesse d'Ahiqar l'assyrien', *Documents araméens d'Égypte* (Paris, 1972), 425–52.

HARRIS, J. R., CONYBEARE, F. C., and LEWIS, A. S., *The Story of Ahikar* (Cambridge, 1913).

KOTTSIEPER, I., *Die Sprache der Ahiqarsprüche*, BZAW 194 (Berlin, 1990).

LINDENBERGER, J. M., *The Aramaic Proverbs of Ahiqar* (Baltimore and London, 1983).

NAU, F., *Histoire et Sagesse d'Ahiqar l'Assyrien* (Paris, 1909).

REINER, E., 'The Etiological Myth of the Seven Sages', *Orientalia* NS 30 (1961), 1–11.

RUPPERT, L., 'Zur Funktion der Achikar-Notizen im Buch Tobias', *Biblische Zeitschrift* NS 20 (1976), 232–7.

VAN DIJK, J., *XVIII Vorläufiger Bericht . . . Ausgrabungen in Uruk-Warka, Winter 1959/60*, Deutsche Orient Gesellschaft Abhandlungen 7 (Berlin, 1962), 43–52.

Aesop

DALY, L. W., *Aesop without Morals* (New York and London, 1961).

GROTANELLI, C., 'Aesop in Babylon' in H. Kühne, H.-J. Nissen, and J. Renger (eds.), *Mesopotamien und seine Nachbarn: Politische und Kulturelle Wechselbeziehungen im Alten Vorderasien vom 4. bis 1. Jahrtausend v. Chr.* (Berlin, 1982), 555–72.

PERRY, B. E., *Babrius and Phaedrus* (Cambridge, Mass., 1965).

Other Court Narratives

COXON, P., 'Another Look at Nebuchadnezzar's Madness', in A. S. Van der Woude (ed.), *The Book of Daniel in the Light of New Findings* (Leuven, 1993), 211–22.

COLLINS, J. J., 'Prayer of Nabonidus', *Anchor Bible Dictionary*, iv. 976–7.

FITZMYER, J. A., and HARRINGTON, D. J., *A Manual of Palestinian Aramaic Texts* (Rome, 1978): Prayer of Nabonidus, 2–4.

GADD, C. J., 'The Harran inscriptions of Nabonidus', *Anatolian Studies* 8 (1958), 58.

GARCÍA MARTINEZ, F., *The Dead Sea Scrolls Translated: The Qumran Texts in English* (Leiden, 1994), 288–90.

PIGULEVSKAYA, N., *Les Villes de l'état iranien aux époques parthe et sassanide* (Paris, 1963).

SACK, R. H., 'Nabonidus', *Anchor Bible Dictionary*, iv. 973–6.

STEINER, R. C., and NIMS, C. F., 'Ashurbanipal and Shamash-shum-ukin: A Tale of Two Brothers from the Aramaic Text in Demotic Script', *Revue Biblique* 92: 1 (1985), 60–81.

VERMES, G., *The Dead Sea Scrolls in English* (3rd edn., Sheffield, 1987), 274–5.

4. Balaam

DAICHES, S., 'Balaam—A Babylonian *bārû*: The Episode of Num. 22,2–22,24 and some Babylonian Parallels', in *Hilprecht Anniversary Volume: Studies in Assyriology and Archaeology* (Leipzig, 1909), 60–70.

GARCÍA MARTINEZ, F., *The Dead Sea Scrolls Translated: The Qumran Texts in English* (Leiden, 1994), 246–59.

HOFTIJZER, J., and VAN DER KOOIJ, G., (eds.), *The Balaam Text from Deir 'Alla Reconsidered* (Leiden, 1991).

HOROVITZ, J., *Koranische Untersuchungen* (Berlin and Leipzig, 1926), 146–8.

LARGEMENT, R., 'Les Oracles de Bile'am et la mantique suméro-akkadienne', *École des langues orientales anciennes de l'Institut Catholique de Paris: Mémorial du cinquantenaire 1914–1964* (Paris, 1964), 37–50.

MARGOLIOUTH, D. S., 'Harut and Marut', *Moslem World* 18 (1928), 67–79.

THACKSTON, W. M., *The Tales of the Prophets of al-Kisa'i* (Boston, 1978).

PIETERSMA, A., *The Apocryphon of Jannes and Jambres the Magicians*, P. Chester Beatty XVI (1994).

VANDERKAM, J. C., *Enoch and the Growth of an Apocalyptic Tradition* (Washington, 1984), 33–43, 114–18.

5. Ashur and Hatra

AGGOULA, B., *Inscriptions et graffites araméens d'Assour* (Naples, 1985).

—— *Inventaire des inscriptions hatréennes* (Paris, 1991).

DALLEY, S., 'Nineveh after 612 BC', *Altorientalische Forschungen* 20 (1993), 134–47.

INGHOLT, H., *Parthian Statues from Hatra* (New Haven, 1954).

POMPONIO, F., *Nabû. Il culto e la figura di un dio del Pantheon babilonese ed assiro*, Studi Semitica 51 (Rome, 1978).

6. Harran and Edessa

AGGOULA, B., 'Divinités phéniciennes dans un passage du *Fihrist* d'Ibn Al-Nadim', *Journal Asiatique* 278 (1990), 1–12.

ARCHI, A., 'Harran in the Third Millenium B.C.', *Ugarit Forschungen* 20 (1989), 1–8.

ATHANASSIADI, P., 'Persecution and Response in Late Paganism', *JHS* 113 (1993), 1–29.

DRIJVERS, H. J. W., *Bardaisan's Book of the Laws of the Countries* (Assen, 1965).

—— *Bardaisan of Edessa* (Assen, 1966).

—— *Old Syriac (Edessean) Inscriptions* (Leiden, 1972).

—— *Cults and Beliefs at Edessa* (Leiden, 1980).

—— 'Bardaisan of Edessa and the Hermetica: The Aramaic Philosopher and the Philosophy of His Time', *Jaarbericht van het vooraziatisch-egyptisch genootschap Ex Oriente Lux* 21 (Leiden, 1970), 190–210, repr. in *East of Antioch: Studies in Early Syriac Christianity* (London, 1984) xi.

—— 'The Persistence of Pagan Cults in Christian Syria', in N. Garsoian, T. Mathews, and R. Thomson (eds.), *East of Byzantium: Syria and Armenia in the Formative Period* (Washington, DC, 1982), 35–43, repr. in *East of Antioch: Studies in Early Syriac Christianity* (London, 1984) xvi.

—— 'Hatra, Palmyra and Edessa', in *ANRW* II.8 (Berlin and New York, 1977), 799–906.

Gignoux, P., 'Incantations magiques syriaques', *Revue des Etudes Juives* (1987).

Green, T., *The City of the Moon God: Religious Traditions of Harran* (Leiden, 1992).

Hadot, I., 'La Vie et l'œuvre de Simplicius', in I. Hadot, (ed.), *Simplicius: Sa vie, son œuvre, sa survie*, Actes du colloque international de Paris, 1985 (Berlin, 1987), 3–39.

Harrak, A., 'The Ancient Name of Edessa', *JNES* 51 (1992), 209–14.

Lloyd, S., and Brice, W., 'Harran', *Anatolian Studies*, Journal of the British Institute of Archaeology at Ankara 1 (1951), 77–112.

Millar, F., *The Roman Near East 31 BC–AD 337* (Cambridge, Mass., and London, 1993).

Pingree, D., 'Indian Planetary Images and the Tradition of Astral Magic', *Journal of the Warburg and Courtauld Institutes* 52 (1982), 1–13.

Pomponio, F., *Nabû: Il culto e la figura di un dio del Pantheon babilonese ed assiro*, Studi Semitica 51 (Rome, 1978).

Segal, J. B., 'Pagan Syriac Monuments in the Vilayet of Urfa', *Anatolian Studies* 3 (1953), 97–119.

—— 'Some Syriac Inscriptions of the Second to Third Centuries A.D.', *Bulletin of the School of Oriental and African Studies* 16 (1954), 13–36.

—— *Edessa, the Blessed City* (Oxford, 1970).

'Harran', in *Reallexicon für Antike und Christentum* xiii. 634 ff.

7. Legacy in the Babylonian Talmud

Alt, A., 'Astrology', *Encyclopedia Judaica* iii. 788–95.

Cavigneaux, A., 'Aux sources du Midrash, l'hermeneutique babylonienne', *Aula Orientalis* 5 (1987), 243–56.

Daiches, S., *Babylonian Oil Omens and the Talmud* (London, 1913).

Farber, W., and Porada, E., 'Lilî, Lilitu, Ardat-lilî', *RlA* vii (1987–90).

Finkel, I. L., 'Necromancy in Ancient Mesopotamia', *Archiv für Orientforschung* 29–30 (1983–84), 1–17, esp. Excursus II, 'The use of a skull in Mesopotamian magical texts, and Jewish parallels for the use of necromancy'.

Handy, L. K., 'Lilith', *Anchor Bible Dictionary* iv. 325.

Hunger, H., 'Kalendar', *RlA* v (1976–80).

Lieberman, S. J., 'A Mesopotamian Background for the So-Called Aggadic "Measures" of Biblical Hermeneutics?', *Hebrew Union College Annual* 58 (1987), 157–225.

Neusner, J., *Judaism, Christianity and Zoroastrianism in Talmudic Babylonia* (New York and London, 1986), esp. 59–62.

Tigay, J., 'An Early Technique of Aggadic Exegesis', in H. Tadmor and M. Weinfeld (eds.), *History, Historiography and Interpretation* (1983), 169–89.

8. Syriac Views of the Assyrians

History of Karka de Beth Selokh, in P. Bedjan (ed.), *Acta Martyrum et Sanctorum* ii. 507.

Acta Mar Behnam, in P. Bedjan (ed.), *Acta Martyrum et Sanctorum* ii. 397–441.

Brock, S. P., 'Christians in the Sassanian Empire: A Case of Divided Loyalties', in S. Mews (ed.), *Religion and National Identity: Studies in Church History XVIII* (Oxford, 1982), repr. in S. P. Brock, *Syriac Perspectives on Late Antiquity* (London, 1984) vi, section vi.

Coakley, J. F., *The Church of the East and the Church of England: A History of the Archbishop of Canterbury's Assyrian Mission* (Oxford, 1992).

Fiey, J. M., '"Assyriens" ou "Araméens"', *L'Orient Syrien* 10 (Paris, 1965), 141–60.

—— *Assyrie chrétienne* 3 (Beirut, 1968), 20–2.

Joseph, J., *The Nestorians and their Muslim Neighbours* (Princeton, 1961).

Acts of Kardagh, ed. J. B. Abbeloos, *Analecta Bollandiana* 9 (1890), 5–106.

Narsai's Eighth Memra on Jonah [Syriac], in A. Mingana (ed.), *Narsai Doctoris Syri Homiliae et Carmina I* (Mosul, 1905), 134–49.

Parpola, S., 'The Murder of Sennacherib', in B. Alster (ed.), *Death in Mesopotamia: Papers read at the XXVIᵉ Rencontre assyriologique internationale* (Copenhagen, 1980) = *Mesopotamia* 38. 171–82.

Pigulevskaya, N., *Les Villes de l'état iranien aux époques parthe et sassanide* (Paris, 1963).

Wiessner, G., 'Die Behnām-Legende', in G. Wiessner (ed.), *Synkretismus-Forschung: Theorie und Praxis*, (Wiesbaden, 1978), 119–33 = *Göttinger Orientforschung* 1.

Yonan, G., *Assyrer heute* (Hamburg, 1978).

VIII

THE SASSANIAN PERIOD AND EARLY ISLAM, c. AD 224–651

STEPHANIE DALLEY

B Y THE TIME THE PARTHIANS GAVE WAY TO THE Sassanians as rulers of Mesopotamia, the physical presence of cuneiform writing and libraries had come to an end. This change is sometimes seen as making a clean break with ancient times. But clear evidence that some major cults continued is recorded in the Babylonian Talmud in the sayings of Rav, who began to teach in Mesopotamia after 219 and founded a new academy there at Sura.

There are five appointed temples of idol-worship. They are: the temple of Bel in Babil, the temple of Nebo in Borsippa . . . (then 3 others, not Babylonian or Assyrian) . . . What is meant by saying that these (temples) are appointed? . . . Regularly all the year round worship takes place in them. (ʿAbodah zarah 11b)

The influence of ancient traditions also persisted, modified by translation and new use, for the cult and oracles of Bel at Palmyra and Apamea, Ishtar at Arbela, Ashur-Bel at Ashur, Shamash-Bel at Hatra, and Sin at Harran, ensured that interest in Chaldaean traditions continued over a wide area. Under Julian the Apostate (331–63) pagan learning briefly enjoyed official favour at Rome.

The early centuries of the Christian era saw titanic struggles between various forms of paganism and newly emerging monotheisms. Manichaeans, Zoroastrians, Gnostics, and various sects of Christianity competed for converts. Each tried to assert its superiority in explaining the nature of divinity, how the world was created and for what purpose. For all of them the origin and nature of evil posed problems. If there was a single god, all good and almighty, how had he allowed the creation of evil? Could a cosmogony be found to account for the paradox? Did man have any personal choice in the direction of his own life, or was he the mere pawn of fate?

Chaldaeans and other pagans of early Antiquity had tackled these questions by describing how creation began, in several alternative accounts. In the Babylonian *Epic of Creation* a primeval pair of deities gave rise to successive generations whose behaviour was imperfect. The Babylonians and Assyrians saw man's role as a finely balanced, unremitting task to maintain the established order and keep chaos at bay. Hence the king annually defeated the powers of chaos at the New Year festival while an *Epic of Creation* was recited. He took the hands of the champion deity Bel (who was Marduk in Babylon but, for instance, the moon-god Sin in Harran) and assumed personal responsibility for maintaining the balance between good and evil, order and chaos. In this way ancient Mesopotamian beliefs embodied a fundamental dualism, not so very different from the Persian beliefs to which the name of the ancient prophet Zoroaster was attached.

The *Epic of Creation* at the Court of Khosroes I

Evidence that knowledge of Babylonian traditions and interest in them continued long after cuneiform died out comes towards the end of the Sassanian period, when Khosroes I (AD 531–79), having taken Antioch, established a cosmopolitan court based at his newly built capital city, Ktesiphon near Babylon. Khosroes I was a broad-minded and cultured king who had received the pagan Athenian philosophers at his court when Justinian banned their teaching at the academy at Athens in AD 529. Among them was its head, Damaskios (458–538), who gathered together ancient cosmogonies, including a passage about Mesopotamian concepts of creation, in his work on first principles. The text shows that Damaskios knew the story of the Babylonian creation epic not from Berossos, but from Eudemos of Rhodes who had worked in Athens with Aristotle more than 800 years earlier.

The Babylonians assume two (principles of the universe), Tauthe (= Tiamat) and Apason (= Apsu), making Apason the husband of Tauthe, and calling her the mother of the gods. Of these was born an only-begotten son, Moumis (= Mummu) . . . From them another generation proceeded, Dache and Dachos (= Lahmu and Lahamu). And again a third (generation proceeds) from them, Kissare and Assoros (= Kishar and Anshar), of whom were born three, Anos (= Anu), Illinos (= Enlil) and Aos (= Ea). And of Aos and Dauke (Damkina) was born a son called Bel.

Not only, therefore, was this centre-piece of Babylonian literature, ritual and philosophy still known, but philosophers from Athens were still interested in it as a theory of creation, nearly 500 years after the last known cuneiform tablet was written.

Babylonian Legacy in Manichaean Scripture

Around AD 216 there was born in Babylonia the founder of a new world religion. His name was Mani. A brilliant painter and illustrator who saw the potential of picture-books for teaching the masses, he began a tradition that is now visible in Persian miniatures and in Buddhist and Jain scriptures and tangkas, the painted linen scrolls used by itinerant religious teachers. Among Persian poets from the tenth century onwards he was legendary as an artist, and Islamic writers often described exquisite beauty by comparison with Mani's paintings, even though he epitomized idolatry.

Mani's father belonged to the sect of Elchesai, baptists whose teaching was taken to Rome by Alkibiades of Apamea-on-Orontes during Trajan's reign. Mani left the sect in order to found his own religious group, beginning his own missionary work in 240, contemporary with the Babylonian Jewish rabbi Rav.

Although Babylon was still, according to Rav, a major centre for idolatry, Mani's inspiration came from Bardaisan (AD 154–222), a religious philosopher who worked in Edessa near Harran and who is variously described as a Gnostic,[1] a Christian humanist, and 'a Babylonian man'. Bardaisan developed a cosmogony that explained the existence of both good and evil from the beginning of creation, and his scheme was taken up and elaborated by Mani.

Mani's foremost disciple Adda composed many fine scriptures, writing in a calligraphic script based on decorative Palmyrene writing. He was also a healer who spent time at the court of Zenobia in Palmyra and cured her sister of an illness when others had failed. Thanks to her patronage the name 'Queen Tadmer' is sometimes found in Manichaean texts; a survival of this time is the story called 'The City of Brass' in the Arabian Nights, which features Queen Tadmer. From Palmyra Adda took his mission southwards to al-Hira, capital city of the Arabian Lakhmid kings where literature and religious freedom flourished.

The Manichaean religion was liberal, tolerant, and pacifist. It rejected the Old Testament utterly and thought that the text of the New Testament was corrupt, but accepted that Jesus Christ was a prophet of God. This allowed its detractors to refer contemptuously to it as a Christian heresy. Mani himself they ridiculed as a man who habitually carried a Babylonian book. His faith developed an ascetic élite. It seems not to have set up churches or monasteries, nor did it make statues of God or the saints, which means that it is almost untraceable by archaeological means. Rulers who levied troops disliked it for its pacifism and for advocating birth control, a Babylonian tenet enshrined in the conclusion to the ancient *Epic of Atrahasis* for the express purpose of preventing over-population. Evangelical Christians and, later, Muslims, hated it for its tremendous success in winning converts world-wide. The repression of Manichaeism in the Christian empire has been identified as 'the spear-head of religious intolerance'.

Saint Augustine of Hippo, when he had converted from being a Manichee to become a Christian in 383, accused the Manichaeans of fatalism. Man's free will was the concept with which Christians evaded the problem of the origins of evil, accusing their rivals

---

[1] See p. 167 for a definition of Gnostics.

of a belief in predestination that precluded freedom of choice for men. This belief was attributed to the Chaldaeans by writers as different as Herodotos and Theodore bar Koni.[2] In fact the Babylonians did not believe that the whole course of a man's life was dictated by the stars or by divine decree, although they were mechanistic in attempting to avoid fate. Divination and omens of all kinds had a strictly limited validity. Even the Tablet of Destinies contained only the potential events of the coming year for the land in a general way. The gods did not inscribe every event for every individual for all time. Potential harm in the near future could be averted by appropriate rituals only if the omens were correctly interpreted; all too often they were confused. Therefore many apotropaic rituals and penitential acts were not specific. The gods might make a new decision at any time if they disapproved of a man's actions. As Diogenes of Babylon pointed out, the different lives and careers of identical twins proved that fates were not inexorably fixed at birth. Besides, the existence of demons was held to account for illness and undeserved misfortune; their wayward acts presented unremitting threats to man's well-being and to the plans of the great gods.

One of the sacred books of the Manichaeans, known as the *Book of Giants*, contained stories about Gilgamesh and his monstrous opponent Humbaba, including how the world was corrupted by lustful giants of divine origin. This contains echoes of a Hittite version of the *Gilgamesh* epic in which Gilgamesh and Enkidu are both giants, and of the Akkadian story in which the lust of Gilgamesh is emphasized. *The Book of Giants* also included an episode relating the tale of the Flood in which the name of the hero who survived by building an ark was the Babylonian Utnapishtim rather than the Jewish and Christian Noah. Long before Mani was born an earlier version of the *Book of Giants*, also featuring Gilgamesh, Humbaba, and Enoch as Enkidu, had been incorporated into an Aramaic version of the Book of Enoch, known from fragments of Dead Sea scrolls written before the time of Jesus. The Manichaean version is known to us from even smaller fragments retrieved from caves and monasteries in the Gobi desert in Central Asia. Enoch himself was partly modelled upon the

antediluvian king of Sippar, Enmeduranki, to whom the gods had revealed the secrets of divination; and partly upon Enkidu from the *Epic of Gilgamesh*. Even in the time of Bardaisan Enoch was acknowledged as the originator of astrology and divination. The link between Enoch and the Manichaeans helps to explain why the latter were condemned as mere magicians and astrologers whose defence against Fate was ritualistic. In the form of the Book of Enoch which Christians used, the chapter about the giants and about Gilgamesh had been cut out. Saint Augustine tells why this was done.

> Now we cannot deny that some things were written under divine inspiration by Enoch . . . But these writings are with good reason not included in the canon of scripture which was carefully kept in the temple of the Hebrew people by a succession of priests . . . Hence discerning authorities are right in their judgement that the writings presented under Enoch's name with those tales about giants not having human fathers should not be attributed to him. In a like manner, many writings are presented by heretics.

Until recently Manichaean scripture was known only from the distortions of its detractors. Many scholars thought that it was essentially Iranian partly because Mesopotamia had been ruled by Iranian kings for so long—Achaemenids, Parthians, and then Sassanians. But recent evidence from papyri has clarified the Babylonian component.

Mani himself, though at times he found favour at the early Sassanian court, was put cruelly to death around 277 by a fervently Zoroastrian ruler, and martyrdom became commonplace for his committed followers. Ruthless persecution was given official standing by Diocletian, who banned the Manichaean faith in 297, and by Saint Augustine. Augustine wrote virulent and widely publicized tracts against the Manichaeans, focusing his attack upon the Manichaean bishop Faustus, whom he described in his best-selling *Confessions* as 'a great snare of the Devil', and 'to so many a snare of death'. Soon a popular genre of literature arose in which 'heretical' bishops were villains and sorcerers, and the legend of Faust in western Europe may have its origins in this famous controversy, helping to ensure that the most ridiculous distortion of Babylonian and Manichaean beliefs became widespread.

---

[2] Theodore bar Koni was a Christian writer of the 6th–7th cent. who gave a detailed account of the main heresies and described the Manichaean cosmogony.

Some groups of Manichaeans retreated to Upper Egypt, where they could share their beliefs in the Babylonian system of natural science and astrology with various tolerant Gnostic sects. Others fled eastwards and joined communities in Central Asia where they found much in common with Buddhists, whose learning had been imbued with genuine Chaldaean scholarship from the time of the Buddha's father.[3] Some travelled on to China, where tales which bear faint echoes of *Gilgamesh* made their way into Chinese legend through the *Book of Giants*, thanks to the practice of translating Manichaean scriptures into whatever language was locally popular.

Eventually the Manichaeans, despite their widespread success in converting people from other religions, and despite the antiquity of their literary traditions, were exterminated by Christians, Muslims, and Zoroastrians, and their scriptures were destroyed. When in AD 923 fourteen sacks filled with Manichaean books were burned in Baghdad, trickles of silver and gold from melted painting ran out from the fire. The faithful were forced to convert or die. Ancient Mesopotamian traditions, espoused by Mani, became abhorrent to the rest of the world and were wiped out. These events, rather than the obsolescence of Akkadian cuneiform, explain why Babylonian literature disappeared completely for some 1,500 years. When the Humanists in late fifteenth-century Europe tried to revive pre-Christian knowledge, there was no distinct Babylonian lore to be found alongside that of Greece, Rome, and Israel. Any surviving remnants were denounced as forgeries. Only the archaeological researches of the past two centuries have been able to revive the achievements of Babylon and Nineveh.

The Idea of Holy Scripture and the Tablet of Destinies

The idea that the gods had a divine tablet, often described as being made of lapis lazuli, upon which in heaven they wrote the destinies for life on earth, was central to Mesopotamian belief. Two myths, the *Epic of Anzu* and the *Epic of Creation*, focus on possession of the Tablet of Destinies. He who holds it controls the universe, and he who loses it is power-less. The gods are thrown into utter confusion when it is stolen by a wicked enemy, for they must then defeat him under impossible conditions. An Iron Age tradition refers to Nabu, god of writing and of wisdom, as controller of the Tablet of Destinies, which was guarded by the Seven Sages and sealed with the Seal of Destinies. What the gods wrote upon that tablet was sometimes divulged to mankind through the markings on the liver and lungs of sacrificial animals, so that a liver upon which omens were read was referred to as 'the tablet of the gods'. In this way holy scripture and divination were very closely linked.

This concept is also found in Jewish traditions. Moses received the Torah direct from God in the form of two tablets of stone containing laws and commandments, inscribed with the finger of God on both sides. The books of Enoch and Jubilees refer to 'heavenly tablets' which include not only laws and a chronicle of contemporary events, but also predictions or revelations for the future.

In Gnostic writings attributed to Hermes it was the emerald tablet of Hermes Trismegistos that contained the secrets of the gods, and was sometimes said to have been sealed with the seal of Hermes. Hermes was called Trismegistos 'thrice great' because he was thought to embody the wisdom of three ancient sages: the Greek Hermes, the Mesopotamian–Jewish Enoch, and the Egyptian god of wisdom and writing Thoth, a conflation reflected in Bardaisan's understanding that Babylonian and Egyptian writings could not be distinguished.

Islam inherited the concept of a holy tablet. It is found in the cosmology of Al-Suyūti describing the tablet and stylus of God who creates by writing upon it, and will continue to do so until the Day of Judgement. The tablet is made of 'hyacinth' on one side and green 'smaragd' on the other, and it contains laws and divine judgements. This is the Book of Fate, mentioned in surah 85 of the Quran, which was considered to be a text transmitted by Gabriel direct from heavenly tablets to Muhammad. Al-Kisā'i described the Preserved Tablet made of white pearl and the pen made of a gigantic gemstone as the first things created by God. Arab tradition regarded Babylonian knowledge as transplanted into Egypt, and described Hermes Trismegistos as a Babylonian who lived in Egypt.

---

[3] See Ch. II, p. 39, and Ch. VI, p. 131.

This key concept is documented over a very long period. It is found in several different languages and religions, both pagan and monotheist. The Tablet of Destinies lingers on as the Book of Fate in the literature of western Europe. Shakespeare puts into the mouth of Henry IV the exclamation (2 *Henry IV*, III. i):

> O God! That one might read the Book of Fate,
> And see the revolution of the times!

Alexander Pope too referred to it in his famous *Essay on Man*:

> Heav'n from all creatures hides the Book of Fate,
> All but the page prescrib'd, their present state.

When Islam distinguished the 'people of the book', namely Jews, Christians, and Sabians, from people whose religions were erroneous, its judgement was in part based upon the very ancient conception that God's will was made known in the first instance through writing. The Sabians were the pagan people of Harran who claimed that the Hermetic writings were their authentic scripture when challenged by Muslims. Although some scholars have thought they invented the claim to avoid persecution, there is in fact reason to think it is true.

A Babylonian Component in Hermetic Writings

The Hermetic writings of late Antiquity are a group of texts that claim authorship from Hermes Trismegistos and consist of philosophical prayers and dialogues, magical formulae, and alchemical works. Many of them were used by Gnostic groups of people, who can be defined by their belief that an individual could reach a higher plane of existence and influence his own destiny through study and contemplation, aided by ascetic techniques and by certain magical procedures and rituals. They exhibit a theory of natural sciences according to which the forces of nature and man's destiny were shaped by seven 'planets'—the sun, moon, and five actual planets according to modern terms—which were the governors of the universe. To those seven planets were individually linked the plants, minerals, and elements which are found on the earth. By manipulating the links through alchemy,

sympathetic magic, and incantation a person could, to some extent, harness the power of the governing forces for his own physical and spiritual advancement. Single items from the stock of their learning look to us like superstition; but viewed as part of a systematic yet flexible application of rules, they belong to a serious and enduring science which had developed over several thousand years. In the words of the philosopher Iamblichos:

Magic investigates the nature, power and quality of everything sublunary; viz. of the elements and their parts, of animals, of all various plants and their fruits, of stones and herbs; in short it explores the essence and power of everything. From hence, therefore, it produces its effects.

In its Babylonian and Egyptian manifestations the system was partly based upon manipulation of words, syllables, and cuneiform or hieroglyphic signs,[4] so it suffered terribly when it was translated into languages written in alphabetic scripts, and would have become an easy target for ridicule had it not been rewritten thoroughly to accord with Greek philosophical taste and style. The problem is described in letter form:

Those who hold opposite principles to start with will say that the style is obscure, and conceals the meaning. And it will be thought still more obscure in time to come, when the Greeks think fit to translate these writings from our tongue into theirs. Translation will greatly distort the sense of the writings, and cause much obscurity.   (*Corpus Hermeticum*, book xvi)

Under this science in its pre-Greek form, however, tremendous progress had been made in major technologies, which seemed to prove its validity. Metalworking (in particular alloying and casting), glaze- and glass-making, and stone-carving had developed as very skilled crafts which had reached a high standard in early Antiquity. They are only now being traced and understood through archaeological science and through the painfully slow reconstruction of Mesopotamian scientific literature, including for instance standard recipes for making glass and glazes. Babylonian 'natural science' combined physics, astronomy, chemistry, botany, and geology in a single conceptual scheme. This is the tradition acknowledged in the medieval *Turba Philosophorum*, which stated that Demokritos, who expounded an atomic theory in the

---

[4] Compare the Stoic technique described in Ch. II, p. 47.

fifth century BC, had received the science of natural things from the Babylonians.

It is common nowadays to separate the philosophical from the alchemical writings in Hermetic traditions, but this is due to modern categorization rather than to any understanding of ancient systems. The Arabic alchemical text known as the *Picatrix* is introduced by a cosmogony in the same way as a Babylonian incantation against toothache. The writings attributed to Zosimos, the famous alchemist who lived at Akhmim (Panopolis) in Upper Egypt during the third to fourth century and who was forced to deny publicly that he was a Manichaean, contain both philosophical and alchemical material. Embedded in an alchemical treatise is a heroic adventure of Zosimos to the ends of the earth, which shows that he, like Gilgamesh, had acquired wisdom by travels and endurance. It was incorporated to show Zosimos' credentials as a sage and an alchemist.[5] The prestige of Hermetic writings was founded upon the belief that the most ancient wisdom was recorded in them, that they had been lost for a while and were later rediscovered. Very often a Hermetic work claimed to have been discovered accidentally, bringing enlightenment to its discoverer. This idea, that very ancient lore written by the sages had disappeared for a while, only to be rediscovered later, is not to be found in the early literature of Egypt or of Israel and Judah, but was formulated in ancient Babylonia. There it was inextricably linked to the story of the Flood, as we know because Berossos relayed the Mesopotamian tradition that writings from before the Flood were buried near Sippar to preserve them and they were dug up again when the Flood receded. Certain Babylonian epics and works of 'science' have colophons in which authorship is attributed to the first sage, Oannes-Adapa, who lived before the Flood; and a whole class of cuneiform narrative literature, including the *Epic of Gilgamesh* and the *Cuthean Legend of Naram-Sin*, begins with the revelation that the story is the secret writings of the hero himself, hidden in a box:

> Look for the copper tablet-box,
> Undo its bronze lock,
> Open the door to its secret,
> Lift out the lapis lazuli tablet and read it,
> The story of that man, Gilgamesh,
> Who went through all kinds of sufferings.

The Egyptians of late Antiquity were presumably aware that their ancient traditions could not account for this important aspect of Hermetic writing. A late attempt to retroject it, and thus to reinforce their claim to Hermes Trismegistos, is evident in the demotic tale of Setne Khamuas, who visits the tomb of the only son of Merneptah and tries to obtain from it an ancient book of magic written by Thoth. The composer of this text in the Ptolemaic period doubtless thought of Merneptah (1224–1214 BC) as representing very early times; but from the view-point of all Egyptian dynastic history he is a latecomer. The prologue to the *Gilgamesh* epic also links the legend with times before the Flood, saying:

> He who experienced the whole gained complete
>   wisdom,
> He found out what was secret and uncovered what was
>   hidden,
> He brought back a tale of times before the Flood.

When Manetho, an Egyptian priest, wrote his account of Egyptian traditions for his Greek patron Ptolemy Philadelphos, he was acting in competition with his slightly older contemporary Berossos. For this reason, and because Jews in Alexandria were keen to connect the biblical story of the Exodus with indigenous Egyptian traditions, he introduced into his account, as a benchmark for very early dynasties, the date of the Flood. It was a useful point at which to separate rulers who were gods or demigods from their mortal successors, but it also introduced a prestigious foreign element into the narrative.

The Mesopotamian component in the philosophical writings which belong to the Hermetic tradition is not easily discerned, nor are the Egyptian and Jewish ones. Scriptures such as the *Perfect Word* (which was written no later than AD 300) and *Poimandres* seem to be at the very least remodelled to accord with Hellenistic tastes, and it is not surprising that an early ancestry for them has been called into question or even rejected outright. The brilliant Greek scholar of the Renaissance, Isaac Casaubon (after whom George Eliot named Mr Casaubon in her novel *Middlemarch*) 'proved' in 1614 that the Hermetic dialogues were bogus creations, long before either Egyptian hieroglyphs or Babylonian cuneiform had been deciphered, and his condemnation has remained

---

[5] See also Ch. II, p. 48 on Apollodoros of Seleukeia.

accepted thinking ever since. Two centuries of scholarship now allow us to make a different judgement from a more solid and objective base.

The tract named *Poimandres* after the name of the character who engages in dialogue with Hermes has recently been compared closely and convincingly with the Slavonic book of Enoch (a reworking of the older book of Enoch, for which Mesopotamian connections have already been discussed). The very name Poimandres has now proved to be an Egyptian rather than a Greek formation as was previously thought. The dialogue of Hermes with Asklepios, the *Perfect Word*, features a god-name which has been recognized as probably Near Eastern in origin.[6] These typical Hermetic dialogues take place between the god Hermes and his son (whether Asklepios or Tat = Thoth, the Egyptian god) who receives paternal wisdom by which he may be able to attain understanding. This may be a vastly elaborated and Hellenized version of the brief dialogue found in Sumerian and Babylonian magical literature, in which the god Ea addressed his son Marduk—Asalluhi, and gave him power to treat a particular disease. One version of this comes from the incantation series *Šurpu* tablet VII. When the sufferer from a disease known as *dimītu* has been described in detail,

Asalluhi looked at him and entered the house of his father Ea and called out: 'Father, *dimītu*-disease has come out from the Abyss.' In addition he said: 'What should I do? I do not know that man, how can he get relief?' Ea answered his son Marduk: 'My son, what do you not know? What can I add for you? Marduk, what do you not know? What can I contribute for you? What I know, you know too.'

It has proved easier to trace Babylonian influence upon the alchemical works attributed to Hermes Trismegistos. The rubric containing injunctions to secrecy in Greek magical papyri can be paralleled word for word in Babylonian colophons, and not in Egyptian texts. The name of the Sumerian Underworld goddess Ereshkigal, has been found in the Greek magical papyri. The scheme of seven planets including the sun and moon is attested in the standard Babylonian astronomical text MUL.APIN, which dates in part at least to the second millennium BC. This text also shows that different colours were assigned to the planets, an idea that plays an important part in planetary superstition. The belief that omens were

given by planetary movements is also well established in Babylonian texts from the early Iron Age.

The *Perfect Word* contains reference to how statues of deities were brought to life and given divine power by ritual. The Babylonians used rituals known as 'the washing of the mouth' and 'the opening of the mouth' in order to put divine life into their idols when they had been made in the workshop and were transferred to a temple; the Egyptians also had such a ritual which is thought to be derived from the Mesopotamian, and the Mandaeans of southern Iraq inherited the practice.

The type of sympathetic magic which pervades Hermetic science was based on the essential connection between a particular planet and certain plants, minerals, and animals. This concept, but with deities who were not necessarily equated with planets, is found in Mesopotamian texts which date no later than the seventh century BC, e.g.:

Tamarisk	Anu
Heart of the date palm	Dumuzi
Soap plant	Ea
Silver	Angal
Gold	Enmesharra
Copper	Ea
Carnelian	Ninlil
Lapis lazuli	Dilibat (Venus)

The same kind of occult sympathy or link lies behind the description of images suitable for use as talismans, for which Babylonian and medieval passages may be compared. The format of the text is the same, and so are many details such as colour, clothing, and objects held in the hand. Names are substituted according to the milieu, in a manner reminiscent of Akkadian magical texts in which 'I, so-and-so son of so-and-so' was written so that the appropriate names for a particular occasion could be inserted.

The form of Narudda of tamarisk, clad in red paste with her proper equipment; you shall draw a design with yellow paste representing a sash around her waist; she wears red head-gear on her head; you shall hang a harp at her left side. (F. A. Wiggermann, *Mesopotamian Protective Spirits* (Gröningen, 1992), 12)

An image of Venus: the form of a woman with her hair unbound riding on a stag, having in her right hand an apple, and in her left, flowers, and dressed in white garments. (*Picatrix* 2. 12)

[6] See Ch. IV, p. 100.

Zosimos transmitted some of this tradition without changing the names of deities. For example, when he equated Bel with tin, Bilati (Belti) with copper, and Nebo (Nabu) with mercury, he was giving a variation upon the same theme, comparable to a Babylonian text which equates the goddess Ninmah with tin and the god Ea with copper.

Quantities of Gnostic writings, preserved on papyri in the Coptic language and recently unearthed in Egypt have begun to revolutionize our understanding of the religious milieu from which Christianity, medieval Judaism, and Islam emerged. Scholars are now trying to trace Babylonian and Manichaean contributions, among others, to Gnostic literature and beliefs.

The Alexander Romance and the Water of Life

Themes from the *Epic of Gilgamesh* were incorporated into the *Alexander Romance*, one of the most widely known pieces of fiction in late Antiquity and the Middle Ages. The composition of some versions can be traced back to the Jewish community in Egyptian Alexandria. The Romance consists of a string of episodes, and was written in many versions and languages from Iran to western Europe. Material was taken, of course, from various biographies of the great man, but its composition also relied extensively on model letters, written apparently in Graeco-Egyptian schools of rhetoric, and supposedly exchanged between Aristotle and Alexander, or between Alexander and his mother Olympias. Model letters of this type are attested in cuneiform from a very early date, including one which was ostensibly written by Gilgamesh himself, known from a tablet of the seventh century BC.

In the *Alexander Romance* the hero, like Gilgamesh and other heroes from very early times, is given one divine parent and acquires wisdom by enduring the hardships of campaigns abroad or travels beyond the boundaries of the known world, and by visiting an even more ancient sage, sometimes alive and sometimes already in his tomb. This sage is named in different versions as Proteus, Enoch, Solomon, and Altinoos, the last being probably a textual corruption for Alkinoos, who was king of the Phaeacians in the *Odyssey*. Historically we know that Alexander, like Gilgamesh, was accorded the honours due to a divine

hero or lesser god. But the connection between the two heroes and their narratives is closer than that, for in one passage Alexander meets Al-Khidr, 'the green one' recognizable as a descendant of Atra-hasis (another name for Ut-napishtim), a wise old man who guides him through darkness in search of the Water of Life. Al-Khidr finds them and drinks to become immortal, but Alexander loses his way and the opportunity is gone for ever.

In this episode are combined two themes from separate Mesopotamian myths. The *Myth of Adapa* describes a story in which a god offered to a mortal the opportunity to drink the Water of Life to make him immortal; and the *Epic of Gilgamesh* relates how the hero acquired the plant of rejuvenation from the bottom of the sea, only to lose it to a thieving snake. The combined themes are ancestral to beliefs of later times. In Al-Khidr we find the Islamic sage or demi-god who alone survived from pagan times into popular religion without, apparently, infringing the monotheism of Islam; indeed, his constant presence gives the authority of a link with time before the Flood that was valuable to early Islam.

In the Water of Life we find a theme linked to baptismal rites. The idea that a particular kind of holy water can bestow everlasting life was taken up by a variety of religious groups. In the community at Qumran before the time of Christ, and among the Elchesaite sect in which Mani was raised, as well as among many others, baptism was one of the rites of initiation by which a person came closer to God. Two kinds were practised: full immersion, and sprinkling, each having antecedents in Assyrian rituals performed in order to purify a man and to free him from evil spells and curses, for the water carried off the evil from his body. The two kinds are represented in two closely associated rituals: *bīt rimki* 'bathing house' and *bīt sala' mê* 'water-sprinkling house', both presided over by the incantation priest or magician, *mašmaššu*. An elaborate series of actions involved progress through a series of seven 'houses', perhaps quite a simple arrangement of chambers or huts, for the ritual was often carried out in open country.

Greek versions of the *Alexander Romance* have largely obliterated the connections with older, Semitic narrative tradition, and the connection with the Water of Life is not so clear. Al-Khidr is renamed Andreas, and we have to use the Arabic and Persian versions to trace the ancestry of the character through the name and the accompanying motifs. Two Hebrew versions, however, add links with Assyrian tradition, for they describe Alexander's meeting with refugees from the time of Assyrian kings—variously Sennacherib and Shalmaneser. This hints at the importance of the deportation policy, carried out so extensively by the late Assyrian kings, in disseminating Babylonian traditions.

The concept of the Water of Life, first attested in the myth of Adapa in Late Bronze Age Babylonian texts, became very important to Gnostics not only in ceremonies of initiation and purification, but also in alchemy. Chemists of late Antiquity called the water of distillation *theion hudor* which means both divine and sulphurous water. It was thought to be related to the water of immortality which was used for baptism and to have a different cosmic source from the waters of chaos. The term has been translated to give *aqua vitae* and whisky (Gaelic *uisgebeatha* = water of life).

The *Tale of Buluqiya*

An Arabic version of the *Alexander Romance*, preserved in a manuscript in Spain, contains passages of narrative which are found almost word for word in the *Tale of Buluqiya* in the *Arabian Nights*, a story which is recognizable as a distant descendant in Arabic of the *Epic of Gilgamesh*. The name of its hero seems to be an abbreviated form of 'Bilgamesh', which is a known variant of 'Gilgamesh'. In that tale, as in Near Eastern versions of the *Alexander Romance*, Al-Khidr appears towards the end of the hero's wanderings over the Seven Seas. His wise companion Affan has already been killed attempting a rash but heroic deed at the tomb of Solomon. Buluqiya is taken on a tour of heavenly regions in true apocalyptic style, and eventually returns home. The giant Humbaba, monstrous guardian of the Pine Forest in the *Epic of Gilgamesh*, is recognizable in the giant who guards the trees of Paradise. Advice to the hero from the wise Queen of Serpents includes an allusion to the plant of rejuvenation, comparable to the way in which Ut-napishtim's wife is responsible for disclosing the existence of that plant to Gilgamesh.

The tale begins with the discovery of hidden writings which reveal to the hero the secret that a new prophet Muhammad will arise; the hero pursues his adventures with the aim of becoming immortal so that he may witness the coming of Muhammad in person. In this way Islam kept a link with both Gilgamesh and Atra-hasis, and countered the claims of Christians that the coming of Muhammad had not been prophesied. Buluqiya is king of the sons of Israel and rules from Cairo. Quite apart from details of narrative which connect the *Epic of Gilgamesh* with the *Tale of Buluqiya*, a number of important concepts are embedded in the latter which date back to Babylonian times.

The revelation of secret writings is, as we have seen, a theme that introduces the genre of heroic biography in cuneiform literature. The cosmic arrangement of the Seven Seas, over which the would-be hero must journey at his peril to reach the tomb of godlike Solomon, has its counterpart in the Mesopotamian *Descent of Ishtar to the Underworld*, in which the goddess descends through seven gates, each guarded by a demon, and finally addresses the ruler of the Underworld.

Buluqiya, when he reads the newly discovered writings, realizes that his father had concealed from him information that should have been in the Torah, and that holy scripture in its present form was deliberately defective. This concept, called *tahrīf* in Islam, made it possible for certain ancient Jewish traditions to be incorporated into Islamic lore, while showing that the Old Testament belonged to a corrupted textual tradition. Islam normally attributed the corruption to Ezra, who had had the scriptures rewritten from memory when he was in exile; but the *Tale of Buluqiya* puts it back to the time of Josiah, a century earlier. The same concern, that textual tradition should convey the words of heaven without omission or addition, is found in the Babylonian *Epic of Erra and Ishum*, attested from the seventh century BC:

> The one who put together the composition about him (Erra) was Kabti-ilani-Marduk, son of Dabibi. He (the god) revealed it to him in the middle of the night, and when he recited it upon waking, he did not omit anything, nor add a single word to it. Erra heard and approved it.

Buluqiya reaches heaven briefly before returning home, just as Gilgamesh reached the near-Paradise where Ut-napishtim with his wife and boatman enjoyed their endless immortality, before being spirited back to Uruk. The pattern of narrative for his ascent has been the subject of a bitter controversy, for it is used to describe the ascent (*mi'raj*) of Muhammad in Islam and the ascent of the poet in Dante's *Divine Comedy*. Which of those two accounts could claim priority and originality was hotly contested between scholars whose clear view of the tradition was hampered on the one hand by the difficulty in giving an accurate date to the Arabic composition (the extant manuscripts being later than Dante) and on the other by ignorance of literary traditions that were neither Christian nor Islamic because they were very much older.

The name of Buluqiya is also found in a rather different composition, where it is given to a Christian monk Bulukhya. The story is told of this monk that he held the secret of why the news of Muhammad's coming had been withheld from the Torah, and imparted it to a very wise Jew from the Yemen, Ka'b al-ahbar, who was then converted to Islam late in life. This tale and a version of the *Tale of Buluqiya* told by the early Arab writer Tha'labī, contain evidence that the story was popular and prestigious among Sufis. Since many early Sufis lived in central and southern Mesopotamia as mystics and theurgists, it seems clear that theirs is one milieu in which tales of Bulukhya/Buluqiya flourished.

Another link which can be traced through the *Tale of Buluqiya* lies in magic and theurgy, by which a skilled practitioner could communicate with God directly. In the Middle Ages, when Christianity and Islam had pushed out both pagan and Manichaean practices, the magical texts and rituals which remained in circulation were regarded as mainly Jewish and Mandaean. Cabbalistic use of the Hebrew alphabet and innumerable angels and demons, named like those in the Book of Enoch, made this identification seem secure. Yet it was an embarrassment that God could be envisaged in human form, seated upon a chariot or throne and living in a palace, for orthodox Palestinian Jewish theology rejected such notions as essentially pagan. Uneasy acceptance or downright rejection was shown towards the type of theurgy known as *Hekhalot* 'Palaces' and *Merkabah* 'Chariot'.[7] Much of this procedure was too dangerous to record in writing, or was written in no coherent form, so that the study of it in modern times has progressed with great difficulty; but a debased form of text was extensively known in the Middle Ages as the *Key of Solomon*. This work has been studied particularly in

connection with the legend of Faust, who sold his soul to the Devil for an advance of pleasure and power, and then could not reclaim it.

The name of Gilgamesh was still known in the Islamic period. Theodore bar Koni named him as the tenth king after the Flood; and an incantation in Arabic, recorded by al-Suyūtī in the fifteenth century, invokes the name of Gilgamesh.

Another cuneiform Mesopotamian story which goes back to the time of Hammurabi, the *Poor Man of Nippur*, has been recognized as an early version of one in the *Arabian Nights*. It tells how a swindler in a position of power is eventually tricked and beaten by his own victim, and was very popular in ancient Babylonia and Assyria. By the sixth century AD it had made its way, appropriately modified, into the Sanskrit *Pancatantra*, and was circulating in other languages in Europe by the thirteenth century. The *Pancatantra* 'Five Books' is an undatable compilation which also includes animal fables in the style of Aesop, upon which ancient Mesopotamian influence is known.[8]

Mesopotamian Themes in Persian Stories

Persian stories occasionally contain themes that come from ancient Mesopotamia. In particular, two tales about the legendary king Jamshid (Yima) bear the traces of influence. In one of them (related in Yasht 19 of the *Avesta*) Jamshid ruled the whole world in peace and health, but after 300 years the population became too dense, so he enlarged the world to make more room for them. This sequence was repeated twice, after 600 and 900 years respectively. The Babylonian *Epic of Atrahasis*, which dates from around 1700 BC, likewise contains a sequence in which the world became overpopulated on three occasions, at intervals of 600 years. Like Jamshid, Atra-hasis lived through them all, but the solution to the problem was quite different, for the gods reduced the population each time with a different devastation: famine, plague, and Flood.

The other story in which Jamshid takes on some of the deeds of Atrahasis is related in the *Vendidad* (*c.* second–third century). Jamshid ruled for a thousand years until the gods planned exceptional hardship

---

[7] See also Ch. II, p. 43.   [8] See also Ch. IV, p. 103 and Ch. VII, p. 146.

from utter cold. Jamshid, being warned, selected pairs of animals and plants and protected them in a cave until the gods relented and warmer weather returned. The cave has replaced the Ark, and cold has replaced the Flood, but in other respects the Babylonian ancestry of the tale has been acknowledged.[9]

A quite different literary composition has been traced back to Mesopotamian antecedents. The text, written in Pahlavi script with some Parthian words, mentions Jamshid's long reign, but is set in the land of Assyria and consists mainly of a dialogue between a talking date-palm and a goat. Plant and animal fables are not known elsewhere in Persian literature, but are known from very early times in Mesopotamia. In format and content this composition has been recognized as a descendant of the famous Babylonian *Dispute between the Palm tree and the Tamarisk*, which was very widely known during the second millennium BC in western Asia. The Persian version may be a Manichaean satire upon Zoroastrian practices in which a goat replaced one of the trees, the better to ridicule the satire's target.

Several Sumerian and Babylonian myths feature the cosmic Anzu bird, an eagle-headed lion with lion's ears and a saw-like beak, notorious for its piercing cry and resembling a large black cloud. The various stories present the creature on the one hand as good, a careful parent who guards the twin mountains at the edge of the world where the sun rises, acting on behalf of Enlil, the chief god of the Sumerian pantheon; and as the heavy mist which hovers over the source of the rivers Tigris and Euphrates. On the other hand they attribute wickedness to Anzu as the betrayer of trust who seized the Tablet of Destinies from its rightful possessor, and had to be defeated in a cosmic battle. In Persian lore some similar stories are told about the Simurgh (Saena) bird, which likewise has the head of an eagle or falcon and the body of a lion. In Sassanian Persia the Simurgh bird is often portrayed like the griffin of earlier western Asia; but towards China it becomes a more decorative bird with pheasant-like tail feathers. In stories preserved in the Shahname there are two distinct Simurghs, though both are described as resembling a large black cloud. The good Simurgh, of non-Zoroastrian origin, is the guardian genius of heroes, who helps Zal and

79. Simurgh bird as shown on a Sassanian silver bowl. The lion's head and ears, on a bird's body, show that it is a descendant of the mythical Mesopotamian Anzu bird.

his son Rustam. The wicked Simurgh, on the other hand, is a monstrous being killed by Isfandiyar in the course of his seven exploits. There are also Kurdish folk-tales in which the Simurgh bird has its young eaten from its nest in a tree by a snake, and then becomes the guardian helper of a hero. Like the eagle in the Babylonian myth of Etana, the Simurgh bird in Kurdish stories carries the hero heavenwards on its back.

There was a Mesopotamian demon Lamashtu who interfered with childbirth and harmed babies and young children. Both by name and by nature she has been recognized in Persian tales as Almasti.

Books of Secrets

Secret knowledge in Babylonian texts is clearly indicated by a colophon which prohibits circulation outside a tiny circle of initiates. This type of colophon was transferred to the Greek magical papyri found in Egypt from the Roman period. The secret cuneiform texts contain a restricted range of information which at first sight seems rather random: lists of gods,

[9] A supposed account by Gurdjieff, of how he heard the *Epic of Gilgamesh* from his father in Armenia early in the 20th cent., is spurious, for it relays errors made by early scholars in trans-

lating certain words that have recently been corrected. Gurdjieff travelled in Mesopotamia between the two world wars with Soviet archaeologists.

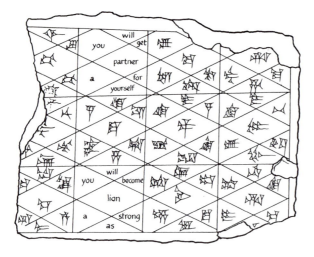

80. Cuneiform clay tablet for telling fortunes. Seleucid period.

stars, cult objects and their equation with minerals or plants, as well as incantations against illness, rituals for making and repairing divine statues, cosmology and theological speculation, mathematical and divination texts. They seem to attempt to systematize the material world and to discover its relationship to the divine world by association of ideas or words or numbers. Such texts appear from the reigns of the Sargonid kings of Assyria onwards, from the eighth century BC, and they often begin with a brief cosmogony. Scholars still barely understand them on a superficial level, let alone the cryptic techniques which underlie the associations.

Long after cuneiform writing died out, various books of secrets or mysteries were transmitted in writing in many different languages. In some cases it has been possible to show that they have an Akkadian basis even though they have developed beyond it in different ways. Some are called 'Book of Secrets' but give no hint as to why their often debased and garbled contents should have the value of secrecy.

One of the seven scriptures of the Manichaeans was called the *Book of Secrets*; although its contents are still unknown, the time of its use helps to bridge the long gap between cuneiform and medieval times.

In Latin and Arabic the composite text known variously as *Picatrix* and *Ghaya* has sources traced back to Uruk in the Seleucid period. There a cuneiform text connects signs of the zodiac with a temple or a city, and with trees, plants, and stones. Intervening

influence is evident, however, for the *Picatrix* inserts names which include Aristotle, Alexander, and Apollonios (of Tyana), and some of the connections are similar to those which characterize the writings of Teukros 'of Babylon', who lived in the first century AD.[10] The Arabic compositions concerned with cosmology were used by Arab alchemists.

The Arabic book 'Secret of Secrets' (Sirr al-asrar) contains a jumble of material, but states at the outset that every phenomenon has a hidden and an overt cause. Known earliest from a tenth-century manuscript, it gives also an exchange of letters between Aristotle and Alexander.

The Jewish *Book of Secrets* (Sefer ha-Razim) was written in Palestine sometime between the first and fourth centuries AD, and includes sections with rituals and instructions for making figurines which have recognizably Mesopotamian antecedents. A part of the *Zohar*, written in Aramaic in late thirteenth-century Spain, was called the 'Book of the Mystery', and was a central writing in kabbalistic mysticism. The Slavonic 'Book of the Secrets of Enoch', also known as the 'Book of Hekhalot', says explicitly why particular kinds of knowledge were selected. They were the names and measurements of heavenly and earthly bodies which Enoch wrote down: 'There have been many books from the beginning of creation, and shall be to the end of the world, but none shall make things known to you like my writings.'

Although only the Slavonic version survives, there are clear indications that the book was written during the first few centuries AD in Greek and in Hebrew. The Ethiopic *Book of the Mysteries of the Heavens and the Earth* contains mainly cosmology and early history. The author Bakhayla Mika'al, to whom it is attributed, is said in the text to be the same as Zosimos, presumably the great mystic and alchemist of Akhmim-Panopolis, to whom many alchemical treatises are attributed.

Last but not least is the 'Book of Secrets' to which the name of Albertus Magnus is attached. It was translated from Latin into English around 1550 AD, and still bears traces of its garbled forebears in giving the names of plants and animals in now incomprehensible 'Chaldaean'. It also includes information on the planets and marvels of the world. Mundane recipes and tricks have replaced the old rituals that breathed

<hr>

[10] See Ch. II, p. 48.

divine life into statues. During the Elizabethan period the genre was caught up in the fashion for encyclopaedic works containing all the information about popular science that well-educated men should know; one Thomas Hill wrote such works and often referred to them as 'secrets', claiming to have taken them from the writings of ancient sages such as Hermes. By this time the label 'secret' is inexplicable without some understanding of the genuinely Chaldaean, esoteric background from which it arose. Instructions such as: 'If this stone be brayed and scattered upon coals in four corners of the house, they that be sleeping shall flee the house', mirror Akkadian instructions in both format and details.

Magicians and Shamans

The words 'magic' and 'magician' are derived from the Persian word *magus*, but it has often been remarked that 'Chaldaeans' in Greek as a word for astrologers or magicians is interchangeable with the word 'Magi'. For lack of early sources written in Persian, it is difficult to assess Persian influence before the Islamic period, and this must be borne in mind when ancient Mesopotamian influence is traced.

A type of biographical legend, called a 'magus legend', is identified by a selection from several characteristics: the hero has a supernatural or mysterious origin, initiation attended by hardships and temptations, distant wanderings, a magical heroic contest, a trial or persecution, a violent, unjust, or mysterious death, and resurrection. It is found narrating the lives of Zoroaster, Cyrus, Pythagoras, Moses, Solomon, Melchizedek, Apollonios of Tyana, and Jesus of Nazareth. Several of these key characteristics are found in cuneiform texts, and are recognizable as forerunners which contribute to the later pattern. The *Legend of Sargon's Birth* has been compared with the story of Moses in Exodus; the life of Enkidu as it is told in the *Epic of Gilgamesh* fits into the pattern; and in the *Epic of Creation* together with the *Ordeal of Marduk* (a curious text in which the virtuous god is imprisoned) the hero-god seems to live his life according to the magus-legend. The Egyptian legend of Osiris, with its strong Syrian connections, also shares many of the characteristic episodes.

Shamans are found particularly among the Turkic peoples of northern Asia, extending from Finland to the Sakhalin Islands. They are selected for initiation to acquire magic power and they may travel to heaven or the Underworld. The mystic journey is closely linked to the epic recital of the person's heroic exploits. Since the phenomenon is found chiefly among illiterate people, it has been described and recorded only recently, so that its antiquity can only be guessed, although some shamanistic practices are described by Herodotos in the fifth century BC.

Certain themes in shaman narratives are strikingly similar to themes of Sumerian and Akkadian myths. The World Tree, the Cosmic Eagle, and a Serpent, often feature together in the shaman's attainment of his other-worldly goal, as they do also in the story of Inanna and the halub tree, of the *Myth of Lugalbanda*, and of the *Legend of Etana*, the latter story being found as far afield as Finland. The shaman often searches for the water and food of life, reminiscent of Adapa's attempt to win immortality.

It is difficult to interpret these similarities with any assurance. In an early phase of scholarship it was thought that diffusion accounted for them, but this view went out of fashion on the assumption that all people think up similar stories independently. One might suppose that shamanism was indigenous in northern Asia and extremely ancient, so that in some way it influenced Mesopotamian myths at their very roots. But one might alternatively suggest that Mesopotamian myth and ritual, spreading abroad in so many ways at many different periods through trade, deportation, into Buddhism from its inception, and finally through the dispersal of persecuted Manichaeans, gave rise to some manifestations recorded much later among shamans. This suggestion, strengthened by a new understanding of the history of Mesopotamia, and returning to the wisdom of earlier scholars, would imply that some forms of shamanism took on Mesopotamian elements.

Islamic Schools

The syllabus of pre-Islamic schools in Mesopotamia survived conversion to Islam. It has long been acknowledged that Greek education made its way into Arab scholarship especially in the fields of philosophy, mathematics, and medicine. Less well known is the component that can be traced right back into the cuneiform schools of the Old Babylonian period.

The *Liber Mensurationum*, written by an unidentified author named Abu Bakr and extant only in a Latin translation, contains a base of material from the Mesopotamian surveyors' training tradition, including techniques of geometrical proof and the setting of riddle-like algebraic problems with no practical application in order to train in methods of calculation. The way in which problems are formulated and expressed in the Latin closely follows Babylonian manuals and school texts.

Format is also the key to the ancestry of the Hippocratic oath. Compare the following:

> I swear by Ashur, Sherua . . .
> and all the gods of Assyria,
> May these gods be our witnesses
> in the presence of the great gods
> of heaven and earth.
> I will keep the oath of this treaty,
>
> I will always serve (king and crown-
> prince) in a true and fitting manner
> and protect them.
> I will not do (anything) that is evil
> and improper to (the king).
>
> Whoever changes, disregards, transgresses
> or erases the oaths of this tablet . . .
> may Ashur . . . decree an evil fate for him.
>
> (Clauses from treaties and loyalty oaths
> from 7th-cent. BC Assyria)

> I swear by Asklepios
> and I swear by all God's saints
> male and female
> and I call upon all of them
> as witnesses
> that I will fulfil this oath
> and this condition.
> I will let (my instructor)
> share in my livelihood.
>
> Things that may harm (patients)
> and do wrong I will avoid
> to the best of my judgement.
> He who keeps this oath
> and does not corrupt it in any way
> will be praised constantly
> by all men in future.
> The opposite applies to him
> who breaks it.
>
> (Ibn Abi Usaibi'ah, *Uyun al-anba* I)

That Arab physicians took over Greek medical treatises attributed to Hippokrates is generally acknowledged, but it is also clear that a part of the Greek Corpus Hippocraticum contains close similarities of form and content with Babylonian medical texts; for instance the type of compilation that describes symptoms in order from head to toe. Far fewer comparisons can be made with Egyptian medical texts.

The career of Ktesias, a Greek doctor who came from Knidos and served the Achaemenid king Artaxerxes II in the fourth century BC, may be one factor in transmission both to and from Mesopotamia. Much earlier, however, the Hittites of Anatolia had translated many Akkadian medical texts, which they added to their own indigenous products. The Mesopotamian texts are certainly the earliest of all, but exceptional doctors of any nationality were in demand by kings of many different countries in the Late Bronze Age, and they acquired their plants and minerals for remedies from far and wide. There is thus a very complex situation in which most countries added Babylonian medical treatises to their own lore. Some Arabic medical lore is therefore likely to stem from Akkadian practices, with or without Greek texts as intermediaries.

An important part of the ancient Mesopotamian curriculum had been training in quantity surveying, much of it very practical: how much seed-corn was needed per field, how many man-hours and cubic measures of soil to dig a canal for irrigation, etc. A composition known as *Nabataean Agriculture* was translated from some language still unidentified into Arabic by Abu Bakr ibn Wahshiya al-Kasdani 'the Chaldaean' during the early Islamic period, and it claimed to have been written 'at a time when a Canaanite dynasty ruled Babylonia'. This description would fit the Old Babylonian period when west Semitic Amorites ruled, among them the great Hammurabi of Babylon. The text is a thorough treatise on land economy, containing anachronisms and interpolations that have led some scholars to deny any link with the Bronze Age and to identify it as a fake of early Muslim date. Others, however, prefer to see an authentic core embellished by subsequent redactors. As early as 1859, when cuneiform studies were in their infancy, the scholar Chwolson noticed that *Nabataean Agriculture* ascribed the introduction of certain medicinal plants to named Babylonian kings in the same way as some Babylonian medical prescriptions are attributed to kings such as Hammurabi or Naram-Sin. From the cuneiform records of Babylonia certain agricultural sections of text are included among many others in the series *Iqqur īpuš* and similar almanac-type compilations. In view of the demonstrable link between Old Babylonian and Arab mathematical texts, it is likely that the Arabic compilation contains genuine, if much reworked, Akkadian material.

Nabataean Agriculture was disseminated widely in tenth-century Europe, and was one of the works that influenced the development of horticulture in the west. A recent assessment of medieval gardens attributes the inspiration and design to Arab and Persian influence rather than to Classical sources. Since the Babylonian Talmud contains many Babylonian plant names, it is possible that Babylonian Jewish academies played an important part in transmission. But more simply, since the Arabic word for 'collector of agricultural taxes', *makis*, is a loan word from Akkadian, an unbroken tradition of agriculture and the state bureaucracy that accompanied it may account for the legacy in Islamic times.

Early Arabic Descriptions of the World

A schematic map of the world has recently been dated quite closely to the late eighth century BC. A later copy which was drawn on clay and labelled in cuneiform has been found, and is in the British Museum. It shows Babylon at the centre of a region which includes the Euphrates and Assyria. A sea surrounds that region, and an uncertain number of other regions, probably seven in number, radiate out beyond the sea as acute triangles, with 'distances between' reckoned in leagues, 'double-hours'. Many of its features have been traced in more ancient

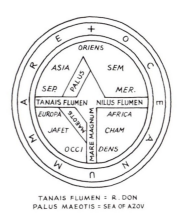

ORIENS
ASIA
SEM
PALUS
SEP.
MER.
TANAIS FLUMEN
NILUS FLUMEN
EUROPA
MAEOTIS
MARE MAGNUM
AFRICA
JAFET
CHAM
OCCI
DENS
TANAIS FLUMEN = R. DON
PALUS MAEOTIS = SEA OF AZOV

82. Map of the world according to Isidore of Seville.

cuneiform literature, and it is notable that Babylon was not replaced by Ashur or Nineveh during the Assyrian empire, which implies that it originated in Babylonia rather than Assyria. The shield of Achilles in *Iliad* 18 likewise showed the world surrounded by ocean: Hephaistos set 'the stream of Ocean around the furthest rim of the cunningly fashioned shield', and an early Greek map drawn by Anaximander of Miletos is said to have shown the earth surrounded by ocean in a similar way.

The geographer Ptolemy (*c.* AD 100–78) in his *Tetrabiblos* described a similar scheme in which the regions of the world were divided for astrological purposes into seven zones called *klimata*, a simplification of his more complex scheme with twenty-four. Other similarities, attributed to him by early Arab writers, cannot be confirmed from his extant writings, but they include features now known from the Babylonian map: a great sea surrounding the earth, and a cosmic mountain; a measurement (of 900 parasangs) is given for each of the *klimata*. *Klima* means a zone

1 Mountain
2 City
3 Urartu
4 Assyria
5 Der
6 (unreadable)
7 Marsh
8 Susa
9 Channel ?
10 Bit Yakin
11 City ?
12 Habban
13 Babylon
14, 15, 16, 17 Salt river
18 Region. 3 leagues between Where sun is not seen
19 Region. 6 leagues between
20 (unreadable)
21 (")
22 Region. 8 leagues between
23 Great Wall

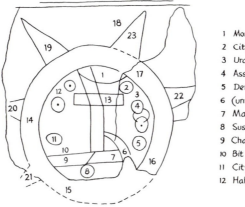

81. Clay map of the world, labelled in Akkadian cuneiform, with newly discovered fragment 'Great Wall' added. Copied from original of *c.*700 BC.

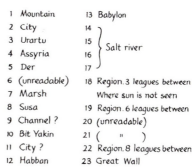

83. Two chalcedony seals, fourth and fifth century AD, showing winged, man-faced bulls.

of latitude which was defined by a rising time and so related to day-length, derived from the shadow given by the gnomon which was invented in Babylonia. Isidore of Seville (c. AD 565–636), the author of the popular encyclopaedia *Etymologies* in which much ancient knowledge was collected, used a similar scheme, as did Agapios, who died in AD 941/2 and came from Hierapolis-Membidj in Syria where paganism survived late.

Early Arabic descriptions show that the tradition came down to them from Babylon. Al-Mas'ūdī, among others, described seven 'climates' (using a word taken over into Arabic from Greek) which were each equated with signs of the zodiac and with one of the seven planets, and each had an area of 700 square parasangs, but the centre of the scheme was still Babylon. According to Mas'ūdī, Babil was the centre of the world, which he compared to the heart in the body, with the other six regions being like the extremities of the body. He conveys, therefore, an ancient tradition which goes back at least to the time of the great Assyrian kings. Persian Islamic schemes divided the world into regions called kishvars which were confused or equated with the 'climates', and had six regions encircling a central region called Babil. Some scholars think that Indian cosmography is also derived ultimately from Babylonian sources.

Architecture and Art

During the early centuries of Islam, many Babylonian and Assyrian monuments were still visible even if their fabric had deteriorated. The old ziggurrat built at Khorsabad by Sargon II late in the eighth century BC had a staircase which spiralled around the outside, and it is thought to have inspired a minaret at Samarra, which similarly has spiral, external stairs. The ground plans of the palaces at Samarra also resemble those of Assyrian kings. At Al-Hira, seat of the Lakhmid dynasty, early Christian churches were built with plans just like ancient Babylonian temples.

In 1904 W. R. Lethaby wrote that 'many of the links in the development and transformation of ancient art must have been irrecoverably lost by the destruction of Eastern cities'. He pointed to the magnificent survivals in stone at Baalbek and Palmyra which influenced Byzantine architectural decoration and the Romanesque style of western Europe. At that time nobody knew that it would prove possible to excavate mud-brick façades from much earlier temples in Mesopotamia which represent pillars as tree-trunks from which foliage bursts forth exuberantly at the crown. It was J. Baltrusaitis in 1934 who showed that many Romanesque motifs in western Europe seemed to come more or less directly from much older Mesopotamian models, especially taken from small objects such as stone seals. Some of these were brought back as precious souvenirs by Crusaders and one at least is still to be seen as a relic from the Holy Land in Palermo cathedral, but he thought the transmission began around 800 BC and continued spasmodically from that time onwards. One can document the presence of Celtic mercenaries and the arrival of a Celtic embassy in Babylon in the time of Alexander the Great; more difficult is to establish the part played later by Armenians, both pagan and Christian, in disseminating ancient Mesopotamian motifs. Norwegians are known to have made up the Varangian guard which served in Byzantium in the eleventh century, and they would have seen antiquities in Constantinople and elsewhere as trophies and curiosities displayed publicly in the cities of the Near East. Some of these adventurers would have taken back souvenirs and the stories that they had heard on campaign, for in that time it was customary for warriors on the march to tell each other tales of the golden past. 'Alongside the men rode Yalan Sina and the warrior Izad Goshasp, who guided the troops by untrodden ways, reciting to them the adventures of the kings of old' (Shah-name 363). This has been held to account for traces of ancient Mesopotamian imagery such as the human-headed bull that are found in the Norse sagas.

FURTHER READING

1. The *Epic of Creation* at the Court of Khosroes I

DAMASCIUS, *Traité des premiers principes*, text L. G. Westerink, trans. J. Combès (Paris, 1986), iii. 165.

GOLDSCHMIDT, L., *Der babylonische Talmud* (Haag, Martinus Nijoff, 1933), vii.

KREBERNIK, M., 'Mummu', *RLA* viii (1995), 415–16.

WEHRLI, F., *Eudemos von Rhodos: Die Schule des Aristoteles VIII* (Basle, 1955).

2. Babylonian Legacy in Manichaean Scripture

ARNOLD, T. W., *Painting in Islam* (Oxford, 1928), esp. 61.

AUGUSTINE OF HIPPO, *City of God* 15. 23, and *Confessions*.

BROWN, P., 'Sorcery, Demons and the Rise of Christianity', in *Religion and Society in the Age of Saint Augustine* (London, 1972), 119–46.

CAMERON, R., and DEWEY, A. J., *The Cologne Mani Codex: 'Concerning the Origin of his Body'* (Missoula, Scholars Press, 1979).

DRIJVERS, H. J. W., 'Bardaisan of Edessa and the Hermetica: The Aramaic Philosopher and the Philosophy of his Time', *Jaarbericht Ex Oriente Lux* 21 (1970), 190–210 (and Variorum Repr., London, 1984).

—— 'Mani und Bardaisan, ein Beitrag zur Vorgeschichte des Manichaismus', in *Mélanges d'histoire des religions offerts à H-C. Puech* (Paris, 1974) (= no. XIII in *East of Antioch*, Variorum Repr. 459–69.)

—— 'The Persistence of Pagan Cults and Practices in Christian Syria', in N. Garsoian *et al.* (eds.), *East of Byzantium* (Dumbarton Oaks, 1982) (and Variorum Repr.).

KVANVIG, H. S., *The Mesopotamian Background of the Enoch Figure and of the Son of Man* (Neukirchener Verlag, 1988).

LIEU, S. N. C., *Manichaeism in the Later Roman Empire and Mediaeval China Manchester*, rev. edn. (Tübingen, 1992), 33–85.

—— 'From Mesopotamia to the Roman East', ch. 2 in collected articles, *Manichaeism in Mesopotamia and the Roman East* (Leiden, 1994), 22–130.

REEVES, J. C., *Jewish Lore in Manichaean Cosmogony, Studies in the Book of Giants Traditions* (Cincinnati, 1992).

—— 'Ut-napishtim in the Book of Giants?', *Journal of Biblical Literature* 112 (1993), 110–15.

RUDOLPH, K., *Gnosis: The Nature and History of Gnosticism*, trans. R. M. Wilson (San Francisco, 1983).

SISTANI, F., Divan (ed.), ʿAli ʿAbd al-Rasuli (Tehran, 1937).

TARDIEU, M., 'L'Arrivée des manichéens à al-Hira', in P. Canivet and J.-P. Coquais (eds.), *La Syrie de Byzance à l'Islam* (Institut français de Damas, 1992), 15–24.

TEIXIDOR, J., *Bardesane d'Edesse: La Première Philosophe syriaque* (Paris, 1992), esp. 71.

3. The Idea of Holy Scripture and the Tablet of Destinies

DALLEY, S., *Myths from Mesopotamia* (Oxford, 1989).

FOSTER, B. R., 'Wisdom and the Gods in Ancient Mesopotamia', *Orientalia* 43 (1974), 344–54.

GEORGE, A., 'Sennacherib and the Tablet of Destinies', *Iraq* 48 (1986), 133–46.

SHAKESPEARE, W., *2 Henry IV* iii.

STARR, I., *The Rituals of the Diviner* (Bibliotheca Mesopotamica 12, Malibu, 1983) esp. 16–24.

THACKSTON, W. M., *The Tales of the Prophets of al-Kisaʾi* (Boston, 1978).

VANDERKAM, J. C., *Enoch and the Growth of an Apocalyptic Tradition*, CBQ monography series 16 (Washington, DC, 1984).

4. A Babylonian Component in Hermetic Writings

BAIGENT, M., *From the Omens of Babylon* (Penguin, 1994).

BARB, A. A., 'The Survival of Magic Arts', in A. Momigliano (ed.), *The Conflict between Paganism and Christianity in the Fourth Century* (Oxford, 1963), 100–25.

BERTHELOT, H., *La Chimie au Moyen Age*, 3 vols. (Paris, 1893) i, p. xv (and compare Livingstone, below, p. 176).

BEST, M. R., and Brightman, F. H., *The Book of Secrets of Albertus Magnus* (Oxford, 1973).

ELIADE, M., 'Hermes Trismegistos', in *Encyclopaedia of Religion* (New York, 1987).

FALKENSTEIN, A., *Die Haupttypen der sumerischen Beschwörung* (Leipzig, 1931), esp. 53 ff.

FOWDEN, G., *The Egyptian Hermes* (Cambridge, 1986), esp. 67.

HUNGER, H., and PINGREE, D., MUL.APIN (Archiv für Orientforschung, Beiheft 24, 1989).

KINGSLEY, P., 'Poimandres: The Etymology of the Name and the Origins of the Hermetica', *Journal of the Warburg and Courtauld Institutes* 56 (1993), 1–24.

LICHTHEIM, M., *Ancient Egyptian Literature*, iii: *The Late Period* (Los Angeles, Calif., 1980), 125–50.

LIVINGSTONE, A., *Mystical and Mythological Explanatory Works of Assyrian and Babylonian Scholars* (Oxford, 1986), esp. 176–9.

MANETHO, *Aegyptiaca*, trans. W. G. Waddell, Loeb edn. (Harvard, 1940).

MEZ, A., *Die Renaissance des Islams* (Heidelberg, 1922), 167.

PEARSON, B. A., *Gnosticism, Judaism and Egyptian Christianity* (Minneapolis, 1990), 136 ff.

PLESSNER, M., 'Hermes Trismegistos and Arab Science', *Studia Islamica* 2 (1954), 45–59.

RUSKA, J., *Tabula Smaragdina* (Heidelberg, 1926).

STARR, I., *The Rituals of the Diviner* (Bibliotheca Mesopotamica 12, Malibu 1983), esp. 16–24.

TAYLOR, T., *Iamblichus on the Mysteries of the Egyptians, Chaldaeans and Assyrians*, 3rd edn. (London, 1968).

THOMPSON, R. Campbell, *A Dictionary of Assyrian Chemistry and Geology* (Oxford, 1936).

WALKER, C. B. F., 'The Second Tablet of ṭupšenna pitema', *JCS* 33 (1981), 191–5.

WENDEL, C., *Die griechisch-römische Buchbeschreibung verglichen mit der des vorderen Orients* (Halle, 1949).

WIGGERMANN, F. A., *Mesopotamian Protective Spirits: The Ritual Texts* (Gröningen, 1992).

YATES, F. A., *Giordano Bruno and the Hermetic Tradition* (London, 1964).

ZIMMERN, H., 'Das vermutliche babylonische Vorbild des Pehtā und Mambūhā der Mandäer', *Orientalische Studien Theodor Nöldeke gewidmet* (Giessen, 1906), 959 ff.

5. *Alexander Romance* and the Water of Life

DALLEY, S., 'The Tale of Buluqiya and the Alexander Romance in Jewish and Sufi Mystical Circles', in, J. C. Reeves (ed.), *Tracing the Threads* (Atlanta, 1994).

GURNEY, O. R., 'The Sultantepe Tablets (continued) VI, A Letter of Gilgamesh', *Anatolian Studies* 7 (1957), 127–36.

—— 'The tale of the Poor Man of Nippur and its Folktale Parallels', *Anatolian Studies* 22 (1972), 149–58.

LAESSOE, J., *Studies on the Assyrian Ritual and Series* bīt rimki (Copenhagen 1955).

RÖLLIG, W., 'Literatur' 4.5 Literarische Briefe, *RLA* vii (1987–90), 57–8.

WILSON, C. A., 'Philosophers, Iōsis and the Water of Life', *Proceedings of the Leeds Philosophical and Literary Society* 19:5 (Leeds, 1984), 103–209.

6. *Tale of Buluqiya*

DALLEY, S., 'Gilgamesh in the Arabian Nights', *Journal of the Royal Asiatic Society* 1 (1991), 1–17.

—— 'The Gilgamesh Epic and Manichaean Themes', *Aram* 3 (1991), 23–33.

7. Mesopotamian Themes in Persian Stories

ARO, J., 'Anzu and Simurgh', in B. L. Eichler (ed.), *Kramer Anniversary vol.*, Alte Orient und Altes Testament 25 (Neukirchen-Vluyn, 1976) 25–8.

BRUNNER, C. J., 'The Fable of the Babylonian Tree', *JNES* 39 (1980), 191–202, 291–302.

CURTIS, V., *Persian Myths* (London, 1993).

HINNELLS, J. R., *Persian Mythology* (London, 1973, 1985).

8. Book of Secrets

BEST, M. R., and BRIGHTMAN, F. H., *The Book of Secrets of Albertus Magnus* (Oxford, 1973).

BORGER, R., 'Geheimwissen', *RLA* iii (1957–71).

BUDGE, E. A. WALLIS, *The Book of the Mysteries of the Heavens and the Earth* (Oxford, 1935).

GREENFIELD, J. C., 'Prolegemenon', in H. Odeberg (ed.), *3 Enoch, or the Hebrew Book of Enoch* (New York, 1973).

HUNGER, H., 'Noch ein "Kalendertext"', *Zeitschrift für Assyriologie* 64 (1975), 40–3.

MANZALAOUI, M., 'The Pseudo-Aristotelean Kitab Sirr al-asrar', *Oriens* 23 (1974), 147–255.

MORFILL, W. R., and CHARLES, R. H., *The Book of the Secrets of Enoch* (Oxford 1906).

NEUSNER, J., *A History of the Jews in Babylonia: Later Sassanian Times* (Leiden, 1970), esp. 344–67.

PINGREE, D., 'Some Sources of the Ghayat al-Hakim', *Journal of the Warburg and Courtauld Institutes* 43 (1980), 1–15.

PLESSNER, M., 'Hermes Trismegistus and Arab Science', *Studia Islamica* 2 (1954), 45–59.

RUSKA, J., *Tabula Smaragdina* (Heidelberg, 1926).

WRIGHT, L. B., *Middle Class Culture in Elisabethan England* (Methuen 1935, Cornell 1964), esp. 562.

9. Magicians and Shamans

HATTO, A. T., *Shamanism and Epic Poetry in Northern Asia* (London, School of Oriental and African Studies, 1970).

BUTLER, E. M., *The Myth of the Magus* (London, 1948/93).

FOSTER, B., *Before the Muses: An Anthology of Akkadian Literature* (Bethesda, Md., 1993).

10. Islamic Schools

CHWOLSON, D., *Über die Überreste der altbabylonischen Literatur in arabischen Übersetzungen* (St Petersburg, 1859). *Encyclopaedia of Islam*, 2nd edn. s.v. Ibn Wahshiyya.

GELLER, M., 'Akkadian medicine in the Babylonian Talmud', in D. Cohn-Sherbock (ed.), *A Traditional Quest: Essays in honour of Louis Jacobs* (Sheffield, 1991).

GOLTZ, D., *Studien zur altorientalischen und griechischen Heilkunde* (Wiesbaden, 1974).

HARVEY, J., *Mediaeval Gardens* (Batsford, 1981).

HOYRUP, J., 'Al-Khwarizmi, Ibn Turk and the Liber Mensurationum: On the Origins of Islamic Algebra', *Erdem* 2 (Ankara, 1986), 445–84.

—— 'Sub-Scientific Mathematics: Observations on a Pre-Modern Phenomenon', *History of Science* 28 (1990), 63–86.

—— 'On the Mensuration of the Liber Mensurationum', *Max-Planck Institute for the History of Science* (Berlin, 1995).

—— '"The Four Sides and the Area", Oblique Light on the Prehistory of Algebra', in *History of Mathematics: Sources, Studies and Pedagogic Integration* (Washington, DC, 1995 or 1996).

KHOURY, R., 'Babylon in der ältesten Version über die Geschichte der Propheten im Islam', in G. Mauer *et al.* (eds.), *Ad bene et fideliter seminandum, Festschrift for K-H. Deller*, Alte Orient und Altes Testament 220 (Neukirchen-Vluyn, 1988), 123–44.

LABAT, R., *Traité akkadien de diagnostics et pronostics médicaux* I (Paris and Leiden, 1951), esp. pp. xxxv–xlv.

SEZGIN, F., *Geschichte des arabischen Schrifttums*, iv (Leiden, 1971), 318 on Ibn Wahshiyya.

WINCKLER, H. A., *Salomo und die Karina: Eine orientalische Legende von der Bezwingung einer Kindbett dämonin durch einigen heiligen Helden* (Stuttgart, 1931), 25.

11. Early Arabic Descriptions of the World

BREHAUT, E., *An Encyclopaedist of the Dark Ages: Isidore of Seville* (New York, 1912).

HARLEY, J. B., and WOODWARD, D., *The History of Carto-graphy*, i–ii (Chicago, 1987–92).

HOROWITZ, W., 'The Babylonian Map of the World', *Iraq* 50 (1988), 147–65.

MILIK, J. T., *The Books of Enoch: Aramaic Fragments of Qumran, Cave 4* (Oxford, 1976), esp. 15–16 n. 3.

PINGREE, D., *The Thousands of Abū Maʿshar* (Warburg Institute, London, 1968).

PTOLEMY, Cl., *Tetrabiblos*, trans. F. E. Robbins, Loeb edn. (Harvard, 1940).

RADTKE, B., *Weltgeschichte und Weltbeschreibung im mittelalterlichen Islam*, Beiruter Texte und Studien, 51 (Beirut, 1992).

12. Architecture and Art

BALTRUSAITIS, J., *Art sumérien, art roman* (Paris, 1934).

COLLON, D., 'Well-Travelled Seals' *First Impressions* (London 1987, rev. 1993), ch. 18.

LETHABY, W. R., *Mediaeval Art from the Peace of the Church to the Eve of the Renaissance* (Oxford, 1904; rev. D. Talbot Rice, 1949).

LEVY, R. (ed.), *The Epic of Kings: Shah-nama the National Epic of Persia*, by Ferdowsi (London, 1967).

MUNDT, M., *Zur Adaption orientalischer Bilder in den Fornaldarsögur Nordrlanda* (Peter Lang, Frankfurt, 1993).

IX

REDISCOVERY AND AFTERMATH

Henrietta McCall

A case scarcely three feet square enclosed all that remained, not only of the great city of Nineveh, but of Babylon itself!

THIS WAS HOW AUSTEN HENRY LAYARD, WRITING at Cheltenham in 1848, described the meagre collection of objects that had till then represented ancient Mesopotamia in the British Museum. At the time, nothing of Assyrian art was known, even by analogy, the architecture of Nineveh and Babylon was a matter of speculation only, and the interpretation of the cuneiform script was in its early stages. But on the eve of the arrival of Layard's first consignment of cases from Nimrud, expectations ran high. George Smith of the British Museum later recalled why their arrival was to arouse such enormous interest and excitement: to scholars and the great Bible-reading public, here was the home of man's earliest traditions, the place where Eden was supposed to have been, where some cities were older than the Flood, the actual birthplace of religious history. Babylonia was 'the first civilized state'; its arts and sciences were, according to Smith, those of the Greeks, and therefore 'our own'.

In France too, only a handful of unclassified cylinder seals bore witness to ancient Mesopotamia, but national pride was stirring. The excavations of Paul-Émile Botta at the site of Khorsabad generated much interest, and the arrival in France of the first enormous decorated slabs was widely reported. European scholars already trying to decipher the unfamiliar wedge-shaped script of Babylon, little realized what a challenge to accepted religious traditions their success would bring.

During the second half of the eighteenth century popular interest in the ancient world was growing. Knowledge about ancient Greece had in a sense never really been lost, and had revived during the Renaissance. Fascinating new evidence about the architecture and ornamentation of Athens was provided by James Stuart and Nicholas Revett's *The Antiquities of Athens*, the first of four volumes of which was published in 1762. After that, and lasting well into the next century there was a European celebration of Greek taste—in architecture, furniture, dress, and literature, as well as an elegant backdrop for paintings. Interest in ancient Egypt, which intensified at the end of the eighteenth century when Napoleon sent a team of scholars up the Nile to record all ancient monuments, and whose work was published in *Description de l'Égypte* between 1809 and 1822, never really threatened this all-consuming passion, and indeed often sat with it in somewhat uneasy harmony, as part of the general interest in Classical Antiquity. Sphinxes, obelisks, and the (literally) odd hieroglyph added a certain exotic element.

Knowledge about ancient Mesopotamia on the brink of rediscovery was actually greater and more colourful than the pathetic display at the British Museum might have suggested. It originated from two different sources, from the Bible and Classical authors on the one hand, and from published works such as Bartholomé D'Herbelot's *La Bibliothèque Orientale* (1697) and the *Arabian Nights*, the first English publication of which appeared about 1712, on the other. D'Herbelot's massive list (in alphabetic order) purported to contain 'Tout ce qui regarde la connoissance des Peuples de l'Orient, Leurs Histoires et Traditions, Véritables ou Fabuleuses . . .'. The *Arabian Nights* pandered to a predilection for oriental fantasy;

many concurred with Sir Richard Burton's description of Baghdad in the days of the mighty caliphs as
a 'worthy successor to Babylon and Nineveh'.

To say confusion reigned about ancient Mesopotamia in the Old Testament and the writings of Classical authors would be an understatement. As has been
seen in Chapter IV, a somewhat haphazard chronology and sequence of events emerged, often based on
conjecture and guesswork. Some writers were more
concerned with entertainment than edification, and
were eclectic, interpreting historical events to suit
their own expositions and plucking names and incid-
ents out of legend. The Bible was equally selective
and the reputation of the Assyrians as bloodthirsty
warmongers in particular owes much to a somewhat
partisan narrative of events. These accounts established a tradition which was to remain more or less
unchallenged until the decipherment of the records
of the ancient Mesopotamians themselves gradually
forced a piecemeal revision of historical events.

The report of Herodotos in Book One of his
History is the first we have regarding ancient Mesopotamia. He begins at the time of the Persian king
Cyrus (559–530 BC) and his conquest of Babylon 'the
most powerful and renowned' city of 'Assyria'. This
enormous and splendid metropolis, divided down the
middle by the river Euphrates, contained two magnificent buildings, a royal palace and a temple of Bel.
This is described in some detail: 'it has a solid central tower, one furlong square, with a second erected
on top of it and then a third, and so on up to eight.
All eight towers can be climbed by a spiral way running round the outside, and about half-way up there
are seats for those who make the ascent to rest on.
On the summit of the topmost tower stands a great
temple'. This was, until the nineteenth century, one
of the more detailed and sober descriptions of Babylon available to writers, travellers, and artists such as
Fischer von Erlach and John Martin. Herodotos himself was considered a reliable source, consulted and
copied by historians in Antiquity and later, until the
British Assyriologist A. H. Sayce did much to dis-
credit the reputation of the aptly-called father of history at the end of the nineteenth century. Herodotos
was also the first to mention the legendary queen,
Semiramis, who was to play such a major role in the
ancients' history of Babylonia. He also gave some
interesting detail of Babylonian dress: 'a linen tunic
reaching to the feet with a woollen one over it, and

a short white cloak on top . . . They grow their hair
long, wear turbans, and perfume themselves all over;
everyone owns a seal and a walking-stick specially
made for him'. He described the Babylonian marriage
market (to be used to such effect by Edwin Long
over 2,000 years later). Not once, however, did he
mention the Hanging Gardens and his promise to
write a history of Assyria never materialized.

The first proper history of Assyria and Babylon we
have was written by Ktesias, a Greek doctor at the
Persian court of Artaxerxes II (404–359 BC). Far from
trustworthy, but full of fascinating information, parts
of his account are preserved in the works of Diodoros
Sikelos and Photius. Ktesias certainly visited Babylon
at least once, at the time of the battle of Cunaxa in
401 BC when Artaxerxes was wounded and Ktesias
attended him there, but the Babylon he describes is
the Babylon of Nebuchadnezzar II (604–562 BC), though
he attributes the splendid buildings to Semiramis.
Ktesias elaborated greatly upon the characters and
doings of Semiramis and Sardanapalos, whose fame
in Classical literature inordinately exceeded the factual part they played in Mesopotamian history, and
he stressed the extravagance and licentiousness of
their behaviour.

Ktesias was the main source for Mesopotamia in
Diodoros' *World History* (in forty books), a work which
inspired his contemporaries and endured through
history to a time when the cuneiform sources could
once again speak for themselves, but he also included
the accounts of, among others, Kleitarchos (a historian who accompanied Alexander and whose exploits
he presented as a romantic and brilliant adventure)
for his description of the walls of Babylon and the
Hanging Gardens. The extra dimensions of depravity with which he surrounded Sardanapalos (who
'outdid all his predecessors in luxury and sluggish-
ness . . . lived the life of a woman . . . practised sexual
indulgence of both kinds without restraint' and who,
not satisfied with throwing himself, his gold and silver and the contents of the royal wardrobe on the
funeral pyre, burnt also his concubines and eunuchs)
were gleaned from Aristobulos and Polybios. He
gave a long history of Semiramis and her rebuilding of Babylon but attributed the Hanging Gardens
to 'a later Syrian king' who wished to please one of
his wives, a Persian by race who longed for the 'distinctive landscape of Persia'. Diodoros understood
that Assyrian and Greek history (as he remarked in

Book 1) were not 'the same thing at all', but as for chronology, he dismissed any attempt to give that type of information. 'There is no special need of giving all the names of the kings and the number of years which each of them reigned because nothing was done by them which merits mentioning' (Book 2).

Later accounts included that of Strabo who described Babylon in Book 16 of his *Geography*, including its walls and listing the Hanging Gardens 'among the seven wonders of the world'. At the time he was writing the city was dilapidated 'partly by the Persians, partly by time', though doubtless to Greek eyes, mud-brick looked unimpressive at any time. Quintus Curtius Rufus described the Hanging Gardens as 'a wonder celebrated in the tales of the Greeks'. Pliny's *Natural History*, published in 77 AD, mentioned the Hanging Gardens but the author's promise to write about them in another book was not fulfilled. He did not allude to Sardanapalos but said that Semiramis had had sexual intercourse with her horse. Arrian described Sardanapalos' tomb at Anchiale with its indelicate inscription. Thus were stereotypes of licentious barbarism introduced by the Greeks and Romans, to be adopted apparently unquestioned by later Christian writers for whom the very names Babylon and Nineveh, Semiramis and Sardanapalos, were synonymous with pagan depravity and impiety.

So the Christian philosopher Athenagoras writing in 177 his *Embassy for the Christians* described Semiramis as 'a lascivious woman and a murderess', naming Ktesias as his source. And Athenaios, who lived at Rome at the end of the second century, the author of *The Deipnosophistae* or *The Sophists at Dinner*, gave a description of Sardanapalos that made all previous accounts of that depraved character look quite restrained:

the king with his face covered with white lead and bejewelled like a woman, combing purple wool in the company of his concubines and sitting among them with knees uplifted, his eyebrows blackened, wearing a woman's dress and having his beard shaved close and his face rubbed with pumice (he was even whiter than milk, and his eyelids were painted).

He also gave a detailed description of the king's funeral pyre:

four hundred feet high, on which he placed a hundred and fifty gold couches and an equal number of tables, these also of gold. On the pyre he constructed a chamber of wood one hundred feet long, in which he spread the couches and lay down; and not only he, but his queen was with him, and the concubines were on the other couches . . . he then roofed the chamber with huge, thick beams, and piled all around many thick timbers so that there should be no exit. In it he placed ten million talents of gold, one hundred million of silver, and garments, purple cloths, and robes of every description. He then gave orders to light the pyre, and it burned for fifteen days.

Not much more restrained was the historian Justinus (third century AD) who made an epitome in Latin of the forty-four books of *Historiae Philippicae* by Trogus Pompeius, a 'gentleman of eloquence'. Justinus 'extracted everything best worth the knowing . . . I have formed as it were a little posy of flowers'. This bouquet described (among other shocking information about Babylon and Assyria) Sardanapalos as 'a man more corrupt than a woman . . . spinning scarlet wool upon a distaff, among companies of whores, and in a woman's habit, exceeding all the women in the softness of his body, and the wantonness of his eyes'. He perished atop his funeral pyre along with all his riches. Both these accounts were to inspire Byron and in turn the painter Delacroix.

As if the Classical sources were not confusing and colourful enough, two very early novels set in the region did little to reveal the true nature of Assyrian or Babylonian civilization, rather they emphasized how disparate and strange they were. The *Ninos Romance*, by an unknown author, written in about the first century BC and set in Assyria, survives only in fragments. It had as its hero King Ninos, aged 17, and as its heroine, Semiramis, his cousin but these were merely historical ciphers in a romantic plot which involved a shipwreck, warfare, and love scenes. *The Babyloniaka* by Iamblichos (*c.* AD 160–80) (quoted at the end of the ninth century by the Byzantine scholar and patriarch Photius) was about two lovers, Sinonis and Rhodanes, who were attempting to escape capture by two eunuchs, Damas and Saca, at the command of the king of Babylon, Garmus, who loved Sinonis. Various magic practices were described and the Babylonian setting was macabre, with tombs, caverns, and the haunts of murderers. For the Greek audience for whom these novels were written, Assyria and Babylon were entirely ornamental settings for what was required from novels: a mixture of psychology, rhetoric, and history. The popular audience was interested in the workings of the human heart, the deliberations, private and public (leading to fine oratory) of the human mind, and an historical framework, preferably suggested by Classical historians.

Travellers to the east were apparently silent between the Classical authors and the first westerner to visit Mesopotamia and record his impressions, Rabbi Benjamin of Tudela, a native of the kingdom of Navarre, probably a merchant. He went on his epic journey from Spain to China, through Europe, Africa, and Asia, between 1160 and 1173. The first printed edition of his *Itinerary* did not appear until 1543, though it was well known to scholars from the thirteenth century. His choice of places and cities visited on the way was doubtless influenced by the Bible. He went to Mosul 'of great extent and very ancient', Nineveh, which 'lies in ruins', Babylon with its ruins of Nebuchadnezzar's palace ('people are afraid to enter it on account of the serpents and scorpions, by which it is infested'), and the Tower of Babel 'constructed of bricks . . . a spiral passage . . . leads up to the summit from which there is a prospect of twenty miles'. It is probable that Rabbi Benjamin's description was based on the remains of the ziggurat at Khorsabad. The publication of the *Itinerary* may have inspired Peter Breugel the Elder to paint two pictures of the Tower of Babel. From the summit of both of his ruined Towers, partly concealed by clouds, a very wide and distant view of the surrounding countryside can be seen, and the people, and boats on the Euphrates look tiny in comparison.

Another traveller, the Dutch plant collector Doctor Leonhardt Rauwolff also found the Tower of Babel, and said it was 'full of Vermin'. His visit to Babylon in October 1574 proved to be a disappointment. He would have failed to recognize 'this Potent and Powerful City' had it not been for 'several ancient and Delicate Antiquities that are still standing hereabout in great Desolation'. These included the bridge described by Herodotos, and what he believed to be the Tower of Babel, whose Vermin he detailed as 'three-headed poisonous lizard-type insects with multicoloured spots on their backs', a description which made his English translator, John Ray, expostulate that this was impossible and that 'Rauwolff was here too credulous and facil'. The ruins led Rauwolff to the melancholy reflection that 'here is a most terrible Example, to all impious and haughty Tyrants . . . that if they do not give over in time and leave their Tyranny . . . God the Almighty will also come upon them'. In December of the same year he also visited 'the Potent Town of Ninive . . . which was the metropolis of Assyria . . . to the time of Sennacherib and his Sons', but noted that 'nothing of any Antiquities' was to be seen. The place was a ruin, as foretold by Nahum, Zephaniah and the pious Tobias. Eventually Tamerlam 'came and took it by storm, burnt it, and reduced it to Ashes . . . that afterwards in the same place grew Beans'.

Following in the steps of Rabbi Benjamin of Tudela and Dr Rauwolff throughout the seventeenth century, a steady stream of travellers found their way to the ruins of Babylon and Nineveh, thrilling in imagination, depressing in reality. Sir Anthony Sherley, ambassador of the King of Persia to the Princes of Christendom, visited Babylon in 1613 and saw the Tower of Babel in ruins, 'As though any earthly foundation . . . could possibly be perpetuall'. At Nineveh, there was 'not one stone standing'. That was the problem: unlike Greece and Rome, or even Egypt which was little explored at the time, there were no vast monumental stone ruins, no picturesque broken columns or collapsed pediments. Mud-brick left an uninspiring legacy above ground.

Pietro della Valle went some fifty years later and in June 1625 found in and around Baghdad inscribed bricks and fragments of black marble 'hard and fine' inscribed with cuneiform. He identified two signs, 'a jacent pyramid . . . and a star of eight points', but the script remained completely impenetrable. His account of his voyage, *Travels into East India and Arabia Deserta* appeared between 1650 and 1663. The final volume, which would have contained the illustrations, was unfortunately never published; later translated editions contained unauthentic engravings.

Another Dutchman and plant collector, Doctor Olfert Dapper published in two volumes his *Naukeurige Beschryving van Asie* in 1680. The second volume described the history and sites of ancient Mesopotamia, and Nineveh, Babylon, and the Tower of Babel were shown in imaginative engravings, in contrast to those of Baghdad and Smyrna which were doubtless accurate representations of what Dapper had actually seen. Another, and most beautiful, attempt was made to do the same thing by J. B. Fischer von Erlach, the architect of the Schonbrunn Imperial Palace, in his *A Plan of Civil and Historical Architecture in the Representation of the Most Noted Buildings of*

Foreign Nations Both Ancient and Modern. Published in five volumes, Book 1 contained 22 plates of ancient monuments 'bury'd in the Ruins of Barbarity . . . restor'd, and set in a true Light' and these included the Hanging Gardens (plate III) and the Temple of Nineveh (plate X). The illustrations in Book 1 made claim to accuracy since their creator was well versed in the ancient literary sources available to him. He cites Ktesias, Quintus Curtius, Strabo, Pliny, Hyginus, and Cassius Dio as well as Herodotos for his illustration of Babylon alone. For the Temple of Nineveh, he used for his artistic reference 'une médaille trouvée près d'une Momie d'Égypte qui selon l'opinion des Connoisseurs est un temple de Ninive'.

Mesopotamia was dramatized from the Classical sources in the last half of the seventeenth century, but it is not clear what critical impact such productions had. In 1647, there were two plays about Semiramis, *La Véritable Sémiramis* by Desfontaines and *Sémiramis* by Gabriel Gilbert, and in 1699, David Lingelbach's *Sardanapalus* appeared. No doubt these rather prosaic titles achieved their aim: these two characters evoked by their very names the perceived spirit of that ancient, violent, and glamorous civilization.

It was now however that the influence of the *Bibliothèque Orientale* (1697) and the *Arabian Nights* (about 1712) began to effect a change in that view of Babylon and Nineveh which had prevailed till then, thanks to the Bible and Classical authors, to which was added the factual accounts of travellers who had gone not only to but beyond Mesopotamia, to the courts of the Ottoman empire. A fabulous setting with wicked sultans, magic carpets, talking animals, and so on became all the rage, seeming to its Christian readership to epitomize oriental delights. A strange but compelling landscape emerged, Mesopotamian and Arabian, where biblical Babylon and Nineveh flourished in the days of the great caliphs.

Those mighty city walls now encompassed hotels and azure-curtained pavilions, kiosks, silk tents, and bazaars; in the Hanging Gardens lounged voluptuous houris in whose great dark eyes languished temptations of the most sensuous kind. Around the Tower of Babel crystal fountains played. Warfare was conducted with fanfares and pomp; any blood that was spilt was as purple as the wine quaffed from massy gold vessels. Luxury and indulgence were everywhere; the very breeze carried sweet scents of cassia and nard. Camels and elephants paraded through the hundred brazen gates and along the broad avenues bordered on each side by jasper pavements. Dulcimers played, and lutes, harps, and cymbals while the snowy hands of virgin slaves waved feathered fans, and bright-eyed concubines performed sensuous dances.

Voltaire was one of the first to weave popular fantasies against this fabulous backdrop. Drawing freely on *The Babyloniaka* by Iamblichos (via Photius), the Quran and the *Bibliothèque Orientale*, he wrote the novel *Zadig* in 1748. Despite these sources, the Babylonian setting of the book lacked any real authenticity. More can be said for his play *Sémiramis* which appeared the same year and was performed at the Comédie-Française to some critical success. The first act took place in front of the palace of Semiramis, with the Hanging Gardens behind, a temple of the magi to the right and a mausoleum ornamented with obelisks to the left. During the fifth act, in this mausoleum of her husband Ninos, Semiramis perishes, as she descends to avenge his shade. The play later inspired Gioacchino Rossini's *Semiramide* which was first performed in Venice on 3 February 1823 and in English at Covent Garden in 1842. In 1845 it was produced in New York. In Voltaire's *La Princesse de Babylone* published in 1768, the setting is again Babylon—Babylon inspired by the *Arabian Nights*, but with a description of the Hanging Gardens closely based on Diodoros.

In rather the same vein, William Beckford wrote *The History of the Caliph Vathek*, published in the original French in 1787 and anonymously in English in 1784. Inspired by the *Arabian Nights*, Beckford produced a fantasy, set in Babylon, about a ninth century caliph, Vathek, much addicted to women and the pleasures of the table, who is induced by a hideous stranger to renounce Mahomet in favour of terrestrial influences. Unfortunately there is very little about Babylon itself but the book survived to inspire Byron who said 'it was one of the tales I had a very early admiration of. For correctness of costume, beauty of description, and power of imagination, it far surpasses all . . . imitations'.

Meanwhile some more hard fact was emerging for those who preferred to see Nineveh and Babylon in more concrete, if somewhat ruined, terms and not as a mere backdrop for fairy tales. Jean Otter published in the same year as Voltaire's *Sémiramis*, his *Voyage en Turquie et en Perse* which gave descriptions of the Tigris and the Euphrates, and described

Nineveh, with an accompanying map. Of real significance though was the publication between 1774 and 1787 of Carsten Niebuhr's *Reisebeschreibung nach Arabien* which contained excellent plates of reliefs from Persepolis. Here at last were imposing stone ruins, remains of great palaces fashioned of fine hard grey marble, built by Darius and Xerxes. Drawings of these showed to western eyes for the first time figures of bearded officials and copies of winged bulls, very similar to those that would soon be found under the ground in Mesopotamia and excite so much interest. Although Niebuhr had also visited Babylon and Nineveh, the only evidence he could provide at this stage was a plan, and a profile of the great mounds. This book made its first appearance in an English translation (by Robert Heron) in 1792. The orientalist G. F. Grotefend (1775–1853) began to study Niebuhr's inscriptions and by 1802 was able to publish his first readings of twelve signs.

For the time being, however, fantasy was more compelling to the reading public than pictures of ruins. One of the greatest influences on western thought about the east was about to make his appearance. In 1815 Byron published his *Hebrew Melodies* which contained the poem *The Destruction of Sennacherib* with its famous first two lines, 'The Assyrian came down like the wolf on the fold, And his cohorts were gleaming in purple and gold'. A year earlier he had written *Vision of Belshazzar* ('Unfit to govern, live, or die') and this in its turn was to inspire two well-known poems and two popular paintings. The subject matter may have been suggested to Byron by Handel's opera *Belshazzar* which had its first performance on 27 March 1745. It had not been a success, only running to three performances. But one critic had liked the 'scornful laughter' of the defiant and decadent Babylonians, in contrast to the Persians who were portrayed as sturdy and uncompromising and the Hebrews who were grave, patient, and dignified. The score relied on Herodotos and the Bible, the best scene being the Writing on the Wall.

Belshazzar was also the hero of a prize-winning poem which was published in 1818. The Revd T. S. Hughes's *Belshazzar's Feast* included 'notes relative to the History of the Babylonian and Assyrian Empires'. He also made an impressive list of his sources which included not only the Old Testament and Classical writers such as Strabo, Herodotos, and Diodoros Sikelos, but also showed that he had read all the most

up-to-date travellers to the region including C. J. Rich (*Memoir on the Ruins of Babylon* 1815) and T. Maurice (*Observations on the Ruins of Babylon* 1816). He had also perused Jacob Bryant's *An Analysis of Ancient Mythology* (1774), and several topographical books on the region by J. B. Bourguignon D'Anville. All this erudite research did not unfortunately prevent him from presenting an Assyria where 'Coral lips waft softer sighs' and the Euphrates as a willowy stream, or from a high moral line which ensured that 'the torrent of guilty pride' would overwhelm Assyria in its 'refluent tide'.

It was, however, Byron's romantic tragedy, *Sardanapalus*, published in 1821 that did most to popularize the idea of decadent and glorious ancient Mesopotamia. The poem caught the public imagination, and though never intended by Byron to be performed, was adapted for the stage by Charles Kean and performed in 1853 and thereafter inspired many a burlesque. The plot closely follows Diodoros, and Byron also acknowledged William Mitford's *The History of Greece* (1784–1818) which took a milder view of a man who was the last king of a dynasty which ended in revolution: 'obloquy on his memory would follow of course from the policy of his successors and their partizans'. This is reflected in Byron's tragedy since Sardanapalos, though lascivious and effeminate, occasionally remembers his kingly status and tries to live up to it.

The tragedy follows the last days of Sardanapalos, doomed to lose his throne in a court intrigue. At first this 'silk worm' shows nothing but frivolity in the face of danger, but when it becomes clear that the battle is lost, sends his wife and sons to safety, then his officers, courtiers, and slaves and he himself majestically commands faggots, pine-cones, and withered leaves to be brought, cedar, precious drugs, spices, mighty planks, frankincense, and myrrh and builds a vast pyre. His successor, the new king Arabaces sends a messenger offering a safe haven as long as the young princes are given up as hostages. Sardanapalos asks for an hour and pretends to consider the offer. Left alone with Myrrha, the Ionian slave girl who has supported him throughout, he makes a final speech:

> —and the light of this
> Most royal of funereal pyres shall be
> Not a mere pillar form'd of cloud and flame,
> A beacon in the horizon for a day,

And then a mount of ashes, but a light
To lessen ages, rebel nations, and
Voluptuous princes. Time shall quench full many
A people's records, and a hero's acts;
Sweep empire after empire, like this first
Of empires, into nothing; but even then
Shall spare this deed of mine, and hold it up
A problem few dare imitate, and none despise.

Myrrha hands him a libation cup; he drinks. They say goodbye. Sardanapalos mounts the pyre and Myrrha fires it with her lighted torch. She springs on to the flames. The poem ends.

The following year the Revd H. H. Milman, professor of poetry at Oxford University, published his dramatic poem, *Belshazzar*. Although the poet, in his preface, said he had adhered strictly to the outline in scripture (the Book of Daniel), he had also availed himself of whatever appeared to his purpose in the profane historians, particularly Herodotos and Diodoros Sikelos. But, he said, the best English account of Babylon was to be found in the learned Dean Prideaux's *Connection of the Old and New Testaments*, first published in 1715. Book 2 of this work dealt with the reign and building works at Babylon of Nebuchadnezzar II and included a description of massive walls surrounded by deep moats, 100 gates all made of solid brass, the Hanging Gardens, and the Tower of Babel 'half a mile in the whole compass, and consisted of eight towers, one built above the other . . . each of them seventy-five feet high, and in them . . . many great rooms with arched roofs supported by pillars'. This is a Babylon of brazen pillars and vessels, of massy gold statues and images, faithfully followed by Milman in his poem. Such an impious creation could not expect to last much longer than Memphis, hundred-gated Thebes, or Assyrian Nineveh:

Babylon! Babylon! that wak'st in pride
And glory, but shall sleep in shapeless ruin.

Shapeless ruins were an awkward problem to the artist John Martin who painted three great canvasses directly relating to ancient Mesopotamia as envisaged by those who read the Bible, *The Fall of Babylon* (1819), *Belshazzar's Feast* (1820), and *The Fall of Nineveh* (1828). 'The mighty cities of Nineveh and Babylon have passed away,' he wrote. 'The accounts of their greatness and splendour may have been exaggerated.

But, where strict truth is not essential, the mind is content to find delight in the contemplation of the grand and the marvellous. Into the solemn visions of Antiquity we look without demanding the clear daylight of truth.' In his paintings, Martin tried to recreate the palaces he imagined had existed at Babylon and Nineveh in their prime, but he necessarily had to rely greatly on imagination, though he made full use of what literary description there was.

For this he turned first to the Old Testament and Classical writers, but neither provided the precise detail which he needed. In 1815 and 1816, C. J. Rich and T. Maurice published their observations at Babylon. Rich included a useful map of the Euphrates showing the existing mound of Babylon, on which he identified sites of the buildings described by Herodotos. It is apparent that Martin was also familiar with the earlier travels of Rabbi Benjamin of Tudela, Rauwolff, Pietro della Valle, Niebuhr, Otter, and Beauchamp, but despite all this, the actual appearance of a Babylonian or Assyrian building was destined to remain a mystery for another quarter century or so, till the excavations of Layard and Botta made tentative reconstruction possible.

Undaunted, and fired by imagination and perhaps to some extent by his childhood years within sight of Hadrian's Wall, ruined but soul-stirring, Martin completed his first great Mesopotamian canvas, *The Fall of Babylon* in 1819. It was exhibited at the British Institution the same year, and sold immediately for 400 guineas. The painting drew large crowds at a time when there was a strong predilection for ancient history brought vividly to life. There were elements in the painting that were reassuringly familiar to the average Londoner, massive embankments, pediments, and terraces, monumentally constructed from solid blackened stone under brooding skies. This was Babylon on the banks of the Thames, built to last. None the less there were also elements that had been carefully researched and faithfully copied from graphic prose, for example the bridge in the painting which was described by both Herodotos and Diodoros Sikelos, of whose works Martin kept copies in his library. And in his painting of the stepped tower or ziggurat he had also taken great care to be historically correct.

Belshazzar's Feast was inspired by the poem of the same name by T. S. Hughes, and was exhibited at the British Institution in 1821. Again the painting enjoyed

84. Print engraving by John Martin of the Fall of Babylon, 1819.

85. Print engraving by John Martin of the Fall of Nineveh, 1828.

an immediate popular success, so much so that a rail had to be erected in front of it to prevent the throng of spectators from pressing in too closely. It was the picture of the year and was later used as a Bible illustration. Martin's sources for the painting were similar to those consulted for *The Fall of Babylon* but he supplemented these with forays into Indian art, justifying this by claiming that

it was the custom of Nebuchadnezzar, the conqueror of Egypt and India, to bring from those parts to Babylon, all the architects, the men of science and handicrafts... therefore I suppose the united talents of the Indian, the Egyptian and Babylonian architects were employed to produce those buildings.

This was a convenient way of expanding the limited information available about Mesopotamian architecture by using his knowledge of Indian forms, a study of which he had made at Sezincote, the Anglo-Indian house in the Cotswolds. His sketchbook for 1817 contains forty pages of drawings made there. Certainly the rounded capitals of the massive colonnades and the stepped arches which join the columns at the far end of the palace look Indian, but the ziggurat again looks surprisingly accurate in those pre-Layard days. The costumes of the figures—long dark cloaks or sleeved robes for the men and white dresses with flowing hair or neatly tied in a fillet for the women—conformed with what Herodotos had described, and were not dissimilar to those depicted on the great reliefs still buried under the mounds.

His last canvas in the towering style of colossal ancient architecture was his most ambitious. Exhibited in the Burlington Arcade in 1828, *The Fall of Nineveh* depicted that most famous of ancient Assyrians, the ubiquitous Sardanapalos. Martin painted his most fantastic city yet as a backdrop for the central scene which was the funeral pyre of this last king. While the victorious enemy streams through the collapsing terraces and colonnades, they are startlingly illuminated by great flashes of lightning. Martin, in the pamphlet he issued to accompany the painting, explained his inspiration:

The style of architecture, particularly of the Egyptian on the one hand, and of the most ancient Indian on the other, has been invented as the most appropriate for a city situate between the two countries, and necessarily in frequent intercourse with them.

This again was a convenient way of avoiding the central problem of what exactly Sardanapalos' palace had looked like.

At the end of the 1820s, Martin abandoned ancient history and turned his skills to designing schemes of modern architecture suitable for a developing industrial nation, and embankments and riverside walks along the Thames. His pictures, with their huge perspectives inspired appropriate styling for the great railways which were just beginning to be built, for example, the battlemented entrance at Edge Hill, Liverpool (strongly reminiscent of *Belshazzar's Feast*), its Moorish Arch, and the terminus of the Liverpool and Manchester Railway. After the discoveries of the real sites of ancient Assyria, Martin's paintings lost their popularity and Ruskin denounced the theatrical revival of dead days and advised artists to concentrate on the present.

The French painter Eugène Delacroix was also inspired by ancient Mesopotamia, and more specifically by Byron. His painting, *La Mort de Sardanapale* was completed in 1827 and presented a bustling scene of most glamorous carnage: five naked or semi-naked dead or dying females, black slaves and eunuchs wielding daggers, massive gold vessels and huge ropes of emeralds, pearls, and rubies filling the foreground, the whole presided over by the recumbent turbanned figure of Sardanapalos, propped on one elbow on an immense bed with elephant heads at its base. Swirling smoke in the top right hand corner obscured what architectural features Delacroix imagined for his Nineveh, but a pediment with figures is discernible and is vaguely reminiscent of John Martin. Byron's tragedy had been translated into French by Amedée Pichot between 1822 and 1825 and Delacroix, an acknowledged admirer of its author, was immediately struck.

Recent research has, however, shown that though Byron was doubtless the inspiration for the painting, the sources were more varied and complex. Delacroix had consulted Diodoros Sikelos and Athenaios, both of whom were indebted to Ktesias, and characterized Sardanapalos as effeminate, dissipated, and addicted to luxury and sexual licentiousness. He had also read the new travel books which showed the ruins of Persepolis in some detail, and had probably referred to volumes of engravings of Etruscan antiquities so popular at the time. In 1864, with more reliable references to hand, Delacroix designed a pendentive for the library of the Palais Bourbon entitled *La Captivité à Babylone*.

Samuel Colman (1780–1845) painted *The Coming of the Messiah and the Destruction of Babylon* in 1828 and *Belshazzar's Feast* about 1832. A native of Bristol, and a Nonconformist, Colman's work was, unlike Martin's, largely ignored in its own day though he painted five pictures with sweeping biblical themes. *The Coming of the Messiah and the Destruction of Babylon* depicts a toppling Tower of Babel somewhat in shadow so its inspiration is hard to attribute, with soldiers in modern dress marching on beleaguered Babylon, so the picture had perhaps wider interpretations. But *Belshazzar's Feast* is truly in the Martin vein with its references to several scenes described in the books of Daniel, Ezra, and Isaiah: Belshazzar quaffing wine from golden vessels stolen from the Temple at Jerusalem, Daniel gesturing to the writing on the wall, and to the right of the painting, the arrival of Cyrus with his victorious troops. There can be no doubt that Colman was familiar with Martin's *Belshazzar's Feast* (which had been exhibited in Bristol in 1825) since the layout of his great hall owes much to the earlier painting and it is possible too that he was influenced by *The Fall of Nineveh* for his serpent capitals. At some stage in its history, the painting was boldly signed 'John Martin RA 1830' but has now been correctly attributed to Colman.

The fall of Nineveh also inspired a poem by the same name and in the same year (1828) by Edwin Atherstone. This was perhaps the last flowering of the great poetic fantasy on the theme and was a worthy finale in the genre. Though the poet acknowledges his sources for the poem as being Prideaux's *Connection*, the Bible (Chronicles, Book of Esther, Daniel, Kings, Judges), Landseer's *Sabaean Researches*, and Xenophon's *Cyropaedia*, the poem is a triumph of imagination in thirty books, full of sprightly damsels with chiming anklets, palaces 'enormous piled', voluptuous music, and myriads of wanton feet going to and fro. The moral is clear, however, that by virtue alone do monarchs sway the hearts of men, and when virtue fails, great empires collapse. The poem ends on a properly virtuous note:

> Where, so late,
> Palace, and tower, and temple; battlement,
> And rock-like wall, deemed everlasting, stood,
> Now, yon black waste of smouldering ashes lay!
> So sank, to endless night, that glorious Nineveh!

The mid-nineteenth century saw the birth of popular travel undertaken purely for pleasure and education by ordinary men or women who had the time and the means. The Grand Tour had of course been part of an upper-class way of life, particularly as part of the education process of its young men, for several decades. Suddenly it became possible for people from more humble circumstances to travel abroad. This was partly because a long period of peace in Europe had brought stability and prosperity, but it was also because the spreading tentacles of railways made it practicable. A pioneer in seeing the potential of this was Thomas Cook, the first travel agent. Born in 1808, in his late teens he became a temperance evangelist and started traversing the country to promote its cause. In one year alone, he travelled 2,962 miles on foot and this set him thinking that there must be an easier way to get about. He arranged his first excursion: a train chartered to take temperance enthusiasts from Leicester to Loughborough, for a return fare of one shilling. From 1845, he was ready to organize his first excursion whose sole object was pleasure, a trip to Liverpool and Snowdonia. From then on tourism never looked back. In 1851, Cook transported 165,000 visitors to the Great Exhibition where they doubtless saw jewellery inspired by Layard's great finds. In 1872 Cook arranged his first world tour which passed through Mesopotamia; but then as now, collapsed mud-brick could not compete with the glorious ruined stones of Italy, Egypt, Greece, Turkey, and the New World, especially when professional travellers and experts working in the area continued to send back such dismal reports.

In 1815 Claudius James Rich, Resident of the Honourable East India Company at the Court of the Pasha of Baghdad published a *Memoir on the Ruins of Babylon*, with three plates, including one of the mound and a view of the embankment and eastern ruins. Extremely erudite and well versed in the Classics, the contemporary accounts and the area itself, Rich concluded sadly that though he 'should have distinguished some traces, however imperfect, of many of the structures of Babylon', it was in the end 'a vast succession of mounds of rubbish'. The following year this report was confirmed by the Revd Thomas Maurice, Assistant Librarian in the British Museum in his *Observations on the Ruins of Babylon as Recently Visited and Described by Claudius James Rich Esq*:

On the far-famed hanging gardens, and the subterraneous vault or tunnel constructed by Semiramis or Nitocris, or the founder of Babylon, whoever he was, there is no necessity to dilate, as every trace of them, except what the idle fancy of travellers has surmised, must long since have disappeared.

In 1821–2 Sir Robert Ker Porter published *Travels in Georgia, Armenia, Ancient Babylonia, etc.* in two volumes. Volume 1 contained many fine plates and a description of Persepolis. Volume 2 described Behistun, Assyria, and Babylonia, including the Tower of Babel, as well as a plan of the ruins and some illustrations of inscriptions and cylinder seals. Ker Porter was familiar with the earlier work of Rich. In 1827 James Buckingham was able in his *Travels in Mesopotamia . . . with Researches on the Ruins of Nineveh, Babylon and Other Ancient Cities* to put all the information thus published on the area to good use. Indefatigable (one night the temperature at midnight stood at 115 degrees F), he collated as best he could all the ancient sources with which he was well acquainted with more modern travellers, including Rabbi Benjamin of Tudela, Rauwolff, della Valle, Niebuhr and Rich. He reported on Mosul, Nineveh 'unquestionably very large; and . . . in the period of its highest glory, a sink of wickedness and abomination', and Babylon, where he tried hard to identify the Tower of Babel, the site of the Hanging Gardens, the tunnel beneath the Euphrates built by Semiramis and the ancient walls. In 1829 he published *Travels in Assyria, Media and Persia*, his account of a journey which took him from Baghdad to Mount Zagros and eventually to Persepolis. Again he tried to relate ancient sources to what he was seeing, specifically the words of Arrian and Diodoros Sikelos on the activities of Semiramis in the area. The book contained many attractive engravings and a colour plate of the author in his travelling costume of purple pantaloons, a green jacket, a red cloak, and a large white turban.

The inspiration for Giuseppe Verdi's opera *Nabucco* was undoubtedly the Bible, though growing interest in the east and Rossini's *Semiramide* probably influenced him in his choice of subject. The first performance of *Nabucco* took place in Milan on 9 March 1842; it was performed in London in 1846 and in New York in 1848. Verdi could hardly have chosen a more topical subject for his opera. 1845 saw the start of Layard's excavations at Nimrud, biblical Calah, and in May 1846 he at last received a long-awaited permit giving him permission to dig for antiquities, and export them to England. In July, he wrote to his aunt Sara Austen in London, 'The discovery is already beginning to make a noise in Europe, and every post brings me letters from people wanting information . . . I only hope that as much interest will be excited in England as on the Continent'. Shortly afterwards, twelve cases of antiquities were packed and placed on huge rafts made of poplar beams supported in the water by inflated skins. Not really cognizant with the significance of Layard's discoveries, and the great expense entailed in their excavation and transportation, the British Museum made a belated and mean-spirited formal offer of help to Layard, the terms of which reduced him to feeling as if he were no better than a 'master-bricklayer'. His uncle almost advised him to present his finds to the French: 'it would serve the Museum right'. Layard persevered and by the end of the year, his uncle and aunt, who lived near the Museum and moved in the highest circles, were able to report, 'All talk to us now about your researches'. The talking turned to clamour in the spring of the next year when on 23 March 1847, the first consignments of bas-reliefs from Nimrud were placed on display at the British Museum. As soon as Layard appeared in person, 'the Ninevite' rapidly became the social catch of the season, invited everywhere. John Murray immediately signed him up for a book on the discoveries.

As a boy, Layard had been influenced by Benjamin Disraeli who had been a close friend of his aunt, and whose graphic descriptions of Turkey and the Holy Land he had found fascinating. In his turn, Disraeli had been inspired by Byron and *The Arabian Nights*. But Layard had a wide knowledge of the ancient history of the Near East, culled from the Bible, Classical authors, Gibbon on the Romans, Laborde on the Crusaders, Burckhardt on the Nabataeans, as well as the most up-to-date information published by Rich —information that was to stand him in good stead on his subsequent travels. Despairing of any success in the law for which his uncle had sponsored him, in 1840 he set off with a friend for India, but fate intervened before he reached his goal and he found himself gazing at the great mounds of ancient Mesopotamia, Ashur and Nimrud and Nineveh, and conceived his first urge to excavate them. Interest in the antiquities of the region was strengthened by meetings with Botta, and his colleagues Flandin and Coste

86. Reconstruction of Nineveh drawn for Layard c.1850.

who were recording the Sassanian sculptures at Taq-i-Bustan. After Layard saw the great rock inscription at Behistun, he abandoned the idea of India, and the friend went on alone. Layard, dressed as a Persian, went to explore Susa. After several months escaping death from hostile tribes, but acquiring in the process valuable first-hand knowledge of them, their ambitions, and intentions, as well as some fluency in their languages, Layard found himself in Constantinople, making a first-hand report to Sir Stratford Canning, the British ambassador. Canning took a fancy to Layard and suggested he enter his service on an unofficial basis. Two years later, news from Mesopotamia of Botta's discoveries at Khorsabad made Layard decide to abandon a problematic life of diplomacy, and throw in his lot with archaeology. Canning generously offered to cover his expenses, at least for the time being.

Meanwhile, the Revd George Badger, one of the Honourable East India Company's chaplains in the Diocese of Bombay, had himself gone to Nimrud. In his book *The Nestorians & Their Rituals* he takes some credit for Layard's having gone to Nimrud since he himself had made a graphic report to Sir Stratford Canning describing the ground literally strewn with fragments of brick, covered with cuneiform inscriptions. This had led directly to Canning 'liberally' sponsoring Layard, 'and we do not doubt that, so far as the records shall be found to have any bearing upon the historical facts handed down in Holy Writ, they will supply an additional and important testimony to the genuineness and authenticity of the Old Testament Scriptures'.

Thanks it was, mainly to Canning but also to Badger, that Layard found himself once more gazing at the enormous mound of Nimrud and dreaming of 'palaces underground, of gigantic monsters, of sculptured figures, and endless inscriptions'. He was not to be disappointed. After only one day's work, using six men, he found two of the most important palaces of the ancient city, to be called the 'north-west palace' and the 'south-west palace'. By the end of the first month, he was uncovering just such gigantic monsters and sculptured figures as he had imagined. From then on, luck and judgement attended all his efforts.

The Political Agent in Baghdad at this time was Henry Creswicke Rawlinson, the man who was to play such a significant part in the decipherment of the ancient Babylonian script. Layard was unable then to read even the names of Ashurbanipal or Esarhaddon and he relied on Rawlinson at the Residency for help. Rawlinson had left England in 1827 to begin a career in the East India Company. He had no knowledge then of any eastern language, and he knew virtually no oriental history. But once in India he taught himself Sanskrit, Avestan, and Persian and in 1833 was posted to Persia. He made copies of the inscriptions at Persepolis, and two years later found himself as military adviser to the Shah's brother at Kermanshah. Kermanshah lies only 22 miles west of Behistun where a great inscription was written on a rock face 122 metres from the ground. There is a frieze of figures quite clearly seen from below: the Persian king Darius standing in judgement over nine rebel chiefs. The inscription is recorded in three languages, Old Persian, Elamite, and Babylonian. The first two were reasonably accessible by agile and somewhat precarious climbing, but the top one, the Babylonian, could only be reached by ropes and ladders and remained uncopied till 1847. Fired by what was going on with the excavations, Rawlinson went back to Behistun and persuaded a Kurdish boy to climb up and over the ledge which separated this inscription from the others, and to make paper squeezes, directions for which Rawlinson shouted out from underneath. Amazingly this method worked: the paper squeezes eventually reached the British Museum where in due course they were deciphered. Fifty years later, they were eaten by mice.

Rawlinson translated the first part, the Old Persian and Elamite versions, in 1837, and sent his translation to the Royal Asiatic Society. Between 1846–50, Edward Hincks (1792–1866) an Irish clergyman also worked on the inscription. He published a Babylonian and Assyrian syllabary which showed that the language (which he called 'Akkadian') was syllabic not alphabetic, and that its script also incorporated signs which were ideograms and determinatives. His work enabled Rawlinson to complete his translation of the third part *On the Babylonian Translation of the Great Persian Inscription at Behistun*, which he published in 1851.

As early as the beginning of 1845, Layard had seen the drawings Eugène Flandin had been making at Khorsabad since May 1844. He had written a series of articles for *The Malta Times* about them which were immediately reprinted in English newspapers and aroused some interest. Layard always believed

that it was these French excavations at Khorsabad that started the great European interest in ancient Mesopotamia, but he also passionately hoped that the British would have the first exhibition of antiquities. Because of the dilatory attitude of the British government, however, who failed to understand the importance of the discoveries, it was in fact the Louvre which was able to display its Mesopotamian acquisitions some three months earlier than the British Museum. And unlike Botta and Flandin, who were generously paid for their work, Layard at first worked for nothing, apart from Canning's sponsorship, and later for a meagre honorarium.

Botta's first consignment from Khorsabad arrived at the port of Le Havre in February 1847 and two new Assyrian rooms in the Louvre were inaugurated by king Louis-Philippe on 1 May, his birthday, before a select audience of scholars. *L'Illustration*, a popular magazine, carried an enthusiastic article on 15 May referring to the fine detail of the limestone slabs, the royal figures, military and domestic particulars, an everyday picture of ancient Assyria. A year later *Le Magasin Pittoresque* gave a summary of the great discovery so far and printed an engraving of the so-called Gilgamesh figure, destined to become the universal favourite of the collection. Still the people did not come: despite having their own special department, the Musée des Antiquités Orientales, the finds were not well displayed and there were no written guides, and very few human ones, to explain the mostly unlabelled exhibits.

In any event, politics were about to overtake archaeology. The Assyrian rooms were closed during the revolutionary months of 1848 and only reopened on 18 March 1849, after which another article in *Le Magasin Pittoresque* fell somewhat short of enthusiasm, damning with faint praise the Assyrians' ability to observe and reproduce nature (frequently making mistakes, thus rendering their figures still and unlifelike) especially in comparison with 'la grande science des proportions qui dirigeait les Egyptiens' and 'le merveilleux accord du style et de la vie qui éclatait dans les Grecs'.

It is clear that even when a more peaceful atmosphere was established outside, and further Assyrian rooms opened from 1857–67, the ambience inside remained lugubrious and unwelcoming. Émile Zola in *L'Assommoir* (1877), the Social and Natural History of a family under the Second Empire, told of a visit to the Louvre by a party of provincial wedding guests. They had come in to avoid the rain, and unaccountably found themselves in the Assyrian Museum which was cold and cavernous, full of stone colossi, silent black marble gods and monstrous beasts, half-cat and half-woman. (It sounds more as if at this point they had strayed into the Egyptian rooms and encountered several statues of Sekhmet.) In any event, they were not impressed: 'Ils trouvaient ça très vilain'. And as for an inscription in 'Phoenician' characters, it was just not possible, 'personne n'avait jamais lu ce grimoire' (illegible scrawl).

Not until early 1883 was a more cheerful and educational background made for the Khorsabad reliefs. The architect Edmond Guillaume (1826–94) advised on the arrangement of the exhibits and Félix Thomas (1815–75) a well-known artist of the time, had earlier designed the decorations: winged bulls, lions and eagles, after Victor Place, in the 'Persian' style. Thomas had in fact been to Mesopotamia in 1853, and had encountered Place on the road to Babylon. He was responsible for two oil paintings based on his travels, *Apparition des taureaux de la porte monumentale de Khorsabad* and *Sentinelle devant les ruines de Ninive*. (Actually they were the ruins of Khorsabad, but Nineveh sounded more romantic.)

In England, by contrast, the arrival of Layard's great finds made an instant popular appeal, though some exalted personages had reservations. William Hamilton, who was a Trustee of the British Museum and who had been partly responsible for the acquisition of the Rosetta Stone and the Elgin Marbles (and who admittedly was described by a Keeper of Manuscripts at the time as a 'prejudiced, ill-tempered partisan') dismissed Layard's discoveries as a 'parcel of rubbish' and 'wished them all at the bottom of the sea'. In fact, he nearly had his wish for on the long watery journey home, from Nimrud to Baghdad, to Basra and the Gulf, to Bombay and then London, the twelve cases of reliefs from the north-west palace at Nimrud had suffered a ducking in sea water, but had arrived intact. Hamilton was determined that no suitable rooms would be provided and that the Museum should be kept 'pure' for Greek objects.

Fortunately, he was overruled and the finds were displayed as soon as space was available. The general public, encouraged by a double-page spread in the *Illustrated London News* which depicted some of the excitements in store, flocked to see the immense and barbaric representations of a race they felt they knew from reading the Bible. The attraction was partly the sheer size of the exhibits, the colossal five-legged winged bulls and lions, the more-than-life-size bearded figures, but it lay also in their calm self-possession, a compelling belief in their own worth.

At first the sculptures were exhibited in the basement under the new Lycian gallery where an attendant was apparently kept fully occupied in escorting visitors to see them. Such was their lure that at the end of 1850, a winged bull and a winged lion from Ashurnasirpal's palace were set up in the front hall, directly opposite the front door, where they successfully lured many visitors into the Museum. The poet Dante Gabriel Rossetti pretended to have undergone a mystical experience as he witnessed the actual arrival of one of these monsters, 'a wingèd beast from Nineveh' 'with dark runes fretted o'er'.

Winged bulls were what seemed to have captured the imagination: *Household Words* published a soliloquy on 8 February 1851 by a W. H. Stone (whose identity is a mystery) in which the bull tells of his birth, of the civilizations he has seen rise and fall, of his transportation to a strange land. Whoever Stone was, he was clearly familiar with ancient history, understood the pathos of a once mighty empire crumbled to dust, and his message carried a warning.

I am the Bull of Nineveh. I was born in the quarries beside the river, the great river . . . As a shapeless block was my substance borne to its place; there did the hands of cunning workmen fashion me; . . . the chisel carved my ear, and I heard; the tool opened mine eyes, and I saw . . . Beside me was a companion like myself; we two guarded the threshold . . . I felt myself the guardian of the nation's history, the emblem of its power, and the thought stamped itself on my features in a smile which has endured till now, proud at once and solemn . . . [Sardanapalos succeeds, and] . . . the sound of music strikes my ear, singing and the voluptuous dance; no more the battle-car, the crash of armies, and the shout of victors . . . [Cyaxares arrives, Ashur falls.] Long did the foreigners hold us; and by degrees the beauty of the ancient work faded: walls crumbled, roofs decayed . . . At length, the building tottered and fell; elsewhere, fire had completed the work of the conqueror; we were left to silent ruin . . . [Time passes, travellers come from far away, then he is uncovered once more] . . . at length the shrouding earth fell . . . Presently came one who seemed a lord . . . Joy was in his face as he gazed on me . . . in his silent steady gaze, I read my changed condition . . . my long slumber, my inglorious waking, and I felt my fallen state. And my shame was clear . . . I was sad, for my pride was fallen. I was borne

87. Assyrian winged bull from the Palace of Sennacherib at Nineveh, *c.*700 BC. Such figures often stand more than 4.0 m. high.

down beside my own ancient river . . . I was tossed many days on the heaving waters. Now I stand in a strange land . . . They say I am far from my violated home, in a city prouder, greater, more glorious than my native realm; but boast not, ye vainglorious creatures of an hour. I have outlived many mighty kingdoms, perchance I may be destined to survive one more.

Canning too found the the winged monster had a contemporary relevance. He wrote to Layard, 'the gigantic bull with a human head—is the very thing for a *British* museum'. And on the subject of Layard's forthcoming book, Sir Charles Alison, the former Oriental Secretary at the British Embassy in Constantinople, gave him some good advice: 'Write a whopper with lots of plates (he wrote); fish up old legends and anecdotes, and if you can by any means humbug people into the belief that you have established any points in the Bible, you are a made man'.

Alison's advice was prescient: when Layard's *Nineveh and its Remains* was published in 1849, the reviews were ecstatic. Printing could hardly keep up with demand. *The Times* called it 'the most extraordinary work of the present age . . . impossible to read his work without finding our minds absorbed in wonder at the development of that period, and

of its works of art'. More than a sight of the objects themselves, the book reached people all over the country and they were insatiable. 20,000 copies were sold in the first four years. It was followed by *Monuments of Nineveh*, a volume of 71 plates of bas-reliefs, ornamentation, and objects (including ivories) found at Nimrud. The next year, W. S. W. Vaux, of the British Museum published *Nineveh and Persepolis* and in May 1851 Layard produced *A Popular Account of Discoveries at Nineveh* which sold well at the Great Exhibition. In 1853 he published *Discoveries in the Ruins of Nineveh and Babylon*.

Some people remained unconvinced, however. At a Select Committee on the National Gallery held in 1853 (the same year that the 'Nineveh Gallery' was opened at the British Museum), Sir Richard Westmacott RA, Professor of Sculpture and creator of *The Progress of Civilization* on the pediment of the British Museum, was grilled by Richard Monckton Milnes as to whether 'the sculptures from Nineveh may deteriorate the public taste and less incline them than they otherwise would be to study works of great antiquity and great art?' To this question, Westmacott replied, 'I think it impossible that any artist can look at the Nineveh Marbles as works for study, for such they certainly are not; they are works of prescriptive art, like works of Egyptian art. No man would think of studying Egyptian art.' Pressed to give an opinion whether people would take an interest in them when compared with the Elgin Marbles, he said, 'No, persons would look at the Nineveh Marbles and be thinking of their Bible at the time they were looking at them; they would consider them as very curious monuments of an age they feel highly interested in; but the interest in the Elgin Marbles arises from a distinct cause; from their excellence as works of art'. Curious but not great art: for the academic élite the hold of ancient Greece was not loosened.

But the Scottish architect Alexander Thomson, so renowned for his work in the Greek revival style that he had acquired the soubriquet 'Greek', designed some buildings for Glasgow in an Assyrian style. One at least still stands: Buck's Head Building at 63 Argyle Street. Its first and second floors are linked by Assyrian columns which ended with broad bracket-like capitals supporting a heavy cast iron balcony. Thomson's inspiration for this and other Assyrian and Babylonian decoration was James Ferguson's *Illustrated Handbook of Architecture* published in 1855, which declared that

The architecture of Assyria is now . . . familiar to us . . . an entirely new chapter added to our history of architecture since the year 1843, and certainly not one of the least interesting, not only from its own intrinsic merits and the beauty of many of its forms, but because of its historic value . . . the parent of all the Ionic forms.

In France, academia worked hard to grapple with the newly found civilization. Beautiful and ruinously expensive books were being published on the French excavations by Layard's old friends, Paul-Émile Botta, Eugène Flandin, and Pascal Coste. The president of the Société Asiatique, Julius Mohl, took a warm interest in the excavations in Mesopotamia. His English wife held a regular salon on Friday evenings in their flat at 120 rue du Bac where she brought together her husband's scholarly colleagues from different disciplines so that they could freely exchange ideas. This doubtless had something to do with the well-organized way in which the French took on ancient Mesopotamia, not least of which were the yearly reports which Mohl delivered to the Société Asiatique, keeping all his confrères throughout Europe up to date with the current situation.

The first mention of Botta was made in the report for the year 1841–2. The French government was determined that these extremely interesting discoveries should come to France. In 1844, it was Botta's finds at Khorsabad that were exciting the whole of Europe, and it was hoped that Paris would soon possess enough sculptures to give substance to the empire of Semiramis. In 1849, Mohl's report was mainly about Layard and his publications. He referred to the immense success of *Nineveh and its Remains* and then he dwelt at some length on *Monuments of Nineveh* which depicted the principal bas-reliefs and inscriptions at Nimrud. Mohl had nothing but praise for the book whose inscriptions had been engraved and published at the British Museum's expense. It was far preferable, he said, even if it resulted in a less magnificent work, that Layard's books should be available to everyone. Botta's was only accessible to a small number of privileged persons. He reiterated this theme two years later, saying 'le format incommode et le prix exorbitant de ce trop magnifique ouvrage' prevented a widespread readership. He also reported on Layard's finds at the mound of Koyundjik, including what he believed to be Assyrian royal archives. He hoped that they would arrive intact in England, and would swell the Assyrian collection at the British Museum, where they would be at the disposal of scholars. They did indeed expand the British Museum's collection of tablets, the sheer quantity of which presented, and continues to present, an enormous task for Assyriologists. Thousands of tablets (many fragmentary) arrived in western Europe at museums which lacked the staff, time, and space to deal with them. Writing in 1925, Sir E. A. Wallis Budge reckoned that from Nineveh alone, the British Museum had 25,000 tablets, not including fragments. Work on these and thousands more tablets from other Mesopotamian sites has not ceased since, but an inordinate amount remains to be done before they yield all their secrets.

Mohl's generous appreciation of the British effort was again expressed at the time of the publication of Layard's *Discoveries In The Ruins of Nineveh and Babylon*. The British had set an example which the French would do well to follow. Both countries had spent roughly equal sums of money for their Assyrian antiquities. But despite the fact that France had the great advantage of having made the discovery, Britain had the richer collection, because money had been wisely spent on excavation and skimped on publication, and in France it was the other way round. In England, the general public could actually afford to buy the books about the discoveries, and they were also accessible in libraries. The beautiful French books were available only in grand libraries ('une curiosité qu'on montre aux voyageurs'), and were so expensive that even the two most deserving men in the world who ought to possess copies, i.e. Layard himself and Rawlinson, could not afford them. This may have been true, but the French achievement cannot be too highly praised: the extreme beauty of the plates has stood the test of time, far better indeed than some of the originals they portray.

Monument de Ninive, published between 1849 and 1850, has five parts. The first two volumes contain magnificent plates from Khorsabad, of façades, elevations and bas-reliefs, some with residual colour, together with details of crowns, jewellery, bridles, and weapons. The third and fourth volumes are devoted to cuneiform inscriptions. In Volume 5, the text speaks of the hitherto incomplete, contradictory, and fabulous information regarding the Assyrians, mainly because of the Bible which had presented a people 'aussi redoutables dans la guerre qu'habiles dans les arts'. In 1851 Flandin and Coste's *Voyage en Perse* appeared, also in five volumes. Though the plates are nearly all of Persepolis, they presented themes that were by then familiar to enthusiasts and scholars alike: winged bulls and lions, palmette and rosette motifs, solid bearded officials wearing long braided robes. It was not until 1867–70 that the last great French publication appeared. This was Victor Place's *Ninive et l'Assyrie* in three volumes. In the introduction to Volume 1, Place spoke of the original discoveries some twenty years earlier, and summarized what had happened since. He was also able to publish, in Volume 2, a cuneiform inscription with both transliteration and translation. Volume 3 contained the plates, of a truly inspirational quality, some in brilliant colour, many of which are imaginative reconstructions of the ruins. He also illustrated cylinder seals and clay tablets.

Layard was not destined to remain at the front of British excavations in Mesopotamia, though his name will always be associated with Assyriology. As early as 1851 he had had enough of excavation, though he continued to write up his discoveries, his last book being *Nineveh and Babylon*, published in 1867. Apart from his publications, he left an architectural sou-

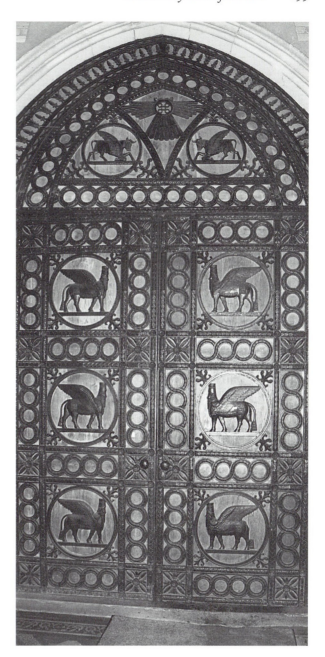

88. Assyrianizing iron gates in the Nineveh Porch at Canford School.

venir, a 'Nineveh Porch' at Canford Court, near Bournemouth in Dorset, the home of Sir John Guest and his wife, Charlotte, Layard's cousin, who were to become his parents-in-law. The Nineveh Porch was actually a small museum built on to the house. The entrance was flanked by a colossal winged bull and winged lion from Nimrud, behind which were hung an enormous and splendid pair of iron-work gates decorated in what was to be the first flowering of Victorian Assyrian revival. Each gate had three large round motifs of winged bulls, each round motif being set into a square bordered by Assyrian rings. At each corner of the square was an authentic floral motif. Above the two leaves of the gate was a semi-circular arch with a winged sun-disk and two kneeling winged bulls without crowns or beards. Inside the museum, there was a fine stained glass window with a palmette and lotus design, executed in brilliant reds and blues, and echoing the gates both in shape and concept. The ceiling, made of wood, was painted midnight blue with golden palmettes, crescent moons, and stars. The ornamentation and decoration and the motifs for the iron-work were based on those found in Chambers B and C at the northwest palace at Nimrud, reproduced in Layard's *Monuments of Nineveh*. A small collection of finds from Nimrud was displayed and there were at least seven large pieces of bas-relief apparently from Sennacherib's palace at Nineveh attached to the walls on either side of the entrance.

Canford Court was sold just before the First World War and became a boys' school. The Nineveh Porch became the tuck shop and this is still its function. The magnificent gates remain, as do the stained glass window and the painted ceiling. Outside can still be traced the outline of Layard's dedication. But of the winged colossi, bas-reliefs, and objects, little is left. The colossi are now in the Metropolitan Museum in New York, the bas-reliefs (all but one) were spotted by none other than Sir Leonard Woolley during a visit to the school in 1956. They were almost unrecognizable under many layers of white paint, and in 1959 were sold for £14,000. The story of what happened to the objects housed there has now been published. As for the remaining bas-relief, it was rediscovered in 1994 and sold to a Japanese religious sect for £7,701,500 in London on 6 July.

Layard's future bride was only 3 years old at the time the Nineveh Porch was built, and 25 when Layard married her in 1869. He was 52, and soon after the wedding presented his wife with an Assyrian bracelet, to be followed by a massive Assyrian-style necklace with matching earrings. Lady Layard described the bracelet in her diary on 23 March 1869, 'Today Henry gave me a bracelet being Esarhaddon's signet which he had found at Nineveh and had set by Phillips'. The large and beautiful carnelian cylinder seal which formed the central part of the heavy bracelet, with a lion's head on either side joined by a hinged gold semicircular hoop, was almost certainly not Esarhaddon's, and it was probably found at Nimrud (in the south-west palace of Esarhaddon), which Layard thought was Nineveh. The necklace and earrings were made to match the bracelet, the whole set being contained in an impressive crescent-shaped box. The heavy necklace was made up of 11 cylinder seals and 4 stamp seals, of chalcedony, agate, and haematite, varying in colour, but mainly white, greyish, blue, and brown. Each cylinder seal was capped with gold and separated from the adjacent one by a gold bead with projecting lotus buds. Three of the stamp seals were suspended from the front of the necklace and were capped with gold loops which hung from lions' heads. The fourth formed the clasp and was set in a twisted goldwork border. The earrings were made of two more cylinder seals again capped in gold, both chalcedony, suspended from lions' heads identical to those of the necklace. Below each seal hung a gold pine cone. The last motif particularly points to the designers and makers having carefully studied the Assyrian reliefs in the British Museum since there was no precedent to this particular shape in jewellery.

Lady Layard wore the whole set when she had her portrait painted in 1870 by the Spanish painter Vicente Palmaroli y Gonzalez in Madrid. She sat for 23 two-hour sessions, wearing a square-necked green velvet dress which admirably set off the somewhat barbaric splendour of these enormous pieces. Queen Victoria reputedly thought well of the jewellery when the Layards went to dinner at Osborne in July 1873. Lady Layard wrote in her diary, 'I wore my Nineveh necklace wh. was much admired and the bracelet passed round for inspection'. The whole set in its original box was bequeathed to the British Museum in 1912.

Splendid though the Layard jewellery was, it was very different from the sort of Assyrian-style jewellery which began to be made about the time of the Great Exhibition in 1851, the fashion for which lasted until the 1870s. This was much more directly influenced by the great bas-reliefs in the British Museum and the Louvre, and was not unlike a miniature version of them, being for the most part gold plaques with tiny replicas of sculptured relief applied to them. Sometimes the replicas were enamelled in primary colours and usually the plaques were bordered with

89. Assyrian revival jewellery, gold, mid-nineteenth century, inspired by sculptures from Nineveh in the British Museum.

authentic-looking Assyrian motifs, sometimes just with false granulation. The gold plaques were easily made into brooches, earrings, and bracelets, sometimes *en suite*. Gemstones were occasionally incorporated into the design.

The nineteenth century as a whole was characterized by a taste for archaeological jewellery i.e. jewellery made in a revival of Classical and other ancient themes. An Archaeological School of Jewellery was founded by F. P. Castellani in Rome in the 1840s, inspired by finds from the Etruscan tombs at Vulci. But it was not only Etruscan finds that inspired jewellers: discoveries from all over the ancient world inspired a taste for jewellery in the Grecian style, the Egyptian style, and finally the Assyrian style. In the 1860s, Castellani's son, Alessandro came to London and opened a successful shop in Piccadilly. His coun-

tryman Carlo Giuliano arrived at the same time and soon set up another shop in Frith Street. The Italians Castellani and Giuliano are certainly the names that come to the fore when revival jewellery is discussed, but the Englishman John Brogden, who worked between 1842 and 1885 was more prominent in Assyrian revival jewellery, more directly influenced by Layard's discoveries of which the British were inordinately proud. Assyrian revival jewellery was displayed at the Great Exhibition in 1851 by Garrard & Co. who displayed a bracelet 'in polished gold, with ruby and brilliant circular centre—from the Nimrud sculptures'. Another firm, Hunt and Roskell had 'Specimens of earrings, in emeralds, diamonds, carbuncles etc., after the marbles from Nineveh'. There was of course plenty of accurate information about for reference purposes and it is certain that designers either went to the British Museum or consulted the relevant books for details. For example, a bracelet made by John Brogden about 1860 is decorated with a scene of Ashurbanipal pouring a libation over his slaughtered prey, one of several lion-hunt reliefs from Nineveh at the British Museum. In similar style, a brooch by an anonymous maker shows the triumphal return of the king after the chase. Attended by court officials, soldiers, and musicians, he pours a libation over a dead lion, although in the original relief it was a bull. The whole was surmounted by the winged head of a lion and surrounded by decorative motifs. The scene was reproduced in *Monuments of Nineveh* (1849). The London firm of J. F. Backes & Co. (later Backes & Strauss) registered seven designs at the Patent Office in July 1872 so as to protect them from copiers, four of which are inspired by bas-reliefs from Mesopotamia. A bracelet based on one of the designs, now in the British Museum, depicts a lion hunt the inspiration for which was taken from a relief from Ashurbanipal's palace at Nineveh, with some additions, for example, the birds flying overhead. Two other designs, one showing a king with two full-size genii figures bearing pine-cones and buckets on his either side, and two further figures of officials beyond them, and another design with a winged bull in the centre, with winged genii to its either side and more officials with swords, are hard to attribute directly, but there are close parallels for these in *Monuments of Nineveh* also. A further design looks distinctly Assyrian: properly accoutred officials carrying a dead lion draped over a thick pole follow a king carrying the head of another dead lion, but such a scene is not a genuine reproduction, though both its subject matter (which suggests similar scenes from the Black Obelisk of Shalmaneser III) and style are certainly possible. As late as the London International Exhibition of 1872 a jewellery firm called Bright & Sons of Scarborough were advertising 'Assyrian-style' jewellery, but the taste for it was declining.

In 1852, Joseph Bonomi published a positive compendium of the story of Mesopotamian discovery so far, together with a resumé of everything anyone had ever wanted to know, with 236 illustrations and maps, entitled *Nineveh and Its Palaces The Discoveries of Botta and Layard, Applied to the Elucidating of Holy Writ*. Such an epitome, together with Layard's own publications, had helped to bring ancient Mesopotamia into sharp focus as far as the great British public was concerned, with all its irresistible connections with the Bible, and it was in droves that people flocked to the Nineveh Court that had been erected in the Crystal Palace for the Great Exhibition.

Henry Layard himself wrote the guidebook for the Crystal Palace Company, John Murray lent illustrations from Layard's publications, and the French and British governments permitted casts to be made of Assyrian sculptures in the Louvre and the British Museum respectively for display within the Court. The Court itself was 126 feet in length and 63 in depth. It had five bays in its frontage and two in its width. It was divided into two apartments, the larger ornamented with casts of sculptures found in the north-west palace at Nimrud, and the smaller being a reconstruction 'as nearly as the dimensions of the room will permit' of one hall at Nimrud with the bas-reliefs placed as closely as possible in the order in which they had been uncovered. Layard was able to assure visitors that the arrangement and contrasts of colours had been carefully studied and to provide them with much fascinating extraneous information, such as the Assyrian way of hunting lions and wild bulls, and their siege methods (with a description of the battering-ram and artificial tower). The Victorian spectator would certainly have felt cheated had no reference been made to biblical records, and the guidebook assured him that recent discoveries most 'completely corroborated' them.

The Nineveh Court at the Crystal Palace inspired at least three panoramas, so popular in those pre-cinema days, one at The Panorama in Leicester Square, entitled *Nimroud, Part of the City of Nineveh*, painted by Robert Burford, assisted by H. C. Selous, and another called *Golden Image in the Plain of Babylon*. A third, 'Daily at the Gothic Hall' at 3 Lower Grosvenor Street, showed the 'Grand Moving Diorama of Nineveh' which had been painted by F. C. Cooper, an artist sent by the Trustees of the British Museum 'to assist Dr Layard', and Mr Cooper also delivered an explanatory lecture. Admission cost one shilling.

Meanwhile, Charles Kean, the great actor manager, was bringing this interest in ancient Mesopotamia to the live theatre with his production of *Sardanapalus, King of Assyria*, a tragedy in five acts first performed on Monday, 13 June 1853. The play was based on Byron's poem but the sets and costumes bore careful witness to Layard's discoveries at Nineveh and had indeed received a 'verdict of approval from the judge most competent to speak with authority upon the surpassingly interesting subject', i.e. Layard himself. There were two main sets, executed by Messrs Gordon, Lloyds, and Days, who had spent many hours sketching at the British Museum, scenery which magnificently suggested the decadent 'Queen of Cities' hurrying to its fall 'by the undue prevalence of luxury and splendour'. These were a glorious diorama of Nineveh on the banks of the Tigris, and the Hall of Nimrod in the Royal Palace 'doomed to conflagration' complete with winged lions and accurately drawn sculptured slabs.

Kean was only too ready to acknowledge his debt to the great discoveries of Layard and Botta. Having been buried for 3,000 years, the finds brought to light the costumes, architecture, and customs of the ancient Assyrians 'so are authentic'. The sculptures in the British Museum had, he said, been 'rigidly followed' thus making it possible to offer a proper dramatization of Lord Byron's tragic poem, hitherto impossible since 'we have known nothing of Assyrian architecture and costume'. He considered himself most fortunate in being allowed to link the 'momentous discoveries of one renowned Englishman with the poetic labours of another'.

Indeed no effort or expense had been spared in achieving his effect, and the reviews that greeted his efforts were for the most part ecstatic. The *Illustrated London News* in a review on 18 June declared it was 'the most magnificent piece of stage-mounting', 'an honour to the national stage of the country'. Charles

90. Hall of Nimrod in the tragedy of *Sardanapalus*, Princess' Theatre, 1853.

Kean, as Sardanapalos, bearded like a figure in ancient sculpture had looked absolutely genuine, but (in its one reservation) the magazine wondered if perhaps the angular positions of limb and body which he had assumed in imitation of those glyptic images had been a little over-zealous. 'The action of Oriental people does not justify this assumption' (it said); 'their manner having a general sweep and roundness'. It did not mention the dancing girls whose costumes Kean had so carefully described in *Lacy's Acting Edition*: 'White merino dresses reaching to the ankle, ample but without under clothes'. Nor do we know what Byron made of the dramatization of a poem never intended to be enacted; he had died of fever at Missolonghi nearly thirty years before.

In France, artistic influences emanating from the great sculptures in the Louvre were harder to attribute. Gustave Doré (1832–63) spent over fifteen years researching his illustrations for an edition of the Bible published in French in 1856. It was followed by other European language editions and a Hebrew edition, and the following year Cassell in England developed a new electroplate process which made it possible for

the original expensive woodcuts to be reproduced indefinitely without loss of quality, thus allowing the English edition to reach a large market. Indeed it became a best-seller throughout the English-speaking world.

The Old Testament illustrations are most pleasing and expressive: 2 Chronicles 9: 1 Solomon receiving the Queen of Sheba has strange winged beasts; Esther 1: 10, 11 The Queen Vashti Refusing to Obey the Command of Ahasuerus has authentic winged bulls, as does Daniel Interpreting the Writing on the Wall (Daniel 5: 5, 25) and Jonah Preaching to the Ninevites (Jonah 3: 3, 4). Persepolitan remains were represented by double-headed columns and winged disks particularly in Esther Before the King (Esther 15: 6, 7), Daniel Confounding the Priests of Bel (Bel and the Dragon 7) and Mattathias and the Apostate (1 Maccabees 2: 23, 24). Babylon Fallen depicted more exotic winged beasts, together with rampant elephants (Revelations 18: 5). Doré was probably familiar with the work of John Martin; his distant turrets of Babylon in Isaiah's Vision of the Destruction of Babylon (Isaiah 13: 20, 21, 22) and terraces of Nineveh

91. Print engraving by Gustave Doré for a Bible illustration, *Jonah Preaching to the Ninevites*, 1856.

in Artaxerxes Granting Liberty to the Jews (Ezra 7: 13) owe something to the earlier artist.

On the other hand, Edgar Dégas's painting *Sémiramis construisant Babylone* (1860) owed nothing to the sculptures in the Louvre. What is discernible in this somewhat cloudy picture looks more Egyptian (lotus frieze) than Assyrian. And an opera *Sardanapale* by Victorin de Joncières and Henri Becque which opened in Paris in February 1867 also had an Egyptian setting with lotus capitals and hieroglyphic inscriptions (and a few Greek pots). The only Assyrian feature was the distinctive beard worn by the king.

The nineteenth century was prone to commemorate in permanent fashion, not only the momentous events of the day, but also its great men and women, with portrait busts and marble sculpture. At first, such celebration pieces were available only to the rich because of the price of marble. About 1843 Thomas Battram, art director of the porcelain firm of Copeland, invented (or at least he is credited with inventing) a new sort of ceramic product which most successfully imitated marble, being white, unglazed, with a fine granular finish. Copeland christened their

new product 'Statuary Porcelain' but later changed its name to 'Parian Ware' to give it classical prestige, claiming it closely resembled white marble from the Greek island of Paros. The new product was easy to use and because it was also very strong, it was possible for the most precise details to be reproduced. It was above all cheap. It was launched on the public at the Great Exhibition in 1851 and thereafter inspired many distinctive and adventurous designs. Most major Victorian figures were reproduced in Parian Ware, from Queen Victoria herself to Charles Dickens and events such as the abolition of slavery in the United States of America were commemorated in huge set pieces. In 1868, A. Hays, an employee in the Oriental Department of the British Museum, and until then not reckoned as a sculptor, modelled a series of Assyrian sculptures based on bas-reliefs in the Museum. The first set consisted of just two figures, Sennacherib and Ashurbanipal (or Sardanapalos as the advertisements were quick to add, well aware of the magic of that name). To these were then added a figure of the Queen of Sardanapalos, a small vase in the form of the head of a winged bull entitled 'Nimrod's Head', and a lion-weight with the name of Sennacherib written in cuneiform and one line of Phoenician. In 1883 the Hays's set was completed with a Winged Human-Headed Bull and a Winged Human-Headed Lion. In 1894 Owen Hale designed a Garden Scene which was actually a plaque ($22 \times 8\frac{1}{2}$ inches (55×22cm.)) depicting Ashurbanipal and his queen feasting in the garden, an accurate copy of the bas-relief found by Layard and in the British Museum. After this, the entire set was reissued by Alfred Jarvis for the princely sum of 11 guineas, though each piece could be purchased individually. A Winged Human-Headed Lion or Bull cost 2 guineas each, but a Lion Weight a mere seven shillings and sixpence.

From the start, the model sculptures attracted encomia. The *Art Journal* described them as 'the most agreeable of ornaments for the drawing-room and boudoir'. The *American Antiquarian* of October 1883 said they were 'faithful reproductions of Assyrian art, and may be safely used by lecturers and teachers'. Even Hormuzd Rassam, Layard's successor at Nimrud, felt he could recommend them to those 'who wished to possess unique representations in porcelain of the renowned Assyrian monarchs, Sennacherib, Sardanapalus, and other objects more especially the well-

92. Assyrianizing Parian Ware figures, launched in 1851.

known Nineveh human-headed Lion and Bull. They reflect great credit upon the designer's skill and good taste for the work of art, and above all the moderate price he has set upon them.'

It is, however, a picture, Edwin Long's *The Babylonian Marriage Market* painted in 1875 (the year after he returned from a tour of Egypt and the Holy Land) which perhaps best encapsulates the Victorian craze for Mesopotamia. Completely different in style from the austere and accurate Parian Ware figures, or the solid gold pieces of jewellery with their splendidly barbaric reliefs, this ravishing canvas owes more to imagination than accurate research, though that had certainly been done. The result is an alluring and seductive scene of pretty and not so pretty girls being sold by auction to a crowd of men. Long had escaped into a world both ancient and oriental where such a shocking event was only to be expected. He had taken as his subject the Babylonian marriage market about which he had read in Herodotos (1. 196) and inevitably he gave it his own gloss. Richard Jenkyns describes the picture as woman portrayed as victim but this would have seemed perfectly natural at the time. What is interesting to the Assyriologist is the evident amount of accurate research of recently available sources. The tiled decoration of palm trees and lions in the background is directly taken from bas-reliefs at the British Museum, the trees perhaps from Sennacherib's palace at Nineveh, the lions, looking somewhat more docile, from Ashurbanipal's, and the whole frieze looking uncannily like the reconstructed glazed-brick panel from the main throne room of the southern citadel at Babylon built by Nebuchadnezzar II and not displayed to western eyes till the beginning of this century. The figures of the men who are bidding for the girls look perfectly authentic, both in visage and costume. The girls are more problematical; unlike the slender but curvaceous females of Egyptian art, so frequently portrayed, there are few representations of Mesopotamian women and those there are look a little formidable. The pretty maidens in Long's picture are designed to attract; the less pretty ones, to the right of the picture (they are painted in descending order of beauty as Herodotos described their auction, pretty ones first), inspire pity or derision depending on the viewer's disposition.

They are all similarly clad, however, in flimsy and clinging white dresses. Gold bangles clasp their bare arms and jewelled fillets their braided hair (which at least looks authentic). They have a girlish air about them: one is admiring her reflection in a hand glass, two others are whispering together. They hug their knees, sitting on tiger skins as they await their turn to be auctioned.

The painting was commissioned by Edward Hermon for a reputed 1,700 guineas, and was exhibited at the Royal Academy. John Ruskin, Slade Professor of Fine Art, described it at great length as 'A painting of great merit, and well deserving purchase by the Anthropological Society' and concluding somewhat sententiously, that nothing had really changed: 'as the most beautiful and marvellous maidens were announced for literal sale by auction in Assyria, are not also the souls of our most marvellous maidens announced annually for sale by auction in Paris and London, in a spiritual manner, for the spiritual advantages of position in society?'

The painting was sold in 1882 for 6,300 guineas, a record price paid at auction for the work of a living British artist. Its new owner was Thomas Holloway, inventor of Holloway's Pills and Ointment. The picture is still in the collection of the Royal Holloway College. Edwin Long died in 1891, ranked as one of the most popular members of the Royal Academy. He also painted *An Assyrian Captive* in 1880.

Not everyone was equally enthusiastic about Mesopotamian motifs. Lord Leighton, in an address to the students of the Royal Academy on December 10th 1883, declared loftily that there was 'nothing in the shape of an Assyrian or Chaldean statue that has come down to us for which any serious merit can be claimed'. He spoke of the 'somewhat truculent' aspect of Assyrian art and complained of the 'grim accentuation' of the reliefs, especially representations of lions. Nothing, he concluded, could compare with the Aryan spirit of fifth-century Greece which represented Simplicity and Truth, and made it supreme.

Nonetheless artists, composers, and architects continued to find inspiration in Mesopotamian sources and reliefs. In France, Georges Rochegrosse painted *La Folie du Roi Nabuchodonosor* in 1886 and *La Fin de Babylone* in 1891. This was praised by Antonin Proust in *Le Salon de 1891* for its abundant detail and for the archaeological research that had been done.

Rochegrosse also illustrated *Hérodias* by Gustave Flaubert the following year; these drawings show some remarkable Babylonian architectural features. Two ceramicists based in Paris, Émile Muller and Léon Parvillée were designing decorative friezes and tiles for floors and the exterior and interior of buildings. From Émile Muller there were tiled friezes which were copies from Artaxerxes's palace at Susa and from Parvillée Frères & Cie could be purchased Assyrian tiles to make borders, surrounds, even floor and chimney decorations for interior and exterior use. In England, Sir Lawrence Alma-Tadema painted *Spring* (1894) with towering pediments and pillars in the style of John Martin and Gustave Doré, Isaac Snowman exhibited a painting called *Sardanapalus* at the Royal Academy in 1900, and F. A. Bridgman *A Royal Pastime in Nineveh*, with most carefully researched bronze gates, in 1901. On 10 March 1875, the first performance of Carl Goldmark's opera *Die Königin von Saba* took place in Vienna. It was performed in New York in 1885 and in London in 1910. Although the music was conventional, the scenery was exotic in the extreme, and contributed to the success of the opera. The designer had clearly done his homework: two magnificent sets show winged bulls, bearded figures, sun-disks and Babylonian roaring lions. The action was set in Jerusalem during the tenth century BC when the Queen of Sheba seduced Assad who was betrothed to King Solomon's daughter. There was an equally magnificent set for the 'Grosse historische Ausstattungspantomime' based on the work of the great German Assyriologist Friedrich Delitzsch performed in Berlin in 1908 entitled *Sardanapal*. The glazed panels have been taken directly from the newly reconstructed Ishtar Gate in the Berlin Museum and there is a pair of distinctly Hittite-looking lions glowering against a back wall.

Assyrian themes even invaded the English social scene as it vied to amuse its illustrious cynosure, the future Edward VII. This was an era of extravagant fancy-dress balls and since historical themes were popular, and there was a limited number who could go dressed as Cleopatra, Semiramis was a more subtle choice. Lady Warwick, one of the Prince's earlier mistresses, made a most decorative Edwardian/Assyrian queen, wasp-waisted and jewel-encrusted, complete with winged disk over her bosom. She had clearly read Diodoros, as the costume was completed by a headdress which consisted of a large white dove.

93. The Countess of Warwick dressed as Semiramis for Mrs Adair's Fancy Dress Ball in May 1903.

Simultaneously with the fashionable craze for all things Assyrian, scholars were making great advances in reading the recondite wedge-shaped script. Rather than confirming accepted beliefs, their success raised difficult questions. The Assyrians were part of the Bible, but what they had to say differed from the Old Testament accounts. New revisions were required. I. P. Cory's *Ancient Fragments* was reissued in a 'New and Enlarged Edition' in 1876, its preface referring to the first publication some fifty years earlier when 'cuneiform research had not yet seen the light' and when 'Nineveh was but a name, and Babylon an abstraction'. In 1872, George Smith, piecing together fragments from the library of Ashurbanipal at Nineveh, suddenly realized that he was looking at something very familiar: an account of a great Flood that had washed away mankind, save for one man, Ut-napishtim, and his wife, and the seeds of a few living things which were preserved in a large wooden boat. The terrible Flood lasted six days and seven nights, after which the boat came to rest on solid mud. Ut-napishtim sent out first a dove, then a swallow, and finally a raven which did not return, having

found dry land. When Smith read a report of this to the Society for Biblical Archaeology in December 1872, his audience was half fascinated, half horrified. This was highly unorthodox. Excitement ran so high that the owner of the *Daily Telegraph*, Sir Edwin Arnold, offered the British Museum 1,000 guineas so that Smith could go to Nineveh and try to find the rest of the tablet.

In Germany, the same controversy was about to erupt with quite violent consequences, involving character slurs, wrecked careers, discredited reputations, and Kaiser Wilhelm II himself. Germany had come late to excavation in Mesopotamia; it was not until 1899 that the newly formed German Oriental Society began examining the ruins of Babylon. In 1903, work started at Ashur, the site with which Germany will always be associated and in 1924 at Uruk (biblical Erech) the home of Gilgamesh, greatest hero of myth. In the field of linguistics, however, German scholars had always been in the forefront. During the 1890s there was a brilliant team of scholars (including Nöldeke and Delitzsch) steeped in the discipline of Semitic languages hard at work on the cuneiform records. But their work, though giving a better understanding of the Old Testament, was hard to reconcile with a literal interpretation of it. Some people went overboard: Hugo Winckler, the Assyriologist and theologian, devised a scheme known as Pan-Babylonism which was based on an idea that 'all myths everywhere can be seen as reflections mostly distorted, of a system which was developed in Babylonia around 3000 BC'. Was the Old Testament then just a collection of old myths with no religious value or truth? Peter Jensen interpreted the ancient *Epic of Gilgamesh* and declared it to be a source for all mythological motifs in world literature, and that the Old and New Testaments should be destroyed as religious texts. Jesus Christ himself was an Israelite Gilgamesh. The biggest storm of all, however, was raised by Friedrich Delitzsch in 1902. In a lecture neatly entitled *Babel und Bibel*, he attempted to put the Bible into a new perspective by showing that Babylonia was the origin of many Old Testament stories and practices. This lecture caused such a controversy that it was still raging a year later when Delitzsch took to the platform once more and told his audience, which included the emperor and the entire German Oriental Society, that the Old Testament must be denied as a divinely inspired book or revelation. This was too much for the Kaiser who hastily dissociated himself from such heresy, declaring 'Religion has never been the result of science' and suggesting that Delitzsch should in future stick to Assyriology and leave theology alone.

In the United States of America, two universities took up the challenge of Near Eastern languages, starting with Hebrew, then embracing Arabic, Syriac, and Coptic, and ultimately Sumerian and Akkadian, the languages of the cuneiform tablets. The University of Pennsylvania opened its faculty first, during the 1880s, and sent its first expedition to Babylonia during the 1888–9 season. Soon major excavations at Nippur yielded a large number of inscribed tablets of all kinds from the temple library. Second in the field but unequalled in its professional attitude towards publication and proper remuneration for its staff was Chicago, where the Oriental Institute was founded in 1919 and has been responsible ever since for the Chicago Assyrian Dictionary. The Chicago Institute also sent fruitful expeditions to Mesopotamia.

Meanwhile, in England, so great was public interest in the new dead language that the Revd Archibald H. Sayce, Professor of Assyriology at Oxford, was prevailed upon to produce an *Elementary Assyrian Grammar*, a handbook for beginners. And in 1902, A. J. Booth, in his *The Discovery and Decipherment of Trilingual Cuneiform Inscriptions*, described how 'Lectures began to be delivered . . . throughout the provinces . . . Whether the new learning would tend to confirm the ancient records or whether it would compel a revision of cherished beliefs began to be debated in many quarters, far beyond the circle of learned societies.'

It was inevitable after the success of Mesopotamian themes and decorations on the stage that they should be used in the cinema, just then beginning to become a commercial proposition. The Italian poet, Gabriele d'Annunzio, worked on the plot and subtitles for *Cabiria*, a film released in 1914, set in the third century BC about Hannibal crossing the Alps and Archimedes setting fire to his ships. Despite the subject matter, stills from the film portray some very fine winged bulls, and the reliefs of warriors look Assyrian in concept, proof that such images were still exciting the popular imagination.

It is, however, the film *Intolerance* which must take credit for the most research and attention to detail paid by anyone to any one film before or since. Running for well over three hours, the theme, which was the intolerance of human beings to one another, was developed by way of four separate stories, one of which was set in Babylon in the time of King Belshazzar and its fall to the Persian king, Cyrus, about 539 BC. The other stories were set at the time of the Crucifixion, the St Bartholomew's Day Massacre in 1572, and in contemporary USA. The research carried out by the director, David Wark Griffith and his assistant director, Joseph Henabery (who also played several vignette parts in the film) for the Babylonian section alone led to the compilation of a scrapbook which eventually weighed over eight pounds. This enormous volume contained illustrations cut out from other books, mainly references to specific objects e.g. armour, chariots, weapons, but it also had a section of pictures painted in the recent past which most memorably conjured up the vision of the Babylon Griffith wanted. The three paintings which unquestionably most influenced him were John Martin's *Belshazzar's Feast*, Edwin Long's *The Babylonian Marriage Market*, and Georges Rochegrosse's *La Fin de Babylone*. This last one had apparently hung in a fashionable New York restaurant where it was probably seen by Griffith.

Not content with accuracy to detail, the enormous whole had to be exact too. Griffith literally reconstructed ancient Babylon in Hollywood, near Sunset Boulevard. The land in those days was a mixture of fields and semi-desert and in an area of some 250 acres, Griffith began building. His first attempt at the city walls he set at half a mile from the main camera station, but realizing this was too close, he moved them so that they were a mile distant. The towers at the corners of the reconstructed city could be seen for miles, and fragments were still standing as late as 1931. The most important structure, however, was the great hall of Belshazzar which could hold 5,000 people at a time without crowding. There was a colossal statue of Ishtar, terraced steps, 50-foot (15-metre) columns topped with larger-than-life-size elephants brandishing one vast front leg. Apart from its principal actors and actresses, the film employed 4,000 extras, and for the scene portraying Cyrus's advance on Babylon and its fall, 16,000 extras were used, making it the cinema's largest crowd-scene. Griffith did not work to a script, and there was no screenplay for this marathon epic.

94. and 95. Two scenes from the film *Intolerance*, which showed the Babylonians as enlightened people.

Despite its length and inevitably poor quality some three-quarters of a century later, the film is a feast for the Assyriologist. It is hard to keep track of all the careful detail as the scene shifts but it is all there: the gates of Babylon, the wall called Imgur-Bel, the winged lions and bulls, Belshazzar impressing his cylinder seal in damp clay, the Persian soldiers taken straight from Persepolitan relief sculpture, the fighting scenes straight from familiar Assyrian panels. And the people look so right (even if the women are again rather too glamorous)—the bearded officials, high priest, soldiers in pointed helmets. One memorable scene when the Mountain Girl (who has been brought to Babylon to be auctioned to a suitable husband) spits with rage at her prospective buyer, then nonchalantly bites in to a large spring onion, before being rescued by Belshazzar, incognito, is taken straight from Edwin Long. For once, the Babylonians are presented in a sympathetic light, decadent perhaps and surrounded by luxury, but also as the unfortunate victims of a marauding and murderous force.

The film was released in the USA during the First World War and distributed in Europe after the war was over. A. H. Sayce was ecstatic. He wrote to Griffith the day after seeing the film,

It is an astounding piece . . . The Babylonian scenes are magnificent, as well as true to facts. I was much impressed by the attention that had been paid to accuracy in detail. The drama is educational in more than one direction, and the interest it must excite in Babylonian history is especially gratifying to the Assyriologist.

The film was also one of the first to use costume to create the illusion of an earlier time. The research that had gone into dressing the entire cast had been painstaking. The men wore woollen robes with heavy embroidery and look completely authentic, as did the soldiers, priests, and kings, but the women suffered the same fate as Long's maidens: they had been prettified to conform with modern tastes and wore flimsy robes that clung or were shaped to the body with jewelled girdles. The women had to be recognizably 'Babylonian' to western eyes, that is exotic, mysterious, and beautiful, and prone to lounge on tiger skins. To an Assyriologist, they merely look oriental. But so successful were the female costumes that they inspired a craze for 'Back to Babylon' dresses and *Photoplay* magazine of April 1917 published sketches of them so that they could be copied by the nimble-fingered at home.

96. American fashions of 1917 inspired by the film *Intolerance*.

The ravages of the First World War and the crumbling of more modern empires pushed aside general interest in ancient civilizations such as Assyria and Babylonia. Gertrude Bell's popular accounts of her intrepid travels among the Bedouin tribes did revive some curiosity in the region and between the First and Second World Wars, the archaeologist R. Campbell-Thompson (with whom both Leonard Woolley and Max Mallowan worked at one time) led a renewal of archaeological interest. The site that captured the public imagination as much as any since Layard's finds at Nimrud was Woolley's excavation at Ur. The Royal Cemetery yielded treasures of brilliant workmanship, and his book about them *Ur of the Chaldees* (1929) went into eight impressions in six years. But the appeal of Ur and its significance were greatly eclipsed by Howard Carter's discovery of the tomb of Tutankhamun. Even Woolley's most romantic assistant at Carchemish, T. E. Lawrence,

97. Assyrianizing motifs on the Pythian building, New York, architect Thomas Lamb, dated 1926, built as the Grand Lodge for the Knights of Pythias.

a Valentino mounted on a camel, failed to galvanize any lasting passion for the region.

The rediscovery of ancient Egypt led to Egyptology, the study of ancient Egypt, and to Egyptomania, the mad fancy for all things in the Egyptian style. Layard and Botta's excavations in Assyria led to Assyriology, the science of ancient Assyria and Babylon, but there is no equivalent to Egyptomania, no Assyriomania. There is a distressing lack of striking material evidence for ancient Mesopotamia, that humanizing element that makes ancient Egypt seem so accessible, so modern, and so amusing. There was certainly no frivolous or fantastic element to the nineteenth-century revival; it was sober, monochrome, and accurately reproduced the originals on to objects of value, made to last. Twentieth-century art nouveau and art décoratif did not sit in natural harmony with Assyrian glyptic. The real ancient Mesopotamians, as opposed to their lurid earlier portrayals in art and literature, were perceived as solid, savage, and sombre, its society as despotic and oppressive —most unsuitable endorsements for cigarettes, ragtime music, or biscuit tins. Their civilization remains a specialist subject.

Nevertheless, comparisons with ancient Egypt do obscure the significance of this civilization for the modern world. When the first palaces, temples, and clay tablets were unearthed in Mesopotamia, no one could have foreseen how extensive and complex the influence of Nineveh and Babylon would prove to be. It has taken five generations of scholars to piece together that inheritance. Only now is the whole picture beginning to emerge and more episodes will unfold in future as the great quest continues. No one concerned with the origins of western civilization can afford to disregard its roots in Mesopotamia, and the legends handed down to us.

It does not matter that there is so little left above ground: no pyramid, no temple, no hypostyle hall, theatre or circus, no forum, no colonnade, only the remains of a few crumbling ziggurats. The visible splendour of proud Babylon and mighty Nineveh may have disappeared from sight but the dusty mounds that remain are linked with the very start of recorded history. Thus their legacy is unassailable, their renown indelible: legendary, glorious, immortal.

FURTHER READING

ATHERSTONE, EDWIN, *The Fall of Nineveh* (London, 1828).
ATTERBURY, PAUL, *The Parian Phenomenon* (Shepton Beauchamp, 1989).

AUBERGER, JANICK, *Ctésias histoires de l'orient* (Paris, 1991).
AULANIER, CHRISTIANE, 'Histoire du Palais et du Musée du

Louvre', *Le Pavillon de l'Horloge et le Département des Antiquités Orientales*, no. 9 (Paris, 1964).

BADGER, REVD GEORGE, *The Nestorians and Their Rituals with the Narrative of a Mission to Mesopotamia and Coordistan in 1842–1844* (London, 1852).

BARKER, DENNIS, *Parian Ware* (Aylesbury, 1985).

BARNETT, R. D., 'Canford and Cuneiform: A Century of Assyriology', *The Museums Journal* 60: 8 (Nov. 1960), 192–200.

—— 'Archaeology in the Levant', in R. Moorey (ed.), *Essays for Kathleen Kenyon* (Warminster, 1978), 172–9.

BECKFORD, WILLIAM THOMAS, *The History of the Caliph Vathek*, ed. R. Lonsdale (Oxford, 1970).

BENJAMIN, Rabbi of Tudela, *Travels* (Constantinople, 1543).

BIGWOOD, J. M., 'Diodorus & Ctesias', *Phoenix* 34 (1980), 195–207.

—— 'Ctesias' Description of Babylon', *American Journal of Ancient History* 3–5: 1 (1978–80), 32–58.

BOHRER, FREDERICK N., 'Assyria as Art: A Perspective on the Early Reception of Ancient Near Eastern Artifacts', *Culture & History* 4 (1989), 7–33.

—— 'The Printed Orient: The Production of A. H. Layard's Earliest Works', *Culture & History* 11 (1982), 85–105.

BONOMI, JOSEPH, *Nineveh and its Palaces, the Discoveries of Botta and Layard applied to the Elucidation of Holy Writ* (London, 1852).

BOOTH, A. J., *The Discovery and Decipherment of Trilingual Cuneiform Inscriptions* (London, 1902).

BOTTA, P.-É., *Monument de Ninive* (Paris, 1849).

—— *Letters on the Discoveries at Nineveh*, trans. Lady Catherine Tobin (London, 1850).

BRYAN, BRUCE, 'Movie Realism and Archaeological Fact', *Art & Archaeology* 18: 4 (Oct. 1924), 131 ff.

BUCKINGHAM, J. S., *Travels in Mesopotamia . . . with Researches on the Ruins of Nineveh, Babylon, and Other Ancient Cities* (London, 1827).

—— *Travels in Assyria, Media and Persia* (London, 1829).

BUDGE, SIR E. A. WALLIS, *The Rise and Progress of Assyriology* (London, 1925).

BURSTEIN, STANLEY M., *The Babyloniaca of Berossus*, Sources from the Ancient Near East 1, fasc. 5 (1978), 5–40.

BURTON, RICHARD FRANCIS, *Love, War and Fancy, the Customs and Manners of the East from Writings on the Arabian Nights*, ed. William Kimber (London, 1964).

COOPER, JERROLD S., 'Posing the Sumerian Question: Race and Scholarship in the Early History of Assyria', *Analecta Orientalia* 9: Festschrift for Miguel Civil (1991), 46–66.

CORY, I. P., *Ancient Fragments*, ed. E. Richmond Hodges (London, 1876).

DREWS, ROBERT, 'Assyria in Classical Universal Histories', *Historia* 14:2 (April 1965), 129–42.

DUNLOP, JOHN COLIN, *History of Prose Fiction* (London, 1888).

FARWELL, BEATRICE, 'Sources for Delacroix's Death of Sardanapalus', *Art Bulletin* 40 (March 1958), 66–71.

FEAVER, WILLIAM, *The Art of John Martin* (Oxford, 1975).

FISCHER VON ERLACH, JOHANN BERNARD, *Entwürff einer Historischen Architektur* (Vienna, 1721).

GADD, C. J., *The Stones of Assyria* (London, 1936).

GERE, CHARLOTTE, *Victorian Jewellery Design* (London, 1972).

GORDON, CYRUS H., *The Pennsylvania Tradition of Semitics* (Atlanta, 1986).

HÄGG, TOMAS, *The Novel in Antiquity* (Oxford, 1983).

HANSON, BERNARD, 'D. W. Griffith: Some Sources', *Art Bulletin* 54 (Dec. 1972), 493–501.

HASKELL, FRANCIS, *Rediscoveries in Art: Some Aspects of Taste, Fashion & Collecting in England & France* (Oxford, 1980).

HOWARD, LILLIAN, 'Back to Babylon for New Fashions', *Photoplay Magazine* (April 1917), 39–40.

HUGHES, REVD. T. S., *Belshazzar's Feast* (Cambridge, 1818).

JENKINS, IAN, *Archaeologists and Aesthetes* (London, 1992).

JENKYNS, RICHARD, *Dignity and Decadence: Victorian Art and the Classical Inheritance* (London, 1991).

JOHNSON, LEE, 'The Etruscan Sources of Delacroix's Death of Sardanapalus', *Art Bulletin* 62 (Dec. 1960), 296–300.

JULLIAN, PHILIPPE, *D'Annunzio* (London, 1972).

KEATES, JONATHAN, *Handel The Man and His Music* (London, 1985).

KLINGENDER, FRANCIS D., *Art and the Industrial Revolution* (London, 1947).

LARSEN, MOGENS TROLLE, 'Orientalism and The Ancient Near East', *Culture & History* 2 (1987), 96–115.

—— 'Seeing Mesopotamia', *Culture & History* 11 (1992), 107–32.

LAYARD, AUSTEN HENRY, *Nineveh and Its Remains* (London, 1849).

—— *The Nineveh Court in the Crystal Palace* (London, 1854).

LEIGHTON, FREDERIC LORD, *Addresses Delivered to the Students of the Royal Academy by the late Lord Leighton* (London, 1896).

LEWY, HILDEGARDE, 'Nitocris—Naqi'a', *JNES* 11 (Oct. 1952), 264–86.

MACGINNIS, J. D. A., 'Ctesias and the Fall of Nineveh', *Illinois Classical Studies* 13: 1 (Spring 1988), 37–41.

MAEDER, EDWARD, *Hollywood and History Costume Design in Film* (London, 1987).

MILLER EDWARD, *That Noble Cabinet: A History of the British Museum* (London, 1973).

MILMAN, REVD. H. H., *Belshazzar A Dramatic Poem* (London, 1822).

MOHL, JULIUS, *Vingt-sept ans d'histoire des études orientales* (Paris, 1879).

MONCKTON, NORAH, 'Architectural Backgrounds in the Pictures of John Martin', *Architectural Review* (August 1948), 81–4.

MUNN, GEOFFREY C., *Castellani and Giuliano Revivalist Jewellers of the Nineteenth Century* (London, 1984).

PHILLIPS, E. D., 'Semiramis at Behistun', *Classica et Mediaevalia* 28–9 (1972), 162–8.

PRIDEAUX, HUMPHREY, *Prideaux's Connection of the Old and New Testaments* (London, 1858).

PROUST, ANTONIN, *Le Salon de 1891* (Paris, 1891).

RAY, JOHN (trans.), *Doctor Leonhart Rauwolff's Travels into the Eastern Countries* (London, 1693).

RHODES, ANTHONY, *The Poet as Superman: A Life of Gabriele d'Annunzio* (London, 1959).

RUDOE, JUDY, 'Assyrian Style Jewellery', *The Antique Collector* (April 1989), 42–8.

—— 'The Layards, Cortelzazzo and Castellani: New Information from the Diaries of Lady Layard', *Jewellery Studies* 1 (1983–4), 59–82.

RUSKIN, JOHN, *Notes on some of the Principal Pictures Exhibited in the Rooms of the Royal Academy* (London, 1875).

RUSSELL, J. M., *Nineveh at Canford Manor, Dorset: The Story of the Nineveh Porch and the Metropolitan Museum Assyrian Sculptures* (Yale, 1996).

SCARISBRICK, DIANA, 'Jewelled Tribute to the Past', *Country Life* (29 Jan. 1981), 244–6.

SIMPSON, M. C. M., *Letters and Recollections of Julius and Mary Mohl* (Orpington, 1887).

SMITH, GEORGE, *Assyrian Discoveries, an Account of Explorations and Discoveries on the Site of Nineveh during 1873 & 1874* (London, 1875).

STERN, SEYMOUR, 'An Index to the Creative Work of David Wark Griffith', Supplement to *Sight & Sound* (April 1944).

STONE, W. H., 'The Nineveh Bull', *Household Words* 46 (8 Feb. 1851), 468–9.

STRANGE, EDWARD F., 'The Scenery of Charles Kean's Plays and The Great Scene—Painters of his Day', *Magazine of Art* (1902), 454–9.

SWANSON, VERN G., *Sir Lawrence Alma-Tadema the Painter of the Victorian Vision of the Ancient World* (London, 1977).

WADE MEADE, C., *Road to Babylon: Development of U.S. Assyriology* (Leiden, 1974).

WATERFIELD, GORDON, *Layard of Nineveh* (London, 1963).

WHIDDEN, MARGARET, *Samuel Colman, Belshazzar's Feast, A Painting in its Context* (Oldham, 1981).

General Index

Very common modern geographical terms, e.g. Mediterranean and Europe, are not included. Owing to the wide range of names used, a term or phrase of orientation is given after many personal and geographical names. Titles of written works and films are *italic*. The following abbreviations are employed: aka = also known as; *fl.* = *floruit*, indicating approximate date of activity; *c.* = *circa*, preceding a cardinal number; c. = century, following an ordinal number; d. = died.

Harran (city in S Turkey, aka Carrhae) 1, 18,
   26, 28–30, 53, 65, 68, 77, 78, 85, 91, 104, 109,
   116, 121, 123, 149, 152, 163, 164, 167, Maps 2, 3,
   5
Harut and Marut (sorcerers) 150
Hasīsu, Hasīsatu (Akkadian 'wisdom'
   personified) 75
Hatra (city in N Iraq) 42, 43, 45, 53, 85, 115–17,
   144, 151, 152, 154, 156, 163, Maps 3, 4
Hattusa (modern Bogazköy, Hittite capital,
   central Turkey) 13, 14, 17, 18, 20, 60, 91,
   Map 1
Hattusili I (Hittite king, fl.1650 BC) 60
Haykar (aka Ahiqar) 146
Hays, A. (sculptor) 204
Hazael (king of Damascus, fl.840 BC) 61
Hazor (city in N Palestine) 20, 57, Map 5
Hebrew (language, people, alphabet) 2, 3, 6,
   38, 39, 57, 60, 61, 66, 68, 75, 77–9, 133, 139,
   140, 143, 144, 147, 148, 155, 156, 171, 172, 174,
   188, 203, 208
Hebrew Melodies (by Byron) 188
Hebron (town in S Palestine) 57, Map 5
Hekataios of Miletos (writer, fl.500 BC) 109
Hekhalot ('Palaces', manuals of Jewish
   mysticism) 43, 172; see also Book of Hekhalot
Helen of Troy 4
Heliodoros (scholar, brother of Ammonios) 135
Helios (sun-god) 116
Hellanikos of Lesbos (writer, 5th c. BC) 109
Hellas 48
Henabery, Joseph (film director) 208
Henry IV, part 2 (by Shakespeare) 167
Hepat (Syrian goddess) 24, 26
Hephaistion of Thebes (writer, fl.415 AD) 133
Hephaistos (god of metal-working) 129, 177
Hera (goddess) 98
Herakles (hero-god) 44, 101, 116
Heraklitos of Ephesos (philosopher, c.540–480
   BC) 132
Hermes (messenger-god) 121, 134, 155, 166, 169,
   175
Hermes Trismegistos 48, 166, 167, 169
Hermetic writings 48, 121, 154, 167, 168
Hermippos (saviour of Aesop) 148
Hermon (mountain in Palestine) 145
Hermon, Edward (patron of arts) 206
Hermopolis (city in Egypt) 27, Map 1
Herodikos (Babylonian writer, 2nd c. AD) 48
Herodotos of Halikarnassos (historian,
   c.490–425 BC) 4, 7, 37–9, 49, 87, 89, 94, 103,
   104, 109, 110, 130, 147, 152, 165, 175, 184,
   186–9, 191, 205
Heron, Robert (translator) 188
Herta (goddess at Palmyra) 50
Hesiod (poet, fl.700 BC) 92, 101, 129
Hezekiah (king of Judah, 722–694 BC) 63, 140
Hierapolis (city in N Syria, aka Membidj,
   Mabbug, Nineveh) 114, 116, 118, 119, 155, 178,
   Map 3
Hill, Thomas (encyclopaedist) 175
Hincks, Edward (scholar) 195
Hipparchos of Rhodes (astronomer, c.190–126
   BC) 48, 114, 134–6
Hippareni (city in S Iraq, aka Nippur) 42
Hippocratic Corpus 115
Hippocratic Oath 176
Hippokrates of Kos (fl.400 BC) 176
Historiae Philippicae (by Trogus Pompeius,
   epitome by Justinus) 185

History (by Joseph ben Gorion) 62
History of Astronomy (by Eudemos of Rhodes)
   40, 110
History of the Caliph Vathek (by Beckford) 187
History of Greece (by Mitford) 188
History of Karka de Beth Selokh 157
Hittite(s) 5, 7, 13, 15, 18–26, 57, 60, 61, 64,
   67–71, 73, 76, 77, 79, 86, 89–93, 95, 97, 100,
   125, 139, 150, 165, 176, 206, Map 5
Holloway, Thomas (inventor) 206
Hollywood (film studios) 208
Homer 48, 85, 91, 92, 129
Horites 60
Hoshang (Iranian god) 155
Hoshea (king of Israel 732–724 BC) 62
Household Words (by Stone) 196
Hughes, T. S. (poet, 19th c. AD) 188, 189
Humanists 166
Humbaba (monster of forest) 4, 43, 101, 165,
   171
Hunt and Roskell (jewellers) 201
Hurrian(s) 15, 18, 19, 23–5, 35, 57, 60, 64, 77,
   Map 5
Huzirina (modern Sultantepe, Assyrian town
   in S Turkey) 18, 26
Hyades (constellation) 129
Hyginus (scholar, c.64 BC–17 AD) 187
Hypsikles of Alexandria (astronomer, fl.c.150
   BC) 134

Iamblichos (author of Babyloniaka Romance,
   2nd c. AD) 185, 187
Iamblichos of Apamea (philosopher, c.250–319
   AD) 52, 103, 167
Ibnahaza (Elamite god) 62
Iberians 39; see also Spain
Ibn Abi Usaibi'ah (writer) 176
Ibn Wahshiya (writer) 78
Idris (aka Enoch) 155; see also Book of Enoch
Iliad 68, 85, 91, 101, 114, 129, 177
Illustrated Handbook of Architecture (by
   Ferguson) 198
Illustrated London News 196, 202
L'Illustration 195
Imgur-Bel (wall of Babylon) 210
Imhotep (Egyptian sage, priest of Heliopolis,
   fl.c.2630 BC) 16
Inanna (Sumerian goddess) 42, 113
Inanna and the halub tree 175
incantations, incantation priests 21, 45, 74, 101,
   143, 144, 156, 167, 168, 170, 172, 174
India(n) 1, 14, 15, 18, 44, 46, 111, 123, 127, 128,
   130–2, 134–7, 141, 142, 154, 191, 193, 194, 195
Indo-Aryan 15, 23, 24
Indo-European (languages) 2, 4, 6, 7, 13, 19, 97
Indo-Iranian 15
Indra (Indic god) 15
Indus river 1, 12, 14, 39, Map 1
Instructions of Shuruppak 70
Interpretation of Dreams (by Freud) 121
Intolerance (film) 208–10
Ionia(ns) (W Turkey and islands) 2, 26, 30, 38,
   91, 93–5, 97, 98, 103, 104, 108, 112, 117, 188,
   Map 3
Ionic (style) 198
Ipiq-Adad (king of Eshnunna) 87
iqqur īpuš (almanac manual) 177
Irad (son of Enoch, city) 68; see also Eridu
Iran, Iranian 9, 12, 19, 22, 26, 35, 38–40, 43, 44,
   57, 95, 108, 128, 130, 131, 137, 141, 144, 165, 170

Iraq 24, 70, 158, 169
Isaac (son of Abraham) 65, 145
Isaac of Antioch (Christian writer, fl. early 5th
   c. AD) 153, 155
Isaiah 68, 73, 78, 156, 192, 203
Isfandiyar (Persian hero, Alexander the Great)
   173
Ishkur (Sumerian storm-god) 20
Ishmael 145
Ishtar (goddess, aka Issar) 10, 21, 24, 38, 41, 42,
   44, 51, 52, 62, 64, 72, 74, 101, 116, 118, 134, 144,
   152, 163, 206
Ishtar's Descent to the Underworld 73, 78, 171
Isidore of Charax (writer, 1st c. BC) 44
Isidore of Seville (encyclopaedist, bishop,
   602–36 AD) 47, 177, 178
Isin (city in central Iraq) 98
Islam(ic) 4, 29, 30, 121, 137, 143, 144, 155, 163,
   164, 166, 167, 170–2, 175, 177, 178
Israel(ite) 2, 3, 5, 26, 30, 43, 57, 60–2, 64, 68,
   70, 76–8, 97, 139, 147, 149, 150, 158, 166, 168,
   171, 207
Issar-Bel (goddess of Arbela) 121, 152
Italy 100, 115, 117, 123
Itapalhum (city-state in NE Iraq, 19th c. BC) 16
itineraries (as texts) 76, 152
Itinerary (by Benjamin of Tudela) 186
Itinerary (by Isidore of Charax) 44

Jacob (son of Isaac) 65, 68
Jacob of Sarug (Christian writer, c.451–521 AD)
   153–5
Jacobsen, Thorkild (scholar) 3
Jain (Indian religion) 164
Jamshid (Persian hero, aka Yima) 172, 173
Jannes and Jambres (magicians) 150
Jared (father of Enoch) 67
Jarvis, Alfred (retailer of sculpture) 204
Javan 73; see also Ionia
Jehoiachin (king of Judah, 598 BC) 29, 43, 63
Jehoiakim (king of Judah, 609–598 BC) 63
Jenkyns, Richard (historian) 205
Jensen, Peter, (scholar) 207
Jerash (ancient Gerasa, city in Jordan) 50
Jeremiah 62, 63, 70
Jeremias, A. (scholar) 2
Jericho (city on Jordan river) 57, Map 5
Jerusalem 2, 3, 29, 38, 43, 60, 61, 63, 75, 76, 78,
   79, 140, 192, Maps 1, 3, 5
Jesus of Nazareth (religious leader) 139, 164,
   165, 175, 207
Jews, Jewish 30, 43, 62, 75, 77, 126, 139, 141,
   143–5, 147, 148, 149, 155–8, 164–8, 170–2,
   177
Job 74, 78, 145
John of Ephesos (Christian historian, fl. late
   6th c. AD) 155
John of Lydia (writer, fl.550 AD) 133, 135
Jonah 157, 203
Jordan river 57
Joseph (son of Jacob) 68, 147
Joseph ben Gorion (historian, aka Yosippon,
   9–10th c. AD) 62
Josephos (historian, c.37–93 AD) 62, 105
Joshua the Stylite (Christian historian, fl. late
   8th c. AD) 155
Josiah (king of Judah, 639–609 BC) 63, 171
Juba II (king of Numidia, 46 BC–23 AD) 113
Jubilees 166
Judaean(s) 38, 62, 63, 139